£21.95
792.95

Restoration Comedy in Performance

The Elements of Drama
The Dark Comedy
The Dramatic Experience
Shakespeare's Stagecraft
Chekhov in Performance
The Challenge of the Theatre
Drama, Stage and Audience
The Shakespeare Revolution
Modern Drama in Theory and Practice
    vol. 1: *Realism and Naturalism*
    vol. 2: *Symbolism, Surrealism and the Absurd*
    vol. 3: *Expressionism and Epic Theatre*
Max Reinhardt
Shakespeare in Performance: All's Well That Ends Well
The State of Drama Study

Restoration Comedy in Performance

J.L. STYAN

Franklyn Bliss Snyder Professor of English Literature and
Professor of Theatre, Northwestern University

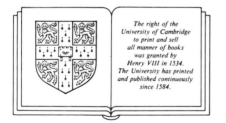

The right of the
University of Cambridge
to print and sell
all manner of books
was granted by
Henry VIII in 1534.
The University has printed
and published continuously
since 1584.

CAMBRIDGE UNIVERSITY PRESS

Cambridge
New York   Port Chester
Melbourne   Sydney

Published by the Press Syndicate of the University of Cambridge
The Pitt Building, Trumpington Street, Cambridge CB2 1RP
40 West 20th Street, New York, NY 10011-4211, USA
10 Stamford Road, Oakleigh, Melbourne 3166, Australia

First published 1986
Reprinted 1989, 1994, 1998

Printed in the United Kingdom by
Woolnough Bookbinding, Irthlingborough, Northants

British Library cataloguing in publication data
Styan, J. L.
Restoration comedy in performance.
1. English drama (Comedy) — 17th
century — History and criticism.
2. Theater — Production and direction.
I. Title
792.9'5   PN 1922

Library of Congress Cataloguing in Publication Data
Styan, J. L.
Restoration comedy in performance.
Bibliography: p.259
Includes index.
1. Theater — Great Britain — History — 17th century.
2. English drama — Restoration, 1660-1700 — History and
criticism. 3. English drama (Comedy) — History and
criticism. 4. Theater — Great Britain — History — 20th century. 1. Title.
PN2592.S74   1986   792'.0941   86 2222

ISBN 0 521 27421 4 paperback

Contents

Contents

Contents

Illustrations

viii

Acknowledgments

For time to read and write, my first debt is to the John Simon Guggenheim Memorial Foundation for its fellowship award in 1983–1984, and to Northwestern University for its additional support. For their generous assistance, I wish to thank many librarians, but particularly those of the British Library, the Bibliothèque Nationale, the Newberry Library of Chicago, the New York Public Library Theatre Collection at Lincoln Center, the Harvard Theatre Collection and Northwestern University Library. I regret that Retta Taney's useful survey *Restoration Revivals on the British Stage (1944–1979)* came to hand after this book was in press. For help at important moments, let me single out for thanks Jérôme Hankins, Linda LaBranche, Norman Spector and Wanderlie Henshaw, whose work of uncovering new sources for the acting of Restoration comedy I came across at the University of Pittsburgh a few years ago. And for countless grateful insights, I remember with pleasure all the students who joyfully tested scenes from the plays in class over the years, beginning with the Yorkshire Summer School of Drama in 1967.

J.L.S.

1. Introduction and approach

This might have been the title of the book, chosen in order to indicate the pleasure to be had in getting to know a unique body of plays – and so perhaps calling up the cynic in every reader and critic. However, the role of celebrant does not altogether fit. It has been left to others to recreate the little world of gifted Restoration actors and actresses which gave the theatre of the time its special sense of occasion. Nor is there any pretence of having reviewed all the plays of the age; rather, in the search for examples, of, say, a lively breeches scene, or a brilliant run of repartee, or a glorious moment of knockabout comedy, the same plays have often come to mind. Nor does the book deal with the talents of individual playwrights, and thereby it commits the sin of seeming to treat one writer very like another, when we all know that Wycherley was not Congreve, nor Etherege Farquhar, if only because the theatre changed a great deal in a generation. Only on occasion is the reader invited to dwell on a single scene which may distinguish the qualities in a particular playwright.

If from time to time this study rehearses some familiar material about Restoration staging and acting conditions, it is because the new task is to ask the pertinent questions about those conditions: what properties made the comedy of the Restoration successful in its own day? And the next question may be the other side of the same coin: why do we find it difficult to recapture those properties in ours?

It is a commonplace that the plots and characters of Restoration comedy largely repeated themselves from play to play for some forty years, in a way which may seem to us to be distinctly uninspired. If there is a provisional conclusion to be drawn from this, it is not that we should look to the plotting and characterization for the answers to our questions, but that we should study what made such repetition *unimportant* to the success of the enterprise. The assumption is that the endless stories of seduction and cuckolding, and the repeated stereotypes of wit and coquette, fop and prude, country wife and country cousin, merely provided convenient pegs on which to hang the true elements of drama offered by Restoration comedy. And where might they be found? In the code of speech and behaviour which lay dormant in the lines, and in whose secrets player and spectator could share – but only through the right sort of performance.

I

So we turn for answers, as so often in the study of drama, to performance. Not only the practice of the Restoration stage itself, but also the experience of those who tried to revive the plays after 1915, may supply the solution. It would be a mistake to ignore what the modern theatre has itself learned about the nature of the genre.

In order to reconstruct the peculiar qualities of a *risqué* sexual comedy through its style of performance, we must turn aside from the kind of anachronistic judgments with which it has been long associated. These are both moralistic (as late as 1919 the Phoenix Society was excoriated for its plans to produce 'the Restoration blackguards Wycherley and Shadwell') and literary (L.C. Knights's now classic piece of misplaced censure that the bulk of this comedy was 'insufferably dull'). For it is hard to think of a style of drama which in its intentions and spirit arose more directly from the special circumstances of its original performance. If drama is an imaginative interchange between its participants on stage and off, a true extension of *homo ludens*, then the Restoration offers an example of one of the most rare games in theatrical history. Played at first in a theatre that was little more than a *salon*, and reflecting the behaviour of an unusually homogeneous audience whose preconceptions the author shared, Restoration comedy rapidly developed an intimate style of speech and behaviour whose private signals were to be understood only in playing them.

Because of significant changes in the conditions of performance by the end of the seventeenth century, especially in the predisposition of the audience, the Restoration comic style was relatively short-lived. The plays continued in some demand into the eighteenth century, but then virtually dropped from the repertoire for 200 years until a few of them were revived in the early years of this century. At that time Restoration comedy was without a known theatrical tradition, unencrusted with the accretions of the stage; it was a lost art form. Yet it is only recently that our interest in the genre has coincided with attempts to understand drama as a self-conscious form in which a play's style is determined by its own laws of performance, its own 'poetics'. In the seventeenth century the illusion of the action could at any moment be fractured, an actor need not always remain in character, and the activity of the audience as much as that of the actors might hold the key to the play. In sum, its text has to be regarded as a framework and not a formula for performance. Restoration comedy was a kind of improvised charade, and, in John Crowne's words in the preface to his masque *Calisto* (1675), the libretto was the 'cold lean carcass of the entertainment'.

2

THE CRITICAL REVERSAL

The arguments that surrounded the revival of Restoration comedy in the early twentieth century were about whether it was necessary to see it on the stage before passing a verdict, and the most direct statement on the matter came from the man who most helped it return to the theatre. In the introduction to his book *The Restoration Theatre*, intended to be the first volume of a complete history of the stage conditions, Montague Summers offered the following admonition:

Without some knowledge, some visualization of Restoration stage conditions the reader of a play by Dryden, Congreve, Otway, or any contemporary, must often find himself hopelessly puzzled and at sea, whilst a piece of stagecraft which is in itself singularly delicate and adroit will appear consumedly clumsy and awkwardly contrived. (p. xv)

This has proved to be ridiculously true, but in the first place the warning was prompted by the savage criticism that had been poured on the plays for a hundred years.

When Lamb excused the Restoration stage as a kind of fairyland in which the rules of right and wrong were irrelevant, he was offering a mildly impressionistic reason, albeit an ill-thought-out one, for his own enjoyment of the plays. It is hard to forget Ivor Brown's remark about Lady Wishfort, that she was 'a very curious kind of fairy'. James Agate pointed out that 'That was only Elia's way', and he added, 'Leigh Hunt and Hazlitt were better champions, since they boggled at nothing and enjoyed their author straightforwardly and for all he was worth' (*Red Letter Nights*, p. 24). But the influence of Macaulay's moral position on the plays ('too filthy to handle and too noisome even to approach') was difficult to shake off. In *The Old Drama and the New* (1923), William Archer also dismissed the best drama of the age as 'that fetid fairyland, that insanitary Alsatia'. More surprisingly, Granville Barker described Wycherley's *Love in a Wood* as 'young men and their mistresses chattering their bawdry and chasing each other through scene after scene, till one asks: How could an audience both be clever enough to understand the story and stupid enough to be interested by it when they did?' This was in his Clark Lectures of 1930, *On Dramatic Method* (p. 121), and, responding in a letter, Gilbert Murray 'agreed violently' with the sentiment. More troubling, perhaps, was Barker's failure to appreciate the point of an acting device like the aside, when in reference to *The Plain Dealer* he applied strangely realistic standards to Fidelia's ringing simplicity with the comment, 'Nobody with any sense of the theatre would employ the aside as clumsily' (p. 123). So much for the author of *The Country Wife*.

3

When the change of attitude came, it was full of contradictions. In his *History of Eighteenth-Century Literature* (1889), Edmund Gosse, the best Restoration scholar of his day, wrote of 'the drama which is read but not acted'. Not unexpectedly, he found Etherege's plays 'marred by a deplorable laxity of tone' and Aphra Behn's suffering from a 'lamentable coarseness'. But in the same book Gosse modified his view of Wycherley's 'indelicacy' with a new critical test: his comedies contained 'very rigorous writing, much genuine wit, and sound satire of the fools and rogues whom the author saw about him' (p. 53). Unforeseen support came from Swinburne, who by 1895 had decided that Congreve was 'the greatest English master of pure comedy' and *The Way of the World* 'the unequalled and unapproached masterpiece of English comedy', and he ranked the playwright with Molière (*Miscellanies*, pp. 52–4). Then in his *Seventeenth-Century Studies* of 1897, Gosse declared that 'the entire neglect of [Etherege's] three plays is an unworthy return for the singular part he played in the creation of modern English comedy' (p. 259), but at the same time observed 'the little graphic touches, the intimate impression, the clear, bright colour of the scenes' in *She Would If She Could*. And he makes an unusual addition: 'The two sprightly girls [Ariana and Gatty] must have been particularly delightful and diverting to *witness*', especially in the party at the Bear (III.3) when the playwright 'with his singular eye for colour, crowds the stage with damsels in sky-blue, and pink, and flame-coloured taffetas' (pp. 272–4, my italics). In sum, Gosse showed notable signs of wanting to apply a test of performance, and by 1912, when he edited the *Everyman* collection of Restoration plays, he actually dismissed Macaulay for going 'much too far in his diatribe' and gave the palm for the best comedy of the time to *Love for Love*, a play hitherto considered to be among the bawdiest.

The test of performance was still to come, and in Montague Summers the plays found their champion. To Archer's assertion that with few exceptions the plays were not worth reviving, Summers responded, 'I don't believe this personally for one moment, not for one moment,' and when he staged *Marriage à la Mode* at the Lyric, Hammersmith in 1920, he wrote confidently, 'For two hundred years everybody has been saying that Dryden's comedies were impossible. We showed them that they were wrong' (Joseph Jerome, *Montague Summers*, p. 42). How are we to see the virtues in the Restoration comedies? – 'This can only be done by producing them.' It was not the whole answer – the magic would not work unless they were produced in a certain way – but the moral objections began to evaporate as soon as the plays were staged. Laughter dispelled prurience. In Walter Kerr's words, 'Nothing that is truly funny can ever be titillating, because the very fact of titillation is being rendered absurd' (*Tragedy and Comedy*, p. 163).

4

THE LIFE IS IN THE STYLE

There were more than 400 plays written between 1660 and 1700, and some 180 playwrights wrote them. Quite a prolific period of theatre. So why did their audience enjoy plays of a kind which suffered so mixed a reception in the long years that followed? The repeated quip that no audience bright enough to understand a Restoration plot could possibly be dull enough to like it, calls for an answer.

The dictum that it is the 'how' and not the 'what' that is the cause of drama was never so true as for the Restoration. Neo-classical theory would have conceded as much: in *The Adventures of a Rake* (1759) we may read, 'When the skill of the player is added to that of the poet, and the one gives utterance to the other's conceptions, it is not the actor or the poet that we hear, 'tis the character of the drama that speaks to us.'

It becomes a matter of overriding importance to identify what Ivor Brown, in reviewing *The Old Bachelor* for the Saturday Review in 1924, called an appropriate 'convention', in this case one in which to act Congreve. The doll-like Araminta and Bellinda, Sylvia and her spinet, did not mix, he thought, with the rough-and-tumble of Captain Bluffe, on this occasion played by Roy Byford who had enjoyed a recent success as Falstaff, and the broad playing of Fondlewife by Hay Petrie, at that time the 'resident clown' at the Old Vic. 'One would give much', wrote Brown, 'to have a glimpse of Drury Lane in 1693. How bluff was Bluffe? How did the ladies move and speak? Was it all riot and ritual? Or was it, as we saw it this week, a marriage, even a polygamy, of styles?' (7 June). Even those who already find the comedies sufficiently full of laughter and delight, tantalized by flirtatious girls or impertinent men (and many may, like Elia, have made their own peace with the devil), feel a need to reconcile the extremes and excesses of so lively a comedy. The solutions will be found in the conventions of the earlier stage.

The frankness of sexual morality in Restoration comedy no longer shocks and distracts the critic and the playgoer. Today our troubles come, not from licentious behaviour on the stage, but from uncommon distortions of the comic mirror. As an audience we have been living too long in the shadow of Ibsen and Chekhov, Stanislavsky and Freud, exposed to the limited kind of dramatic style which has been unnaturally perpetuated by the proscenium arch and the photographic actuality of film and television. An aside on television is all but ineffective, and a wink at the audience in the theatre is still thought by some to be unforgivable: both 'break the illusion'.

Play implies interplay, and the proper study of drama is a study of the interplay between stage and audience. The Restoration especially enjoyed a comedy of non-illusion. It was replete with stage convention and practice which deny any idea that the drama sought some kind of realism – conventions which included prologues and epilogues, soliloquies and asides, winks and double-takes, glances and throw-aways. All were at work linking the stage and the audience, so that the drama was less a realistic portrait of Restoration life than a stage image, at best an extension of its self-image. The comic stage held no mirror up to nature, but, to echo Swift, was 'a sort of glass, wherein beholders do generally discover everybody's face but their own'. In his *Amusements Serious and Comical* (1700), Tom Brown's lively assessment was, 'The playhouse is an enchanted island, where nothing appears in reality what it is, nor what it should be' (Amusement IV).

We can reconstruct the seventeenth-century playhouse, but we cannot bring back the audience and spirit of the time. When we see a Restoration comedy on the stage today, it is done in circumstances quite alien to the originals. We often see, in fact, a museum piece, a display of colourful costumes, period poses and drama school manners. The interplay between actor and spectator is missing, and with it the experience of the comedy. A play in performance is like an electric circuit in which the vital current flows from the stage to the audience and back again. If in this century the circuit is broken, judgments will go wildly astray, and we may well wonder whether something so narrowly of its own time can have value for us three hundred years later.

In *The Country Wife*, II.I the charming actress Elizabeth Boutell introduced Margery Pinchwife to the audience with the line, 'Pray, sister, where are the best fields and woods to walk in, in London?' The line is addressed to Alithea, Margery's sister-in-law and a London lady who 'knows the town'. On a simple level this is an adequate 'situation' line for a new character who must convey the idea that she is from the country; innocent Margery believes all the world to be an extension of the country life she knows best. There is a good joke in this suggestion of the disparity between town and country ways, and that is the literary explanation of the line. But there is a far better one just beneath the surface. As Margery provocatively displays her new dress, her audience must also wonder about her reasons for wanting to walk out, and the sight of the knowing surprise in Alithea's raised eyebrows, together with a glimpse of the outraged face of Pinchwife as he eavesdrops on his wife from the stage door in the proscenium, prompts and guides the delighted response of the audience.

Although it appears that Boutell managed to maintain her independence as an actress more than most, it is not to be forgotten that she was in demand as a person in her own right. Thus the same line takes on new, extra-dramatic dimensions. The intimate conditions of the Restoration playhouse lend her words the implicit qualities of an innuendo or an aside – here a simple matter of a glance of the eyes and an inflection in the voice. So another laugh was intended to follow the first as the actress plays to the pit, her question, now doubly provocative, addressed to every man – and woman – in the audience. Alithea at this moment becomes a go-between, and her quizzical smile in turn a response to the house's roar of approval at the question. At the same time Pinchwife's rage becomes that of every close husband, his gesticulation increasing in its threat the louder the audience laughs at him.

It was all a game, and in ways like this the Restoration comic stage established one of the most extraordinary games in the history of the theatre.

THE PLAYGOERS: A HOMOGENEOUS AUDIENCE

There is no need to re-open the issue of the composition of the audience, its representativeness, its relationship with a licentious court and its qualities as a coterie. Let us lay the ghosts of Allardyce Nicoll, who in his *History of English Drama* (vol. I, p. 8) argued for an *élite*, court audience, and Emmett Avery, who in 'The Restoration Audience' thought it was wider. It is sufficient that for a particular social group the playhouses were on a pleasure circuit that included the parks and the brothels, the gaming-houses and the bagnios. For if we accept Avery's argument that the audience also contained a good number of professional men and their wives – administrators, writers, doctors, lawyers, parliamentarians and men of affairs, as well as a few merchants – Nicoll's idea that the nobility and their ladies were at the centre of things is not exploded. Avery's playgoers shared the same privileged background and by no means made the audience more representative of the people of London. In any case, there is no reason to doubt that the playwrights, like the actors, aimed their wit at the highest social level of the house, indeed, at the better-paying part of the audience. John Dennis believed that when a majority of men of taste and culture 'declared themselves upon any new dramatic performance, the town fell immediately in with them' (*Critical Works*, vol. II, p. 277).

Everything points to this extraordinary fact about Restoration drama: that the social attitude of its audience was the narrowest in the history of the public theatre. The Restoration was certainly not going to produce the range of dramatic interest found in the Elizabethan theatre. Nevertheless, its special homogeneity enabled author and audience to create a social comedy in which the performance jokes would be frankly 'in-house'. Just as at a private party the familiarity of one guest with another removes certain inhibitions which would otherwise spoil the fun, so homogeneity in the theatre encourages a free expression of feeling and opinion. Paradoxically, therefore, the narrow social representatives of the Restoration playgoers made for an excellent audience.

The writers themselves, men of high birth like the Duke of Buckingham, Sir Charles Sedley and Sir George Etherege, or courtiers like Dryden and Wycherley, were members of the same set, and as such they could serve as both its mouthpiece and its critic. This final element of homogeneity produced a drama of unique mutuality, and so in yet another way the conditions were ripe for a drama played as a social game.

THE BEHAVIOUR OF THE AUDIENCE

Dryden's concern in his preface to *The Conquest of Granada* notwithstanding, that the poet should 'endeavour an absolute dominion over the minds of the spectators', much evidence has been collected that by any modern standards Restoration playgoers were uncommonly ill-behaved. Visitors to London, essayists and diarists, authors in prologue, epilogue and scenes from many of the plays themselves, all paint an alarming picture that attests to a rare lack of decorum in the house. It seems that rapport with the actors and actresses extended to the spectator's jumping on the stage itself and visiting the rooms behind the stage, while pit, box and gallery enacted a drama of their own. Here is a small sample of the evidence in order to colour in the picture.

Henri Misson's *Memoirs* give a first impression of the scene in the pit, which he described as an 'amphitheatre' of green cloth-covered benches without backs. It was a place where 'men of quality, particularly the younger sort, some ladies of reputation and virtue, and abundance of damsels that hunt for prey, sit all together..., higgledy-piggledy, chatter, toy, play, hear, hear not' (Summers, *Restoration Theatre*, p. 31). Hear and hear not? – continuity of attention is not characteristic or prescriptive at a Restoration comedy, and we may wonder at the unusual challenge to the players.

A variety of more or less cynical reasons have been ascribed to the playgoers for going to the play. In the fourth of his *Amusements* Tom Brown is confident that their behaviour comes of empty heads. His enchanted island of a playhouse is

frequented by persons of all degrees and qualities whatsoever, that have a great deal of idle time lying upon their hands and can't tell how to employ it worse. Here lords come to laugh, and to be laughed at for being there and seeing their qualities ridiculed by every worthless poet. Knights come hither to learn the *à la mode* grin, the antic brow, the new-fashioned cringe, and how to adjust their phiz to make themselves as ridiculous by art as they are by nature.

Hither come the country gentlemen to show their shapes, and trouble the pit with irrelevances about hawking, hunting, their handsome wives and their housewifery. There sits a beau like a fool in a frame, that dares not stir his head nor move his body for fear of incommoding his wig, ruffling his cravat, or putting his eyes or mouth out of the order his *maître de danse* set it in; whilst a bully beau comes drunk into the pit, screaming out, 'Damn me, Jack, 'tis a confounded play, let's to a whore, and spend our time better.'

Aping Dekker's *The Gull's Hornbook* of 1609, Samuel Vincent in 1674 offered London *The Young Gallant's Academy*, in which chapter v gives some ironic 'Instructions for a young gallant how to behave himself in the playhouse'.

Let our gallant (having paid his half-crown, and given the door-keeper his ticket) presently advance himself into the middle of the pit, where having made his honour to the rest of the company, but especially to the vizard-masks, let him pull out his comb, and manage his flaxen wig with all the grace he can. Having so done, the next step is to give a hum to the China orange-wench, and give her her own rate for her oranges (for 'tis below a gentleman to stand haggling like a citizen's wife) and then to present the fairest to the next vizard-mask .... Let him but consider what large comings-in are pursed up sitting in the pit. .

   1. First, a conspicuous eminence is gotten, by which means the best and most essential parts of a gentleman, as his fine clothes and peruke, are perfectly revealed.

   2. By sitting in the pit, if you be a knight, you may happily get you a mistress.

(Summers, p. 322)

In all this the plays themselves are scarcely mentioned; at best the reason to go to the play is 'to hoard up the finest play-scraps' he can find, 'upon which his lean wit may most savourly feed for want of other stuff'.

In a multitude of references to the gentleman playgoers, the plays themselves seem to join in a common joke. This is Lansdowne's *The She-Gallants*:

They spread themselves in parties all over the house; some in the pit, some in the boxes, others in the galleries, but principally on the stage; they cough, sneeze, talk loud, and break silly jests; sometimes laughing, sometimes singing, sometimes whistling, till the house is in uproar; some laugh and clap; some hiss and are angry; swords are drawn, the actors interrupted, the scene broken off, and so the play's sent to the devil. (III.1)

And Cibber's *Love's Last Shift*:

SIR NOVELTY FASHION. Then you must know, my coach and equipage are as well known as myself; and since the conveniency of two playhouses, I have a better opportunity of showing them; for between every act – whisk – I am gone from one to th'other: – Oh! what pleasure 'tis, at a good play, to go out before half an act's done!

9

NARCISSA. Why at a good play?

SIR NOVELTY FASHION. O! madam, it looks particular, and gives the whole audience an opportunity of turning upon me at once: then do they conclude I have some extraordinary business, or a fine woman to go to at least: and then again, it shows my contempt of what the dull town think their chiefest diversion . . . . (II.I)

The shaft of satire in such accounts is not to be ignored, but their chief suggestion is of a drama which is serving more than a dramatic end. More, that playwright, actor and audience alike implicitly acknowledge this wider role.

The playbills often carried a useless warning, 'No person to stand on the stage'; but any beau might take it upon himself to use the stage for self-display. Here Berenice describes the behaviour of Lord Brainless in D'Urfey's *The Marriage-Hater Matched*:

From the box, whip he's in the pit, from the pit, hop he's in the gallery, from thence hey pass between the scenes in a moment, when I have seen him spoil many a comedy, by baulking the actors' entrance, for when I have eagerly expected some buffoon to divert, the first nauseous appearance has been my Lord. (II.I)

Nor would such a gentleman, pursuing his ends as patron of the arts, hesitate to make free also with the tiring-rooms. Selfish enters '*bawling*' in Shadwell's *A True Widow*, 'I have enjoyed the prettiest creature, just now, in a room behind the scenes' (act IV). Colley Cibber complained bitterly of the difficulty of acting if the players had no privacy.

If they wished, amateur critics in the pit would quite disregard the efforts of the actors on the stage. The Prologue to Etherege's *The Comical Revenge* complains,

> And gallants, as for you, talk loud i'th'pit,
> Divert yourselves and friends with your own wit.

Such playgoers could, according to the Prologue to Cartwright's *The Ordinary*,

> sit out a play of three hours long,
> Minding no part of't but the dance or song.

It comes as no surprise to learn that when such an audience was actually displeased with a production, there was no restraining its hissing and clapping.

Life in the auditorium was much enlivened by the presence of women who had no intention of watching the play, for in the pit the orange-girls and ladies of the town had a free run. Again, there is an abundance of evidence in the plays for this rival activity. Thus the Prologue to D'Urfey's *Don Quixote* reported,

> The orange-miss, that now cajoles the duke
> May sell her rotten ware without rebuke.

There is much more like this, and the best collection of sources may be found in Summers's chapter III in *The Restoration Theatre*, 'The audience pleased and displeased'. Rival attraction indeed, and Betterton made the point explicitly through his character Brittle in *The Amorous Widow*: ''Tis a better entertainment, than any part of the play can be' (act II).

Any effect of stage illusion was impossible under such circumstances. Indeed, we might ask what kind of dialogue, what kind of play, was it necessary to write in order to compete with such real-life attractions? If nothing else, the stage had to satisfy an audience in a very special mood, and certainly not attempt to suppress its pleasure in playgoing. There is only a problem, however, if one sees the play and its audience set in some sort of adversary position. If the activity on the stage is an extension of the activity in the auditorium, then both are at one, and this condition will dictate the way the actors play to their audience through the medium of the play.

The behaviour of the Restoration audience has been assumed to represent a display of disrespect for the art of the theatre. However, turn the coin and such apparent lack of decorum could be the ultimate sign of a theatre of non-illusion. If an audience enjoys such freedom, it is also enjoying an unusual sense of possession and belonging, holding the drama in a special affection, that of an audience which has completely accepted its own participatory role in the business of playmaking. Another paradox.

A SELF-CONSCIOUS THEATRE

In his controversial essay, 'On Some of the Old Actors', Lamb also touched on the nature of dramatic 'fancy' and illusion. The audience, he felt, had to be 'a party to the scene'. The audience for whom the early comedians wrote, Dryden, Etherege, Shadwell, Wycherley, was involved in the game.

As late as 1702, Farquhar declared in his *Discourse*, 'The rules of English comedy don't lie in the compass of Aristotle or his followers but in the pit, box, and galleries.' This is not an oblique reference to the intransigence of 'the drama's patrons' with their catcalls, the annoying habit of pelting the stage with orange-peel and the cabals arranged to kill a new play, but to a more interior factor the playwright was well aware of, the cheerful and cheeky break-up of the unities. This casual treatment of the rules was occasioned not by a desire for realism, but by a freedom of time and place and plotting expected in a comedy in which the audience was a full partner. Farquhar writes of commonplaces in no commonplace manner:

– The poet expects no more that you should believe the plot of his play than old Aesop designed the world should think his eagle and lion talked like you and I.
– There are several improbabilities, nay, impossibilities, that all the criticisms in nature cannot correct.
– The whole audience at the same time knows that this [Alexander] is Mr Betterton who is strutting upon the stage and tearing his lungs for a livelihood.
– I may travel from Constantinople to Denmark, so to France, and home to England, and rest long enough in each country besides. But you'll say: How can you carry us with you? Very easily, sir, if you be willing to go.
– Whereabouts are you now, sir? Were not you the very minute before in the pit in the English playhouse talking to a wench, and now, *presto pass*, you are spirited away to the banks of the river Nile.

The self-conscious quality in Restoration comedy may be ascribed not only to a dual consciousness in the actor, but also to the same affliction in the spectator as he shifts in and out of the processes of the play in performance.

The playhouse after 1660 scarcely encouraged illusion of the hypnotic variety, if only because the same chandeliers that illuminated the actor also illuminated his audience, and performance in conditions of overall lighting and intimate space is of a special order. An actor working inside an illuminated picture-frame stage cut off by a wall of darkness tends to play in his own world, that of the fictional play. Without such a refuge, he tends to play in the real world of the audience, as Grotowski found: 'Once a spectator is placed in an illuminated zone, or in other words becomes visible', he wrote in *Towards a Poor Theatre*, 'he too begins to play a part in the performance' (p. 20). This and other physical characteristics of the playhouse dictated the kind of dialogue written, the kind of playing and the kind of attention bestowed on it.

S.L. Bethell's conclusions about the Elizabethan stage in his *Shakespeare and the Popular Dramatic Tradition* speak also for the Restoration: 'The inability [of the Elizabethan theatre] to produce an illusion of actuality', he argued, 'was wholly to the good. . . . The audience are vividly aware of acting in progress and the communication, through their co-operative goodwill, of a work of dramatic art.' He goes on to suggest a virtue in this theatre of non-illusion which must apply with special force in the case of comedy when he says that 'this double consciousness of the play world and real world has a solid advantage of "distancing" a play, so that the words and deeds of which it consists may be critically weighed in the course of its performance' (pp. 29–30). Comedy works, as Brecht confirmed, when an audience is not emotionally involved with the drama, and the best of its kind is rich with undercutting and alienating devices of speech and action which keep the spectator aware that he is at a play and hold him in a critical frame of mind; he is given the freedom to laugh.

In the new jargon, we are skirting the hazy but exhilarating universe of 'metatheatre', where actor and audience alike self-consciously indulge the imaginative pleasures of dramatic pretence. Actors in their masks of character let it be known that *they* know they are on a stage. Spectators gladly call for the improbable and the impossible. The stage gains another degree of intimacy with those who watch it by having them share the moment-by-moment activity of creating the drama. The author develops a special skill in commenting, slyly or openly, on his own business as a craftsman, as if he were on the stage himself. The style of writing, of acting and of viewing all undergo a transformation, and what might have been taken to be secondary characteristics of the art of drama begin to command the whole event.

One transparent feature of the Restoration comic stage is the constant reference to the existence of the playhouse itself, together with all its multifarious doings. It is not surprising that this is also an age of burlesque, which is metatheatre at its most outrageous. Burlesque soon erupts with Davenant's *The Playhouse To Be Let* (1663), an entertainment using its whole first act as a framing device in which lowly playhouse workers, tirewoman, charwoman, housekeeper, player, musician and dancing-master, discuss their situation before the drama's 'teeming muse, big with imagination', throws out a medley of comedy and farce, heroic and burlesque opera.

The impulse towards parody comes to early maturity with Buckingham's *The Rehearsal* (1671), which mocks the conventions of comedy's tragic counterpart unmercifully. The burlesque spirit continues throughout the period with a stream of playhouse jokes, parodied heroics and mock critiques in the manner of Molière, like the well-known discussion of the morality of *The Country Wife* in *The Plain Dealer*. In this atmosphere, quips about the players and playgoers themselves between the stage and the house were commonplace. Upon the suggestion that the actor playing Don Diego in *The Gentleman Dancing-Master* is 'a very good fool', James Nokes as Monsieur de Paris returns immediately, 'Nauh, nauh, Nokes is a better fool' (III.1).

The famous fourth act of Shadwell's *A True Widow* provided quite a Pirandellian experience for the playgoers at Dorset Garden in 1678. The author brings almost his whole cast of characters, more than twelve, on stage as if *'into the playhouse, seating themselves'*, ostensibly so that

Isabella, masked, may spy on Bellamour's activities when he goes to the play. Dialogue is at first provided in fragments, as if the on-stage audience has broken into some five smaller groups, and when several supers enter, the lines widen in their reference to embrace both the stage audience and the real one:

Several young coxcombs fool with the orange-women.
ORANGE-WOMAN. Oranges! will you have any oranges?
1ST BULLY. What play do they play? Some confounded play or other.
PRIG. A pox on't, madam! What should we do at this damned playhouse? Let's send for some cards, and play at lang-trilloo in the box. Pox on 'em! I ne'er saw a play had anything in't; some of 'em have wit now and then, but what care I for wit?

And,

1ST BULLY. Damme! when will these fellows begin? Plague on't! here's a staying.
2ND MAN. Whose play is this?
3RD MAN. One Prickett's – poet Prickett.
1ST MAN. Oh, hang him! Pox on him! he cannot write. Prithee let's to Whitehall.

There is more like this until, '*The play begins. Enter Lover and Wife*', who introduce a typical Restoration comedy situation of cuckolding. They do so in very dry prose, dull enough to provoke the following:

1ST MAN. Damme! I don't like it.
2ND MAN. Pox on the coxcomb that writ it! there's nothing in't.
1ST MAN. Gad, I love drums, and trumpets, and much ranting, roaring, hussing and fretting, and good store of noise in a play.

When the hapless husband enters, the lover kicks him several times, and this is followed by some silly business with two lovers hiding and squabbling under a table. However, the audience on stage has lost all interest by this time.

2ND MAN (*to a vizard*). Gad! some whore, I warrant you, or chambermaid in her lady's old clothes. (*He sits down and lolls in the orange-wench's lap.*)
3RD MAN. She must be a woman of quality; she has right point.
4TH MAN. 'Faith! she earns all the clothes on her back by lying on't.

Meanwhile Prig '*raps people on the backs, and twirls their hats, and then looks demurely, as if he did not do it*', until a fight breaks out and the play-within-the-play breaks up. Between the inner and the outer plays there is a slight echo of the theme of jealousy (Isabella's of Gartrude, Bellamour's of Stanmore), but it would be a mistake to look for the correspondences of Jacobean double plotting; the fun lies in the cracked mirror that Shadwell holds up to the behaviour of the real audience for it to enjoy.

Restoration comedies, moreover, had little need to set up such frames for a play-within-a-play: the way they were presented prompted elements of metatheatre spontaneously. The foolish pretensions as a 'virtuoso' of Dryden's Sir Martin Mar-all gave the author an immediate opportunity to pretend to mock his own play:

WARNER. Madam, there's a coach at door to carry you to the play.
SIR MARTIN. Which house do you mean to go to?
MILLISENT. The Duke's, I think.
SIR MARTIN. It is a damned play, and has nothing in't.
MILLISENT. Then let us to the King's.
SIR MARTIN. That's e'en as bad.

(III.1)

The joke lay in the fact that the audience was actually watching *Sir Martin Mar-all* at the Duke's Theatre. In act V of *The Gentleman Dancing-Master* Wycherley contrives to ridicule his own play and cast a barb at his possible critics all at one stroke. Asked what she is thinking of by the man who has gained access to her by pretending to be her dancing-master, Hippolita replies,

I am thinking if some little filching inquisitive poet should get my story, and represent it on the stage, what those ladies, who are never precise but at a play, would say of me now; that I were a confident coming piece I warrant, and they would damn the poor poet for libelling the sex.

This kind of wit deserves to be recognized as of a different order: *pace* Cocteau, not wit in the theatre, but wit of the theatre.

At about this time the plays of Etherege and Wycherley were equally rich in playhouse wit, and in instance after instance the unexpected superimposition of the actual on the fictional was good for a laugh. In act V of *She Would If She Could* everyone can enjoy Gatty's discussion of dissembling – both on and off the stage. 'I hate to dissemble when I need not', she says to Ariana. ''Twould look as affected in us to be reserved now we're alone as for a player to maintain the character she acts in the tiring-room.' In *The Country Wife* Sparkish says he dislikes playwrights for making him sound so like a fool:

DORILANT. But the poets damned your songs, did they?
SPARKISH. Damn the poets! They turned 'em into burlesque, as they call it. That burlesque is a hocus-pocus trick they have got, which, by the virtue of *hictius doctius, topsy-turvy*, they make a wise and witty man in the world a fool upon the stage, you know not how; and 'tis therefore I hate 'em too, for I know not but it may be my own case.

(III.2)

That little hesitation by poor Sparkish in his last line is a brilliant touch. As choice is the instance of Mrs Loveit in *The Man of Mode*, who can accuse Dorimant of going behind the scenes and fawning upon 'those little insignificant creatures, the players' (II.2) when she is a player herself. As late as *The Way of the World* Congreve has Witwoud complete the ensemble of act v with the remark, 'What, are you all got together, like players at the end of the last act?' Such intrusive playhouse references are irresistible to an audience, and shade easily into the cuts at actual social behaviour which permeate every text.

RECREATING THE PERFORMANCE

To reconstruct even fragmentary moments from period comedy in its original playhouse is not easy, but the attempt must be made if its demise is to be prevented. The following is a rather uneven list of external sources which can occasionally supplement a study of the text and assist in building up a picture.

- In the modern theatre the promptbooks with which director and actor work are comparatively informative about today's stagecraft. In the seventeenth century there are disappointingly few that have survived, and these offer little more than a smattering of technical details – cues for scene changes, music, discoveries, entrances and exits, and an occasional amendment or cut in the printed text. Charles Shattuck would say that we must make do with crumbs.
- There was no formal reviewing of plays at this time, but there were a number of diaries, letters, memoirs, travel-books and other reports by contemporary playgoers and visitors (Pepys and Evelyn, for example, but also foreign observers like the Grand Duke of Tuscany Cosmo the Third, Henri de Valbourg Misson and Gaston Jean-Baptiste Cominges), and also impressions supplied by such satirists as Ned Ward and John Gay scribbling vividly about turn-of-the-century London. Even then, such literature yields precious little on the acting of comedy. When modern commentators like Alan Downer and Philip Highfill discuss the style of Restoration acting, they write of the tragic stage, and then chiefly after 1700. Highfill makes the point in his essay, 'Performers and Performing': 'Comic styles are almost impossible to discriminate for purposes of discussion today. They were imitated and inherited and were developed within confines of "type" just as were the broad "lines" of tragic heroes, heroines, and villains' (in Robert Hume, ed., *The London Theatre World*, p. 163, n.116).
- The recognition of the particular actors and actresses, with their individual qualities and contributions to a production, for whom a

play was written or with whom it was cast, will speak for the
continuity of a stage tradition. However, even here, such knowledge will often merely affirm that stock characters and performances were the staple of the Restoration comic stage, and tell us
too little about the essential variations that emerge when different
personalities recreate the parts. Yet such variations on familiar
themes are the lifeblood of a comic repertory.

- The courtesy or etiquette books of the day, often published in Paris
  and translated for the London reader, can establish a norm of polite
  behaviour, and certain works happily constitute a unique resource:
  one thinks particularly of Antoine de Courtin's *The Rules of
  Civility* (1671), the anonymous *The Art of Making Love, or, Rules
  for the Conduct of Ladies and Gallants in Their Amours* (1676), Jean
  Gailhard's *The Compleat Gentleman, or, Directions for the Order of
  Youth as to Their Breeding at Home and Travelling Abroad* (1678)
  and the Abbot Jean-Baptiste Morvan de Bellegarde's books of
  Reflexions upon Ridicule and *Reflexions upon the Politeness of
  Manners* (1706–7), not to mention other popular compilations like
  Le Mercure Galant (1672), which can lay claim to be the first
  international fashion magazine.
- It is productive to look at prints of the costumes and clothing of the
  time. These often suggest something of the characteristic posture,
  movement and gestures of a Restoration lady or gentleman. For
  this approach I am indebted to the work of Wanderlie Henshaw,
  who pioneered the study of graphic sources as a way of visualizing
  the activity on the Restoration stage. She drew especially on the
  rich resources of the Cabinet des Estampes of the Bibliothèque
  Nationale in Paris, particularly the etchings of the brothers
  Bonnart, Jean Dieu de Saint-Jean, Nicholas Arnoult, Jean Le
  Pautre and others. The several books on the arts of fencing and
  dancing can also supplement our picture of the stage. With all this,
  however, we must concede Lyn Oxenford's cautionary note in
  Producing Period Plays, where she writes, 'All period movement is
  partly guesswork based on pictures and the fact that the human
  body has not altered basically' (p. 186). Nevertheless, some
  familiarity with the restrictions of weight and other features of the
  clothing of the day – a familiarity especially to be gained by wearing
  it – can be an enormous help in bringing Restoration characters to
  life.

All this may not amount to much that is tangible, but such resources
increase our chances of pulling together the relevant details of performance, in order to match them with the evidence of the printed text of the

plays themselves. This less literary reading of the lines, taken together with whatever experience and insight are to be gleaned from twentieth-century productions and their reception by modern audiences, can be a spur to our better appreciation of what happened on the comic stage of the Restoration.

2. The playhouse and the performance

It is in the nature of drama for its actors to find a space to work almost anywhere, and one of the more extraordinary features of Restoration London, robbed of its playhouses, was its initial choice of the Tudor tennis court. Roofed and with a surrounding gallery surmounted by high windows, not only was this the most readily adaptable structure for the occasion, but it came closest to the fashionable indoor theatres many remembered from the years before Cromwell. It also proved to be a starting-point for the new theatres that grew up in the next hundred years, and it might be claimed that the effects of putting on plays in a tennis court determined the kind of play and performance offered the public for generations to come.

It is easy to tear down a theatre, immensely more difficult to open one. 'To appease and avert the wrath of God', the decree of Cromwell's parliament had closed all of London's theatres within a month of the end of the Civil War in 1642; in 1648 they were destroyed. It was no surprise that when Charles II was restored to his throne, he as promptly issued the Royal Grant of 21 August 1660 giving Thomas Killigrew and Sir William Davenant 'power and authority to erect two companies of players' and 'to purchase, build and erect, or hire at their charge, so they shall think fit, two houses or theatres'. Both companies, the King's Men (His Majesty's Servants) under Killigrew and the Duke's Men (the company of the King's brother, James, Duke of York) under Davenant, chose a tennis court, just as the 'stroller' actor–manager George Jolly had done in exile in Krachbein in Germany and as Molière had done in Paris when in 1658 he hired the Jeu de Paume des Mestayers.

In 1660 Killigrew quickly adapted Gibbons's tennis court in Vere Street for his first Theatre Royal; on 20 November Pepys pronounced it 'the finest playhouse, I believe, that ever was in England', which seems a questionable statement about so makeshift a theatre. In 1661 Davenant adapted Lisle's tennis court in Lincoln's Inn Fields, and there he produced *The Siege of Rhodes*, evidently with scenery that took longer to set up. The comedies occasionally include jokes about the use of tennis courts located in the shadowy district of Covent Garden and rubbing shoulders with alehouses and brothels, but the two leaders of the English theatre had set a pattern.

1 Wren's Drury Lane design redrawn

We may surmise that it was the size of the tennis court that had the
immediate appeal for actor and spectator alike. Edward Langhans has
recently summarized our conjectures about its dimensions in his chapter
'The Theatres' in Hume's *The London Theatre World*. Gibbons's tennis
court was 70 by 25 feet externally, with a stage area 22 feet deep by 14 feet
wide, and Lisle's tennis court was not much bigger, 75 by 30 feet, with its
stage 34 by 20 feet. Neither had a capacity of much over 400 persons.
These theatres were soon to be replaced by Davenant at Dorset Garden in
1671, and, after his Bridges Street Theatre Royal of 1663 was destroyed
by fire in 1672, by Killigrew with the same dimensions in the new Theatre
Royal at Drury Lane in 1674. The size of these two stages increased to 51

2 Wren's Drury Lane theatre imaginatively recreated

by 30 feet and 66 by 31 feet respectively, with the house capacity more than doubling. However, in order to survive a difficult time of half-empty houses, the two companies joined forces in 1682. It should be emphasized in all this that, if it was the intimacy of the tennis courts that first attracted the actors, this quality remained. Langhans makes the specific point that 'the crucial distance from the stage to the back of the front boxes did not increase' (p. 42).

21

Such intimacy dominated performance throughout our period, and the theatrical principle behind the Restoration tennis court was simple. Divided in two where the net would have been, the available space was given half to the actors, half to the audience, so that the important characteristic of this theatre was a deep and prominent apron or forestage which projected into the pit past the side-boxes, and dwarfed – literally putting into the shade – the space behind it where scenery might have been set. Two or three doors were placed on both sides of the proscenium arch, so that when the curtain was drawn up an actor would find himself playing out into the house as soon as he entered. Richard Leacroft has thus expressed it: 'The proscenium, or actors', stage is seen to be completely within the limits of the auditorium' (*The Development of the English Playhouse*, p. 96).

Time after time stage directions urge the actor to '*come forward*' or '*advance to the front of the stage*', especially, as we shall see, after a discovery, when we might read, '*They come forward, and the scene shuts behind them*' (this taken from act v of Vanbrugh's *The Confederacy*). It was a more striking intimacy than that enjoyed by the theatres of the Elizabethans. Within the dimensions of the tennis court it would have seemed that the players were performing in the same room with the spectators, especially when the whole space was lit by the same tallow candles in wall-brackets and one or two chandeliers, none of which could be snuffed until the end of the play. The playhouse provided one arena for all.

The actors were sharply aware of the change in playing conditions when, near the end of the century, Christopher Rich cut back the vital apron at Drury Lane in order to increase the size of the pit. The actor, manager and playwright Colley Cibber was certainly angry, and here again is the well-known comment from chapter 12 of his *Apology*:

When the actors were in possession of that forwarder space to advance upon, the voice was then more in the centre of the house, so that the most distant ear had scarce the least doubt or difficulty in hearing what fell from the weakest utterance: all objects were thus drawn nearer to the sense; every painted scene was stronger; every grand scene and dance more extended; every rich or fine-coloured habit had a more lively lustre: nor was the minutest motion of a feature (properly changing with the passion, or humour, it suited) ever lost, as they frequently must be in the obscurity of too great a distance: and how valuable in advantage the facility of hearing distinctly is to every well-acted scene, every common spectator is a judge.

Particularly in a comedy, a lively scene would hardly have taken place in the darker recesses of an upstage area. Cibber reminds us that in the close conditions of the first Restoration theatres, every gesture could count and the smallest glance be seen, a slight inflection of a line could reverberate in its comic context and an aside might positively explode into the house.

THE STAGE DOORS

All entrances on to the stage were made through the doors built into the proscenium arch, with access immediately onto the apron; the scenic area remained behind the actors. For a hundred years these doors were known as the 'stage doors', usually four in number.

The actor's pattern of movement was determined by these downstage entrances. Since the actor emerged so close to the audience, his first words were not infrequently an aside, as when Horner in *The Country Wife* immediately draws the audience into his wicked scheme on introducing the Quack:

A quack is as fit for a pimp as a midwife for a bawd; they are still but in their way both helpers of nature. (I.I)

It was no different at the end of the period, as when Silvia in *The Recruiting Officer* wastes no time in explaining her appearance in the uniform of an ensign:

Had I but a commission in my pocket, I fancy my breeches would become me as well as any ranting fellow of 'em all, for I take a bold step, a rakish toss, a smart cock, and an impudent air to be the principal ingredients in the composition of a captain.

No doubt she attempts a delightful impersonation of Captain Plume before she spots Rose and turns from the audience thus,

What's here? Rose, my nurse's daughter. I'll go and practise. Come, child, kiss me at once. (IV.I)

A stage door could serve as a realistic door to house or chamber, as when Miss Prue's Nurse begins act III by discovering Tattle inside Prue's room in *Love for Love*, or in *The Relapse*, III.3 when Young Fashion, in pursuit of Miss Hoyden's fortune, is greeted at his door by her father Sir Tunbelly, '*with his servants armed with guns, clubs, pitchforks, scythes, etc.*'

It was, however, in most frequent use as the door of a 'closet'. What had been an inner chamber or private room since the fourteenth century could also be a cupboard after 1616, and even a water-closet after 1662, 'a closet of ease'. It is understandable therefore that hiding in a closet took on increasingly farcical implications. The girls Ariana and Gatty discover Courtall and Freeman hiding in a closet in act V of *She Would If She Could*, the same 'wood-hole', we may assume, that had concealed Mrs Sentry and Freeman in act I. Closets also became the convenient repository for hidden chaplains in *The Man of Mode*, v.2, and in Shadwell's *The Squire of Alsatia*, II.I. Mrs Termagant hides in the one already occupied by Lucia, whom she '*pulls out by the hair*', suggesting all the elements of a French farce. And hiding for lascivious purposes, with a deal of peeping no doubt, is commonplace by the time of Vanbrugh's *The Provoked Wife*, when Heartfree and Constant slip into Lady Brute's closet to escape from her husband Sir John, only to be discovered when '*he bursts open the door with his foot*' (v.2).

Nevertheless, the permanent presence of the stage doors had the chief effect of making them seem to disappear, like the proscenium arch itself. Moreover, their formal symmetry, a quality echoed in the use of the Elizabethan stage doors, could lend an amusing balance to the business of a scene. In act II of Dryden's *The Wild Gallant* opposite doors permit a farcical encounter in the 'darkness' between Loveby and Failer, as the stage directions suggest: '*Enter Loveby solus, in the dark, his sword drawn, groping out his way. Enter Failer at t'other end of the stage*'. There is an echo here of the ancient *commedia dell'arte* business of swashing blows in the dark, found also in the silly fight between Lysander and Demetrius in Shakespeare's wood near Athens.

If Buckingham's *The Rehearsal* made a point of ridiculing this symmetry by having four soldiers enter at one door and four at another (II.5), it could also create lively patterns of artificial movement, as when in *She Would If She Could* Ariana and Gatty are chased by Courtall and Freeman back and forth across the stage through the doors as if they are on the 'walks' of Mulberry Garden:

ARIANA. Look, look yonder, I protest they chase us.
GATTY. Let us bear away then; if they be truly valiant they'll quickly make more sail and board us.
The women go out, and go behind the scenes to the other door. Enter Courtall and Freeman.
FREEMAN. How fleet they are! Whatsoever faults they have, they cannot sure be broken-winded.

And so on, until the inevitable clash of the sexes upon this unusual direction:

Enter the women, and after 'em Courtall at the lower door, and Freeman at the upper on the contrary side.

(II.I)

The chase through Mulberry Garden seems realistic enough, and yet its abstract form nicely increases our amused perspective on the rites of courtship.

THE BALCONIES

Each stage door in the Restoration playhouse had a balcony built above it, so that the actors automatically enjoyed the use of a second level in close proximity with the apron and the audience. Throughout the period, as in the Elizabethan theatre, a balcony is referred to also as 'above' or as a 'window'. Richard Southern's assumption in his *Changeable Scenery*, p. 134, of 'a scenic window cut in the back shutters' seems unwarranted. On occasion the balcony was hung with a curtain as if it were a window, as in *The Rover*, II.1 where Angellica and Moretta draw a silk curtain across it, and in Mary Pix's *The Deceiver Deceived*, act V, where it is again supplied with '*a curtain to draw*'.

The balcony had a wide variety of uses, all of them suggesting an element of comic improvisation. When fiddlers play below, a lady may appear on it, as does Lady Faddle and her maid Bridget in Crowne's *The Country Wit*, act II. It is just the place for 'coquetting', and Lady Lurewell uses it for this in Farquhar's *The Constant Couple*, III.3. And it is very convenient for eavesdropping on those on the apron below, as Hypolita, Flora and Trappant find in Cibber's *She Would and She Would Not*, act I.

The balcony is also a good place from which to drop and throw things. Dryden has Wildblood and Bellamy serenading Theodosia and Jacinta '*above*' in *An Evening's Love*, II.1, until '*Jacinta throws down her handkerchief with a favour tied to it*'. Less romantically in D'Urfey's *Madam Fickle*, v.2, Zechiel from a balcony '*takes orange-peels out of his pocket, and throws at Captain Tilbury*' on the jolly line, '''Tis my father and drunk as a wheel-barrow.' Or, in reverse, Sir Nicholas Gimcrack avoids the oranges thrown at Sir Formal Trifle by staying '*above*' in Shadwell's *The Virtuoso*, act v.

The balcony also invited the actor's physical prowess. Courtine appears to have climbed Sylvia's balcony overlooking the Piazza in Covent Garden in Otway's *The Soldier's Fortune*, IV.2, causing her to '*squeak*'. The balcony doubles as a prison in Robert Howard's *The Committee*, and in act v Careless makes his escape when he '*lets down the ladder of ropes*'. A rope-ladder appears again in Pix's *The Spanish Wives*, II.5 when Camillus and Friar Andrew descend into an orchard and '*come down the wall by a ladder of ropes*'; unfortunately, '*when the Friar is halfway up, the ladder breaks, and falls down*'. A cry of 'Thieves! thieves!' is heard within and the unhappy Friar '*gets up [a] tree*'. Did the same balcony serve as the tree? The one on the other side of the stage?

In his early comedies between 1667 and 1672 Dryden seems to have been taken with this feature of the stage; it is brought into the action in

Secret Love, Sir Martin Mar-all, An Evening's Love and *The Assignation*. He can claim originality for the celebrated Cyrano scene in *Sir Martin Mar-all*, v.1, in which he makes extensive use of opposite balconies, and calls for no less than three in simultaneous use. The inept Sir Martin is determined to woo the lovely Millisent with music and song, but since he cannot play or sing 'one stop', he takes his man Warner's good advice:

Get up into your window, and set two candles by you, take my landlord's lute in your hand, and fumble on't, and make grimaces with your mouth, as if you sung; in the meantime, I'll play in the next room in the dark, and consequently your mistress, who will come to her balcony over against you, will think it to be you; and at the end of every tune, I'll ring the bell that hangs between your chamber and mine, that you may know when to have done.

So Millisent and Rose enter *'with a candle by 'em above'*, the candle of course signifying that it is dark.

ROSE. We shall have rare music.
MILLISENT. I wish it prove so; for I suspect the knight can neither play nor sing. . . .Peace, I hear them beginning to tune the lute.
ROSE. And see, madam, where your true knight Sir Martin is placed yonder like Apollo, with his lute in his hand and his rays about his head.
Sir Martin appears at the adverse window, a tune played; when it is done, Warner rings, and Sir Martin holds.

All goes well until Warner sings the song, appropriately entitled 'Blind love'; Sir Martin is so enraptured at the sight of the lady that he forgets his cue:

The song being done, Warner rings again; but Sir Martin continues fumbling, and gazing on his mistress.
MILLISENT. A pretty humoured song: – but stay, methinks he plays and sings still, and yet we cannot hear him. Play louder, Sir Martin, that we may have the fruits on't. . . .
SIR MARTIN (*peeping*). Ha! what do you say, madam? How does your ladyship like my music?
MILLISENT. O most heavenly! just like the harmony of the spheres that is to be admired, and never heard.

After this, the action continues on the stage below where his rival and three bailiffs take up the plot. In its day, with Nokes in the title part, this play was a winner, as witness Pepys, who on 16 August 1667 declared it 'the most entire piece of mirth . . . that certainly was ever writ', and Downes records that it earned the company 'more money than any preceding comedy' (p. 28).

THE SCENERY

Of slightly more consequence is the 'scenery' on the Restoration stage, although seventeenth-century texts refer only to the 'scene', and the modern idea of scenery is not thought of until a century later.

If in tragedy and opera there was a growing interest in creating effects of spectacle like fire and storm, in the comedies scenic decoration was only vaguely supplied by painted side-wings and shutters set in perspective, together with a backing of shutters that could be drawn together across the stage in grooves. An actor might be 'discovered' by opening such shutters, upon which he would come forward without breaking the flow of the action. Since curtains were not used between the acts, scene-shifting was done in full view of the audience. In *Changeable Scenery* Richard Southern believes that 'it is scenery in the stage sense of the decking of a stage, but not scenery in the landscape sense of a background seen behind people' (pp. 114–15). Thus here again there is no concept of realistic illusion. Sets were used again and again, at best merely suggesting an indoor or an outdoor scene, and the disappearing perspective, together with the rigid symmetry, provided only a representative, not a particular, background. At one point in *The Beaux' Stratagem*, act IV, we learn that Gip *'goes behind the side-scene and listens'*, but the actor is never encouraged to work in the upstage scenic area in any realistic way.

Stage directions indicating the scene are so few as to imply that location was not a big consideration. The texts carry only general suggestions about place, and are at best a loose guide, not for painting, but acting. After interior rooms and chambers, gardens and arbours are the most common, indicating the kind of movement and behaviour to be adopted, while other locations like taverns and eating-houses partly suggest the expected props and business. We have to wait for the eighteenth century for more variety: *The Recruiting Officer* sets its major scenes daringly in a provincial market-place and the neighbouring courthouse.

Any detail in the setting is always supported by the action that follows on the stage. John Tatham's *The Rump*, which calls for *'a piece of wood . . . painted like a pile of faggots and fire, and faggots lying by to supply it'*, ends with a dance round this painted bonfire. When in Shadwell's *The Squire of Alsatia*, II.2, the lines suggest that dinner is served 'in the next room', we read *'Enter four servants with four dishes of meat, who cross the stage'* in the Elizabethan way. Again, it is not until the next century that a setting grows more particular. Farquhar supplies *'a room miserably furnished'* for the sponging-house of *The Twin Rivals*, IV.3, and to encourage the impression he litters his stage with *'trunks, bandboxes, and other luggage'*. *'A tapster with a bottle and glass'* establishes Boniface's inn in the first scene of *The*

Beaux' Stratagem. It is interesting that some of the apparatus of later, more realistic, scene-setting starts to appear at about this time: 'relieves', or cut-out pieces like ground-rows, and even an early form of back-cloth wrapped on rollers begin to fill out the picture we associate with a more representational scene.

DISCOVERIES

The upstage discovery area is of little interest as an acting space, but shuttered scenery had been in use since it was introduced into the masques of Inigo Jones and John Webb, and was particularly useful when a tragic tableau was wanted. In Settle's *The Conquest of China by the Tartar* a fine example is offered by the line, 'See there the ruins of your sinking state', whereupon '*The scene opens, and is discovered a number of murdered women, some with daggers in their breasts, some thrust through with swords, some strangled, and others poisoned; with several other forms of death.*' When in this way shutters, suspended in grooves, could be slid on and off quickly, new scenes could be set one behind the other in readiness; there could be as many as four pairs of these shutters, and so four discoveries. The scene '*opens*', '*draws*', '*shuts*' or '*changes*' – all are in reference to the same device.

A street scene could change to a room in a house in a moment, or the necessary props could be quickly arranged for eating and drinking. Crowne's *Sir Courtly Nice* opens in Covent Garden, but on the cry, 'Open the door!', '*the scene is drawn*' revealing Lord Bellguard's servants, 'a company of crooked, withered, ill-looking fellows' at breakfast; Vanbrugh's *The Confederacy*, v.2 has '*Araminta, Corinna, Gripe and Money-trap are discovered at a tea-table, very gay and laughing.*'

Among many examples, these are some of the more interesting ones: in Shadwell's *The Virtuoso*, II.2 '*the scene opens and discovers Sir Nicholas Gimcrack learning to swim upon a table*', his teacher advising him to 'observe the frog!' In Crowne's *City Politiques*, act IV, perhaps just as laughable, '*The scene is drawn: Florio and Rosanna are discovered sitting arm in arm*', the very picture of a debauch and a wanton locked in an amorous embrace. Almost as eye-catching is the famous scene v.5 in Cibber's *The Careless Husband*, in which '*The scene opens, and discovers Sir Charles without his periwig, and Edging [his wife's maid] by him, both asleep in two chairs .... Then enter Lady Easy, who starts and trembles, some time unable to speak;*' after a pathetic speech she '*takes a Steinkirk [cravat] off her neck, and lays it gently on his head*', whereupon he wakes up a rake reformed – all this, according to Boswell, the true story of one Colonel Brett and his wife. The provocative discovery of a lady's bedchamber had become popular by the time of Vanbrugh's *The Relapse* (IV.3) and *The Provoked Wife* (III.3).

If many scene changes were managed by opening or closing the shutters, others were neatly effected in the Elizabethan style by verbal suggestion alone. In Crowne's *The Country Wit*, act IV, a knock on the proscenium door to introduce Lady Faddle, and the street has become the interior of her house. In Shadwell's *A True Widow*, act III, Gartrude enters to Theodosia and Isabella with the line, 'O sister, come hither! here are four men measuring of swords; I believe they are going to fight in the next field', whereupon: '*Enter Carlos, Prig, Stanmore, and Young Maggot, as in the field*', and the change is made. Speed was of the essence, but the need to bring on clumsy props like tables and chairs no doubt determined that the groove-and-shutter technique would survive for some years before drop-curtains and flying scenery came into use. It is fair to conclude that the chief virtue of the Restoration discovery was not scenic at all, but one of sustaining continuity and pace – a desirable quality in farce and light comedy. In *Changeable Scenery* Southern writes nostalgically of the passing of the visible scene-change, speaking of 'the old, quick-fire, continuous varied shows of the Stuarts and the Georgians, where so much was packed into the time' (p. 24).

FAMILIAR LOCATIONS

An empty stage can assume a location anywhere, but the Restoration comic playwright frequently made a point of calling up places that were well known to his audience, all part of the technique of inducing its self-conscious activity of mind. A play might even use its chief location for a title, like Sedley's *The Mulberry Garden*, Wycherley's *Love in a Wood; or, St James's Park*, Shadwell's *Epsom Wells* and *The Squire of Alsatia* (i.e., Southwark), John Dover's *The Mall* (a walk in St James's Park) and William Mountfort's *Greenwich Park*.

References in the dialogue to actual places are legion, and Wycherley especially enjoyed dropping names. His *Love in a Wood* and *The Gentleman Dancing-Master* names several places of assignation in their first scenes: in the former My Lady Flippant 'in distress for a husband' declares,

Have I not constantly kept Covent Garden Church, St Martin's, the playhouses, Hyde Park, Mulberry Garden, and all the other public marts where widows and maids are exposed?,

and in the latter Hippolita and Prue complain immediately of the places they have been forbidden:

HIPPOLITA. Not suffered to see a play in a twelve-month! –
PRUE. Nor to go to Ponchinello nor Paradise! –
HIPPOLITA. Nor to take a ramble to the Park nor Mulberry Gar'n! –

3 St James's Park, by John Kip, 1713

PRUE. Nor to Tottenham Court nor Islington! –
HIPPOLITA. Nor to eat a sillybub in New Spring Gar'n with a cousin! –
PRUE. Nor to drink a pint of wine with a friend at the Prince in the Sun! –
HIPPOLITA. Nor to hear a fiddle in good company! –
PRUE. Nor to hear the organs and tongs at the Gun in Moorfields! –

This dialogue constitutes quite a 'What's On in London'.

In act I of *The Country Wife* Wycherley soon has Sparkish disclose the whereabouts of the unconscionable Horner:

Said I, 'I know where the best new sign is.' 'Where?' says one of the ladies. 'In Covent Garden,' I replied. Said another, 'In what street?' 'In Russell Street,' answered I. 'Lord,' says another, 'I'm sure there was ne'er a fine new sign there yesterday.' 'Yes, but there was,' said I again, 'and it came out of France, and has been there a fortnight.'

Just a step, it seems, from the theatre in Drury Lane where the audience sat. All this before Sparkish and Dorilant discuss where to dine: 'At

Chateline's?' – 'Yes, if you will.' – 'Or at the Cock?' – 'Yes, if you please.' –
'Or at the Dog Partridge?' And no sooner are we introduced to the women
in act II than Alithea tells Margery where to go in London: 'Why, sister,
Mulberry Garden and St James's Park; and for close walks, the New
Exchange.'

Such lines have the simple effect, at the very least, of making the
audience feel at home, and no doubt it expressed its approval vocally. In
his *Restoration Theatre* Summers suggests that the scene-painting in a
play like *The Mulberry Garden* would have been authentic: 'The
presentment of any well-known centre, part of the town or other view was
very exact' (p. 219). However, the joy of these familiar references did not
lie in seeing them in paint, but in their power to charge the imagination –
the audience knew the territory, and what to expect of it.

Mulberry Garden, the New Exchange, Vauxhall, even the wilds of
Kensington in Sedley's *Bellamira*, and other fashionable 'walks' come up
again and again in the comedies. Etherege's *She Would If She Could*
managed to range over Mulberry Garden in act II, the New Exchange in
act III and the New Spring Garden (Vauxhall) in act IV. Such resorts were
indeed in regular use at this time by ladies and gentlemen of reputation,
including dukes and duchesses. In the sixth of his *Amusements* Tom
Brown slyly explains: 'We have divers sorts of walks about London; in
some you go to see and be seen, in others neither to see nor be seen, but,
like a noun substantive, to be felt, heard, and understood.' A sense of these
places is important for an appreciation of Restoration performance.

Each venue had a slightly different character. Mulberry Garden, where
Victoria and Olivia walk in act I of Sedley's play of that name (itself an
adaptation of Shirley's *Hyde Park*), and where the amorous chase is
pursued throughout *Love in a Wood*, was a walk in St James's Park,
popular because of its ability to conceal what was going on. According to
Ned Ward's *The London Spy*, it was blessed with an abundance of trees
and bushes which afforded a happy hunting-ground in spring and
summer. He offered this poem:

> S ure art and nature, nowhere else can show
> A park where trees in such true order grow.
> I n silver streams the gentle Isis here
> N o banks o'erflows, yet proudly swells so near,
> T he pleasing cup does just brimful appear.
>
> J n summer's longest days, when Phoebus takes
> A pride to pierce the thickest shades and brakes,
> M ay beauties walk beneath a verdant screen,
> E xempt from dust, and by the sun unseen.

S o thick with leaves each plant, so green the grass,
S ure mortal never viewed a sweeter place.

P revailing ladies meet in lovely swarms,
A nd bless each day its umbrage with their charms.
R ev'rence the Stuarts' name for this hereafter
K ing James the First clubbed wood, his grandson Charles found water.

There in acts III and IV of *Love's Last Shift* Loveless and Young Worthy
go a-whoring, and Sir Novelty Fashion mistakes his mistress Mrs Flareit
in her mask. There in act II of *The Provoked Wife* Lady Fancyfull and her
French maid choose to take to the 'green walk' to look for conquests. And
there in act II of *The Way of the World* we first meet Millamant 'full sail'.
These imaginary walks served the stage like a ballroom, allowing ladies
and gentlemen to assemble, separate, mix and assemble again.

The New Exchange was an arcade in the Strand with galleries of shops
above it. In *She Would If She Could*, act III, we actually meet a Mrs
Trinket and a Mrs Gazette selling their wares. The millinery and trinkets
and ballads of the New Exchange made it a special attraction for the ladies,
whose presence in turn attracted the men. But again there was more than
met the eye, as Ned Ward explains:

We moved leisurely along the Strand, meeting nothing remarkable until we came
to the New Exchange, into which seraglio of fair ladies we made our entrance, to
take a pleasing view of the cherubimical lasses, who, I suppose, had dressed
themselves up for sale to the best advantage, as well as the fopperies and toys they
dealt in . . . . The chiefest customers they had, I observed, were beaux, who, I
imagined, were paying a double price for linen, gloves, or sword-knots. (p. 162)

Moreover, as may be judged from act III of *The Country Wife*, in which
Horner is seen '*hailing away Mrs Pinchwife*' into 'the next walk', whence
he carries her up 'into the house next to the Exchange', this venue had the
additional convenience of being adjacent to the brothels of Covent
Garden.

To name Covent Garden was in fact to be a little more *risqué*. With its
'Piazza' or 'Square' it was situated in a district to the east of Drury Lane
notorious for its narrow streets and alleys in the older part of London.
This was the red-light district, and in play after play an edge was added to
the story by naming it. It was here that Horner had his lodgings, and there
the ladies followed him. Here Sylvia and Courtine of *The Soldier's
Fortune* make their assignation in act III and enjoy it in act IV. And here Sir
Courtly Nice in Crowne's play, III.2, will not drink French wine ('Deuce
take me, sir! if the clowns don't press all the grapes with their filthy naked
feet . . .; no wonder we are poisoned with their wine.')

Back west again to the close walks of the New Spring Gardens in Vauxhall, across the Thames at Lambeth, which were accessible by boat or coach and grew increasingly fashionable. The reason is not far to seek, and Tom Brown again explains:

Both sexes meet and mutually serve one another as guides to lose their way; and the windings and turnings in the little wildernesses are so intricate that the most experienced mothers have often lost themselves in looking for their daughters.

Evelyn liked it there: 'Went to New Spring Garden, Lambeth, a pretty contrived plantation' (2 July 1661). So did Pepys: 'And so up by water and to Fox Hall, where we walked a great while, and pleased mightily with the pleasure thereof, and the company there, and then in, and ate and drank, and then out again and walked. It beginning to be dark, we to a corner and sang, that everybody got about to hear us' (14 May 1668). But Rakehell the pimp deploys his forces here in *She Would If She Could*, and Pepys also reports a few incidents in which gallants 'were ready to take hold of every woman that came by them' (30 May 1668). On 1 June he witnessed two ladies being accosted, and on 27 July he writes, 'How rude some of the young gallants of the town are become, to go into people's arbours where there are no men, and almost force the women.'

Vanbrugh dramatizes such an incident in *The Provoked Wife*, IV.4, when Lady Brute and Bellinda go to Spring Garden to meet Constant and Heartfree. Bellinda is concerned that 'It's almost dark, nobody will know us', but not so the Lady, who confesses, 'I dote upon this little odd private corner. But don't let my lazy fancy confine you.' So it is that when Bellinda has walked off with Heartfree, Constant seizes Lady Brute:

LADY BRUTE (*aside*). Poor coward virtue, how it shuns the battle. – O heavens! let me go!
CONSTANT. Aye, go, aye. Where shall we go, my charming angel? Into this private arbour. Nay, let's lose no time. Moments are precious.
LADY BRUTE. And lovers wild. Pray let us stop here, at least for this time.
CONSTANT. 'Tis impossible. He that has power over you can have none over himself.
LADY BRUTE. Ah, I'm lost!

With its ornamental lake and fountains, a tavern and an orchestra, flowery walks and arbours, Vauxhall grew more elegant as other pleasure gardens were opened in the eighteenth century.

From the ranks of London's taverns, each is to be identified by its particular tone and style. When all the villains in *The Squire of Alsatia* are found drinking and whoring at The George in Whitefriars, enough has been said. When Dorimant in *The Man of Mode* chooses to dine at Long's or Locket's, we may be sure these are the resorts most in vogue, and it is

4 Vauxhall Gardens, a general prospect by S. Wale

interesting that twenty years later Lord Foppington of *The Relapse* finds reason to complain of the cost of a meal at Locket's – 'where you are so nicely served that, stap my vitals! they shall compose you a dish no bigger than a saucer which shall come to fifty shillings.'

THE MUSIC

It may be surprising to find that, for an entertainment that is often remembered for its verbal wit, Restoration comedy was notably musical, and that from the beginning a small orchestra, 'a consort of musicians' – probably a few strings, with oboe, flute and bassoon – formed a regular part of every production to serve the needs of the play. An overture played in the audience and the Prologue, for in the play-scene in *A True Widow* is found the stage direction, '*They play the curtain-time, then [the on-stage spectators] take their places.*' Accompanied songs and musical entr'actes punctuated every performance, and the Restoration actor and actress was obviously expected to be able to sing.

The place where the musicians were seated had traditionally been in a music gallery above the stage, but on 8 May 1663 Pepys records that at the Theatre Royal, Bridges Street, it was, for an unknown reason, below the stage, that is, in the pit: 'The music being below, and most of it sounding under the very stage, there is no hearing of the basses at all, nor very well of the trebles, which sure must be mended.' By the time of Buckingham's *The Chances* at Drury Lane in 1666, again the '*music plays above*' in act IV. And when the Dorset Garden Theatre opened in 1671, it too was blessed with a music gallery above the proscenium arch, as the decorative panels for *The Siege of Rhodes* appear to confirm by the musical instruments painted on them. Brecht would have approved the fact that Restoration musicians were at all times in full view of the spectators.

Musicians might also appear on the stage proper. Dancing and singing-masters would have their own: '*two flutes and a thorough-bass*' for Betty's singing lesson in II.1 of *The Squire of Alsatia*. And '*instrumental and vocal music*' is appropriately introduced by Dryden for his nunnery scene in *The Assignation*, v.2. When in Shadwell's *The Sullen Lovers* Sir Positive At-all, the 'foolish knight, that pretends to understand everything in the world', attempts musical composition in II.3, the stage direction has, '*Enter fiddlers and play a ridiculous piece of music*'. The orchestra must have relished its opportunity to contribute to the enormity of Sir Positive's eccentricity. Was a similar bit of nonsense, we may wonder, introduced into act II of Crowne's *The Country Wit* when Jack Merry brings in 'the fiddles' to serenade Lady Faddle on her balcony?

The extensive use of music, dance and song in the comedies must indicate the lightness of their tone and style, a matter easily passed over in reading them. Dances and jigs were introduced into every kind of play to add to the entertainment, and these were frequently remarked by Pepys, who seemed always to approve of what he called 'a variety of divertissement'. Matching this, vocal and instrumental music became increasingly popular both as entr'acte amusements and as integral to the plot, foreshadowing the growth of interest in opera as a form in the next century. According to Pepys's entry for 12 February 1667, Thomas Killigrew was particularly keen to promote Italian music and singing, 'a very noble undertaking' at which Pepys was 'mightily pleased'. The presence of so much music in the comedies should, if nothing else, remind us that the show on the stage was almost as unreal and full of conventions as opera itself.

LIGHTING AND EFFECTS

The Restoration playhouse was lit by daylight from its windows, supplemented by a chandelier or chandeliers hung in the centre of the building from the proscenium arch. One chandelier is pictured in the frontispiece to *Troilus and Cressida* in Rowe's *Shakespeare* of 1709 and that for Francis Kirkman's *The Wits* of 1672 has two, like the Cockpit at Court in Whitehall, for which the Lord Chamberlain mentions 'a couple of fair brass branches for lights' (Boswell, *The Restoration Court Stage*, p. 16). These candles were hung in front of the curtain over the apron, and lit before the curtain was raised. They were also supplemented by footlights, or 'floats', so-called because they were simply candles floating in troughs of water, or else lights made from cotton wick threaded through corks floating in oil, an invention from Paris. Six of these are illustrated in *The Wits* drawing, situated at the foot of the apron where the actors needed them in order to be seen. A danger of fire was constantly present, and candle snuffers would stand close to hand.

The arrangement of the lights ensured that the main acting area was well downstage on the apron; like moths to a flame, the actors were drawn towards the best-lit spot, reinforcing their sense of playing to the audience. That audience would of course see better when the actors were closer. And since the same lighting also illuminated much of the house, the actor, like his predecessor on the unroofed Elizabethan stage, would feel that he was working in the same room with the spectator, sharing the activity of playing and playgoing.

The burning candles, which were made from mutton fat, produced a characteristic haze of smoke after the start of the performance, and coughing and spitting mixed with the general chatter of the audience.

Crowded into so small a space, the ladies and gentlemen suffered the obnoxious fumes from these candles mixed with the smell of their own unwashed bodies and the latrines in the passageways that ran behind the boxes and the gallery. It is understandable that people resorted to perfuming their persons heavily and sniffed pomanders and snuff throughout the performance – all of which contributed to the peculiar odour and noise of the Restoration playhouse.

On the stage itself only modest lighting effects were possible with the aid of hand-held candles, lanterns and torches, although it is striking how frequently a playwright called for a night scene. Dimming the lights had to wait until the eighteenth and nineteenth centuries, although Summers believes that effects of darkness could have been induced in the Restoration by lowering the floats or removing candles (*Restoration Theatre*, pp. 273–4). In a theatre lacking illusion, it is more likely that a hand-held light, together with mimed activity on the stage, would have been sufficient to give an impression of darkness. Candles light the way to bed in many plays, and '*torches appear*' in *Marriage à la Mode*, IV.1, to introduce a court masquerade, while in *The Country Wife*, V.3, linkboys with torches indicate that it is night.

The comedies made good use of effects of darkness in a variety of ways. The business of groping in the dark is introduced by Dryden in *The Wild Gallant* (1663) at the beginning of the period as we saw (p. 24), and the same trick is still in use at the end when Carlos and Angelina wander in the dark before they embrace in act IV of Cibber's *Love Makes a Man* (1700). The fun here lies in the fact that, while the actor pretends to see nothing, the audience sees everything. In more complicated situations like those in *She Would If She Could*, act V and *Love in a Wood*, II and V, the simulation of darkness encouraged the use of the whole stage for apparently random amorous encounters. Darkness also assists scenes of mistaken identity, like that in which Manly intends to replace Fidelia in Olivia's bed in *The Plain Dealer*, IV.2, and in which Sir Formal Trifle takes Sir Samuel Hearty to be a woman in Shadwell's *The Virtuoso*, IV.1. Naturally, Mercury is better able to assume Sosia's shape with the aid of '*a dark lanthorn*' in act II of Dryden's *Amphitryon*. And candles and darkness are good for provocative love-scenes, as when Loveless tries to seduce Berinthia in *The Relapse*, IV.3, and another Loveless in Cibber's *Love's Last Shift*, IV.3, makes love to his own wife Amanda by mistake.

There is on record an unusual instance for a comedy of an attempt to simulate flames in Behn's *The Younger Brother*, III.3, at Drury Lane. The scene is set in '*a garden by night*', and we read, '*Enter Lady Blunder in her nightgown*' crying 'Fire! Fire! Fire!' Servants run in and out with trunks and Manage her maid cries, 'Oh heavens! My lady Mirtilla's chamber's all on flame.' To this point words and movement have done it all, but then comes, *'Prince Frederick and Mirtilla appear at the window, the flame behind 'em'*, whereupon they descend by ladder. With memories of the Great Fire still lingering, the audience must have been arrested by such an effect, although we may never know whether or not it was all done by paint.

RESTORATION SETTING ON THE MODERN STAGE

Putting Restoration comedy across to a twentieth-century audience begins with the style of the acting, but the sort of stage and setting the actor is working with is also important. A spirit of interaction with the audience is noticeably fostered by certain features of the original playhouse, and if this spirit is in any degree to be recreated, some of those features should be found within the modern framework. This is the justification for raising the matter here at the beginning of this study. It is not a factor that has greatly exercised producers of Restoration comedy since the time of the first modern revivals in the 1910s and 20s, although there have been desultory attempts to reconstruct doors in the modern proscenium arch, and occasionally a pattern of wings and shutters has been simulated as a decorative backing.

The first Stage Society and Phoenix revivals were always short of funds and always on the move between one borrowed theatre and another; the Sunday performances between 1915 and 1925 found temporary homes in the Queen's, the Aldwych, King's Hall, Covent Garden, the Lyric, Hammersmith, the New Oxford, the Shaftesbury, Daly's and the Regent Theatre. It was perhaps more by chance than judgment, therefore, that the early productions were blessed with a fairly bare stage, and that the burden of artistic success fell on the shoulders of the actors themselves. Then, after a few of the comedies became accepted into the modern classical repertory (*The Country Wife, The Beaux' Stratagem* and *Love for Love* soon became the leading three – see Appendix B), an embarrassing self-destructive, self-conscious spirit in their staging, costume and décor invaded the Restoration revivals, a trend reinforced by Nigel Playfair's successful, pioneering productions at the Lyric, Hammersmith. The approach was not that of 'Let's put on a Restoration comedy', but of 'Let's *pretend* to put on a Restoration comedy.'

When the *Times* critic A.B. Walkley saw the Stage Society's *The Double Dealer* in 1916, he at once recognized the need for authenticity. Congreve wrote his comedies, he said, 'for the stage and not for the study, for *his* stage, of course, not for ours, for the "platform" stage, not the "picture" stage.' In the following year the Society produced *Love for Love*, and

Walkley pursued the same point; he pleaded that the producer not apply 'some wretched criterion of "realism", which no one had ever heard of in Congreve's day'. He was happy to praise *The Beaux' Stratagem* in 1919 for 'the simplicity of the setting', which lent 'unusual prominence to the dialogue'.

Nevertheless, the unexpected success of Playfair's *The Beggar's Opera* in 1920, and the run of talented designers and directors after the war, continued the revivals on an erratic course. For the Phoenix's production of *Amphitryon* in 1922, Norman Wilkinson's imaginative setting was found to be 'ingenious and beautiful', and Harvey Braban as a foppish Jupiter 'descended from the clouds in a kind of house-painter's cradle to the toot of a motor-horn', according to the *Era*. In the Phoenix's *Country Wife* in 1924, Baliol Holloway as Horner was made up to look like Charles II.

Playfair himself offered *The Way of the World* with Edith Evans as Millamant at the Lyric, Hammersmith, in 1924. He was a witty director, and he employed for the occasion an equally witty designer, Doris Zinkeisen, who supplied a very elaborate and colourful stage picture. In chapter x of *The Story of the Lyric Theatre* Playfair records that he was aware of the unlucky history of the play, which 'had never failed to lead to bankruptcy'; he therefore 'burlesqued the plot considerably, and treated it as a joke'. Servants lit candles in quartet formation, and everyone who was not speaking struck attitudes with an arm raised or an elbow stuck out. A small quartet of musicians was dressed in the style of the period, and remained visible throughout to play Frederic Austin's music. Such 'period' flourishes reflected a kind of silly pedantry. According to the *New Statesman*, the performance was highly balletic, with 'continual efforts to be pretty', and in a leading article for *The Observer* of 24 February, Lennox Robinson condemned the production for its 'quaintness' and its costumes for being 'quaintly bright'. All the dresses were 'as gorgeously polychromatic as possible,' wrote Walkley in *The Times*, and pronounced it, 'a rattling, jaunty, jigging, almost jazzing revival'; in a word, the play was '*fantasticated*' (my italics). Nevertheless, the production was again a great success, and exercised a strong influence on subsequent Restoration productions. It was a success, and that counts for something, but it was at the price of neglecting that essential bite found in the best of Restoration comedy.

Playful colour and rococo fantasy became its curse. Wilkinson's design for *The Assignation* by the Phoenix in 1925 had, according to the *Spectator*, a 'delightful and ingenious' garden set, and another that was a 'beautiful painted chamber with a frieze of dolphins'. The ghost of Playfair's *The Beggar's Opera* seemed to haunt the stage, and a troubled

5 Scene design by Rolf Gerard for *The Constant Couple*, Arts Theatre, 1943

6 Scene design by René Allio for *The Recruiting Officer*, Old Vic, 1963

Ivor Brown followed its uneasy trail from production to production. The emphasis in *The Country Wife* at the Everyman in 1926 was wholly misplaced: 'The setting was too airy and made Restoration London look as clean to the eye as it cannot have been to nose and touch', he complained in the *Saturday Review*; 'Miss Fremantle's design graciously filled Hornerdom with soap and sunlight; no doubt they were needed.' Ten years later he reviewed the same play at the Old Vic for *The Observer*, and reported that the designer Oliver Messel had given the age 'a wash and brush up', creating an 'illusion of an Alsatian operetta, in which Lady Fidget can pass for a whimsical sprite instead of for a brazen profligate'. The same 'fantastication' afflicted Rex Whistler's designs for Gielgud's *Love for Love* in 1943, and Anthony Quayle's exuberant *Relapse* at the Lyric, Hammersmith, in 1947.

Walkley's term 'fantastication' exactly pinpointed what had become a decorator's substitute for a satisfactory Restoration setting and staging. The seductive dangers of the picture-frame stage had taken possession, falsely recalling the colourful toy theatres of the Victorian playroom (see plates 5 and 6).

3. The actor

THE PRIMACY OF THE ACTING STYLE

The burden of a play's success falls on the performance of the actor, and even after a good director has applied his skills and insights, this is especially true of comedy and farce. Eric Bentley went so far as to suggest that 'farce concentrates itself in the actor's body' (*The Life of the Drama*, p. 251), and it is not hard to see that physical movements, gestures and facial expressions are inevitable extensions of the special persona the comedian and farceur must assume. This is quite apart from the presence and magnetism of the individual actor on the stage.

Yet there are other non-literary considerations to exercise us in making an assessment of what counts in the performance of comedy. The degree of reality or unreality in the assumed persona is discrete from what are usually taken to be the elements of 'character' in a play. Any realism of physical behaviour in a comic character is absolutely determined by the attitude of the audience to the comedy as a whole, the image of life it is prepared to accept before the comic process can work. While never closing the necessary gap between real behaviour and stage behaviour, the Restoration actor was nevertheless presenting his distinguished spectators with a kind of portrait of themselves in intimate playing conditions, so that his speech and behaviour, his dress and style, might be closely scrutinized in every minute detail at once for their authenticity and for their divergence from the norm. Writing in *The Revels History* for 1660–1750, Marion Jones believes that the Restoration theatre was not a literary theatre, but 'predominantly an actors' theatre, based on an intimate and complex relationship between the human beings on the stage and in the house' (Loftis *et al.*, p. 133). The elusive details of this proposition remain to be spelled out.

The issue of establishing a working relationship with an audience emerged forcibly when the attempt was made to revive the plays in the twentieth century. The Stage Society and Phoenix actors were hard put to create their own style and standard of acting when faced with the need to reconcile the old comedies to an audience for the most part unfamiliar with them.

In the beginning the Stage Society assembled a jumble of styles, as if experimenting with what could be shared with its audience. The earliest modern revival was of *The Recruiting Officer* in 1915, and *The Observer* reported that 'some were for formal old comedy, some for old comedy brushed up, some for modern with no touch of old, some for the deadly serious and some for the utterly farcical'. It was not uncommon to fall back on the ways of modern drawing-room comedy, and in *The Sunday Times* Sydney Carroll, reviewing the Society's *The Provoked Wife* in 1919, complained of 'those who conceived their performances in the modern drawing-room spirit, who were hurried in speech, slovenly and undistinguished in manner, and consequently created a sense of dullness'. Reviewing the Phoenix's *Love for Love* in 1921, the same critic invoked Shaw's requirement of an operatic style for his own plays, and called for 'a bravura style' of artificial acting, one of 'immense verve and speed and a brilliant disregard of reality'. He went on to distinguish those actors who were too natural and those who 'wavered between artifice and reality' from those who achieved a comedic relationship with the audience, naming Ernest Thesiger's Tattle and Athene Seyler's Mrs Frail for their success in capturing the right degree of mannered acting and formal speech. Eventually, in 1934, Baliol Holloway's production of *The Country Wife* displayed an all-round vigour of style to match Wycherley's own quenchless energy, and after the Second World War the team-playing of the Royal Shakespeare Company in Trevor Nunn's *The Relapse* in 1967 achieved a consistency of stylistic exaggeration missing from more naturalistic productions. It is still not uncommon to spatter a Restoration comedy with nervous titters and self-conscious winks from the beaux whenever the word 'cuckold' is spoken.

'The achievement of style is the final stage in this struggle to be articulate', wrote the old trouper W. Bridges-Adams, former director of the Shakespeare Memorial Theatre, and he makes no apology for emphasizing the importance of the acting style in his essay *Looking at a Play*. There he argues that even a well-trained Shakespearian actor may fall flat in Goldsmith and Sheridan, and 'a virile Hotspur may find his fingers are all thumbs when he attempts the no less virile Charles Surface'. But neither will the polish of modern comedy serve:

There are easy-mannered comedians who find themselves as flummoxed as the Shakespearians by the paraphernalia that an eighteenth-century walking gentle-man carried as a matter of course. It is comparatively easy to handle a cigarette-case with dexterity, but in the manipulation of a snuff-box and handkerchief there is a mysterious and skilled technique. New and disquieting horizons open on the discovery that at fifty pounds a week one is not perfect in the management of a clouded cane, as the old phrase went. And these things are the ABC of the business, a detail compared with the *panache* and breeding that must pervade the whole man if we are to feel that he is something more than a charming person in fancy dress. When old stagers shake their heads over eighteenth-century comedy as though it were a lost art, they know what they mean, if we don't. They are thinking of style. (p. 29)

This chapter and the next will be given to the endlessly demanding business of being a Restoration lady or gentleman, beginning with the latter. A 'beefwitted' Robert Loraine as Mirabel stood no chance, for all his swagger, against Edith Evans' Millamant in Playfair's *The Way of the World* in 1924. And in playing the old comedies today, it is the men who have shown themselves less at home than the women, who seem to have been far less bewitched by their costumes and paralyzed by their props when interpreting a Restoration text.

THE ACTOR IN COSTUME

Being a Restoration gentleman on or off the stage began with his clothes, and although it is possible to point to other drama in which a sumptuous costume display counted for much, there never was such a peacock excess as on the Restoration stage. If the popular image of the beaux of Charles II's time is one of fussy effeminacy, it is with some justice. Even Pepys, himself no slouch, writes on 1 May 1669 that he was afraid to be seen in his best suit 'of flowered tabby vest, and coloured camlet tunic, because it was too fine with the gold lace at the bands', and Evelyn wrote of 'the fantastic habits of the time'. The norm of sartorial elegance for the man, dictated by the court fashions of Louis XIV of France and the itch to dispel dreary memories of the puritanical Commonwealth, grew more and more colourful and decorative. The clothes called such attention to themselves that they spoke eloquently of character and attitude as soon as the actor stepped on the stage, and the actor's knowledge of how, or how not, to wear them provided a regular source of satirical comment in the dialogue. Regrettably, in the modern revivals it was a matter for praise if the actors wore their finery simply as if they were used to it.

In *A Short Discourse on the English Stage* (1664), Richard Flecknoe, himself a playwright, compares former theatres with those of his period and notes that 'ours now for costume and ornament are arrived to the heights of magnificence'. Many of the costumes were in fact the gifts of noble patrons, including the King himself, and the two companies set great store by their wardrobes. As with the Elizabethan and Jacobean companies, the costumes were worth more than the play, and by the eighteenth century it was customary in a death scene to lay down in solemn style a green baize carpet so that clothing should not be spoiled.

In brief summary: by 1690, decorum required that a man wore his long coat loosely shaped to the body and reaching down to his knees. Its cuffs were fantastically wide, and its pockets, unnaturally low about the legs, had great flaps from which a large handkerchief might hang. The whole brocade garment was heavily embroidered with silver and gold, and several yards of fine lace and silk ribbon would trim the shirt, breeches and hose beneath it. Since the breeches did not hide the feet, shoes became a focus for attention, and could feature prominently high red heels and a garnish of ribbons. The male fashion was for long hair falling about the shoulders and tumbling down the back, and by the end of the century it was necessary to lend nature a hand with a full-bottomed wig which could supply the necessary masses of curls. To cover such a wig, only a large plumed hat seemed appropriate, although underneath all this a man's head would be cropped, which necessitated his wearing a skull cap in private.

If in real life clothes could reflect the wearer's personality, they nevertheless severely restricted the movements of his body. On the Restoration stage, however, costume could be made to speak a vivid and colourful language louder than any gesture. In his letter 'Concerning humour in comedy', Congreve, himself the acknowledged master of verbal wit among his contemporaries, recognized that 'ridiculous dress or clothing . . . goes a good way in some received characters', and that 'undoubtedly a man's humour may incline him to dress differently from other people'. No playwright could resist the invitation of such grotesque clothing, and no comic actor would waste the opportunity lent him. This is the sentiment we hear behind Sir Joslin Jolley's comment in *She Would If She Could*, III.3, when he finds the rake Sir Oliver Cockwood doing penance: 'he is a little fantastical now and then, and dresses himself up in an odd fashion. But that's all one among friends . . . .'

Thus when rhinegraves, petticoat breeches of German origin, were worn like a skirt before 1675, and Antoine de Courtin in his popular *Rules of Civility* was complaining at this time about breeches 'worn an ell wide at the knee' (p. 90), the comic stage would present them extravagantly wide. When the jackanapes coat was later shortened to reveal the lace of the shirtfront and sleeves, an absurd brevity would mark the stage traveller from Paris. As pockets slipped lower and lower, and the peruke grew higher and longer, as fashion demanded lacquered red cheeks and beauty spots became as acceptable for men as for women, excesses of every kind would reveal the fop's lack of decorum.

If we except the obvious xenophobic jokes about French and Spanish dress – one thinks of Monsieur de Paris and Don Diego in *The Gentleman Dancing-Master* – the range of deviation from the acceptable norm extended from characters deliberately set up for social ridicule, like the old cuckold or the uncouth country cousin, to others vain and self-

7 Cavalier en escharpe

8 Les cinq sens

9 John Gielgud as Mirabell, *The Way of the World*, Lyric Theatre, Hammersmith,
1953

conscious about their appearance, like the fops and beaux. All fell short as much in their dress as in their manners. At one extreme Sir Wilfull Witwoud in *The Way of the World* wears a drab riding habit that is topped with mud on boots and breeches. He cries out to be 'smoked', and with the sure eye of a comedian Congreve drops him neatly into the company of his finical half-brother Witwoud and the refined and fragile lady Millamant. At another extreme the fop, who early appeared in James Howard's *The English Monsieur* and quickly came to ripe perfection as Sir Fopling Flutter in *The Man of Mode*, might be considered the natural product of an age so intent upon the way it dressed, but he could not be dismissed from the English stage for 200 years. His French excesses in fullness of wig, length of coat, abundance of ribbon and lace, and display of jarring colours, were instantly risible. No doubt Ernest Thesiger's exquisite performance as Tattle in 1921 could be attributed in no small part to the glories of his orange stockings, his brocade waistcoat, his white fur muff and the wonderful plume on his hat.

The business of putting on these clothes was so elaborate that the *levée* became a frequent occasion for satire, as in *The Character of the Beaux* (1696), which selected for comment 'a nice, affected beau' –

one who from ten till twelve, receives visits in bed, where he lies most magnificently with a long periwig neatly laid over the sheets, extravagantly powdered and exactly curled . . . . When the clock has struck twelve, that his two hours have expired, he begins to rise, and with much ado, about three is dressed, which we must allow to be but a very short time, considering how many little piddling insignificant things he has to adorn himself withal; as perfuming his clothes, using washes to make his hands white, beautifying his face, putting on two or three little patches, soaking his handkerchief in rose-water, powdering his linen which he pretends to stink of soap, he's not able to bear it; and chiefly tying on his cravat, which perhaps is done and undone a dozen times, before it sets with an air according to his mind. (p. 11)

The length of time taken in dressing offered a good opportunity for receiving visits, and in the comedies a dressing-room scene served both for dramatic exposition and for witty gossip. Such scenes of rising and dressing are found in abundance throughout the period.

A True Widow opens confidently with

STANMORE. Come, Bellamour; what, not dressed yet?
BELLAMOUR. There is a respect due from a country gentleman to a new suit and
    peruke; they must not be hastily put on.

In III.2 of *Sir Courtly Nice*, the gentleman of the title is discovered dressing with '*men and women singing to him*', an amusing refinement in keeping with his character. *The Twin Rivals* begins efficiently,

The curtain drawn up discovers Young Wouldbe a-dressing and his valet buckling his shoes.
RICHMORE. No farther yet, Wouldbe? 'Tis almost one.

Wouldbe looks forlorn and his clothes unimpressive: the audience soon learns that he lost his money gambling the night before. But when he has cheated his brother of his inheritance, this opening is balanced in act III by another *levée*, one which is presented in splendid style and with '*several gentlemen whispering him by turns*', all begging his favours.

The finest achievement in comic dressing-scenes must be that of Lord Foppington in *The Relapse*, 1.3. Not only does Vanbrugh take us through a sequence of hilarious encounters between the fop and his tailor, his shoemaker, his hosier and his wigmaker, but the whole gang of tradesmen is used both to reveal the fop for what he is, and, as an on-stage audience, to make him seem an even bigger fool than he is. The scene itself is cleverly constructed, like Brecht's classic treatment of robing the Pope in scene 12 of *Galileo Galilei*, where a pompous man is built up as a caricature from the skin. Foppington enters from his bed, anything but the dignified figure he has chosen for himself. He is yawning and in bare feet, nightgown, bald pate and nightcap (a combination Wycherley had tested for Alderman Gripe in *Love in a Wood*, act IV). Foppington calls first for his page, and starting with a dawdling entrance, that individual begins to develop the picture of ridicule and contempt in which his own servants hold their master:

LORD FOPPINGTON. Page –
PAGE. Sir.
LORD FOPPINGTON. Sir! Pray, sir, do me the favour to teach your tongue the title
    the king has thought fit to honour me with.
PAGE. I ask your lordship's pardon, my lord.

The Page's repetition of 'lord' sounds increasingly hollow as the dialogue continues.

When Foppington is alone and waiting for attention, Vanbrugh employs a simple and effective ruse. He has his actor, undressed as he is, behave as if he were already fully dressed and at the court reception planned for the evening:

Well, 'tis an unspeakable pleasure to be a man of quality, strike me dumb! My lord – your lordship – my lord Foppington. Ah, *c'est quelque chose de beau, que le diable m'emporte*. Why, the ladies were ready to puke at me whilst I had nothing but Sir Navelty to recommend me to 'em. Sure, whilst I was but a knight I was a very nauseous fellow. Well, 'tis then thousand pawnd well given, stap my vitals.

As he greets his imaginary idolators on this side and that with a wave or a

10 Colley Cibber as Lord Foppington in *The Relapse*, 1696

11 Donald Sinden as Lord Foppington in *The Relapse*, Royal Shakespeare
Company, Aldwych Theatre, 1967

nod, he must of course comport himself with appropriate pomp, in spite of his bare feet and night attire, so showing the immediate discrepancy between the real and the imaginary figure, between what we see and how Foppington sees himself. Comic distancing rarely achieves such precision. Now the ironic servility of the tailor who begins the process of dressing him ('My lord, I ask your lordship's pardon, my lord. I hope, my lord, your lordship will please to own, I have brought your lordship as accomplished a suit of clothes as ever peer of England trod the stage in, my lord . . . .') can know no bounds, and the incongruity between Foppington's outward appearance and the normal concept of a noble gentleman is complete. The magnificent clothing of his disguise has actually revealed more of the true man.

The act of dressing in Restoration comedy might be considered to be not unlike that of preparing for a dramatic performance itself, one in which the world and the audience sat ready to take critical note of every detail of a gentleman's dress and outward show.

DORIMANT GREETS THE NEW DAY

Etherege opens the first act of *The Man of Mode* with an easy confidence:

A dressing-room. A table covered with a toilet; clothes laid ready. Enter Dorimant in his gown and slippers, with a note in his hand made up, repeating verses.

A tasteful *levée* is a pleasing way to exhibit one's rakish hero in a comedy, and Dorimant the private man will be amusingly exposed by means of a trivializing dressing scene, so that the play's amiable libertine may strike a comic balance between sympathy and censure. According to John Dennis, Dorimant was modelled on the Earl of Rochester himself, with Betterton the first of actors playing Rochester the first of rakehells; but in effect the character is fashioned to fit the secret image of every man in the audience, with the playwright carefully selecting what he wants his audience to perceive.

An impudent Prologue bows himself off with a flippant couplet:

> Since each is fond of his own ugly face,
> Why should you, when we hold it, break the glass?

The same tone of assurance is heard again as soon as Dorimant makes his nonchalant entrance as from his bed, reciting, also impudently, a line or two from a poem by Edmund Waller, the fashionable poet of the day. It is a poem, surprising to relate, about war with Spain, England's ancient enemy:

> Now, for some ages, had the pride of Spain
> Made the sun shine on, half the world in vain.

12 Homme de qualité en robe de chambre

Dorimant is no Lord Foppington; he saunters across the stage in a leisurely manner, one quite out of keeping with the heroic sentiments of the poem. It is also at odds with the letter he has received from Mrs Loveit, which he now holds between thumb and forefinger as if it is infected. 'What a dull, insipid thing is a billet-doux written in cold blood, after the heat of the business is over!' He is as indifferent to the letter's contents, and to its author, as he is to the war with Spain.

The few props on stage and the actor's state of undress signify in the conventional way that the scene will introduce the absorbing business of dressing (in 1971 the Royal Shakespeare Company production had Alan Howard sitting in his bath-tub). The scene will also show Dorimant's casual management of his servants and the characteristic reception of his visitors; he will make his arrangements for the day ahead. It will also incidentally demonstrate to the curious members of the audience, and especially to the ladies, how among the stylish set a gentleman's morning is conducted. This is to be Dorimant facing the new day, one day like any other; it will be a man's scene to a fault, full of a gentleman's habits and prejudices, in its details of behaviour calculated to be irresistible to the viewer. In this way the playwright will get his play off to an unhurried, but engrossing, start.

Significantly, Dorimant speaks his first lines alone on the stage, addressing the audience directly, confident that everyone will accept him at face value. Male and female alike feel the shameless challenge when he intimates, with a wry smile and a faint bow, that he has finished with his former mistress Loveit: 'Faith, women are i'the right when they jealously examine our letters, for in them we always first discover our decay of passion.' By these unceremonious remarks and the brazen tone of his voice, the actor establishes a rapport with the audience, and, disarmingly, Dorimant's informal dress will allow him to lounge across a chair in a way not to be seen again in the play. His first thoughts on waking are on women and on himself, but not necessarily in that order.

His priorities are soon apparent. When Handy, his valet, tells him that his footmen are either asleep or 'poaching after whores' – doubtless taking their cue from their master – and that his choice of service lies between 'swearing Tom, the shoemaker' and 'Foggy Nan, the orange-woman', a creature who is evidently bawd first and fruit-seller second, he turns naturally to the Orange-Woman. The brief introduction of one such as Foggy Nan is not intended to fill out some realistic picture of seventeenth-century low-life, but to place the rake in a scandalous setting, for the bawd counters his insults with a revealing familiarity. Etherege now marks his man by verbal juxtapositioning. First Dorimant quietly rolls his tongue round an unexpected outpouring of supercilious vituperation, calling the wretched woman 'that overgrown jade with the flasket of guts before her', and then he promptly caps this with a smooth line or two from a love lyric by Waller:

It is not that I love you less,
Than when before your feet I lay –

Finally, all in the same breath, he shifts back to the coarseness of 'How now, double-tripe, what news do you bring?' Wrapping the thought in so bland a voice displays his mind, and the same indifference with which he dismissed Loveit is felt in the way in which he follows the delicate lines of poetry with the abuse of the fruit-seller.

The sexual *double entendres* which surround the subsequent discussion of fruit are quite in key with the unblushing frankness of Etherege's presentation of Dorimant. All is done in slow time, nothing sensationally, all at the leisurely pace of a late riser. Now Foggy Nan serves also to introduce Harriet, the play's heroine, with the same lack of ceremony; she is 'a young gentlewoman lately come to town . . . with a hugeous fortune'. Dorimant is interested, but he gives nothing away of his feelings; 'Is she handsome?' is all he asks. Nor does the pace quicken as he takes the peach he is offered; he sinks his teeth into it voluptuously and persists with his attitude of insouciance. 'This fine woman, I'll lay my life, is some awkward, ill-fashioned country toad.' The city joke is accentuated no doubt by another casual bite of the peach. However, it seems that this 'country toad' has already scored points off him in his absence; she had spotted him when he 'fooled' with some woman in the New Exchange, the choice of word undermining the elegant figure he would have preferred to cut. Harriet had also been watching him, and had accurately captured his manner in a clever imitation of his gestures. How disagreeable! When the Orange-Woman reports that Harriet 'acted with her head and with her body so like you', she probably offers a little performance of her own, one even less flattering.

This Dorimant, so elegant a beau, so distant a lover, is evidently already a vulnerable target among his inferiors. So the slender plot is laid while the routine and gossip of the morning, reproduced in its precise tone and detail, is so punctuated with the business of dressing that it need not be a play at all. Dorimant will receive his friends Medley and Bellair; at the same time an impertinent shoemaker will fit his new shoes and Handy will dress him and perfume his clothes. At length the gentlemen agree to dine at Long's, and the exposition of the play seems complete. Dorimant is just about to depart, however, when Etherege plays a new card. A footman enters bearing a chilling little scrap of paper, which, for all its brevity, adds another dimension to the picture of Dorimant, especially when he reads it aloud in the same dry, slightly mocking, voice:

13 *The Man of Mode*, act 1

I told a you you dud not love me, if you dud, you would have seen me again ere now. I have no money and am very malicolly. Pray send me a guynie to see the operies. Your servant to command, Molly.

This sorry little begging-letter tells the whole story of Dorimant's cavalier treatment of his whores, and the *débonnaire* gentleman who strolls off with Medley, singing and in the best of spirits, must strike one as a rather smaller man.

The little piddling details of dressing have been going on throughout the act, and not much seems to have been accomplished for twenty minutes' playing time. Yet the endless background chatter is not merely there to accompany the ritual of dressing; it is the ritual of dressing that dominates the chatter, with the comic effect of reducing Dorimant's management of his women for his pleasure to the level of putting on his clothes. The image of the egotistical lover planning his amours of the day is set in piquant counterpoint with the manner of his fussing with his clothes. Thus costume comments on character in a richly theatrical way, and the fine clothing with which Dorimant exibits himself signals his preposterously selfish attitude to life.

HIS PERSONAL PROPS

A Restoration gentleman's personal accessories were few, but in social situations they could grow enormously in importance to him. Certainly, what an actor did with his hat and sword in those days mattered far more than how an actor manages his teacup and saucer, or his cocktail and cigarette, today. In his pocket or sleeve was always a handkerchief awaiting his proper attention, and indoors or out he might carry a cane, his gloves or his muff. A graceful arch of the wrist when plucking, flicking or waving his gloves or his handkerchief took not a little skill, and such items afforded his hands a kind of extra vocabulary by which their owner could express himself more eloquently, emphasizing one point or demolishing another.

Smoking (a long clay pipe lit with a taper) was less of a social practice and was enjoyed only at home, but snuff was everywhere increasingly in use from Wycherley to Farquhar, and even more after 1700 than before, for ladies as well as for men. The ritual of the snuffbox – tapping the lid, pinching and sniffing, closing the box and flicking the dust from wrist or cuff or sleeve with the handkerchief – would all be timed to punctuate one's speech with grace and aplomb. The snuffbox could be a pleasant source of comedy if it were mislaid (Clodio loses his in Cibber's *Love Makes a Man*, III.4), and if the snuff-taker chanced to sneeze it would be the occasion for general mirth, as we learn from the dancing-master Rigadoon when Mockmode takes his snuff and sneezes in Farquhar's *Love and a Bottle*, I.2:

RIGADOON. O Lord, sir, you must never sneeze: 'tis as unbecoming after orangerie as grace after meat.
MOCKMODE. I thought people took it to clear their brain.
RIGADOON. The beaux have no brains at all, sir; their skull is a perfect snuffbox.

Since the actor played exclusively in 'modern dress', he supplied his own more personal items, his wig and hat, gloves and scarves, shoes and stockings. But certain of these personal accessories were required of a gentleman, and accordingly what he did with them acquired a special importance in performance. This was notably true of his wig, his hat and his sword.

Wigs came into fashion from the example of Louis XIII, who lost all his hair from an illness in 1633, so that the full-bottomed periwig soon became *de rigueur* for any gentleman who wished to pass as such. This adornment quickly reached monumental proportions, with Paris dictating its development curl by curl. At first the curls fell over the shoulders and down the back, but having gone far enough in that direction, they then stood up in two points and finally divided into three tufts (the *binette*). These great perukes were such formidable objects that they acquired a dramatic life of their own, and it is not surprising to find in many of the plays that the sheer business of wearing them, combing and caring for them, became a lively topic of conversation, if not a delicious source of comedy. The actor had to know, at the very least, to hold his head upright, and if he must move it from side to side to do so gently, so that his nose and mouth should not be smothered and his eyes should see. Should it be necessary to make a deep bow, a decorous toss of the head was needed, and in Dryden's epilogue to Etherege's *The Man of Mode* he describes how Sir Fopling Flutter would do it:

> Another's diving bow he did adore,
> Which with a shog casts all the hair before,
> Till he with full decorum brings it back
> And rises with a water spaniel shake.

As might be expected, Etherege is the writer to enlighten us on matters concerning the peruke. We may guess how indispensable it was from hearing Rakehell's lesson in fashion given to Sir Oliver and Sir Joslin in *She Would If She Could*, III.3. Never try to make love without a wig, he urges:

A lover had better appear before his mistress with a bald pate [than without a wig]: 'twill make the ladies apprehend a savour, stop their noses, and avoid you: 'Slife,

14 Officier du roy:
taking snuff

15 Habit d'espée en esté:
combing the peruke

love in a cap is more ridiculous than love in a tub, or love in a pipkin . . . . Here's a peruke, sir . . . . 'Tis the best in England. Pray, Sir Joslin, take him in your hand, and draw a comb through him [here the wig is personalized]; there is not such another frizz in Europe . . . . Pray, Sir Oliver, do me the favour to grace it on your head a little [Sir Oliver does so] . . . . You never wore anything became you half so well in all your life before.

No beau would walk out without a comb about his person, although to use it in public was a mark of ill-breeding and disrespect, for some beaux wandered 'from one playhouse to the other playhouse, and if they like neither the play nor the women, they seldom stay any longer than the combing of their periwigs' (Gatty in *She Would If She Could*, 1.2). Ranger and Dapperwit fight over a comb in *Love in a Wood*, III.1 in order to 'prune and flounce' their curls ready for Miss Lucy's arrival. Shadwell completes the picture of indecorum in *A True Widow* when Selfish, 'a coxcomb conceited of his beauty . . ., always admiring and talking of himself', is reported to be 'combing his peruke below stairs'; whereupon, '*Enter Selfish, sets his peruke, and bows to the glass*' saying, 'You fat fellows have always glasses that make one look so thin' (act I). He is matched in Shadwell's *The Volunteers* by Trim, another coxcomb who '*struts and cocks, setting his periwig and cravat-string, admiring himself*' (act III).

A small, but not unimportant, refinement was introduced later – powder. In *Trivia: or, The Art of Walking the Streets of London* (1716), John Gay tells us that when the fop had 'veiled his empty head' with 'mantling peruke', he also powdered it, presenting the world with another hazard:

> Him, like the miller, pass with caution by,
> Lest from his shoulder clouds of powder fly. (p. 17)

These extraordinary wigs were ready-made for farce. In act III of *A True Widow* Stanmore mortifies Selfish when he '*fillips him and pulls off his peruke*', and in act V the audience is delighted to discover that Young Maggot keeps verses under his. In the scene of Lord Foppington's *levée* in *The Relapse*, donning the peruke is made the climax of the action:

LORD FOPPINGTON. Come, Mr Foretop, let me see what you have done, and then the fatigue of the morning will be over.

FORETOP. My lord, I have done what I defy any prince in Europe to out-do; I have made you a periwig so long, and so full of hair, it will serve you for a hat and cloak in all weathers.

LORD FOPPINGTON. Gad's curse! Mr Foretop, you don't intend to put this upon me for a full periwig?

FORETOP. Not a full one, my lord! I don't know what your lordship may please to call a full one, but I have crammed twenty ounces of hair into it.

LORD FOPPINGTON. What it may be by weight, sir, I shall not dispute; but by tale, there are not nine hairs on a side.

FORETOP. O Lord! Why, as God may judge me, your honour's side-face is reduced to the tip of your nose.

LORD FOPPINGTON. My side-face may be in an eclipse for aught I know; but I'm sure my full-face is like the full moon.

Lyn Oxenford suggests in *Playing Period Plays* that 'the moment when the new wig is actually placed on the head should take place in breathless silence and then be broken by the fop giving a short, sharp scream' (p. 242). This nonsense was bettered only by the powdered wig Colley Cibber wore as Sir Novelty Fashion in his own *Love's Last Shift*, act II; this wig became legendary after it made its entrance onto the stage carried in a sedan chair by two footmen to the ecstatic applause of the audience.

The Phoenix revivals were wise to make much of the Restoration periwig, and 'Tarn' in the *Spectator* was among those who were greatly diverted by seeing shepherds in periwigs in Dryden's *Marriage à la Mode* in 1920, and in the same author's *Amphitryon* of 1922 by witnessing a 'very amusing conversation between a bewigged Mercury and a whip-cracking Phoebus as to the "goings-on" of their father Jupiter', all in preparation for the descent from above of a bewigged Jupiter himself (3 June).

The Restoration beau was only slightly less preoccupied with his hat. This was another excessively awkward object, a large beaver with a buckle to hold in place a plume of feathers (if they were tall enough, the very ones, according to Addison in the *Spectator* 42, that might symbolize a hero in tragedy). In the beginning of the period it was worn both indoors and out as a matter of course; Pepys at one time complained that he caught a cold when he flung off his hat at dinner. Naturally, the civilities that went with it were endless, every one fit for comedy on its own account. From some of the rules laid down by Antoine de Courtin in his *Nouveau Traité de la Civilité Française* (1676), this is a fair selection:

Q. May a youth wear his hat far down over his eyes?
A. No, that is the sign of a rogue or a traitor who doesn't wish to be recognized.

Q. May he wear it far up on his forehead?
A. No, that looks like effrontery.

Q. If he is standing and obliged to remain uncovered, how should he hold his hat?
A. After having modishly doffed it, he should turn the inside toward himself, he will place it under the left arm or in front of his left hip, and he will keep both hands still.

Q. What faults should he avoid concerning the hat, when he is standing uncovered?
A. 1. He will not turn it in his hands.

2. He will not play with it.
3. He will not put it in front of his mouth.
4. He will not carry it turned out like a beggar who asks alms.

Q. When should he cover himself when he is with persons who are superior to him?

A. It is an incivility to cover himself without their order, and even then he will not cover himself until he has been asked two or three times. (In *Love Makes a Man*, III.4 Don Duart says to the fop, 'Sir, in Lisbon, no man asks me a question covered' and '*strikes off*' his hat).

Q. Should he uncover all the time, as at each word he says, at every response he makes?

A. No, to uncover incessantly is to render oneself troublesome.

(trans. Nancy Henshaw, 'Graphic Sources', pp. 180–90).

It should come as no surprise to learn that there was also a special relationship between the hat and the sneeze: 'If his lordship chances to sneeze, you are not to bawl out, "God bless you, sir", but pulling off your hat, bow to him handsomely, and make that observation to yourself.'

If such unwieldy headgear presented a constant problem to the wearer, this was doubled when hat and wig came into conflict. Repeated covering and uncovering put the stability of the peruke at hazard, and it therefore became the fashion to carry one's hat to avoid disordering one's curls, as Ward's *The London Spy* reports: 'A very gaudy crowd of fellows were walking backwards and forwards with their hats in their hands, not daring to convert 'em to their intended use, lest it should put the foretops of their wigs into some disorder' (pp. 155–6). Here again Restoration fashion granted its comic stage yet another gift.

Swordsmanship was part of every gentleman's education, and he wore a sword at all times, until the practice was discouraged by Beau Brummell at the turn of the next century. Needless to say, a sword constituted a further demand on propriety of behaviour. Its sheath was under a man's coat, and it was necessary to swing the baldric to the side if he was not to find the sword dangling between his legs; at table he had to take care that it did not pluck at the skirts of the ladies or trip up the legs of the footmen. At his best, a gallant would wear it with a jaunty swing, and it would help him cut a dashing figure. Nancy Henshaw sums up the ever-present hazards for the actor: 'It clatters, it bangs into people and things, it catches on doors and furniture, it gets tangled in his legs and clothes, it takes up too much room'; the practised actor, however, 'uses the space around him differently; he uses, in fact, more space' (p. 198). Lacking elegance, a gentleman with a sword at his waist would look very funny indeed.

When the occasion arose to use a sword on the stage, anything short of quick, confident handling would always, then as now, be a source of laughter. Draw, guard, thrust and parry must be right, and in duels and skirmishes comedy exploited the range of possibilities. Comic duels were therefore not uncommon, like that between Palmer the 'gamester' and the foolish knight, fat Sir Nicholas Cully in *The Comical Revenge*, III.4–5. Shadwell arranged another between Ninny, his 'conceited poet', and Woodcock, 'a familiar loving coxcomb, that embraces and kisses all men', to bring to an end *The Sullen Lovers*; his clowns '*fight at a distance*', like Sir Andrew Aguecheek and Viola, which will suggest the kind of knock-about comedy called for. In the fight which concludes *A True Widow*, Bellamour quickly vanquishes Selfish, who pleads for mercy with the imperishable line, 'Do not kill me; consider how the ladies will hate you, if you should.'

Many years later, in his letter of 27 September 1749 to his Dear Boy, Lord Chesterfield was still sounding a warning against clumsiness in the use of those personal accessories necessary to a gentleman:

The very accoutrements of a man of fashion are grievous incumbrances to a vulgar man. He is at a loss what to do with his hat, when it is not upon his head; his cane (if unfortunately he wears one) is at perpetual war with every cup of tea or coffee he drinks; destroys them first, and then accompanies them in their fall. His sword is formidable only to his own legs, which would possibly carry him fast enough out of the way of any sword but his own.

THE STYLE IS THE MAN

It appears from Gildon's *Life* that the greatest actor of the day, Thomas Betterton, had much to say about acting tragedy, but nothing about comedy. Perhaps he had little need to do so, because the rules of social behaviour imposed upon the Restoration gentleman in public were themselves quasi-histrionic to begin with. They were partly determined by the extraordinary garments he wore, which dictated his posture, gesture and carriage, his every move, on and off the stage. His wig insisted that he hold his head high at all times; the lace on his sleeves required him to hold his arms away from his body, and toying with his cane or flourishing his handkerchief gave his hands thus poised something to do; the weight of his coat required a swinging stride that came close to a swagger, or, with the shorter steps of a fop, a mincing walk. He would have to sit forward on his chair, carefully balancing, but never crossing, his legs, and making no violent movement which might strain his breeches. When standing, his weight would fall on the back leg, and, tensing the calf muscles of the other, he would always seem to be posing to display his well-turned 'parts'. Harriet's advice to Young Bellair in *The Man of Mode* supplies a living picture of the young man about town:

Your head a little more on one side. Ease yourself on your left leg and play with your right hand . . . . Now set your right leg firm on the ground, adjust your belt, then look about you . . . . Smile, and turn to me again very sparkish. (III.1)

All in all, a Restoration gentleman had to know how to wear his clothes, and not let them wear him.

Most of the rules of behaviour were self-inflicted, and it is these that set the standard without which any comedy of social or sexual manners could not begin. As the many popular books of etiquette suggest, there were rules for every gesture and movement from greeting a friend to fighting a duel. Some admonitions are obvious, like this edited sample from Antoine de Courtin's *The Rules of Civility*, 1671:

- No yawning, no spitting in the fire, no snoring, sweating, gaping or dribbling, snapping fingers, scratching, pulling out hairs.
- Do not pull a man by his buttons.
- When you have blown your nose in your handkerchief, look not into it as if there were a jewel dropped out of your head.

Others call for more circumspection:

- No whistling, singing 'for your divertissement', no breaking out in violent and loud laughs, no bawling 'as their throats would split'.
- 'The man which caresses, or expresses much fondness, for his wife before company makes himself ridiculous.'
- On coming up close to your face: 'you are to pray heartily their breath may be sweet, or you're a dead man'. (pp. 28ff)

The social traps are endless and ubiquitous.

Rules, however, lie only on the surface. As never before, a man was conscious of his whole body, and in his recent study *The Fall of Public Man* Richard Sennett sees the body at this time as a mannequin which provided a form of expression in itself: 'the body seemed to have become an amusing toy to play with' (p. 65). If with more reverence, this observation is well in accord with attitudes to social intercourse found repeatedly. How a man should stand, walk and sit was a matter of infinite concern, and the most commonplace posture or motion was seen as an occasion to give and take aesthetic satisfaction. It is significant that the best contemporary commentary on how a man should daily comport himself is to be found in the manual of the dancing-master Kellom Tomlinson, *The Art of Dancing* (1735, but written somewhat earlier). Chapter 1 is entitled 'Of Standing':

I apprehend it to be necessary to consider the grace and air so highly requisite in our position, when we stand in company; for, having a true notion of this, there remains nothing farther to be observed, when we enter upon the stage of life, either in walking or dancing, than to preserve the same . . . . Let us imagine ourselves, as so many living pictures drawn by the most excellent masters, exquisitely designed to afford the utmost pleasure to beholders: and, indeed, we ought to set our bodies in such a disposition, when we stand in conversation, that, were our actions or postures delineated, they might bear the strictest examination of the most critical judges.

In order to attain a 'fine and becoming presence', Tomlinson then supplies the details for several positions:

Those for conversation, or when we stand in company, are when the weight rests as much on one foot as the other, the feet being considerably separated or open, the knees straight, the hands placed by the side in a genteel fall or natural bend of the wrists, and being in an agreeable fashion or shape about the joint or bend of the hip, with the head gracefully turning to the right or left, which completes a most heroic posture.

He continues in this style, describing the second position as having the hands on the hips and the legs apart; the third, 'the hands being put between the folds or flaps of the coat, or waist-coat, if the coat is unbuttoned, with a natural and easy fall of the arms from the shoulders, this produces a very modest and agreeable posture'; the fourth has the feet apart again, 'the weight of the body resting on the contrary foot . . . with the toes handsomely turning out, the hat under one arm, and the other in some agreeable action' (pp. 3–4).

Tomlinson's chapter II is entitled 'Of Walking', and begins:

In walking with a good grace, time and harmony must be observed, as well as in dancing. For example, the setting down or receiving the poise at the end of the step, is upon *One*; the taking up the disengaged foot, by a gentle and easy raising the heel and pointing the toe, in one entire motion, which is the manner of taking up the foot to step, is upon *Three*; and *Two* is the coming up of the disengaged foot, after the step has been made, which may be continued faster or slower, but must always be in one certain time, counting *One*, *Two*, and *Three*, as in music. (p. 6)

This, and much more, he says, 'must necessarily add great beauty to our walking'. The emphasis was always on the studied grace and ease of the gentleman's carriage and gait if gravity and nobility were to be preserved. And if walking was a challenge, so much more difficult was sitting. There could be no flopping or lounging. It was first necessary to lift the coat-tails, correct the fall of the sword and hold the back of the chair more or less at the same time; with eyes up and back straight, the body would then be lowered slowly on to the edge of the chair; and finally one leg would slide forward cautiously as the other took the weight of the body. A gentleman was of course obliged to rise whenever someone else rose or entered, but no matter how often this happened, the object was always to achieve an effortless flow of movement.

When the comedies were first revived in this century, critics wondered whether men and women actually uncovered, bowed and curtsied as often as they did on the stage. Such salutation was indeed constantly and diligently practised, by man to man, by husband and wife, and by son and daughter, and a gentlemen would always bow to a lady and kiss her hand. However, these gestures had a significance that went beyond mere politeness. Nancy Henshaw has expressed it well:

At this point in English history, an honour or reverence was a public performance requiring impeccable choice, timing and execution. The guidance of a dancing-master was needed for its perfection. Like formal conversation or dancing, the making and returning of honours was one of the arts of aristocratic living. It also provided a veritable index of breeding by means of which persons of quality recognized and communicated with each other. By the nice regulation of these studied gestures, they courted superiors, acknowledged inferiors and accepted equals. (pp. 115–16)

The implications in this for comedy are limitless. A gentleman who affected to know everybody like Sir Courtly Nice was obliged to show his presumption physically, and was a fit subject for laughter: 'Sir Courtly is so civil a creature, and so respectful to everything that belongs to a gentleman, that he stands bare to his own periwig.' In the same play, on the other hand, Surly is his opposite, because he 'uncovers to nothing but his own nightcap, nor to that, if he be drunk, for he sleeps in his hat' (act I). The fop Witwoud and the boor Petulant from *The Way of the World* make a comparable contrast in manners. In Crowne's *The English Friar*, act II, Lord Stately is comic because he makes his salutations with too much deliberation:

LORD STATELY. I make distinctions of persons, and whenever I uncover to any man I weigh my hat.
BELLMOUR. Weigh your hat, my lord?
LORD STATELY. Aye, with gold weights. To a nobleman I give an entire behaviour (*puts his hat low*). To all gentlemen I give only a kind of demicoster (*poises his hat over his shoulder*). To a common fellow I give a bend of my brim and a cock; the bend to show my courtesy, the cock to show my quality and my superiority.

When the 'ceremonious' Lord Plausible takes his uncomfortable leave of Manly in the first scene of *The Plain Dealer*, he attempts up to seven salutations in a row.

Throughout the period men who were good friends might kiss and embrace in public. However, from the way this salutation is used in many plays we may suspect that a joke is intended. When Dorimant and Medley kiss in *The Man of Mode*, act I, the tone of the Orange-Woman's comment is unmistakable: 'Lord, what a filthy trick these men have got of kissing one another!' – and '*she spits*'. In *The Old Bachelor*, act III, the blustering Sir Joseph Wittoll's 'Come let me kiss thee' to his comic counterpart Captain Bluffe must also be ridiculous, like Sir Willfull's attempt to embrace Witwoud in *The Way of the World*, III.3, when in an excess of revulsion Witwoud exclaims, 'You think you're in the country, where great lubberly brothers slabber and kiss one another when they meet, like a call of serjeants. 'Tis not the fashion here; 'tis not indeed, dear brother.' And in act III of *The Recruiting Officer* the foppish Captain Brazen is so liberal with his kisses that he is a source of embarrassment to Silvia, who in her breeches part must maintain her disguise as an ensign.

16 Brazen embraces Plume: Laurence Olivier and Robert Stephens in *The Recruiting Officer*, Old Vic, 1963

No gesture was more flamboyant than the bow proper, which Tomlinson considered to be 'very grand, noble, and highly ornamental'. It was performed in all its glory by bringing the hand or the hat from the chest (as if to say 'my heart is yours') to a graceful sweep towards the floor with the palm of the hand or the rim of the hat upwards ('and I lay it at your feet'). Such a flourish might be repeated several times, like Witwoud's first entrance with his 'Afford me your compassion, my dears! Pity me, Fainall! Mirabell, pity me.' Witwoud spins round the stage with one sweep to all assembled, followed by particular sweeps to Fainall and Mirabell, each more generous than the last. And on the comic stage the style and pace of the bow could immediately communicate an attitude. Manly's perfunctory salute to Olivia in *The Plain Dealer*, or Dorimant's to Loveit in *The Man of Mode*, II.2, on 'What, dancing the galloping nag without a fiddle?' before she '*flings away*', would in each case mock the lady mercilessly. A trickle to the floor would be the wit's jocular response to the fool, while a slow, deep bow could suggest warmth of regard and sincerity of feeling, the depth measuring rank and respect. Again, a quick tilt of the back and neck would be insulting, while a cringe would seem like hypocrisy.

All Restoration courtesies and salutations were of course to be echoed by the words spoken, but they were especially to be seen in the gestures and the eyes, and if the actors did not attend to a careful standard of social manners in performance, the result could be a clown-show. Balletic in movement, colourful in speech, freely acknowledging the close presence of the audience, the comic acting style of the period was designed to appeal irresistibly to the eye and the ear, and aimed to establish the range of attitudes appropriate to the social situation of the immediate moment.

THE BEAU ASSUMES HIS ROLE

The years of the Restoration scintillate with fops and beaux, coxcombs and gallants, as Misson attests in his *Memoirs*: 'The playhouses, chocolate-houses, and parks in spring, perfectly swarm with them: their whole business is to hunt after new fashions' (p. 16). The gallant or the rake provides the pattern or standard, of course, in every comedy; he is the leading man, the Courtall and Freeman, the Dorimant and Horner, the Careless and Valentine, the Loveless and Heartfree, the Aimwell and Archer, barely distinguishable in character one from another, his name boldly stating his comic function and usually suggesting his two-dimensional limitations. But in play after play the beau or the fop seems to proliferate; he is a 'debauch' who often gives debauchery a bad name. In *The Relapse* Berinthia contrasts the beau with real men she calls 'the beaux' antipathy':

These have brains: the beau has none.
These are in love with their mistress: the beau with himself.
They take care of her reputation: he's industrious to destroy it.
They are decent: he's a fop.
They are sound: he's rotten.
They are men: he's an ass. (II.1)

Nevertheless, these simple distinctions disguise the fact that in performance the beau can be endearing, and his less foolish counterpart a positive
villain.

Yet there is little to choose between the morality of the beau and that of
the gallant. Both are equally selfish, and neither feels the need to be
faithful to a mistress. In matters of wit, Congreve admitted in his
dedication to *The Way of the World* that it is not easy 'to distinguish
between the character of a Witwoud [a would-be wit] and a Truewit', and
indeed in that play Witwoud's performance regularly eclipses that of
Mirabell. Etherege knew also that even his Dorimant must eventually
surrender the stage to his man of mode, Sir Fopling, and perhaps held the
latter back for that reason. In matters of the heart, the beau yields nothing
to the gallant. He may seem to rival the ladies in effeminacy, but he is no
homosexual, and we have Sir Fopling's word for it that swordsmanship
was as much his concern as dancing. Either beau or gallant will toy with
his cane or flourish his handkerchief or drawl out his lines, but the former
was usually the source of better theatre, and in a recent article, 'A Few
Kind Words for the Fop', Susan Staves has reminded us that his role was
ever popular with actors and audiences.

So it is no wonder that fops and beaux proliferate on the stage, even in
the same play. In Shadwell's *The Sullen Lovers* the author parades at least
four of them, all to annoy Stanford, the sullen lover of the title. The
dramatis personae include:

SIR POSITIVE AT-ALL, a foolish knight, that pretends to understand everything
in the world, and will suffer no man to understand anything in his
company.
NINNY, a conceited poet, always troubling men with impertinent discourses of
poetry, and the repetition of his own verses.
WOODCOCK, a familiar loving coxcomb, that embraces and kisses all men.
HUFFE, an impudent, cowardly hector, that torments Stanford with coming to
borrow money.

Since the differences between these characters are chiefly verbal, the
individual talents of the four comedians playing them will be hard put to
distinguish their basic physical affectations as beaux.

From the many satirical descriptions of the physical behaviour of the
beau at his worst I choose one from Paris and one from London. *Le*

Mercure Galant ('containing many true and pleasant relations of what hath passed at Paris') tells of a particular beau who kept four great looking-glasses in his closet with which to cultivate his fantasies:

He concluded that gay and fine people made many more conquests than others: he believed he saw already a great plume wagging in his hat, and his coat glittering all over with embroidery, that it out-vied the sun, wherever he went; he fancied all eyes followed him, and he could not doubt but his manly presence ... must capture the stubbornest hearts, and make the ladies fall flat before him .... He smirks and smiles, imagining he sees among them a great many pretty women, and those thoughts egg on others which fill his whole brainpan full of a thousand ravishing conceptions. (pp. 84–6)

In the *London Spy* Ned Ward writes of the character of the beau with a kind of celebratory joy that is hard to match:

He is a Narcissus that is fallen in love with himself and his own shadow. Within doors he's a great friend to a great glass; without doors he adores the sun like a Persian, and walks always in his rays. His body's but a poor stuffing of a rich case, like bran to a lady's pin-cushion, that when the outside is stripped off, there remains nothing that's valuable. His head is a fool's egg which lies hid in a nest of hair. His brains are the yolk, which conceit has addled.

He's a strolling assistant to drapers and tailors, showing every other day a new pattern and a new fashion. He's a very troublesome guest in a tavern, and must have good wine changed three or four times, till they bring him the worst in the cellar, before he'll like it. He's a bubble to all he deals with, from his wench to his periwig-maker, and hates the sordid rascal that won't flatter him ....

He is always furnished with new jests from the last new play, which he most commonly spoils in repeating. Though his parents have given him an expensive education, he's as dumb to rhetoric as a fool to reason; as blind to philosophy as an owl in the sunshine; and as deaf to understanding as a priest to charity. He's a coward among brave men, and a brave fellow among cowards; a fool amongst wise men, and a wit in fools' company. (pp. 280–1)

The French connection in mode of dress and manners could be fully documented from a multitude of sources. Whether the Englishman liked it or not, Paris set the standards, and the English beau emulated the French *marquis*, as Dorimant reports of Sir Fopling: 'He went to Paris a plain bashful English blockhead, and is returned a fine undertaking French fop' (*The Man of Mode*, IV.1). The source of comedy in the French joke lay in a persistent Francophobia, and *The Character of the Beaux* 'written by a young gentleman' adopts the style of many similar sneers:

The French being naturally a sort of finical, fantastic, ridiculous creatures, are always very busy in emulating one another's fooleries, but particularly to exceed each other in dress; and their chiefest endeavours are, who shall be most foppish. (p. 90)

However, the prejudice of the English towards the French is well mixed with a subtle Francophilia, so that the actor playing the beau had not only to imitate the Frenchman, but also know at what point to prompt admiration as well as to induce ridicule.

Any fashions from abroad were an immediate target. In *The Gentleman*

17 Paul Scofield as Witwoud, *The Way of the World*, Lyric Theatre, Hammersmith, 1953

Dancing-Master Wycherley found a perfect formula for laughter by thrusting Hippolita's father, who calls himself 'Don Diego' and is 'much affected with the habit and customs of Spain' together on the same stage with her intended, one Monsieur de Paris, a man 'mightily affected with the French language and fashions'. An elementary knowledge of Spanish hose, which clung to the thighs, and of French pantaloons, which flew out round the knees like wide petticoats, made a battle of the breeches easy to anticipate. After Don Diego *'walks leisurely round the Monsieur, surveying him, and shrugging up his shoulders whilst Monsieur makes legs and faces'*, comes this:

MONSIEUR. Have you not the admiration for my *pantaloon*, Don Diego *mon oncle*?
DON DIEGO. I am astonished at them *verdaderamente*, they are wonderfully
    ridiculous.
MONSIEUR. Redicule, redicule! ah – 'tis well you are my uncle, da – Redicule, ah –
    is dere any ting in de universe so *gentil* as de *pantaloons*? any ting so
    ravissant as de *pantaloons*? Auh – I could kneel down and varship a pair of
    gentil pantaloons. Vat, vat, you would have me have de admiration for dis
    outward skin of your thigh, which you call Spanish hose, fie, fie, fie – ha,
    ha, ha!
DON DIEGO. Dost thou deride my Spanish hose? young man, haugh?
MONSIEUR. In comparison of *pantaloon* I do undervalue 'em indeed, Don Diego,
    mon oncle, ha, ha, ha! (act III)

This use of costume was little short of an exhibition of clowns, complemented by the zany behaviour of Monsieur, no doubt acting with 'the head, and the feet, and the hands, and the tongue, all going together', as the priceless Marquis is characterized in Farquhar's *Sir Harry Wildair*, act III.

Monsieur's lines remind us that French and the affectation of French provided another target for laughter, and frequently an hilarious mixture of tongues could result. *The Character of the Beaux* does not miss this side of the fop, who was

always endeavouring to speak fine, and unintelligibly of word, not being a master of his own language, [and] intermixes it with bombast Latin, and scraps of French, that the ladies may take him for a man of parts, and a true linguist. (p. 18)

Cibber's Sir Novelty Fashion has it all, as the ladies remark:

NARCISSA. Oh! such an air! so becoming a negligence! Upon my soul, Sir
    Novelty, you'll be the envy of the *beau monde*!
HILLARIA. . . . You, sir, are an ornament to your clothes.
SIR NOVELTY. Then your ladyship really thinks they are – *bien entendue*!
HILLARIA. *A merveil, monsieur!*

(*Love's Last Shift*, II.I)

An interesting variation occurs in *The Beaux' Stratagem*, where Count Bellair, the foppish French officer held prisoner at Lichfield, must speak a parody of English in his fleeting amorous encounter with Mrs Sullen. He opens the attack by speaking of her 'killing' eyes:

> Would your ladyship be as ready to apply the remedy as to give the wound? Consider, madam, I am doubly a prisoner; first to the arms of your general, then to your more conquering eyes. My first chains are easy – there a ransom may redeem me; but from your fetters I never shall get free. (III.3)

No pidgin French is needed here to convey the extravagance of his accent and its lilt, and when Archer later attempts such prattle himself, he seems to echo this colourful French count.

SIR FOPLING INTRODUCED

The Man of Mode is a great play of *haute couture*. It begins by offering in its prologue a triplet which draws attention to the sartorial competition between the actors and their fine audience:

> But I'm afraid that while to France we go,
> To bring you home fine dresses, dance, and show,
> The stage, like you, will but more foppish grow.

And in a few moments Etherege is sharing his preoccupation with clothes with the help of his rake Dorimant, who readily confesses, 'I love to be well dressed, sir, and think it no scandal to my understanding.' Yet this is only in preparation for introducing the one 'great critic in these matters', Sir Fopling Flutter, whose performance as the godling genius of the sartorial art peaks the play and takes on the spirit of opera and ballet both.

In Sir Fopling Etherege designed 'the very cock-fool of all those fools', and the pattern for many who followed, but the audience has to wait until the very middle of the play (III.2) before it is allowed to see the man of mode himself. The news that he has arrived 'piping hot from Paris' has of course been a topic of conversation from the first act:

YOUNG BELLAIR. He thinks himself the pattern of modern gallantry.
DORIMANT. He is indeed the pattern of modern foppery.
MEDLEY. He was yesterday at the play, with a pair of gloves up to his elbows and a periwig more exactly curled than a lady's head newly dressed for a ball.
YOUNG BELLAIR. What a pretty lisp he has!
DORIMANT. Ho, that he affects in imitation of the people of quality of France.
MEDLEY. His head stands for the most part on one side, and his looks are more languishing than a lady's when she lolls at stretch in her coach or leans her head carelessly against the side of a box i'the playhouse.
DORIMANT. He is a person indeed of great acquired follies.

The actor is being given his cues for performance, and the 'great acquired follies' are soon to be demonstrated.

In the gossipy world of Lady Townley's salon, old and young, male and female, discuss the scandals of the town. The style of their talk is not that of Sheridan's scandalous school, exaggerated to the point of affectation; rather, it is as unaffected and natural as its author can make it, for it is normality that is to provide the setting for Sir Fopling's abnormality. In the simple structure of Lady Townley's scene, built by simple entrance cues, they speak of Dorimant's reputation, and lo! Dorimant enters. They speak of fools, and behold! Sir Fopling is announced. That the audience is to be included in the tattling is suggested early in the scene when Lady Townley levels the remark at the spectators that, 'next to the playhouse' her house is 'the common refuge of all the idle young people'. Then, when Dorimant and Medley lay their plan for Sir Fopling's arrival by agreeing to 'soothe him up in his extravagance' that he may 'show the better', the audience has been implicitly invited to join the general conspiracy against him.

The qualities of Sir Fopling Flutter are devised to exhibit the excesses of the Frenchified Englishman superimposed upon the conventional extravagances of the beau. The joke is stock, but nonetheless delightfully anticipated and savoured. In addition, the foolish knight is to a more subtle degree amusing because he will show none of the aggressive superiority expected of the stereotype. He is all innocence in his vanity, and so inseparable from his clothes that they seem the only proper extension of his personality; the actor playing Sir Fopling will *act* his costume. The author does not describe the performance for fear of usurping the image the actor presents; nevertheless, there are one or two devices by which Etherege assists the conduct of the stage.

Sir Fopling's every entrance in the play is magnificent. (In the Royal Shakespeare Company's production of 1971 Terry Hands had John Wood appear in the fourth act like the Sun King, carried on a chariot of fire designed like a sunburst.) Here at his first appearance Etherege is content to let the actor and his preposterous costume strike the eye of the beholder, merely adding to the picture a puny pageboy, presumably brushing or otherwise fussing him as he high-steps in. He treads nicely with his feet as if the floor were 'paved with eggs', and, as his name suggests, flutters onto the stage like a gaudy butterfly. Then, all joy at seeing the smiles of the assembled company, he greets each in turn:

(*To Lady Townley*) Madam, I kiss your hands. I see yesterday was nothing of chance: the *belles assemblées* form themselves here every day. (*To Emilia*) Lady, your servant. – Dorimant, let me embrace thee.

76

He sweeps a bow to Lady Townley, catching and raising her hand to kiss as he rises. He repeats the performance without the kiss but with a deeper bow to Emilia, the younger lady. Next, twirling across the stage, he salutes Dorimant with a bow and an embrace, claiming him as a Francophile like himself.

He is blissfully unaware that the ladies are pulling faces behind his back as they express the feelings of the audience, and oblivious to the disclaimers with which Dorimant tries to escape his endearments. Then he is back to Emilia with a compliment on her lace, and finally on to Medley with another embrace:

Forgive me, sir; in this *embarras* of civilities I could not come to have you in my arms sooner.

The reprieve was short-lived, and soon accompanied by a compliment on Medley's equipage spoken in order to elicit another on his own, a new carriage he calls his 'gallesh' (*calèche*). It is an entrance that is nothing short of a dance, and the stage is alive with his ribbons and plumes and flourishes.

The assembled company ply him with French words and phrases in order to spark his performance as a beau, but he will not be drawn by sarcasm and instead revels in their attention. The loud ironic asides passed between the ladies ('He's very fine' – 'Extreme proper!') are intended also for Sir Fopling's ears, but such is his vanity that he hears them only as praise and suspects no treachery. As Lady Townley and Emilia retreat to the fringes of the apron to give him space to exhibit himself, their broad glances lightly invite the audience to share the mockery with them.

Now in exacting detail the playwright passes in review every item of dress the fop is wearing. The on-stage audience encourages him by its assiduous concern and exaggerated interest, but every time he has an endearing way of turning each comment to his advantage. He fingers his coat:

SIR FOPLING. A slight suit I made to appear in at my first arrival – not worthy your consideration, ladies.

This is an outrageous example of false modesty, for the suit is marvellously extravagant in its colour and trim.

DORIMANT. The pantaloon is very well mounted.
SIR FOPLING. The tassels *are* new and pretty.

More than happy to agree, he assists with the inspection of the details.

DORIMANT. That's the shape our ladies dote on.
MEDLEY. Your breech, though, is a handful too high, in my eye, Sir Fopling.
SIR FOPLING. Peace, Medley, I have wished it lower a thousand times; but a pox
    on't, 'twill not be!

He accepts the criticism dolefully, but he is secretly proud of a garment
that seems to have so independent an existence. Every remark is grist to
his mill and he betrays his pleasure at every attention he receives by
responding with a display that takes in his whole person from tip to toe.
His delight is childlike and infectious. Who would have Sir Fopling other
than he is?

The examination continues, its particulars growing finer and faster as
Sir Fopling is pleased to give credit to each famous Paris merchant in turn.
His four mock admirers vie with one another to recite the list of his
glittering accessories, until they have their victim posturing and gesticu-
lating and prancing on each line.

LADY TOWNLEY. The suit?
SIR FOPLING. Barroy.
EMILIA. The garniture?
SIR FOPLING. Le Gras.
MEDLEY. The shoes?
SIR FOPLING. Piccar.
DORIMANT. The periwig?
SIR FOPLING. Chedreux.
LADY TOWNLEY. ⎫
                  ⎬ The gloves?
EMILIA. ⎭
SIR FOPLING. Orangerie.

Sir Fopling is word-perfect, and the voices of the ladies chime on the last
item to suggest the pitch of excitement to which the exchange has risen.
The lines aspire to some strange exotic music, with his voice seeming to
sing out his ecstacy of self-satisfaction. At this moment, all our little
perceptions of his vanity are focussed and clarified in one unexpected
remark:

Dorimant, I could find it in my heart for an amusement to have a gallantry with
some of our *English* ladies.

So! Fopling's magnificent display is after all rooted in his desire to flirt.
The laughter at the revealing bathos of his line is warm and kindly. For all
his ostentation, he is one of them. And yet, in so clothes-conscious an age,
would the Restoration audience probably not have been as much
consumed by curiosity over the latest fashions from France as by laughter
at the fop's eccentricities?

The play must go on. Dorimant seizes his chance to punish Loveit: Sir Fopling should 'confirm the reputation of his wit' by a gallantry with a lady of quality who would be worthy of his conquest; 'Besides, I hear she likes you too.' The lie is enough to decide Sir Fopling in his intention, and St James's Park is fixed upon for the assignation. A call to his page, the briefest gesture of departure, and Sir Fopling Flutter has gone, unable to think of anything but the next challenge of society. A fading '*Au revoir*' is all he leaves behind as a remembrance of his devotion to France. They laugh at him when he has gone, but Emilia, we suspect, has the truth of the matter when she says, 'However you despise him, gentlemen, I'll lay my life he passes for a wit with many.' A creature of such irrepressible comic humour will be welcome everywhere, and certainly in the theatre.

THE ACTOR SHARES HIMSELF WITH THE AUDIENCE

A picture of the beau taken only from books of etiquette and manuals of dancing is flat and colourless; even in Restoration comedy typical behaviour, should that ever exist, would be poor stuff. It is important to gain a sense of the actor at work, and therefore his contribution to the life of the comic theatre must take account of what passes between the stage and the audience. Yet some scenes seem on the surface only occasions for beaux to 'comb their heads and talk'. If, however, the actor, blown up in his costume and loaded with his personal accessories, is also animated with lines that are physically alive with glance and gesture, an audience can be ingeniously brought into his circle of acquaintance, and a scene which at first seems to be static can be fully alive and enjoyable for its own sake when it is shared.

Congreve is one who has a talent for such apparently static conversation pieces. He assembles his gentlemen, perhaps 'rising from cards' in a chocolate-house, or joined by others who have been sporting themselves somewhere else, and he dares to set them to talking. For an example a few lines from the opening act of *Love for Love* will serve. It happens that Athene Seyler played in the Phoenix production of this play in 1921, and in a letter to Stephen Haggard in *The Craft of Comedy* indicates the informal look of the scene as she remembered it:

The men are disposed about the stage in the easy attitudes of men talking intimately together. Scandal is perhaps stretched on a settee, feet up on the arm. Valentine may be in a chair with legs thrust out in front of him and feet crossed. Tattle, who is extravagantly dressed, corseted and obviously made-up, is leaning negligently on the overmantle of the fireplace. (p. 70)

The furniture here belongs to a modern treatment of the play, but the approach succeeds in making the scene human.

Tattle is the 'half-witted beau, vain of his amours, yet valuing himself for secrecy', and he is discoursing of his conquests with the other sex. His tone is bland, his gestures dismissive, until he carefully chances to mention 'a certain woman of quality'. Nothing new in that, suggests Scandal.

TATTLE. Yes, yes, everybody knows – no doubt on't, everybody knows my secrets. But I soon satisfied the lady of *my* innocence; for I told her – Madam, says I, there are some persons who make it their business to tell stories, and say this and that of one and t'other, and everything in the world; and, says I, if your grace –

SCANDAL. Grace!

TATTLE. O Lord, what have I said? My unlucky tongue!

VALENTINE. Ha, ha, ha!

As he takes centre-stage, Tattle grows more and more casual in speech, every phrase an evasion or a little lie – 'no matter for that' . . . 'everybody knows' . . . 'no doubt on't' – and every motion an ironic throw-away as he tries to catch the interest of his listeners. He perhaps offers a glance over his shoulder to see how his words are being taken. He passes on a little more information more pointedly with 'Madam, says I . . .', but his hands have already dismissed it when he says 'and say this and that of one and t'other'. Finally he seems to drop the key words 'your grace' with total nonchalance, except for the almost imperceptible reverence he would make at the mention of her rank. That his conquest was a lady of quality is the news he is determined to convey, and when Scandal sits up and echoes him and Valentine falls back laughing, their reaction reflects that of the audience exactly.

Like Scandal and Valentine, the audience wants to know more.

VALENTINE. Well, but how did you acquit yourself?

TATTLE. Pooh, pooh, nothing at all, I only rallied with you. A woman of ordinary rank was a little jealous of me, and I told her something or other; faith, I know not what. Come, let's talk of something else. (*Hums a song.*)

SCANDAL. Hang him, let him alone. He has a mind we should enquire.

By this time Tattle would have had everyone hanging on his words, if only Scandal had fed him the question he wanted so badly. Instead, Tattle has to wait, displaying his dress, humming his song, all with an air of immense satisfaction; but he waits in vain. The audience on and off the stage cheats him by holding its peace, laughing at his annoyance, and indeed at its own self-constraint.

Such deceptively clever lines are animated, not by vigour of a pressing situation or physical action, but by the sweet flow of genial humour; not by wit and word-play, but by a common humanity revealed in a shrug of the shoulders, a flick or droop of the fingers, a lassitude in the wrist or arm, a toss or brush of a stray lock in the peruke – small gestures performed for those who would recognize them, submitted for everyone's scrutiny and judgment.

Etherege is another excellent presenter of the Restoration comic mode. A courtier and noted wit himself, he created his best play by displaying those attitudes he could share with an audience he knew as one of them. Conceived as a delicacy for the court of Charles II, *The Man of Mode* held audiences for a hundred years. As in Congreve, throughout the play the life-style of London's *beau monde* is closely delineated, and its scenes follow the endless round of the pleasure-seekers by day and by night from the Mall to the salon and presumably to the bedchamber. More pertinently, Etherege acknowledges the presence of his audience by the relationships he sets up between the men and women on his stage, themselves conveyed persuasively by the hundred and one details of dress and behaviour which punctuate every scene.

Dorimant is in top form when Loveit is in her jealous fit in II.2. The cause of all her distress is announced, and he enters with Waller's verses on his lips as always, this time with lines so ironic for the situation that there can be little doubt he passes them directly to the audience on entrance:

> They taste of death who do at heaven arrive;
> But we this paradise approach alive.

He has therefore submitted his case to the house before he punctiliously bows to his mistress and offers to kiss her hand as if nothing were wrong. He performs the salutation splendidly, but naturally '*she flings away and walks on*', all but inviting his sarcasm:

I fear this restlessness of the body, madam, (*pursuing her*) proceeds from an unquietness of the mind. What unlucky accident puts you out of humour – a point ill-washed, knots spoiled i'the making up, hair shaded awry, or some other little mistake in setting you in order?

This mockery is again, one must think, delivered to the audience, and especially to the ladies. Dorimant is then challenged to explain why he has ignored Loveit for two days, and his answer is appallingly frank: 'We are not masters of our own affections; our inclinations daily alter . . . . Human frailty will have it so, and who can help it?' This with a careless gesture of angelic innocence aimed at the gallery as if to acknowledge the Deity.

Dorimant returns to studying his lace, for he well knows that his remark is calculated to provoke the unhappy lady further. Who was the woman he was with at the play? she demands. And again the roguish honesty of 'The devil was obstinate and would not tell me . . . I did all I could to know' is half to the audience, which enjoys his joke. His wide-eyed pretence of simplicity in amorous matters produces in Loveit the desired result; she bursts out with 'Hell and furies!', '*tears her fan in pieces*' and dissolves into tears. Her gesture is one of sheer frustration in the face of this infuriating man. Whereupon from Dorimant comes the icy line, 'Spare your fan, madam. You are growing hot and will want it to cool you.'

Throughout this quarrel between the former lovers, Bellinda has been standing to one side in silent triumph, the immediate author of the clash. With Loveit defeated, Dorimant now turns with his next salute to the second lady. But he has seen the smile on Bellinda's face, and his bow is equally impertinent: 'Bellinda, you are the devil that has raised this storm.' He knows, and she knows he knows. The mock anger with which he now addresses her is a witty gallantry, as the audience hears from his caressing tones:

Here I vow revenge – resolve to pursue and persecute you more impertinently than ever any loving fop did his mistress, hunt you i'the Park, trace you i'the Mall, dog you in every visit you make, haunt you at the plays and i'the drawing-room, hang my nose in your neck and talk to you whether you will or no, and ever look upon you with such dying eyes till your friends grow jealous of me, send you out of town, and the world suspect your reputation. (*In a lower voice.*) At my Lady Townley's when we go from hence.

It is a long caress, and with such smooth and musical sentences he dares to make his next assignation in Loveit's presence. How neatly Dorimant has managed his two women at one and the same time, emerging quite unscathed!

Loveit in her fury now pursues him, but, not unlike Célimène to the importunate Alceste, Dorimant responds with devastating directness. How can she expect him to be constant at his years? And his phrase actually insinuates that she has passed the age when the game can be played dispassionately: 'You might as well expect the fruit the autumn ripens i'the spring.' Again he passes his bland little truism through the audience for its approval. Loveit has trapped herself by her own weakness, and she has no recourse but to dismiss him. He is delighted to bow out, freedom regained. Yet, however, she cannot let him go so easily, and calling him back she both demeans herself further and gives him the chance to accuse *her* of infidelity. In the eye of the spectator, no doubt they are two of a kind. So it is that a new twist is introduced into the story: Dorimant implies that she has lent a kind ear to an admirer who is none other than Sir Fopling Flutter, and –

I would not have a woman have the least good thought of me that can think well of Fopling. Farewell!

His parting sally, insulting as it is, is irrefutable, and her mortification is complete. The audience shares his triumph.

Etherege allows his delighted audience to imagine for itself a last glimpse of Dorimant in this scene when Pert reports that he has gone, and it can do so in precise detail by this time:

PERT. When I told him you desired him to come back, he smiled, made a mouth at me, flung into his coach, and said –
MRS LOVEIT. What did he say?
PERT. 'Drive away'; and then repeated verses.

18 Homme de qualité chantant

'Repeated verses'! – they are almost audible. The audience sees his careless smile, and the cheeky expression on his face. It sees his flying coat-tails and his lace and curls as he skips into his carriage with a nonchalant signal to the coachman. It may even be able to supply another polished line or two from Waller to meet the special occasion of his escape. It can do all this because the playwright has supplied an exactly observed style and tone for the actor playing the part, enabling the audience to take its Dorimant to itself.

A BRIGHT DANCE OF LIFE

In the early years of the twentieth century a well-motivated realism could be said to set the standards for playwriting and acting, and when in 1934 *The Times* reviewed *The Country Wife* at the Ambassadors' Theatre, it betrayed the critical awkwardness that playgoers were still feeling in the presence of Restoration comedy. Discussing the characters, the correspondent typically sought excuses for their cardboard qualities:

They are puppets and, therefore, in the human aspect, dull; but they are puppets by design, fitted to a convention consistently maintained, and considered as talking-machines they are astonishingly ingenious. (3 March)

The hoary question whether a puppet could be a satisfactory stage character was still at issue. That most comedies before the twentieth century could not function if their creatures were anything more than two-dimensional seems not to have occurred to the critics.

It is an incontrovertible fact that the Restoration stage for the most part dealt in stereotypes. The characters' names immediately conveyed their roles, which were assumed like a mask as quickly as possible by the actors, and as quickly registered by the audience. Think of the legion of fops and fools alone: Dapperwit, Sparkish, Selfish, Prig, Tattle; Sir Courtly Nice, Sir Mannerly Shallow, Sir Humphry Noddy, Sir Joseph Wittol. Each is gloriously circumscribed by his name every time he is addressed or appears. When the types repeated from play to play, the authors working 'to force their characters out of complaisance to their actors' (according to John Dennis's *Critical Works*, vol. I, p. 418), less and less subtle individuality of character was the result. Such creatures certainly could not support the analysis applied to the modern problem play. When Congreve tried to paint one or two of his characters more in the round, like Mirabell and Mrs Fainall in *The Way of the World*, they seemed to step out of the frame of their play and put its consistency of style at risk.

It must be concluded that the Restoration actor actually embraced the

19 Ernest Thesiger as Sparkish, with Iris Holey as Mrs Dainty Fidget, *The Country Wife*, Old Vic, 1936

puppet-like qualities of his character with gratitude and enthusiasm. Indeed, the limited range of wits and fops and cuckolds, repeated in play after play, smacks more of the actors' company associated with the *commedia dell'arte* or even the Victorian repertory troupe. Such companies, fixed entirely by the regular needs of casting, merely shuffled their players as each new play called merely for minor variations in plotting.

For the men, roles were established chiefly to supply the broad contrasts of age, attitude and marital status, but the range was quite wide. Brutish husbands were fashioned like Squire Sullen in *The Beaux' Stratagem* and Sir John Brute in *The Provoked Wife*. The latter opens his play uncompromisingly:

What cloying meat is love, when matrimony's the sauce to it. Two years' marriage has debauched my five senses. Everything I see, everything I hear, everything I feel, everything I smell, and everything I taste – methinks has wife in't. No boy was ever so weary of his tutor, no girl of her bib, no nun of doing penance, nor old maid of being chaste, as I am of being married. Sure there's a secret curse entailed upon the very name of wife.

When Garrick played Sir John in 1758, he was 'such a joyous, agreeable, wicked dog, that we never think we can have enough of his company' (*London Chronicle*, 7 October). In the right hands, such a part could dominate the stage.

The lecherous old man was as much a joke as his female counterpart, the superannuated prude. Before Lord Drybone makes his entrance in his nightgown in Crowne's *The Country Wit*, act II, Betty's introductory comment is, ' 'Tis a man, and not a piece of parchment that I value.' Sir Arthur Oldlove in D'Urfey's *Madame Fickle* is actually portrayed as 'an antiquary . . . ridiculously dressed, hung with medals' (III.1). The same author's *A Fond Husband* offers a gaggle of old lechers, beginning with Peregrine Bubble, 'a credulous fond cuckold'; then Old Fumble, 'a superannuated alderman, that dotes on black women [i.e., brunettes]. He's very deaf and almost blind; and seeking to cover his imperfection of not hearing what is said to him, answers quite contrary'; and finally Sir Roger Petulant, 'a jolly old knight of the last age', who orders his nephew Sneak to tell him what women are laid to his charge, and gets the answer, 'What women! 'Bud are you ignorant? Hum. Nan, Pagg, Joan of the dairy, Sara, Jenny, Dorothy, Mary, Bridget.' But there are few such grotesques to match those in *The Soldier's Fortune*, which boasts the one-eyed Sir Davy Dunce and Sir Jolly Jumble, a notorious voyeur who keeps a 'table book' of virgins to hand (IV.1).

When an Irishman appears on stage, as in Robert Howard's *The Committee* and Shadwell's *The Amorous Bigot*, he is usually 'Teague', the sobriquet for any uncouth Irishman of the time, like the more modern 'Paddy'. It was in this period that the stage Irishman developed the characteristics that carried him successfully across the comic stage for two centuries: a dreadful brogue bristling with oaths, red cheeks, red hair, bloated eyes and a face of diabolical cunning.

Any new comic characters conformed to the broadest style, like the Falstaffian Dominic of Dryden's *The Spanish Friar*, described first in blank verse by Pedro in act I, where he is to be seen

> Come puffing with his greasy baldpate choir,
> And fumbling o'er his beads in such an agony,
> He told 'em false, for fear. About his neck
> There hung a wench, the label of his function,
> Whom he shook off, i'faith, methought, unkindly.
> It seems the holy stallion durst not store
> Another sin before he left the world.

In act II a servant adds to this caricature when he announces,

There's a huge, fat, religious gentleman coming up, sir. He says he's but a friar, but he's big enough to be a pope; his gills are as rosy as a turkey-cock; his great belly walks in state before him, like an harbinger; and his gouty legs come limping after it: never was such a tun of devotion seen. (II.3)

The phrase 'larger than life' must surely apply here, but for all the joy of Dryden's Rabelaisian eye Friar Dominic treads the same boards as Jack Pinchwife, Alderman Gripe and a hundred other prodigies.

The spirit of caricature on the Restoration stage is elusive and stage directions are scanty. Sometimes the behaviour books of the time possess a sense of the stage themselves in characterizing the manners of the beau or the puritan or the country squire, and the one human aberration universally deplored is that of 'affectation'. In his *Reflexions upon Ridicule* Bellegarde is scathing on anyone who does not conform to his ideal of social correctness, and he is merciless with those who affect 'a finical air' and make use of 'studied grimaces':

People corrupted with the vice, have nothing natural in their way of talking, walking, dressing, turning their eyes or head, these are motions unknown to other men. In order to speak, there needs no more than to open the mouth easily, and without pains; but they seek a mystery in it, they seem to be moved with springs; it would grieve them to laugh, or cough, or spit like the vulgar, their disguise reaches even to the sound of their voice. (p. 78)

Bellegarde finds that affectation is 'the falsification of the whole person', and might almost be giving instructions to the actors in their search for the delightful excesses of the comic stage.

The comic performance was one of display – display of clothes, of behaviour, of a man's suitability or unsuitability as a sexual partner, of his quirks and quiddities. When Congreve was first revived by the Stage Society in and after 1916, this element of exhibition struck the *Observer's* critic forcibly. He reviewed the strange rainbow of Touchwoods and Plyants and Froths in Allan Wade's producton of *The Double Dealer* and noted 'how masterfully Congreve *shows them off*' (my italics), and was astonished at the way the text could 'leap to life' (26 May 1916). When *Love for Love* was the next year produced at the Aldwych, it was admired as

an inexhaustibly living spectacle of high-coloured male and female characters acting and reacting in a bright dance of life. The spendthrift, the coquette, the boor, the hoyden, the old fool, the discreet but corruptible wife, the man-hunter, the fop, the cynic – here they all are, as large as life and just as much more natural as makes them good company in the theatre.   (22 April 1917)

The reviewer echoed John Palmer's view in *The Comedy of Manners* (1913) that 'life is accepted and observed – not as a problem, but a pageant' (p. 191), and praised this production because it did not interrupt what he called 'the moving dance, which must never threaten for an instant to run down'. And in the long view, the theatre which sees no place for the bright dance of life is already dead.

4. The actress

The presence of women on the English stage for the first time accounts for many of the new ingredients found in the comedy of the Restoration, and more than supplies an explanation for much of the streak of self-conscious exhibitionism running through the plays. Yet the new actresses hardly brought a feminine delicacy or compassion to the relationships between characters, as might have been expected. Instead, they had much to do with a persistent element of cynicism both in writing and performance that surpassed anything that had gone before. It is therefore appropriate first to review the unusual circumstances that surrounded the Restoration actress in order to judge her contribution.

Men and boys had played the female parts since the religious drama of the middle ages, and only in court masques did the ladies play any role at all. French actresses had been drafted into London in the 1600s, and were quickly run off the stage, as an eye-witness reported:

Glad I am to say that they were hissed, hooted, and pippin-pelted from the stage, so that I do not think they will soon be ready to try the same again.

(W. Macqueen Pope, *Ladies First*, p. 25)

The puritan William Prynne spoke for the common view when he asserted that all women players were 'notorious whores'. In *Histriomastix, the Players' Scourge* (1633) his invective against actresses was taken to cast an aspersion on Charles I's Queen Henrietta Maria, who had played a part in the masque *The Shepherd's Paradise*. For implying that a royal lady was an actress, Prynne lost his ears and was pilloried and fined £5,000. Yet it was in this controversial context that Charles II dared to introduce women on to the public stage.

On the one hand, Charles probably saw, and would understandably have been entertained by seeing, women on the stage during his exile in France, Italy and Holland. On the other, although the King's Company had four boys when Charles first commissioned it, in England the elaborate training of boy actors to play women's parts had ceased during the Interregnum. The time was ripe, and Charles cleverly found a reason for having female parts played by women as morally compelling as the one that had formerly prevented this: he argued that it was just as offensive for the male sex to wear skirts as it was for the female sex to display itself in public. He therefore issued the royal patent of 1662, which contained the following operative sentence:

Forasmuch as . . . the women's parts [in many plays] have been acted by men in the habits of women, at which some have taken offence, . . . we do . . . permit and give leave that all the women's parts to be acted in either of the . . . two companies from this time to come may be performed by women.

Although we cannot be sure of the first occasion when an actress took the stage professionally, in no time at all, it seems, women seized their opportunity.

Margaret Hughes is on record as having appeared with the King's Company in 1660 in *The Moor of Venice*, a play which stood to gain a good deal in sexual suggestion from the presence of a female Desdemona. Thomas Jordan's 'A Prologue to introduce the first Woman that came to Act on the Stage in the Tragedy, called The Moor of Venice' in *A Royal Arbour of Loyal Poesie* (1664) expresses the extraordinary interest the town took in the event:

> I come, unknown to any of the rest,
> To tell you news; I saw the lady drest:
> The woman plays today; mistake me not,
> No man in gown, nor page in petticoat:
> A woman to my knowledge; yet I can't
> If I should die make affidavit on't.

The first actresses won their audiences by their charm and good looks, and soon established themselves as indispensable to the success of a production. 'In this reforming age / We have intents to civilize the stage.' In the words of Rosamund Gilder, they were 'a glittering and light-hearted band' (*Enter the Actress*, p. 143).

The recruitment of the protégées of the new companies began in earnest, and while some of them had pretensions to gentility, many were little more than prostitutes. Those who had fallen on hard times were like Charlotte Butler, who was reported by Cibber in chapter v of his *Apology* to be 'the daughter of a decayed knight' and recommended to the Duke's Company by the King himself; or like Elizabeth Barry, who was the daughter of a cavalry colonel who had lost his fortune during the Civil War. Those who had fallen further still were often poor but pretty girls in their teens who had an abundance of talent on and off the stage. Nell Gwyn's career was characteristic in its pattern: she started work as an orange-girl with the King's Men under Killigrew, took naturally to the stage, became the mistress of her leading man Charles Hart, graduated to the bedchamber of a member of the audience, Lord Buckhurst, for £100 a year, that gentleman allegedly consoling himself with the title of the Earl of Middlesex when she heard the call to the bedchamber of the King himself; in his *History of My Own Times* Bishop Burnet declared her to be 'the indiscreetest and wildest creature that ever was at court' (vol. 1, p. 483). In the same company, Anne Reeve became the mistress of its principal playwright, John Dryden.

On 18 September 1666 John Evelyn explained in his diary why he seldom went to the theatre:

Foul and undecent women now (and never till now) were permitted to appear and act, who inflaming several young noblemen and gallants, became their misses, and to some, their wives. Witness the Earl of Oxford, Sir R[obert] Howard, Prince Rupert, the Earl of Dorset, and another greater person than any of them, who fell into their snares, to the reproach of their noble families, and ruin of both body and soul.

'Misses' regarded themselves as a cut above the professional whores, and they were frequently chosen, according to Cibber, 'to calm and mollify the cares of Empire'; for them the stage offered the shortest path to a 'keeper' or a husband. When Mrs Squeamish of *The Country Wife* exclaims against 'keeping little playhouse creatures', the actress playing the part (one Mrs Wyatt) was of course in the running herself. For the good bishop, the playhouses had become 'nests of prostitution' and the stage itself was 'defiled beyond all example' (p. 495). The rapid turnover of the cast-lists suggests that many of the new actresses achieved their object, and years later Cibber as a manager was still complaining of losing promising young actresses, 'the many frail fair ones . . . who, before they could arrive to their theatrical maturity, were feloniously stolen from the tree' (*Apology*, p. 303), or who, in John Downes's words, were 'by force of love erept the stage' (*Roscius Anglicanus*, p. 35).

EXPLOITING THE ACTRESS

Every actor expects to be 'exploited'; his individual talents as interpreter of his lines, as well as his particular presence as a person, are among his qualifications for the stage. It is another matter if an actress should find herself in a lubricious scene and required to perform provocatively because of her sex. Suggestive behaviour on the stage has vulgarized many a play in this century as in others, or, as Steele acknowledged in the *Spectator* for 28 April 1711, it may help it on its intended course:

I, who know nothing of women but from seeing plays, can give great guesses at the whole structure of the fair sex, by being innocently placed in the pit, and insulted by the petticoats of their dancers; the advantages of whose pretty persons are a great help to a dull play. When a poet flags in writing lusciously, a pretty girl can move lasciviously, and have the same good consequences for the author.

There can be little doubt that characterization and casting in Restoration comedy often turned on the new element of an actress's sexuality.

Exploitation of the actress was a first consequence of her visible assets, primarily her shoulders and breasts. In an age of full-length dresses *décolletage* assumed a special importance, if we may judge by the portraits of the period; on the stage itself an actress's costume would have been still more revealing. The bosom was a valuable commodity, as appears from a book of *Coffee-House Jests* in 1677:

A gallant once meeting in Covent Garden with a handsome, and as it seems, smart lass, with her naked breasts appearing very largely; says he, I pray, mistress, is that flesh to be sold? No, says she, no money shall buy it. Well, says he, then let me advise you, if you will not sell, you should shut up your shop. (p. 31)

Crowne's *City Politiques* is not therefore exceptional in its interest in these matters, when in act III the 'debauch' Florio tells breathlessly how in the street he was attracted by 'a young woman with naked – pooh! – breasts' which she said she had uncovered to please her husband –

so I said her husband was a wise man to make his wife show her – pooh! – her breasts in such a town as this; such treasure would invite pickpockets enough to rob him of it. And thus with this wanton woman I wasted my – pooh! – my spirits.

This is more lip-service than anything else, although in v.2 the foppish Craffy admires Rosaura in her presence by exclaiming, 'She's the handsomest woman in the world; what breasts she has!' The truth is that in itself the bosom may be good for beating in tragedy, but in comedy it usually refuses to be anything other than funny.

The Restoration stage invented the device that might be called 'the bosom as letterbox'. The business of concealing a letter in one's bodice recurs in several plays with the principal virtue of drawing comic attention to a lady's *décolletage*. In act I of *The Comical Revenge* Amelia puts Beaufort's letter lovingly next to her heart, and in act II of *She Would and She Would Not* Viletta slips Octavio's billet hastily 'into her bosom'. In act IV of *The Country Wife* Margery manages to exchange one letter for another (two in the bodice at one time!) with her back to her husband and, of course, her front in full view of the audience. The courtesans of the masquerade in *The Rover*, I.2 pin inviting messages 'on their breasts' for anyone to read at closer view. Years later a natural consequence of the epistolary novel was Pamela's habit of concealing her scribbling in her bosom; but reading about it is not the same thing at all.

The rest of a lady's body was more difficult to expose or reveal. If an actress wore only petticoats or nightgown, walking and dancing could hint at more of her charms. However, the shape of her legs would have remained obscure for many more years had it not been for the expedient of the 'breeches part', the subject of a later commentary. Suffice it to say that the majority of Restoration comedies had at least one actress appear in male costume in order to show off her hips and calves and a pair of neat ankles. Pepys's reaction to seeing a play with a woman on the stage in man's clothing for the first time was that she 'had the best legs that ever I saw, and I was very well pleased with it' (28 October 1661). On one occasion in 1664 Killigrew dared to present *The Parson's Wedding*, a bawdy farce in which *all* the parts were played by women, male as well as female.

Opportunities for the prurient abounded in the new conditions, and (briefly to state the obvious) the curtsy itself was, in varying degrees in its execution, a strong invitation to view, while the breeches part usually came to an uproarious conclusion when the pretty young man was discovered to be a female upon removing her peruke and feeling or seeing her breasts. Simulated pregnancy was not unknown on the Elizabethan and Jacobean stage, but it now took on more realistic proportions: Dryden's *The Wild Gallant* has Constance enter 'as with child' in IV.1, and in V.4 of *The Comical Revenge* Wheadle goes so far as to stroke Grace's belly. Salacious possibilities were limitless. *The Assignation* must have created a sensation in act IV when Laura and Hippolita set forth on their amorous expedition both dressed as nuns.

The chief physical advantage of the Restoration actress over the boy player of the Elizabethans lay in her looks. The fashionable female attributes of the period may be deduced from such contemporary accounts as the Comte de Grammont's *Memoirs*, in which the young women who were presented to the King are described *seriatim*. A girl would be, for example, blessed with eyes that were 'languishing' or 'roguish' or 'sparkling with wit and vivacity', and one Miss Frances Jennings was particularly pleasing because 'her gestures and her every movement were so many delightful surprises' (somewhat alarming, this). In Dryden's *Secret Love* Nell Gwyn played Florimell and Charles Hart, her lover in real life, played Celadon. When the two flirt in act I, words gild the lily:

FLORIMELL. What kind of beauty do you like?
CELADON. Just such a one as yours.
FLORIMELL. What's that?
CELADON. Such an oval face, clear skin, hazel eyes, thick brown eyebrows, and hair as you have for all the world . . . . A turned-up nose: that gives an air to your face: Oh, I find I am more and more in love with you! a full nether-lip, an out-mouth, that makes mine water at it: the bottom of your cheeks a little blub, and two dimples when you smile; for your stature 'tis well, and

for your wit 'twas given you by one that knew it had been thrown away upon an ill face; come, you are handsome, there's no denying it.

Such luscious lines delivered to the lady herself must have elicited a charming pantomime from her.

Modern actresses also seized the new opportunity to play the coquette in a way that few contemporary plays allowed. Reviewing *The Gentleman Dancing-Master* in 1925, *The Times* remarked on 'the opportunities for display and the almost impish delight with which ladies of spotless reputation take to representing ladies by no means so immaculate' (21 December); these old plays were a fine gift to any actress with a stylish sense of provocative behaviour.

Two other points are worth making about the early revivals. First, the critics tended to give more attention to the actresses than to the actors, as if they were writing in the time of Charles II. The refrain is that the men are too solemn and 'obviously ill at ease' (*The Times* on *The Way of the World*, 15 May 1918), that the ladies 'outshone' the men (*The Times* again on *The Double Dealer*, 16 May 1916), that they were 'stronger' (the *Nation and Athenaeum* on *The Chances*, 4 February 1922) and that they 'carried off all the acting honours' (*The Observer* on *The Country Wife*, 24 February 1924). For Ivor Brown in the *Saturday Review*, *The Country Wife* had an 'airy witty side to it, and this is far better presented by the women than by the men' (18 December 1926). The second point is that, while there were occasional failures among the new actresses – Cecily Byrne's suggestion of a modern miss was out of place for the part of Araminta in *The Old Bachelor* in 1924, and as Millamant in *The Way of the World* in 1948 Faith Brook was considered to have shown off too self-consciously – individual performers emerged with new honours from the Restoration experience, notably Helen Haye, Athene Seyler, Cathleen Nesbitt, Edith Evans and Isabel Jeans.

'Every actress her own Millamant' was *The Times*'s verdict on the first Phoenix revival of *The Way of the World* in 1918 (15 May), because 'the tradition of the part had been lost'; the writer indicated that Ethel Irving had some years before (at the Court Theatre in 1904) 'delighted the town with a Millamant of her own invention, a roguey-poguey Millamant', and now Edyth Goodall was 'brimming over with fun' as 'a chaffing minx'. This general judgment could be applied equally to the numerous coquettish parts found everywhere in the plays, since each provided the actress with a frame to fill with her own intuitive sense of a coquette. Thus Athene Seyler's Melantha in *Marriage à la Mode* in 1920 was, according to *The Times*, 'a perfect thing, the very quintessence of fun', and as 'that arch-coquette Doralice' Cathleen Nesbitt was 'a little triumph of dainty roguishness' (10 February). In the *annus mirabilis* of 1924 there were two exquisite performances: Edith Evans as Millamant and Isabel Jeans as Margery Pinchwife.

Nigel Playfair had chosen Edith Evans to play Millamant at the Lyric, Hammersmith, following her sparkling success as Cressida for William Poel. In his Journal for 8 February Arnold Bennett wrote that she gave the finest comedy performance he had ever seen on the stage. A.B. Walkley of *The Times* had one of the happiest evenings he remembered spending in the theatre; her Millamant was 'a dainty rogue, an imp of mischief' and she had given 'a delicious performance'; he could not forget her icily understated exit line in act IV, spoken in response to Sir Wilfull when he is a little drunk: 'Sir Wilfull grows very powerful.' The actress was completely in tune with her words, so that for Hubert Griffith of *The Observer* 'one hung upon the lips of her Millamant and delighted in her', and he was 'strangely moved' by the power and beauty of Evans's own personality as she transformed Millamant 'into a poem' (10 February). Ralph Wright of the *New Statesman* thought hers the most delightful piece of acting he had ever seen, and that she was

the perfect and graceful mistress of every situation in which she found herself. Her voice, her coquetry, her hasty tenderness and still more hasty withdrawal, her pretty affectation, her use of her fan, her little run across the stage, her quickness of apprehension, and that fascinating gift she has of betraying in her face a brilliant thought before she gives it utterance – all these and a hundred other details of intelligent acting were at her continual command. (16 February)

Here then was a performance in the tradition, one may imagine, of Bracegirdle, Oldfield, Woffington, Pritchard and Abington.

The Congreve had opened on 7 February, and ten days later at the Regent Theatre the Phoenix Society presented *The Country Wife*, a resurrection for the play after its bloodless adaptation as *The Country Girl* by Garrick. When Summers and his director Allan Wade found Isabel Jeans, Wycherley had found his first modern Margery Pinchwife. Ralph Wright again:

Miss Isabel Jeans played the part with a sort of innocent and affectionate naughtiness that was very attractive. She was not as innocent as she pretended to be, one knew, but she was innocent. Or rather she was only ignorant and the quickest scholar imaginable. It was her ignorance that made her let the cat out of the bag so continually, but when put to it she showed the sharpness of her wits, and her childish delight in them, with the utmost effect. Her first letter scene . . . was a perfect piece of acting. The way she showed protest, submission to force, bewilderment, then a dawning sense of a way out, and finally childish triumph, was a lesson in the portrayal of unsophisticated emotions. She was young, lovely and as full of tricks as a monkey. (23 February)

Edward Shanks in the *Outlook* of the same date was also entranced by Jeans's performance in Margery's letter scene:

I do not think I have ever before seen a whole theatre rise spontaneously in applause at a mere change of expression. But the movement of Miss Jeans's features from doubt to the efficacy of a lie to complacency at its success was irresistible.

What else was she capable of? In *The Sunday Times* James Agate answered, 'It may be that as Lady Macbeth she would say, "Give me the daggers, sweet bud", with the same air of roguish innocence. Even so, I vow I should be enraptured' (24 February). This was the best thing the Phoenix had done, and Wycherley's comic genius was reclaimed, like Congreve's, by the actress.

DRESS AND UNDRESS

Le Mercure Galant in 1678 describes with enthusiasm a lady's *manteau* for winter: 'Il est de gross satin de Florence, couleur de musc, brode de frye de couleurs modestes, qui sont le violet, le gris de lin, et la couleur de Prince' (p. 208). Translation seems unnecessary; the emphasis is on colour. In the Restoration it was the vogue to dazzle the eye with a rainbow of reds, yellows, blues and greens. In Bathsua Makin's concern 'to revive the ancient education of a gentlewoman' in her *Essay* of 1673 she is warm in her criticism of women with ostentatious clothes and painted faces, which were 'not truly to adorn, but to adulterate their bodies' (p. 22).

The street girls may have lacked high style, but they too gloried in their appearance, which was as gaudy and flamboyant as they could make it. Ward in *The London Spy* conveys the impression vividly:

As we stumbled along my friend bid me notice a shop wherein sat three or four very provoking damsels, with as much velvet on their backs as would have made a burying-pall for a country parish, or a holiday coat for a physician, being glorified at bottom with gold fringes, so that I thought at first they might be parsons' daughters who had borrowed their fathers' pulpit clothes to use as scarves to go a visiting in . . . I asked my friend what he took them for; he answered, they were a kind of first-rate love-bird by their rigging, of about a guinea purchase . . . .

By help of paint, powder and patches, they were of a waxwork complexion, and thus dressed: their under-petticoats were white dimity, embroidered like a turkey-work chair, or a fool's doublet, with red, green, blue and yellow; their pin-up coats of Scotch plaid, adorned with bugle lace; and their gowns of printed calico. But their heads were dressed up to the best advantage, like a vintner's bar-keeper or a church-warden's daughter upon an Easter Sunday. (pp. 23, 26)

20 Edith Evans as Millamant, *The Way of the World*, Wyndham's Theatre, 1927

21 Pamela Brown as Millamant, *The Way of the World*, Lyric Theatre, Hammersmith, 1953

The Restoration actress no doubt also erupted on to the stage in colour, but what she wore dictated rather more how she moved.

She covered herself first in a loose shift or chemise (if of course she had not slept in it the night before), one made of Holland linen (if she could afford it). Her bodice was rectilinear and cut low to permit the appropriate *décolletage*, which might be enhanced by teasing Venetian lace at the edges. This was all she wore to protect her skin from the wooden or bone stays that made up her corset back and front. This she proceeded to lace up so that her spine was straight and her breasts made prominent: it was the most essential of all her garments, for it governed her shape and general appearance, and controlled her every movement.

In her letters on 'Fans, Trains and Stays', Athene Seyler insists that it is not the dress one wears that is important, but what is worn underneath. The Restoration lady, like her predecessors and successors of the sixteenth and eighteenth centuries, made it her aim to be straight, slim and poised. Today a woman would find these stays tiresomely restricting: when Yvonne Arnaud played Mrs Frail in John Gielgud's production of *Love for Love* in 1947, he recorded that no one could persuade her to wear them (*Stage Directions*, p. 68).

The Restoration lady's bell-shaped *manteau* or gown, all done in lace, brocades and satins, had its skirt separated in front, and sometimes caught up to show her petticoats, highly decorative items in themselves. Softer gowns became fashionable in the last quarter of the century, borrowing their names from the French vogues of the time: *Innocentes, battantes, déshabillés, négligées* and *robes de chambre* – supposed to have been invented by Madame de Montespan to hide her pregnancies. Sleeves came only to the elbows, allowing the lace of the chemise to be seen below it. In public she wore a train, which she replaced with a more comfortable gown at home. Stockings were held by a garter above or below the knee, and her shoes, graced with high heels of some $1\frac{1}{2}$ inches, would limit her freedom in walking. Out of doors she wore additional items according to the weather; the melancholy Emilia of *The Sullen Lovers* calls for her maid to bring her 'hoods and scarfs' when she wants to walk abroad (III.1).

It goes without saying that she had to acquire a certain skill in moving and turning in order to bring her train to heel without knocking over her chair, and she had to kick her skirt in front to avoid treading on it. When she sat down, she was unable to forget her corset, and felt more comfortable if she sat on the edge of the chair. If she leaned backwards or slumped forwards in her seat, she would be poked by her stays, and when she sat down in her voluminous skirts, she was always in danger of missing the chair altogether.

'Undress' was the term for anything short of being fully dressed, and applied to men as well as women. A man could be in undress if he wore no wig, and a lady if she wore no *manteau* or other long overdress. Therefore it was normal to be undressed in a morning gown, and it was possible to be undressed out of doors; indeed, there was a fetching 'pastoral' fashion in the next century which permitted a lady to walk out wearing a milkmaid's hat and her petticoats charmingly tucked up. It is of course a different matter when Cleonte is *'discovered in her nightgown at a table, as undressing'*, with Silvio *'all undressed, gazing wildly on Cleonte'*, ready for the love-scene of II.6 in Behn's *The Dutch Lover*, or when Amanda is in her antechamber *'loosely dressed'* in Cibber's *Love's Last Shift*, IV.3, where Loveless speaks passionate words to her in the dark. At such times undress was a signal to the audience to expect something untoward.

In *The Craft of Comedy* Seyler offered this advice to the modern actress of period drama:

I should say that a woman ought to *dance* as she moves in a seventeeth-century play, to *sail* in an eighteenth-century one, to *swim* in a nineteenth-century dress (with tiny, even steps under crinoline or bustle) and to *stride* in the twentieth century. Roughly, then, she wouldn't be out of period. (p. 65)

The basic silhouette of a lady's dress in much of the Restoration and eighteenth century was full-skirted, with the waistline coming naturally where the waist was and the skirts hanging comfortably to the floor. This lent the wearer an easier movement that did not belong to the Elizabethan farthingale or the Victorian crinoline. Flowing from the waist, an actress's dress responded to each twist and turn on the stage in a way that could pleasingly suggest both an elegant carriage and the motion of the body beneath. Every step was reflected in the swing of her skirt, which could trace an arabesque of curves. Lifting the skirt and setting it down again with a delicate gesture of the hands was almost a balletic movement designed to display her gorgeous clothes and her sparkling self.

It is agreed that no playwright of the time equalled Congreve in giving his lines the kind of dancing movement intended for Ann Bracegirdle when she played Millamant. Her famous first entrance is of course indicated before she is seen: 'Here she comes, i'faith, full sail, with her fan spread and her streamers out.' After that, she is plied with lines which put her in motion like a living doll. Asked by Mrs Fainall why she was so long, she answers, 'Long! Lord, have I not made violent haste? I have asked every living thing I met for you; I have enquired after you, as after a new fashion.' These lines invite an appeal to the audience, then to those around her, and finally a return to her questioner. When Mincing offers a convenient explanation, that she 'stayed to peruse a pecquet of letters', Millamant's dance begins again:

Oh, aye, letters; I had letters. I am persecuted with letters. I hate letters. Nobody knows how to write letters; and yet one has 'em, one does not know why. They serve to pin up one's hair.   (*The Way of the World*, II.4).

Each statement is a little step and a turn, as if she is harassed on all sides, each mention of 'letters' a mild gesture of despair, until finally she comes

22 Femme de qualité
en stenkerke et falbala

23 Femme de qualité
allant incognita par la ville

to rest on the outrageous conceit of her last line, almost thrown away as it is: 'They serve to pin up one's hair.'

THE TOILETTE

Millamant was thinking of her morning's labours when she spoke of pinning up her hair. A Restoration lady gave up her whole morning to her toilette, which consisted not so much in dressing as in mending her hair and face, a matter of endless concern and discussion. The burdens of the toilette are pleasantly described in *The Gentleman Instructed* (1716):

24 Femme de qualité en déshabillé reposant sur un lit d'ange

What is the grand occupation of the day? Between eight and nine in comes my lady's woman to range in order and method all the little trinkets of the toilet. She chuckles together a whole covey of essences and perfumes, she commands combs to their posts, pomatums to theirs . . . . I have seen a *corps de reserve* upon a sideboard ready for sudden occasions. A French glass *à la mode* commands the *corps de battaille*; at his back the patch-boxes march, powders and essences advance, combs enter upon duty . . . . Now my lady brandishes the combs, and the powders rise in white clouds in the apartment. She trims up the commode [head-piece], she places it ten times, unplaces it as often without being so fortunate as to hit upon the critical point. (p. 117)

The comedies include many female dressing-scenes, and many jokes are enjoyed at the ladies' expense. The best of these is in *The Way of the World*, III.1, where the first view of Lady Wishfort as she attempts the impossible repairs at her toilette was an automatic choice for Congreve:

LADY WISHFORT. I have no more patience. If I have not fretted myself till I am pale again, there's no veracity in me! Fetch me the red; the red, do you hear, sweetheart? An arrant ash-colour, as I'm a person! Look you how this wench stirs! Why dost thou not fetch me a little red? Didst thou not hear me, mopus?

PEG. The red ratafia does your ladyship mean, or the cherry brandy?

LADY WISHFORT. Ratafia, fool? No, fool! Not the ratafia, fool. Grant me patience! I mean the Spanish paper, idiot; complexion, darling. Paint, paint, paint, dost thou understand that, changeling?

After Wishfort has lost her temper at news of Mirabell's faithlessness, her first thought is of her 'economy of face' and the 'cracks discernible in the white varnish'.

A first essential for a toilette scene was such a glass as Wishfort snatches from Foible later in the scene, and, happily, it was among the easiest of props to bring on to the small stage. As here, a hand prop would often suffice, but a stage prop standing on floor or table would present no difficulty. It would not be hung: Sir Fopling's convenient complaint to Dorimant in *The Man of Mode* is,

Why hast not thou a glass hung up here? A room is the dullest thing without one . . . . In a glass a man may entertain himself . . . . Correct the errors of his motions and his dress. (IV.2)

A glass warns the audience to expect affectation and pretence. In D'Urfey's *Madam Fickle* the lady of the title calls for her glass as she waits for Bellamore like a spider waiting its prey (II.2). A glass also establishes a character's self-conceit, like that of Lady Fancyfull in *The Provoked Wife* when she looks '*affectedly*' in her glass on the priceless line, 'I'm almost afraid it flatters me, it makes me look so very engaging' (I.2).

25 Dame de qualité a son lever

The two scenes of Loveit's and Harriet's toilette afford a clear contrast between the conceited female and the free spirit represented by Harriet, who refuses to throw herself at Dorimant as Loveit does. The latter introduces herself to the spectator in II.2 by *'pulling out her pocket glass and looking in it'*, after which her character is developed by placing her in the obligatory toilette scene. Harriet is seen for the first time in act III, also being dressed for the day ahead, but when she refuses to allow her hair to be arranged, her difference from her rival is immediately apparent:

BUSY. Dear madam, let me set that curl in order.
HARRIET. Let me alone, I will shake 'em all out of order!
BUSY. Will you never leave this wildness?
HARRIET. Torment me not.
BUSY. Look, there's a knot falling off.
HARRIET. Let it drop.
BUSY. But one pin, dear madam.
HARRIET. How do I daily suffer under thy officious fingers!
BUSY. Ah, the difference that is between you and my Lady Dapper! How uneasy she is if the least thing be amiss about her!

These two scenes are set back to back to some purpose.

It is hard to be sure which preoccupied a lady more, her face or her 'head'. Make-up was used by both men and women until the nineteenth century, so that the female felt impelled to eclipse the male. In comedy, the larger the number of pots and powders, pins and paints, the richer the humour. First the skin was plastered and washed with a white-lead varnish which, like Wishfort's, reduced the features to an immobile mask; she might also paint her hands white to match her face. The lips were next painted with Spanish red, and then the cheeks were 'inlayed' with a red gum applied shinily with the little finger. An older woman might also insert 'plumpers' inside her cheeks to fill out the cavities. While it cannot match Pope's first canto to Belinda, the following satirical piece from *Poems on Affairs of State* (1705) summarizes the work of the actress at her toilette while her leading man waits:

His royal consort next consults her glass,
And out of twenty boxes culls a face.
The whit'ning first her ghastly looks besmears,
All pale and wan th'unfinish'd form appears;
Till on her cheeks the blushing purple glows,
And a false virgin modesty bestows;
Her ruddy lips the deep vermilion dyes;
Length to her brows the pencil's touch supplies,
And with black bending arches shades her eyes.

Well pleas'd, at length the picture she beholds,
And spots it o'er with artificial molds.

(p. 486)

When Pepys saw Mary Knepp and Nell Gwyn on 5 October 1667, he was repelled: 'But Lord! to see how they were both painted would make a man mad, and did make me loath them.'

The white face would then be decorated with black silk patches, some two or three, chiefly to emphasize its pallor, even if in *The London Terrefilius* (1707) Ned Ward noted that 'patches on her white lead face, some big, some little, look like so many raisins and currants floating in a porringer of rice-milk' (part III, p.19). Sometimes a patch conveyed a secret message of intent: one at the corner of the eye suggested a passionate nature, one in the centre of the cheek the lady's gaiety, one on the nose her pertness. There was room for invention, but if all were applied together the opposite sex might have found the message confusing. In Dryden's *Secret Love* the Queen uses her patches to combat her melancholy mood, and she '*plucks out her glass, and looks sometimes on herself, sometimes on her rival*', saying, 'Methinks a long patch here beneath [my] eye / Might hide that dismal hollowness' (III.1).

Misson in his *Memoirs* almost suggests that patching *à la mode* could be useful for comedy when he writes, 'The use of patches is not unknown to the French ladies, but she that wears them must be young and handsome. In England, young, old, handsome, ugly, all are bepatched till they are bed-rid. I have often counted fifteen patches, or more, upon the swarthy wrinkled phiz of an old hag three-score and ten, and upwards' (p. 214). No doubt the comediennes who played the superannuated ladies of the comedies would have added a few more for theatrical effect.

A lady's hair also cost her time. At the beginning of the period she aimed at a studied negligence, with crimped serpentaux puffs and curls tumbling carelessly about her forehead, face and neck. Studies of Nell Gwyn and others flaunting little ringlets give a good impression of the style. A little later the curls were teased and padded out over the ears for a more horizontal effect. After 1670, the object was an appearance of even greater negligence, when the *hurlupée* or *hurluberlu* ('scatterbrain') image called for a simple mass of curls to crown the face.

About ten years later (*c.* 1678) the shape of the head began to change, and for thirty more years a head-dress or 'commode' was carefully built up with a fontange, defined by François Boucher in his *History of Costume in the West* as 'a complex scaffolding of locks completed with a cap that crowned the head in a veritable architecture of muslin, lace and ribbons mounted on brass wire' (p. 262). The fontange sat high on a lady's head like a Spanish mantilla tilted a little forward. Such a head-dress, precarious with its wires and starches, insisted that she held her head up straight; any untoward nodding would produce the effect of little boats on a choppy sea. This was the price she paid to compete with the periwig.

The toilette was not a ritual observed for its own sake; its purpose was to catch fish of the other sex, and book II of Charles Hopkins's poem *The Art of Love* (1700) reminds the ladies of this.

> Yet female warriors, haste, to arms, to arms,
> Put on your smiles, your glances, and your charms,
> Paint, patches, pins, and all the little rest,
> Which must be done e'er beauty can be drest,
> Flames in your eyes, and coldness in your breast,
> Put on a modest mildness with your dress,
> Put on those somethings which I can't express.
> Let all with artful negligence be done,
> Put every charm, put the whole woman on. (p. 2)

However, the torments of the Restoration lady were not yet over.

THE FAN

A Restoration lady did not consider herself ready to face the world when she had arranged her hair and her face. She had yet to choose her necklaces, bracelets and rings. If she intended to walk or to ride out, she had the task of choosing her reticule, pomander and parasol. If the weather threatened, she would be troubled with her fichu, her hood and her muff. The list of her personal accessories is a long one. Of all these items, however, there were two which served a special purpose, and if she where to conduct her social life with any success they demanded her special attention. These indispensable items were her fan and her vizard mask, and they naturally had much work to do in the comedies.

For some two hundred years a lady indoors or out without her fan was 'undressed'. The first folding fan appeared towards the last quarter of the seventeenth century, and it was this instrument, which could be opened and shut, manipulated and flourished, that served the actress so well on the stage. Used carelessly, it could distract attention and obliterate speech; used carefully, it could attract attention and speak for itself. In her letters on the art of period acting in *Theatre Arts* Athene Seyler ventured the opinion that the use of the fan followed the spirit of the times:

For instance, the use of a fan must have indicated and reflected the same attitude towards life as shown in the style of the hairdressing, of the clothes and of the dances of any given age. The late seventeenth-century women wore a mass of shaking curls, bared their bosoms and evidently had flung themselves out of

26 Dame se promenant à la campagne: the parasol

Puritanism with a gay vengeance. So what more reasonable than to suggest in a Restoration play that one should flirt one's fan and flutter it gaily around one's curls, or gaze archly over it? (p. 21)

Seyler's talents as an actress did the rest.

Edith Evans used to say that 'the only thing you can't do with a fan is fan yourself' (*Plays and Players*, December 1976, p. 39). If it was not for fanning, then what was it for? In *Playing Period Plays* Lyn Oxenford offers this: 'The fan can almost be classed as a weapon: it was used for skirmishes, pitched battles and absolute surrender. It had as much life as a tame bird; it was never the metronome, beating relentlessly' (p. 185). The battles she refers to are those of the sexes. Addison's delightful *Spectator* paper of 27 June 1711 supports this view, and the relevant passages are reproduced here:

Women are armed with fans as men with swords, and sometimes do more execution with them . . . . To the end, therefore, that ladies may be entire mistresses of the weapon which they bear, I have erected up an academy for the training of young women in the *exercise of the fan*, according to the most fashionable airs and motions that are now practised at court . . . .

When my female regiment is drawn up in array, with everyone her weapon in her hand, upon my word to *handle their fans*, each of them shakes her fan at me with a smile, then gives her right-hand woman a tap near the shoulder, then presses her lips with the extremity of her fan, then lets her arm fall in an easy motion, and stands in a readiness to receive the next word of command. All this is done with a close fan, and is generally learned in the first week.

The next motion is that of *unfurling the fan*, in which are comprehended several little flirts and vibrations, as also gradual and deliberate openings with many voluntary fallings asunder in the fan itself, that are seldom learned under a month's practice . . . .

Upon my giving the word to *discharge their fans*, they give one general crack that may be heard at a considerable distance when the wind sits fair . . . .

There is an infinite variety of motions to be made use of in the *flutter of the fan*. There is the angry flutter, the modest flutter, the timorous flutter, the confused flutter, the merry flutter, and the amorous flutter. Not to be tedious, there is scarce any emotion in the mind which does not produce a suitable agitation in the fan; insomuch that I only see the fan of a disciplined lady, I know very well whether she laughs, frowns or blushes. I have seen a fan so very angry, that it would have been dangerous for the absent lover who provoked it to have come within the wind of it; and at other times so very languishing, that I have been glad for the lady's sake that the lover was at a sufficient distance from it. I need not add that a fan is either a prude or a coquette, according to the nature of the person who bears it.

Addison's fantasy would be less laughable were not so much of it true. Opened or closed, the fan actually developed a secret code of signals in the nineteenth century. On the stage it had the power of accentuating a line or a silence, and when it described a figure in the air it could replace a whole speech. With a flick of the wrist the fan could close or open by its own weight, and make a point in a uniquely staccato fashion. In 'Graphic Sources' Henshaw summarizes its function:

The fan was a means of expressing character and emotion; it embellished and punctuated conversation, besides being a conversation piece; it provided lovers with intimate yet polite things to do with their hands; and in addition to all this, it was to its lady, cigarette, cocktail and worry-stone all in one. (p. 245)

It was, indeed, a direct extension of a lady's personality, and at all times signalled her mood. A slow wafting of air indicated her thoughtful assent, an energetic pumping her anger or embarrassment. A glance of the eyes along the line of the open fan could show her interest in a lucky mortal on the other side of the room or the stage; another inch and he could be excluded from all further communication. By a dexterous switching of the fan from one side of her face to the other, a lady could even conduct two

28 Femme de qualité
en déshabillé de vestalle:
with fan and mask

28 Femme de qualité
en déshabillè de vestalle:
with fan and mask

intimate but independent conversations, spoken or silent, on either side of her at the same time.

The *locus classicus* for the use of the fan is in *The Man of Mode*, III.1, where Young Bellair instructs Harriet how to show that she is in love.

YOUNG BELLAIR. At one motion play your fan, roll your eyes, and then settle a kind look upon me.

HARRIET. So.

YOUNG BELLAIR. Now spread your fan, look down upon it, and tell the sticks with a finger.

HARRIET. Very modish.

YOUNG BELLAIR. Clap your hand up to your bosom, hold down your gown. Shrug a little, draw up your breasts and let 'em fall again, gently, with a sigh or two, etc . . . .

HARRIET. 'Twill not be amiss now to seem a little pleasant.

YOUNG BELLAIR. Clap your fan then in both hands, snatch it to your mouth, smile, and with a lively motion fling your body a little forwards. So! Now spread it, fall back on the sudden, cover your face with it, and break out into loud laughter – Take up! Look grave and fall a-fanning of yourself. Admirably well acted!

The number of references to the fan in the texts is few – because it was in constant use. But it was not for tearing or hitting, and when it is mentioned in the stage directions, the occasion is sensational. Melinda, the heiress in *The Recruiting Officer* who wants a husband in general and Worthy in particular, is seen *'fretting and tearing her fan'* in frustration when that gentleman is not more forthcoming (IV.2). When Sir Charles Easy flirts with the coquette Lady Betty Modish in Cibber's *The Careless Husband*, IV.1, she betrays her loss of decorum:

SIR CHARLES. O that I were your lover for a month or two.

LADY BETTY. What then?

SIR CHARLES. I would make that pretty heart's blood of yours ache in a fortnight.

LADY BETTY. Hugh – I should hate you, your assurance would make your address intolerable.

SIR CHARLES. I believe it would, for I'd never address you at all.

LADY BETTY. O! you clown you! (*Hitting him with her fan.*)

As he grows impertinent and she loses her modesty, her fan loses its subtlety.

When Mrs Loveit *'tears her fan in pieces'* in *The Man of Mode*, II.2, this extraordinary gesture comes at a crisis of events for her. When she first flings on to the stage she is folding into her pocket the letter that was earlier read back to Dorimant its author for his amusement. Now we watch its effect. With one hand she is 'putting up' the letter and with the other she examines herself in her pocket-glass. 'I hate myself, I look so ill today', she says, and her first reaction to the letter is a concern with her appearance. The rival whom Loveit does not yet suspect next trips in with an elaborate display of regret at not having visited for two days, whereupon Loveit must exchange her glass for her fan. The visitor is Bellinda, who explains to us behind *her* fan the true reason for her coming in a perfidious aside: 'Now to carry on my plot; nothing but love could make me capable of so much falsehood. 'Tis time to begin, lest Dorimant should come before her jealousy has stung her.' So Bellinda *'laughs and then speaks on'*, and the fans of the two women who exude friendship and mutual consolation against *that* statement perfectly articulate the world of deceit they both inhabit.

Bellinda next probes the wound she perceives the letter to have caused. She imagines she saw Loveit at the play, since Dorimant was there with 'a lady masked, in a pretty *déshabillé'*. She lightly touches Loveit's dress, and that lady immediately feels the pain:

MRS LOVEIT (*aside*). Dorimant at the play entertaining a mask! Oh, heavens!
BELLINDA (*aside*). Good!

Their fans are still up, and the quick asides trigger the passion that exists beneath the surface politeness. At first Loveit turns away, and the fan is still coolly protective. 'Did he stay all the while?' she asks, for she would dearly like to know how the affair progressed. But Bellinda's answers are bland and soon provoke a torrent of abuse: 'Shame and confusion be ever in her face when she shows it!' The line is compact of sudden movement, the defences of her fan abandoned. Dorimant's casual entrance is timed to bring on the final explosion, and so the innocent fan falls the victim of her wrath in a destructive gesture so violent that it discredits its owner forever in the eyes of the audience. In any case, by this time it has lost all its magic properties as a weapon of dissimulation.

THE MASK

The mask was as important among a lady's personal accoutrements as her fan. She could hold it in her hand or up to her face as she chose, or she could fix it in place with pins, or by a little handle which she pushed into her hair; she could could even hold it in her teeth by a button. It came into vogue quite early in the period. On 12 June 1663 Pepys reported that he saw Lady Mary Cromwell masked at a play, and added that wearing a mask 'of late is become a great fashion among the ladies'. In his *History* Bishop Burnet recorded for 1668,

At this time the court fell into much extravagance in masquerading; both King and Queen, and all the court, went about masked, and came into houses unknown, and danced there with a great deal of wild frolic. (Vol. 1, p. 482)

29 Lady with muff wearing mask

30 Dame allant à la campagne: holding mask

Men might also wear the mask, and in *A French Ambassador at the Court of Charles II* Cominges records that one night after leaving St James's Palace Lady Castlemaine was accosted by three noblemen who were masked (p. 91). The mask had become something more than a prop for a masquerade: it became a toy with which to play adult games.

In the beginning it was probably used to protect a lady's make-up from the ravages of the outside air, but it soon became the instrument by which she could pass incognito in public. Cibber wrote in his *Apology*, 'I remember the ladies were then observed to be decently afraid of venturing bare-faced to a new comedy, till they had been assured they might do it without the risk of an insult to their modesty' (p. 147). The playhouse scene in *A True Widow* gives a fair idea of the way a lady might employ her mask at a play, with the consequences for her friends and neighbours. When Isabella and Gartrude, the sober and the silly sisters, take their seats in masks, they are well aware they are playing a game of deceit:

ISABELLA. By being masked, I shall observe Bellamour's actions.
GARTRUDE. Now nobody will know me; they'll take me for you in this petticoat.
ISABELLA. If you hold your tongue, sister, but [i.e. only] that makes a great difference between us.

Meanwhile their various beaux are all delightfully at a loss:

BELLAMOUR. I wonder Isabella is not here, Stanmore; I am so damnably in love . . . .
STANMORE. My mistress [Gartrude] is not here neither . . . . I have a most abominable lust to her . . . .

And a little way off two other gentlemen are equally perplexed:

YOUNG MAGGOT. I wonder pretty Mistress Gertrude is not here.
SELFISH. I am amazed at it: for I knew she was to come . . . .

The masking game was complicated by the fact that the prostitutes who frequented the playhouses themselves wore masks as the sign of their trade (their nickname was 'vizards'), and a woman of quality who went to the play in a mask was for all practical purposes choosing to compete with them for the attention of the men. The mask obliterated all distinctions of rank, and, on Pinchwife's authority in *The Country Wife*, 'Masks have made more cuckolds than the best faces that ever were known' (III.1). They were also the source of other errors, and in *Epsom Wells*, act 1, Woodly tells a sad tale:

I have had two damned unlucky adventures. The first vizor mask I pursued after, I had followed her a furlong, and importuned her to show her face; when I thought I had got a prize beyond my hopes, proved an old lady of three-score, with a wrinkled pimpled face, but one eye, and no teeth; but which was ten times a worse disappointment, the next that I followed proved to be my own wife.

However, this particular game came to an end with Queen Anne's edict of 17 January 1704, which commanded that 'no woman be allowed or presume to wear a vizard mask in either of the theatres' (*Daily Courant*, 24 January).

Clearly, a mask on the stage was worn only for the fun of taking it off again at the right moment, and this sportive use of it is frequent throughout the comedies. *Secret Love* begins straight off with a masking scene. *'The scene is walks near the court'*, with Florimell and Flavia in masks, and the initial exercise is one of how to confuse the male sex. Thus Celadon addresses the two fair unknowns as one, and with a single innuendo for both:

CELADON. Cannot I serve you in the gentleman's room, ladies?
FLAVIA. Which of us would you serve?
CELADON. Either of you, or both of you.
FLAVIA. Why, could you not be constant to one?

This challenge to Celadon's freedom of choice produces a flirtation in which all are coy about losing their freedom:

FLAVIA. You are as unconstant as the moon.
FLORIMELL. You wrong him, he's as constant as the sun: he would see all the world round in twenty-four hours.
CELADON. 'Tis very true, madam, but, like him, I would visit and away.
FLORIMELL. For what an unreasonable thing it were to stay long, be troublesome, and hinder a lady of a fresh lover.

Already these two are well in tune, and from their asides (Florimell, 'He fits my humour rarely'; Celadon, 'A rare creature this!') it is clear that the masking game has served its purpose by attracting the two principals. Inevitably the man then wants to see the lady's face to see the 'blind bargain' he has. Celadon moves to a point by slyly offering to allow 'the most handsome' to take him, tempting Florimell to disclose herself by flattery:

FLORIMELL. What kind of beauty do you like?
CELADON. Just such a one as yours . . . .

It is difficult for the poor man to sound genuine when he can see nothing.

FLORIMELL. Can you settle your spirits to see an ugly face, and not be frighted, I could find in my heart to lift up my mask and disabuse you.
CELADON. I defy your mask, would you would try the experiment.

FLORIMELL. No, I won'not; for your ignorance is the mother of your devotion to me.

Celadon has lost again.

Next year Etherege tried a variation on this simple pattern of teasing. In *She Would If She Could* he takes his scene to Mulberry Garden at night, and works with two pairs of lovers, matching Ariana and Gatty with Courtall and Freeman. The girls had complained of being 'mewed up' like birds in a cage, and envied the menfolk their freedom. Their solution is to walk out in masks, so that the men are 'only acquainted with our vizards and our petticoats'. Thus begins the chase of II.1:

Enter Ariana and Gatty with vizards, and pass nimbly over the stage.
FREEMAN. Ha, ha. How wantonly they trip it! There is temptation enough in their very gait to stir up the courage of an old alderman. Prithee let us follow 'em.

So the girls succeed in gaining their temporary advantage over the men by their anonymity, although of course they fully intend to be caught.

FREEMAN. Are you so wild that you must be hooded thus?
COURTALL. Fie, fie. Put off these scandals to all good faces.
GATTY. For your reputations' sake we shall keep 'em on. 'Slife, we should be taken for your relations if we durst show our faces with you thus publicly.
ARIANA. And what a shame that would be to a couple of young gallants! Methinks you should blush to think on't.

But the girls agree to see them again provided they swear to be true, and the real joke emerges when the men are introduced to the very same girls that evening, now respectably *without* masks.

The embarrassment of the male is sometimes exchanged for that of the female, as Behn demonstrated by her manipulation of the device in *The Rover*. This is a play in which one Neapolitan carnival masquerade follows another in a plethora of disguisings and mistaken identities. Not unexpectedly, Florinda dons a mask in order to pursue Colonel Belvile, avoiding the eyes of her Spanish brother Don Pedro, who intends her for his friend Don Antonio. The result is that in IV.5 she runs the risk of rape, and in act V comes perilously close to an incestuous attack from her brother:

Enter Florinda running, masked, Pedro after her.
FLORINDA (*aside*). Good heaven defend me from discovery!
PEDRO. 'Tis but in vain to fly me; you're fallen to my lot . . . .

The lubricious situation is characteristic of Aphra Behn.

Twenty years later Vanbrugh is still arranging for the crisis of a comedy to be a chase in the park, and making use of masks to resolve the action. In

The Provoked Wife Bellinda and the unhappily married Lady Brute decide to use masks to cement their relationship with Heartfree and Constant:

BELLINDA. But, pray, how shall we contrive to see these blades again quickly?
LADY BRUTE. We must e'en have recourse to the old way: make 'em an appointment 'twixt jest and earnest, 'twill look like a frolic, and that you know's a very good thing to save a woman's blushes.
BELLINDA. You advise well; but where shall it be?
LADY BRUTE. In Spring Garden. But they shan't know their women till their women pull of their masks, for a surprise is the most agreeable thing in the world. (III.3)

They send a note to their beaux, and all is set for the grand recognition in IV.4. However, they had not reckoned with intruders.

First Lady Fancyfull, who wants Heartfree for herself, with her Madamoiselle in tow, follow the men in masks of their own, and eavesdrop on the encounter ('We'll slip into this close arbour.') To complicate things further, Lady Brute and Bellinda have chosen not only to be masked, but also poorly dressed, the better to deceive their lovers. As a consequence, not only do the men back off ('How now, who are these? Not our game, I hope.'), but Sir John Brute himself enters drunk, and mistakes his wife and niece for whores:

What a pox! Here's Constant, Heartfree, and two whores, egad. O you covetous rogues; what have you never a spare punk for your friend? But I'll share with you. (*He seizes both the women.*)

The ladies are naturally alarmed by premature discovery by the wrong man, and when Heartfree and Constant decide that it is a capital idea to resign them to Sir John, they take fright:

LADY BRUTE. Why sure, you won't leave us in the hands of a drunken fellow to abuse us?
SIR JOHN. Who do you call a drunken fellow, you slut you? I'm a man of quality; the king has made me a knight.

So it turns out that, to save themselves, Lady Brute must run to Constant *'twitching off her mask and clapping it on again'* to undeceive him, and Bellinda must do the same with Heartfree. Finally, it is left to Lady Fancyfull and Madamoiselle to cap the joke when they *'bolt out upon them and run over the stage'*:

LADY FANCYFULL. Fe, fe, fe, fe, fe.
MADAMOISELLE. Fe, fe, fe, fe, fe.
CONSTANT. Death and furies, who are these?
LADY BRUTE. O heavens, I'm out of my wits; if they knew me, I'm ruined.

So the young ladies who had set out with such a confident plan '*exit running*' and leave Lady Fancyfull with the profound thought, ''Tis a prodigious thing how women can suffer filthy fellows to grow so familiar with 'em.'

In these merry scenes of masking, the playwrights knew they had a formula which worked well and would do so again. In every one of them the audience has the pleasure of knowing from the start who is deceiving whom. Although there is no chance that the mask will return to fashion as a plot device, a modern audience has no difficulty in relishing the game of comic disguise in Restoration comedy as readily as it can that of mistaken identities in *The Comedy of Errors*.

THE STYLE OF THE ACTRESS

A lady's presentation of herself in public in the Restoration period was spared the constraints imposed by the social forms of the Elizabethans, as well as those that closed in upon her in the eighteenth and nineteenth centuries. The theatre projected a little of the ways of a Rosalind and the wit of a Beatrice without the proprieties of a Teazle and a Maria, and the result was a series of delightfully extroverted free spirits: Melantha and Florimell, Ariana and Gatty, Harriet and Emilia, Angelica and Millamant, Amanda and Berinthia, Lady Brute and Bellinda, Mrs Sullen and Dorinda. Then there is that other order of Margery Pinchwife and Miss Prue, Rose and Cherry.

The behaviour of these girls moved just beyond the social sanctions of the day, and was an entertainment in itself. When in *The Man of Mode*, II.1, Medley has his little joke with Emilia about *The Art of Affectation*, an audience hearing his account of a stylish modern lady would recognize what it had seen in play after play. The book, he says, was

written by a late beauty of quality, teaching you how to draw up your breasts, stretch up your neck, to thrust out your breech, to play with your head, to toss up your nose, to bite your lips, to turn up your eyes, to speak in a silly soft tone of a voice, and use all the foolish French words that will infallibly make your person and conversation charming; with a short apology at the latter end, in the behalf of young ladies who notoriously wash and paint, though they have naturally good complexions.

It is a likely description of the way Mrs Loveit behaved in the play, but much of it would also fit Bellinda and Harriet and Emilia herself. What all these young women shared was a stageworthy self-assertion of endless fascination.

When Athene Seyler wrote of a mass of shaking curls and a bared

31 Un cavalier et une dame beuvant du chocolat

bosom, she was thinking of the impression she herself aimed to create on the stage. Hubert Griffith's comments on her Lady Fidget for *The Observer* of 24 February 1924 may supplement the picture:

Every gesture was an exquisite conceit, each look and speech a world of wit. And when she shook her spaniel curls, pointed her monitory forefinger or arched still more her saucy eyebrows, high comedy was in full flower.

Seyler had grasped the idea that a Restoration performance was an exhibition. Nevertheless, as she is the first to argue, any such behaviour must fall within the limits set for a woman of the period. This section, therefore, will survey the kind of posture and movement, carriage and curtsy the Restoration actress had in her arsenal of attributes when she played the coquette with the spectator.

A provocative presentation of the female lead was common to every play. The first few moments of *The Provoked Wife* are given to the boorish Sir John Brute, but only to prepare the major assault made by his wife '*sola*' as a blatant appeal to the sympathies of the audience. 'I thought I had charms enough', she pleads, and the choice of word is important. So she considers revenge:

But some comfort still: if one would be revenged of him, these are good times. A woman may have a gallant and a separate maintenance too . . . . Let me see. What opposes? My matrimonial vow? Why, what did I vow? I think I promised to be true to my husband. Well; and he promised to be kind to me. But he han't kept his word. Why then I'm absolved from mine. Aye, that seems clear to me . . . . Virtue's an ass, and a gallant's worth forty on't.

Each question, each pause for thought, is passed through the audience for its expected approval. When Bellinda her confidante joins her, they proceed immediately to discuss coquetry and the possibility of an intrigue. In spite of appearances to the contrary, Lady Brute insists that she is no coquette, and then reverses herself:

'Tis true, coquetry is one of the main ingredients in the natural composition of a woman, and I as well as others could be well enough pleased to see a crowd of young fellows ogling and glancing and watching all occasions to do forty foolish officious things.

She is directly addressing the pit.

Another level of coquetry is soon presented in the person of Lady Fancyfull at her toilet, with 'How do I look this morning?' as she studies herself in her glass. This new charmer seems to steal the show *pro tem*: 'Is it possible my eyes can be so languishing, and so very full of fire?' For one of her best moments this lady is even granted a 'running' entrance in III.1: '*Enter Lady Fancyfull, who runs first to Lady Brute, then to Bellinda, kissing 'em'*. Lady Brute comments for the house, 'What an inundation of impertinence is here coming upon us!' But as Fancyfull explains,

Why really, to confess the truth to you, I am so everlastingly fatigued with the addresses of unfortunate gentlemen, that were it not for the extravagancy of the example, I should e'en tear out these wicked eyes with my own fingers, to make both myself and mankind easy.

The wicked eyes she is conscious of match the way she moves.

Her entrance was eye-catching because it was not the usual way for a lady to enter a room. Rather more majesty in posture and movement was the style she aimed to achieve, something that every young gentlewoman learned as part of her upbringing, and which the dancing-masters' manuals address in detail. In John Essex's *The Dancing-Master* (following the French of P. Rameau), we find,

If she holds her head upright, and the body well disposed, without affectation, or too much boldness, they say, There goes a stately lady. If she carries it negligently, they accuse her of carelessness; if she pokes her head forward, of indolence; and in short, if she stoops, of thoughtlessness, or want of assurance; and so on. (p. 22)

Like a latter-day goddess her head would be poised proudly, with her shoulders down and her arms tucked back and hands to the front. In his *Letters* Muralt supports this picture of the Englishwoman when he describes those he saw: 'They walk together, for the most part without speaking; they are always dressed and always stiff', and he adds chillingly, 'I doubt they would not stoop to take up a flower from under their feet' (p. 15). In *A Walk to Islington* the satirist Ned Ward conveys the same impression:

> Her arms by her side are so formally posted,
> She looks like a pullet trussed up to be roasted.
> True dancing-school breeding in her is recorded;
> The swell of her bubbies, and jut of her bum
> To the next brawny stallion cries, Come, my dear, come.   (p. 5)

If, to set against this, the actress introduced a modish swing and swirl of her body, the audience would know that the promenade was only the beginning of something else.

The coquetry that accompanied her walking started with the curtsy. A daughter would curtsy to a parent, a wife to a husband, and all women to their superiors; and they would do so on arrival and on departure, on entrance and exit. A backward curtsy was accomplished by a gentle lifting of the side of the skirt, taking a step back on one foot and bending the knees with a little push of the skirt to the rear. A forward curtsy slid one foot forwards rather than backwards, and a curtsy *en passant* called for only 'a

32 The curtsy and the bow: *The Constant Couple*, Arts Theatre, 1943

moderate inclination' without stopping. In a deep curtsy there could be no handling at the waist and none of that swaying which occurred if the feet were in the wrong place.

On the stage the town lady distinguished herself from the country girl by the grace with which she executed her salute. And her curtsy had work to do beyond the merely conventional reverence: it conveyed meaning and feeling also. According to Antoine de Courtin in his *Rules of Civility* it should not be 'short and precipitate, but grave and low, if there be room' (p. 26). A quick bob was an insult, where the slow descent of a deep curtsy, held in place for some little time, could bespeak passion and sincerity. The lady's eyes had yet another function while this was going on, as this account from de Lauze's *Apologie de la Danse* suggests:

When she begins [the curtsy], it is necessary to look at the company, but in order not to depart from modesty, in bending the knees, she must lower the eyes with the body, which, on finishing, will be raised again, without stopping to regard any person fixedly, for that savours of effrontery. (p. 131)

In addition, Tomlinson in his *Art of Dancing* sees the gesture as an opportunity for flirting, and he gives much of his space to what a lady does when she is in the interesting position of subjection:

The courtesy, or respect, which a lady pays to those of either sex, is by a graceful bending of the knees, accompanied with a becoming and suitable disposition of the different parts of the body: as, having the hands before them, in some agreeable posture supporting, as it were, the slanting or falling shoulders, which, at the same time, lengthen and more gracefully expose a fine neck, as well as a beautiful face composed of so many delicate and charming features, with which they are unusually adorned by the bounty of nature.

He goes on,

A modest look or direction of the eye, an agreeable smile or a lively and pleasant aspect, with a chin neither poked out nor curbed in, but the whole countenance erect and graceful, will add a lustre to the whole, where any of these are wanting, whether in one sex or the other. (p. 9)

In Seyler's account of the manners of the period, culled from playing the parts herself, she lists the display of 'charms', provocative glances over her fan and, especially, inviting poses, and the most important of these was the deep curtsy for its power to display the actress's bare shoulders and frivolously shaking curls (*The Craft of Comedy*, p. 63). The most famous description of all stage curtsies is that of Colley Cibber's memory of how Susanna Mountfort played Melantha in act II of *Marriage à la Mode* when she receives Palamede with his father's letter of introduction:

33 Dames en conversation aux Tuilleries

She reads the letter ... with a careless, dropping lip and an erected brow, humming it hastily over as if she were impatient to outgo her father's commands by making a complete conquest of him at once; and that the letter might not embarrass her attack, crack! she crumbles it at once into her palm and pours upon him her whole artillery of airs, eyes, and motion; down goes her dainty, diving body to the ground, as if she were sinking under the conscious load of her own attractions; then launches into a flood of fine language and compliment, still playing her chest forward in fifty falls and risings, like a swan upon waving water. (p. 96)

In this performance Cibber believed he had seen 'the most complete system of female foppery that could possibly be crowded into the tortured form of a fine lady.'

Restoration playwrights are conscious of the workings of coquetry, and demonstrate it in action on the stage. In *The Man of Mode* we saw how Etherege contrives a scene in which Young Bellair instructs Harriet in the art of flirting (p. 111). Dorimant is also fascinated by her behaviour and accuses her of deliberately attracting men: 'How wantonly you played with your head, flung back your locks and looked smilingly over your shoulder at 'em' (III.3). For her part, Harriet knows how to tease Dorimant by a *pretended* seriousness when he wishes to speak of his love for her: 'I will put on my serious look, turn my head carelessly from you, drop my lip, let my eyelids fall and hang half o'er my eyes – thus.' Dorimant is quite non-plussed by this demonstration: 'Why do you not begin?' she asks (IV.I).

Cibber offers his own portrait of the coquette when Young Worthy describes Narcissa to her face in *Love's Last Shift*:

Why, madam, I have observed several particular qualities in your ladyship, that I have perfectly adored you for; as, the majestic toss of your head; – your obliging bow-curtsy; – your satirical smile; – your blushing laugh; – your demure look; – the careless tie of your hood; – the genteel flirt of your fan; – the designed accident in your letting it fall, and your agreeable manner of receiving it from him that takes it up. (II.I)

The stage direction that precedes this pretty picture tells Narcissa to imitate Worthy's words 'in dumb show' as he speaks, so that the verbal account is reinforced by her acting. Coquetry, pretence and play-acting are thus shown to be all of a kind.

There are many expedients to which the coquette may resort. Mrs Christian in Dryden's *Sir Martin Mar-all* 'plays the innocent' in act I in order to catch Lord Darmouth. In *Love for Love*, act III, on the other hand, Mrs Frail has to force the pace with flagrant flattery in order to make an impression on the dull-witted Ben. When she begins her campaign of 'wheedling', as she calls it, the occasion calls for some heavy strokes from Congreve's delicate pen:

BEN. Mayhap I have no mind to marry.
MRS FRAIL. That would be a pity, such a handsome young gentleman.

And,

BEN. Mess, you're a tight vessel and well rigged, and you were but as well manned.
MRS FRAIL. I should not doubt that if *you* were master of me.

Before long she is appealing to his weakness with a tearful 'If you should forsake me after all, you'd break my heart', and 'Will you love me always?'

Yet this would be dull stuff without the actual contribution of the actress –
in Seyler's words, 'frankly enjoying her power of repartee and with
sparkle all over her, nodding fontange, eyes, fingers, fan and toes alert and
merry' (*The Craft of Comedy*, p. 76). In drama, speech and action are
inseparable; in coquetry, they are one.

DEPARTURES FROM ACCEPTABILITY

Women on the stage infinitely extended the scope of sexual comedy, and
overnight the battle of the sexes became more urgent in impact. On a
sliding scale of acceptability, the Restoration audience could now review
in order a theatrical hierarchy of prudes and pretenders, female fops and
country girls, fools and innocents, with a variety of flirts and whores to
complete the gallery. The hierarchy was established according to the
values, not of virtue or vice, but of intelligence or stupidity, elegance or
inelegance in conducting themselves.

Near the bottom of the scale come the two 'common women of the
town', Mrs Flirt and Mrs Flounce, in *The Gentleman Dancing-Master*.
They serve first to fill out the day-to-day life of Gerrard and Martin, the
heroes of the piece. Before the two women enter the 'French House' where
the gentlemen eat, the waiter gives a sense of what may be expected of this
ill-mannered pair by reporting that 'they'll kick me downstairs' if he tries
to keep them out; when he shuts the door on them, ''*tis thrust open again*'
and they land him a blow as they sweep in. They shamelessly wear their
vizards and they know what they want: 'the brisk Hoazas of seventeen or
eighteen'. They set their caps at Monsieur de Paris, who has invited their
attention by peeping under Flounce's scarf to view her 'déshabille', as he
calls it. Then follows,

MONSIEUR. Do you love me?
FLIRT. Indeed I cannot help telling you now what my modesty ought to conceal,
    but my eyes would disclose it too. I have a passion for you, sir.
MONSIEUR. A passion for me!
FLIRT. An extreme passion, dear sir, you are so French, so mightily French, so
    agreeably French; but I'll tell you more of my heart at home: come along.
    (1.2)

After making so unconscionable a tryst, the Frenchified fop and this
brazen Flirt deserve one another. Flounce and Flirt are seen again at the
end of the play when they try to blackmail Monsieur and manage to break
up his engagement to Hippolita.

An unblushing Mrs Termagant appears in Shadwell's grossly Jon-
sonian *The Squire of Alsatia*. She is an extraordinarily violent lady who, all

in II.I, *'falls into a fit'*, *'flies at'* Belfont jun., *'hides in his closet'* and *'pulls Lucia out by the hair'* – there never was such a shrew. And if we remember the West Country wench Mary the Buxom in D'Urfey's *The Comical History of Don Quixote*, it is because Colley Cibber relished how she was played by Susanna Mountfort: 'a young todpole dowdy, as freckled as a raven's egg, with matted hair, snotty nose, and a pair of hands as black as the skin of a tortoise, with nails as long as kite's tallons upon every finger'. And was this the lovely Melantha? Mary the Buxom was vulgar enough to call down the wrath of Jeremy Collier. Grotesque characters such as these verge on caricature and perhaps linger on the periphery of social form.

More central to several of the comedies in the early years is the female fop. In *Marriage à la Mode* the role of Melantha is that of a *précieuse ridicule* and a would-be gentlewoman. She is at once the coquette of youth and beauty, and a silly woman affected by all things French, so that her gushing Francophilia undercuts the pleasure taken in her sexuality and results in a curiously ambivalent perception of her. Palamede has the task of trying to flirt with a girl who speaks another language. First played in 1672 by Boutell, Melantha was a prize for actresses for years, including those in the Cibber versions of the eighteenth century. When recreated by Seyler in 1920, *The Times* found her 'a perfect thing, the very quintessence of fun' (10 February). Summers's programme note believed 'it is obvious that from Melantha Congreve took many a hint for Millamant'; if so, such hints had little to do with her foolishness.

At the beginning Dryden almost stifles his character in French. Her first words in act II on Rhodophil, for example, are, 'Let me die but he's a fine man; he sings and dances *en Français* and writes *billets-doux* to a miracle.' Her conversation with Palamede turns on the latest dances, plays and ballets, all French, until she hears that 'the new prince is just passed by the end of the walk', and immediately the snob in her takes charge and she departs, *'exit running'*. Her habit of running certainly enlivens her words, and the next moment she returns in the same style, running to embrace Doralice; when Artemis, then Amalthea, enter, she runs to each in turn; and when she hears that the prince is coming again, again it is *'exit running'*. Doralice asks Palamede why he does not follow her, and his quick rejoinder is, 'Follow her? Why, at this rate she'll be in the Indies within the half hour.'

Act III finds her at her French lesson with the help of her maid Philotis, who has 'drained all the French plays and romances' to fuel Melantha's daily consumption of new words, and only then does she practise her 'postures', pulling faces into a glass. But Dryden finally strikes gold when he explores and extends her affectation. Alone on the stage, she imagines a meeting with her lover in which she plays both the parts:

'Rhodophil, you'll wonder at my assurance to meet you here; let me die, I am so out of breath with coming that I can render you no reason for it.' Then he will make this *repartie*: 'Madam, I have no reason to accuse you for that which is so great a favour to me.' Then I reply, 'But why have you drawn me to this solitary place? Let me die but I am apprehensive of some violence from you.' Then, says he, 'Solitude, madam, is most fit for lovers; but by this fair hand –' '–Nay, now I vow you're rude, sir. O fie, fie, fie; I hope you'll be honourable? –' '– You'd laugh at me if I should, madam –' '– What do you men to throw me down thus? Ah me! ah, ah, ah!'

It is Melantha's best moment, noticeably when there is no need for her to speak French. The pantomime enacts her silly thoughts, and suddenly her character becomes theatrically complete.

Only slight variations in female foppery produce bold designs and new opportunities for the actress. Less benign by far is the Olivia of Wycherley's *The Plain Dealer*. Drawing upon Molière's *Le Misanthrope*, she is a disturbing mixture of Célimène in her attractiveness and Arsinoé in her prudishness; she has a more vicious tongue and a sharper bite than Melantha could ever have. When she is introduced in act II, Wycherley's technique is to have her deny everything she is, with her cousin Eliza as a corrective; it is for the actress playing Olivia to make plain the opposite of what she says.

OLIVIA. Ah, cousin, what a world 'tis we live in! I am so weary of it.
ELIZA. Truly, cousin, I can find no fault with it but that we cannot always live in it. For I can never be weary of it.
OLIVIA. O hideous! You cannot be in earnest sure when you say you like the filthy world.

These opening lines supply the code: in her languishing tone and gesture, Olivia is indulging herself to the full.

The playwright proceeds to touch on one foppish characteristic after another, an appalling catalogue of pretensions:

ELIZA. But is it possible the world, which has such variety of charms for other women, can have none for you? Let's see – first, what d'ye think of dressing and fine clothing?
OLIVIA. Dressing! Fie, fie, 'tis my aversion. But come hither, you dowdy, methinks you might have opened this toure [an added hairpiece] better. O hideous! I cannot suffer it! D'ye see how't sits?

The pattern is simple: in spite of Olivia's protests and expostulations about dressing, she fusses over Eliza's hair, and at the same time manages to put her down. Then she insists that clothes are also her 'aversion', but it turns out that she bought seven new gowns that month, and is pleased to display her latest acquisition. The dialogue lists everything a female pretender professes to despise, but in practice desires. It offers a complete programme for malicious railing, on balls, plays, masquerades, then on husbands, marriage and lovers.

LETTICE. But what does your ladyship think of a liberal, handsome young lover?
OLIVIA. A handsome young fellow, you impudent! Be gone, out of my sight. Name a handsome young fellow to me! Foh, a hideous, handsome young fellow I abominate. (*Spits.*)

When Olivia's closest interests are touched, she grows shrill, and the contradictions in her attitude are recognizable in the clever oxymoron of a 'hideous, handsome' young fellow and her loss of self-possession.

Olivia and her overheated feelings shade into the least acceptable, and most laughable, of female aberrations, those of the maiden lady of 'high profession and low practice', as she is aptly identified. She is the prude who lacks any redeeming feature in her hypocrisy, and if less subtle is consequently far more animated. She is first recognizable by her name, Lady Loveall in *The Parson's Wedding*, Lady Vaine in *The Sullen Lovers*, Lady Loveyouth in *The Humorists*, Lady Plyant in *The Double Dealer*, Lady Wishfort in *The Way of the World*, and many more. When Shadwell writes his notes on Lady Vaine, he comes straight out with, 'A whore that takes upon her the name of a lady, very talkative and impertinently affected in her language, always pretending to virtue and honour.'

This prude is the frequent subject of the character studies of the time. In *Reflexions upon Ridicule*, Bellegarde is at first quite generous:

A woman, who for a long time has had the reputation of beauty, would at last distinguish herself by her devotion, when she can no longer be handsome. It mortifies her to lose the empire she obtained over hearts, and she tries to establish another kind of dominion over minds . . . . She must now act another part, and change her batteries, when the fire of her eyes is extinguished, and her face is upon the decay. (p. 91)

Here prudishness is attributed to the onset of *anno domini*, over which a fading beauty can after all have no control. In the second part of his *Reflexions* (1707) Bellegarde draws her character from her inappropriate excess of make-up:

What can be more disgusting and loathsome, than an old woman daubed and plastered, and who has filled up the wrinkle of her forehead with pomatum and ceruse? Who could forbear laughing to see old Emilia's glaring cheeks? Her face resembles a death's-head, painted white and red; and yet she thinks of pleasing, and will still see the world, upon which she dotes now more than ever. (p. 224)

The comic stage employs the signals of powder and paint with cruel glee.
The unfortunate among older ladies are so afflicted with the affection

34 La folie pare la décrépitude des adjustements de la jeunesse

of virtue that they must be constantly on the alert for men who they believe harbour designs upon their persons. One thinks of Lady Dunce of *The Soldier's Fortune* and her memorable line spoken when men try to flirt with her, 'Curse on my fatal beauty!', a line which W. S. Gilbert could not resist putting in the mouth of his Idyllic Poet in *Patience*, Archibald Grosvenor: 'A curse on my fatal beauty, for I am sick of conquests!' In *The Double Dealer*, Congreve loads unforgettable lines on Lady Plyant when

130

Mellefont tries to speak of her daughter, while in her perfervid imagination Lady Plyant thinks he wants herself.

MELLEFONT. Madam, pray give me leave to ask you one question –

LADY PLYANT. O Lord, ask me the question, I'll swear I'll refuse it; I'll swear I'll deny it – therefore don't ask me, nay you shan't ask me, I swear I'll deny it. O Gemini, you have brought all the blood into my face; I warrant I am as red as a turkey-cock; O fie, cousin Mellefont!

MELLEFONT. Nay, madam, hear me; I mean –

LADY PLYANT. Hear you, no, no; I'll deny you first and hear you afterwards. For one does not know how one's mind may change upon hearing – Hearing is one of the senses, and all the senses are fallible; I won't trust my honour, I assure you; my honour is infallible and uncomeatable.

MELLEFONT. For heaven's sake, madam –

LADY PLYANT. O name it no more – Bless me, how can you talk of heaven! and have so much wickedness in your heart? (II.5)

Perfection in this kind is realized in Lady Wishfort in *The Way of the World*, acts III and IV, that 'antidote to desire' who bursts into life when she prepares for a lover. The fact that the object of her attention is an impostor only makes her more ridiculous. It does not help her self-possession, although it will surely help the work of the actress, that Wishfort is tipsy from cherry brandy when she contemplates the visit:

But art thou sure Sir Rowland will not fail to come? Or will he not fail when he does come? Will he be importunate, Foible, and push? For if he should not be importunate, I shall never break decorums. I shall die with confusion, if I am forced to advance. Oh no, I can never advance! I shall swoon if he should expect advances. No, I hope Sir Rowland is better bred than to put a lady to the necessity of breaking her forms. I won't be too coy neither. I won't give him despair; but a little disdain is not amiss, a little scorn is alluring.

'A little scorn becomes your ladyship', is Foible's response. And later Wishfort asks her maid how she looks, and seems well pleased with the reply, 'Most killing well, madam.'

Well, and how shall I receive him? In what figure shall I give his heart the first impression? There is a great deal in the first comparison. Shall I sit? – No, I won't sit – I'll walk – aye, I'll walk from the door upon his entrance; and then turn full upon him. – No, that will be too sudden. I'll lie – aye, I'll lie down – I'll receive him in my little dressing-room; there's a couch – yes, yes, I'll give the first impression on a couch. – I won't loll neither, but loll and lean upon one elbow, with one foot a little dangling off, jogging in a thoughtful way – yes – and then as soon as he appears start, aye, start and be surprised, and rise to meet him in a pretty disorder – yes – oh, nothing is more alluring than a levee from a couch in some confusion. – It shows the foot to advantage, and furnishes with blushes, and recomposing airs beyond comparison. Hark! There's a coach.

35 Mrs Pitt as Lady Wishfort, *The Way of the World*, act III

Such speech is completely expressive and stageworthy. The words carry:

- a complete development in range of feeling from apprehension to exhilaration, and Wishfort's voice is heard in all its shades and tones in every line.
- an implicit statement of the lady's pretended modesty ('I shall never break decorums') together with the double image of how she appears and how she is.
- a total embodiment of gesture for performance, from 'die with confusion' (flutter of hands and fan) to 'I won't be too coy neither' (flutter of eyelids and curls) to 'a little disdain . . . a little scorn' (stiffening into respectability once more).
- a happy use of props, especially her glass and her costume (her 'pretty disorder', with a demonstrative flurry like that of a young girl).
- a physical enactment of her prolific imagination as she practises her poses and postures, and at the same time projects what she hopes the future will bring. And all the while Foible is used to orchestrate the reactions of the audience through her ironic comments ('a little scorn becomes your ladyship' . . . 'most killing well, madam.')

From such lines a great performance can come: that of Elinor Leigh, the first Wishfort, adept at rendering 'modest stale maids that have missed their market' and at painting 'the blind side of nature' (Cibber, p. 93). Or of Margaret Yarde for Playfair's revival in 1924, a she-dragon of desire, 'flamboyancy itself', in the view of A.B. Walkley of *The Times* (8 February). Or of Edith Evans, a creature of raddled pathos in John Burrell's production of 1948. Or of Margaret Rutherford for John Gielgud in 1953, now, according to Ivor Brown in *The Observer* for 22 February, 'a magnificent picture of an ample and downy pillow craving a head to be laid on it'. The variety of Wishforts from dragons to pathetic pillows begins to belie the thinking that she is a cardboard figure of two dimensions (see plates 36 and 37).

THE BREECHES PART

For much of its history the theatre has unblushingly enjoyed the business of changing sexes by changing clothes. As in Elizabethan times, the Restoration actor might play in skirts for broad comic effect, like Sir Samuel Hearty in *The Virtuoso*, 'a brisk, amorous, adventurous, unfortunate coxcomb' who chooses to pursue his ends 'in woman's habit', so that in iv.1 Sir Formal Trifle mistakes him for a real woman in the darkness. Mrs Mandrake the midwife in *The Twin Rivals* was traditionally played by a man, a Mr Bullock in the first production. Moreoever, according to J.H. Wilson, there were some fourteen plays written in the period for an actress to play the leading man, a tradition which has persisted into modern times with the principal boy of pantomime (*All the King's Ladies*, p. 81). And in revivals of certain of Shakespeare's comedies, of course, a girl also appeared in breeches – Rowe's edition illustrates a Rosalind in breeches, tricorn and peruke.

Yet one of the most striking departures arising directly from the presence of the actress on the Restoration stage was the 'breeches part', and a large number of new plays were contrived so that a girl would have to dress as a man. This practice was unrelated to the happy convention in Shakespeare of presenting the boy actor first as a girl in skirts and then as a boy in doublet and hose. Julia, Portia, Rosalind, Viola and Imogen all explore the ambiguities of representing both male and female simulta- neously, forcing comparisons of attitude and action, but these were attitudes and actions of the mind, not the body. The breeches part of the Restoration was introduced first for the youthful actress to display as much of the female anatomy below the waist as a man's dress would allow; in an age when women wore their skirts to the ground, a shapely ankle or calf was provocative and 'a pair of Holland thighs' would be sensational.

Wilson counted no fewer than 89 of the 375 new plays written and produced between 1660 and 1700 with breeches parts (p. 73). They were clearly a lively new attraction, and Pepys, not unexpectedly, was quick to keep note: on 23 February 1663 he saw Moll Davis 'in boy's apparel, she having very fine legs, only bends in the hams, as I perceive all women do'. Nell Gwyn was especially adept at such parts, and Pepys very much approved her role as Florimell mimicking the manners of a beau in *Secret Love* – 'when she comes in like a young gallant; and hath the motions and carriage of a spark the most that ever I saw any man have. It makes me, I confess, admire her' (2 March 1667). Betterton in his *History of the English Stage* records that Elizabeth Boutell was 'low of stature, had very agreeable features, a good complexion, but a childish look' (p. 21); she was just right for breeches parts, and the one play of John Corye, *The Generous Enemies*, has a very pointed epilogue for Boutell's part of Semena, previously disguised as Lysander:

> As woman let me with the men prevail,
> And with the ladies as I look like male.
> 'Tis worth your money that such legs appear;
> These are not to be seen elsewhere:
> In short, commend this play, or by this light,
> We will not sup with one of you tonight.

36 Edith Evans as Lady Wishfort, *The Way of the World*, New Theatre, 1948

37 Margaret Rutherford as Lady Wishfort, *The Way of the World*, Lyric Theatre, Hammersmith, 1953

Like Susanna Mountfort, she was one who could carry on what Cibber interestingly called 'a secret dialogue' with the audience when in breeches.

Rich possibilities for theatrical sensation arose with the epicene roles. An actress in breeches could take the house by storm in her own right, like Nell Gwyn. Or by chasing her lover to discover his true intentions, she might trespass dangerously upon male preserves. When Margery Pinchwife is disguised in boy's clothing, Wycherley can begin a delicious process of teasing until she gives herself away. When Fidelia becomes Captain Manly's pretty pageboy in *The Plain Dealer*, she finds herself in the pathetic situation, not wholly unlike that of Viola in *Twelfth Night*, of doing duty as his procuress while at the same time risking the attentions to her person of both Olivia and Vernish.

The audience knew to expect the eventual discovery of the actress's disguise, and pleasurably anticipated the way it would be done. The chosen moment always involved her flinging off her hat and peruke, or having them flung off for her, so that her hair would fall down at a shake of the head, like Bellamira's in Sedley's play of that name (III.4). For Fidelia's discovery Wycherley added a new touch when Vernish '*pulls off her peruke and feels her breasts*'. From those on stage the cry would go up, as in Behn's *The Younger Brother*, 'By heaven, a woman!', or words to that effect.

In *Secret Love*, v.1, Florimell offers a good example of the kind of swagger and style an actress might assume with her male attire. Dryden puts the actress through her paces in an amusing sort of rehearsal when she appears '*in man's habit*', produces a comb and a mirror and says to herself,

Save you, Monsieur Florimell! Faith, methinks you are a very jaunty fellow, *poudré et adjusté* as well as the best of 'em. I can manage the little comb, set my hat, shake my garniture, toss about my empty noddle, walk with a courant slur, and at every step peck down my head. If I should be mistaken for some courtier now, pray where's the difference?

She checks her peruke with the comb, arranges her hat and its plume, and finally begins to stroll about with a swing of the hips as if she were dancing the courant.

When her beloved Celadon enters with two rivals, Olinda and Sabina, she proceeds to flirt with them herself as a way to keep them off him, adding to her affected gait a voice that purrs its compliments as she '*walks with them*':

FLORIMELL. They are the greatest beauties I confess that ever I beheld.

CELADON. How now, what's the meaning of this, young fellow?
FLORIMELL. And therefore I cannot wonder that this gentleman who has the honour to be known to you should admire you . . . .

The girls respond with pleasure to the flattery, but Celadon is incensed at being outdone by the attractive stranger.

CELADON. Pish, thee! a young raw creature, thou hast ne'er been under the barber's hands yet.
FLORIMELL. No, nor under the surgeon's neither as you have been.
CELADON. 'Slife what wouldst thou be at? I am madder than thou art!
FLORIMELL. The devil you are; I'll tope with you, I'll sing with you, I'll dance with you, – I'll swagger with you –
CELADON. I'll fight with you.

Upon this offer to fight, Celadon's hand threateningly on the hilt of his sword, Florimell must quickly talk her way out of a ticklish situation: 'Out upon fighting; 'tis grown so common a fashion, that a modish man contemns it.'

In the muddled masquerade of *Marriage à la Mode*, IV.3, Doralice's disguise as a man finds her awkwardly placed in a male environment, an eating-house with bottles of wine on the table; but she is able to test Palamede because she is free to say what she otherwise could not: 'Were I a woman, O how you'd admire me!' And she risks putting words into his mouth: ''Tis almost parktime' and 'Shall we go out of the pit and go behind the scenes for an act or two?' Only when she has revealed her identity to Palamede by plucking off her wig and quickly replacing it, may the same disguise permit him to kiss her on the hand and the lips in front of her husband Rhodophil. That gentleman, meanwhile, has Palamede's mistress Melantha '*in boy's habit*' with him, so that Rhodophil is enabled to embrace her in front of him: ''Twill be the prettiest juggling trick to cheat him when he looks upon us.' The audience now sees two men and two boys on the stage, and both Palamede and Rhodophil think that one of the boys is a girl. Dryden concludes his scene of mixed identities with a very mixed-up joke:

PALAMEDE. What shall we do with the two boys?
RHODOPHIL. Let them take a lodging in the house till the business be over.

Now Doralice and Melantha must wriggle out of a critical situation of their own making:

DORALICE. What, lie with a boy? For my part, I own it, I cannot endure to lie with a boy.
MELANTHA. Let me die if I enter into a pair of sheets with him that hates the French.

In *She Would and She Would Not* the difficulties that arise from a girl's wearing breeches are exploited remorselessly from the first act to the last. In the very first scene Hypolita and her maid Flora enter *'in men's habits'* in order to pursue Hypolita's betrothed, Don Philip. The embarrassments begin at an inn where Trappanti, a sort of Truffaldino, servant of two masters, offers to shave her. In act II she finds herself in a sword fight with Philip's brother Octavio over the affections of Rosara. In act III Rosara's father chooses Hypolita for her husband, while the latter must act the breeches part in good earnest in order to maintain her disguise, thus: when the two girls are alone, Hypolita remains distant – she *'stands for some time mute, looks carelessly at Rosara, and she smiles as in contempt'*; when the father returns, Hypolita must kiss and embrace Rosara warmly to impress him – and thus, and thus, and thus'. In act IV Don Philip offers to despatch her as an impostor, and *'seizes her, and holds the sword to her breast'* while she throws herself trembling at his feet. Not until act V is the poor girl released from the comic terrors of her disguise.

A comically acute instance of sexual embarrassment is developed in *The Recruiting Officer*. Silvia, in love with Captain Plume, follows her best inclinations and offers to join the army *'dressed in man's apparel'*. With some swagger and more trepidation she announces herself in III.2 as 'Jack Wilful at your service', telling Plume and Brazen that 'he that bids me fairest shall have me'. Farquhar then offers these lines:

BRAZEN. Sir, I'll prefer you; I'll make you a corporal this minute.
PLUME. A corporal! I'll make you my companion; you shall eat with me.
BRAZEN. You shall drink with me.
PLUME. You shall lie with me, you young rogue. (*Kisses her.*)

Silvia hops away smartly, lucky not to have been discovered; but her induction into the military has only just begun.

Act IV finds her practising 'the principal ingredients in the composition of a captain', 'a bold step, a rakish toss, a smart cock, and an impudent air'. When she spies the country wench Rose, she continues her studies: 'Come, child, kiss me at once. (*Kisses Rose.*)' It is but a short step further when Plume offers Rose to her as a bribe: 'Si vous voulez donc vous enroller dans ma companie, la sera à vous.' It is an offer she cannot refuse. The obligatory scene with Rose takes place offstage, but in act V Silvia enters as from bed after a tormented night (a scene 'corrected' out of the second and third quartos.). Periwig, hat and sword lie on a table, and Silvia walks shakily down to the audience in her nightcap.

SILVIA. I have rested but indifferently, and I believe my bedfellow was as little pleased. Poor Rose. Here she comes. Good morrow, my dear, how d'ye this morning?

But Rose enters in a fury.

ROSE. Just as I was last night, neither better nor worse for you.
SILVIA. What's the matter? Did you not like your bedfellow?
ROSE. I don't know whether I had a bedfellow or not.
SILVIA. Did not I lie with you?
ROSE. No. I wonder you could have the conscience to ruin a poor girl for nothing.

Comment would be superfluous.

The breeches scene in act III of *The Country Wife* may be the cleverest in the canon of Restoration comedies. It has the virtues of an inverted game of hide-and-seek, since instead of having the female deceive and chase the male, the male pretends ignorance of the truth while the female

38 Helen Cherry in breeches as Silvia, with Edward Byrne (Brazen) and Trevor Howard (Plume), *The Recruiting Officer*, Arts Theatre, 1943

in breeches only half-heartedly tries to deceive him. All the time, of course, the audience has the pleasure of knowing the truth better than anyone. In order to throw the men off the trail of his new young wife Margery, Pinchwife has instructed her to pose in public as her own brother. He believes that breeches will be a safer disguise than a mask; the audience knows they will present a greater challenge to the hunter. Act III.2 takes the scene to the New Exchange, where all can meet and mingle, and so they do. At the first encounter with Horner, Margery strides and postures splendidly like a young man, although she begins to give her

39 Maggie Smith in breeches as Silvia, with Lynn Redgrave (Rose), *The Recruiting Officer*, Old Vic, 1963: 'I wonder you could have the conscience to ruin a poor girl for nothing.'

identity away by showing uncommon interest in the ballads and plays she finds there, and Pinchwife increases Horner's suspicions by being strangely protective and pulling her away. At this point Horner and his friends do not know the truth for certain.

At the second encounter Horner takes the initiative with a devilish series of tricks designed to test the sex of this charming young man.

- He first *'takes hold'* of Margery, using excessive politeness – 'this pretty gentleman' – in her hearing. The touch and tone are enough to discompose her performance as a boy, and she may betray herself again with a giggle and a wriggle ('She carries it so sillily' from Pinchwife).
- Horner tries again, repeating the provocative word that worked well before: 'Who is this pretty young gentleman?' . . . 'I never saw anything so pretty in all my life.' Margery now forgets her duty and turns to jelly, while Pinchwife, caught in his own trap, must release her to maintain the deception.
- Horner goes a step further: 'He is very like her I saw you at the play with, whom I told you I was in love with.' Margery, suitably aroused, at last breaks into speech with an aside: 'I love him already too.' Now it is she who wants the truth to come out ('How she gazes on him!'). It has been well said that never before was a fortress so unwilling to be defended.
- Horner next calls his friends to help him compare the brother with the sister, and as the pace picks up Harcourt and Dorilant assist in Margery's physical trial: 'She is as like him *here* as can be' (is this her face, her bosom, her bottom?). And she certainly proves herself to be a creature 'of flesh and blood'.
- Horner's pleasure in teasing Margery is doubled by his ability to torment Pinchwife at the same time, so that the latter's frenzy grows, his wild asides registering the imminence of discovery like a pressure valve.
- Horner asks Margery to present his 'humble service' to his sister (the *double entendre* heard in his voice). In her blissful confusion, does she bow or does she curtsy? And he is able to address his endearments to her under Pinchwife's nose with 'You have revived the love I had for her at first sight in the playhouse.' She responds as in a trance: 'But did you love her indeed, and indeed?'
- Comes the final test. Horner kisses her ('Give her this kiss for me'), not once, but three times, with Margery protesting more and more feebly as her disguise falls away. Then for further kissing she is spun from Horner to Harcourt to Dorilant and back in a balletic whirl of giddy pleasure, with the unhappy Pinchwife giving chase in vain, always a pace or two behind.

40 Ruth Gordon as Margery Pinchwife, *The Country Wife*, Old Vic, 1936

5. Stage and sexual tactics

In her letters to *Theatre Arts* Athene Seyler is persuaded that any movement and gesture in the seventeenth century needs space. On the small stage of the Restoration playhouse they especially call for an acting area uncluttered with furniture. Not only did the voluminous costumes of the well-dressed men and women of the time demand spatial freedom, but so too did the patterns of movement that belonged to the social encounters found in play after play.

Those plays which expect their actors to simulate a crowded salon or a busy New Exchange or a milling St James's Park are made up of a good deal of ambulatory comedy, often performed in pairs crossing and passing on the perimeter of the apron nearest the audience in the pit. Dryden's *Secret Love*, act III, is set in 'the court gallery', and the scene typically has the direction, '*Enter Celadon, Olinda, Sabina: they walk on the stage together, he seeming to court them.*' It is a display, chiefly in pantomime, of what the audience would recognize as a familiar social situation. His *An Evening's Love* opens with women '*passing by*', and as they walk '*they pull up their veils, and pull 'em down again*'.

Such activity had its basis in real life. Henshaw maintains that the promenade was 'particularly conducive to refined conversation' and had little in common with what we now call 'going for a walk': 'it was done with as much sense of form as if it were a dance' ('Graphic Sources', p. 307). Walking in a formal seventeenth-century garden, with its symmetrical flower-beds and its geometrically pruned trees, was likely to be as fraught with proprieties and as rigidly patterned as a neo-classical work of art. Nor were 'chance' encounters on such walks left to chance, any more than the secret signals exchanged between the sexes were particularly secret. In *The Art of Love* (1700) Charles Hopkins indicates lightly how the sexes might behave if they were to see and be seen, even when the lady was masked:

> As you pass by, the subtle fair shall turn,
> She hopes you know her noted garments worn.
> Seem not to know, let no salute be paid,
> But rally, mildly sharp, the masking maid.
> Perhaps the kind attendant shall display

Restoration comedy in performance

Her waving handkerchief, to court your stay.
If the white flag flies waving to the field,
The warrior knows the charming fort will yield.
The maid, perchance, with an alluring grace,
Grants some quick sketches of her simp'ring face,
Whilst her spread fan, held cunningly, is born,
(That very fan you had so lately torn)
Becks with her hand, and now turns short, now stands;
Do you return her beckons with your hands.

(p. 77)

The action on stage of walking and observing, pausing and saluting,
inviting and beckoning, was important to the audience's recognition and

41 Dame en manteaux et gentilhomme allant par la ville

understanding of the organization of the sexes in the play. In Shadwell's *The Sullen Lovers*, II.3, the morose couple Stanford and Emilia at first break the rules when they *'walk up and down, and take little notice of one another'*, but the business of perambulating itself anticipates that some encounter will follow, and indeed their more lively opposite numbers Lovel and Carolina plan to bring their friends together. When in the next act Emilia announces strangely that she intends to 'take a walk in the fields' on her own, the audience cannot fail to watch for some special encounter with Stanford.

In Farquhar's *The Inconstant*, act III, Mirabel and Bisarre are to be seen *'passing carelessly by one another'*; but again the strong visual suggestion is that significant signals are to be sent and received, and so their subsequent asides confirm:

BISARRE (*aside*). I wonder what she can see in this fellow to like him?
MIRABEL (*aside*). I wonder what my friend can see in this girl to admire her?
BISARRE (*aside*). A wild, foppish, extravagant rakehell.
MIRABEL (*aside*). A light, whimsical, impertinent madcap.

The symmetry of the asides (and presumably the gestures) also reminds the audience of the artificial formality of the action.

Etherege introduces his own characteristic device, that of mutual mimicry, into the 'little harmless discourse in public walks' provided for Dorimant and Harriet when he has them disparage one another as they walk:

DORIMANT. I know you are greedy of the praises of the whole Mall.
HARRIET. You do me wrong.
DORIMANT. I do not. As I followed you, I observed how you were pleased when the fops cried 'She's handsome, very handsome, by God she is!' and whispered aloud your name – the thousand several forms you put your face into; then, to make yourself more agreeable, how wantonly you played with your head, flung back your locks, and looked smilingly over your shoulder at 'em.
HARRIET. I do not go begging the men's, as you do the ladies' good liking, with a sly softness in your looks and a gentle slowness in your bows as you pass by 'em. As thus, sir. (*Acts him.*) Is not this like you?

(*The Man of Mode*, III.3).

Without recourse to a breeches part, Harriet mimics the beau to his face – and to the audience for its delighted comparison with the Dorimant it already knows. But only after he has dared to mimic her own pretty behaviour.

Letting the young men and women loose in park or mall was an efficient tactic to reveal their intentions and serve their ends, flirtation or assignation. *Love in a Wood* provides a strong example of the business of

promenading at its most tantalizing, and it has two major scenes, II.1 and
v.1, located in St James's Park at night, excellent territory for 'coursing'.
In the first of the scenes the young men of the town 'ramble' on from the
French House, with Lady Flippant's song about hateful wives still in our
ears. They promptly comment on the virtues of walking in the Park:

RANGER. Hang me if I am not pleased extremely with this new-fashioned
    caterwauling, this midnight coursing in the Park.
VINCENT. A man may come after supper with his three bottles in his head, reel
    himself sober, without reproof from his mother, aunt, or grave relation.
RANGER. May bring his bashful wench, and not have her put out of countenance
    by the impudent honest women of the town.

After this story of self-indulgence, the audience knows just what to
expect.

Soon comes the direction, '*people walking slowly over the stage*', and
these prompt a spiteful comment or two before Ranger departs in hot
pursuit of a wench. Another moment and his mistress Lydia and my Lady
Flippant are also seen '*walking over the stage*', with Lydia looking for
Ranger. When the ladies '*go off*', Vincent and Dapperwit follow them,
whereupon the ladies re-enter and the men '*walk slowly towards them*'.
This change in the wind flutters the dove-cote:

FLIPPANT. Do they come? are they men certainly?
LYDIA. Prepare for an assault, they'll put you to't.
FLIPPANT. Will they put us to't certainly? I was never put to't yet; if they should
    put us to't, I should drop down, down, certainly.
LYDIA. I believe, truly, you would not have power to run away.
FLIPPANT. Therefore I will not stay the push. They come, they come, oh the
    fellows come!

So my Lady Flippant runs off with all the others in tow, the flurries of
skirts and ribbons this way and that giving the broad impression of an
ornate, if amorous, sport played among the imaginary trees and bushes, a
kind of *tableau vivant*.

Flippant's behaviour develops ludicrously when she hits on Sir Simon
Addleplot, and the chase continues with Ranger replacing Vincent in the
pursuit of Lydia. However, nothing has really changed, and the best part
of the entertainment lies in observing the coming and going of the pairs,
building up a polite excitement which culminates in a dance by torchlight
for the final breathless clash of the sexes:

FLIPPANT (*to Lydia*). Nay, if you stay any longer, I must leave you again.
VINCENT. We have overtaken them at last again, these are they, they separate too,
    and that's but a challenge to us. (*Flippant going off.*)
DAPPERWIT. Let me perish, ladies –

LYDIA. Nay, good madam, let's unite, now here's the common enemy among us.
VINCENT. Damme, ladies –
DAPPERWIT. Hold, a pox you are too rough, let me perish, ladies.
LYDIA. Not for want of breath, gentlemen, we'll stay rather.
DAPPERWIT. For want of your favour, rather, sweet ladies.

It is difficult to describe the course of this hectic action, but its elements of comedy may be traced:

- The twin groups are at first separated, the women coming to rest with Flippant in earnest consultation with Lydia while glancing over her shoulder, the two women representing in their attractive persons at once the need to escape and the wish to stay.
- The men pause apart when they see their prey has temporarily come to a halt, and they consolidate their gains, rejoin forces, collect themselves, renew the attack.
- The pairs come together momentarily, and the audience senses a resolution to come.
- Flippant's motion towards departure threatens the success of the enterprise for everyone, divides the men, and calls up a protest from Lydia which compels her companion to hesitate.
- The men's breathless exasperation is resolved by a turn of wit: the ladies will stay because they choose to do so, the men because they desire their favours, and, in polite terms, both parties are satisfied.

The whole episode represents in little an amusing image of sexual tactics appropriate to the everlasting battle. The audience follows the chase through all its stages, the indecision and hesitation, the protest and pretence, the tension and final gratification.

THE SPACIOUS ENTRANCE AND EXIT

The intimate stage with its proscenium doors opening straight onto the apron invited a sensational personal entrance by the actor that the later proscenium stage could not emulate. A beau's entrance exploited to the full the elaborate salutation of uncovering, bowing and kissing, and the dialogue usually indicates how the *entrée* is to be made in the spirit of the moment. Lord Foppington's entrance in Cibber's *The Careless Husband*, II.2, is particularly spectacular as curls and feathers fly with every flourish:

My dear *agréable! Que je t'embrasse! Pardi! Il y a cent ans que je ne t'ay vu* – My Lord, I am your Lordship's most obedient humble servant. [Let me kiss you! By Jove! It's been a hundred years since I saw you.]

Cibber wrote the lines for himself, and with them he filled the stage. By contrast, Sparkish in *The Country Wife* blows in like a gust of wind:

How is't, sparks, how is't? Well, faith, Harry, I must rally thee a little, ha, ha, ha! upon the report of the town of thee, ha, ha, ha! I can't hold i'faith; shall I speak?

(act I)

Or a curt, repetitive style can be laughable, like Novel's in *The Plain Dealer*: 'Servant, servant, my lord' (IV.2); or Monsieur de Paris's in *The Gentleman Dancing-Master*: '*Serviteur, serviteur*' (act I). The extenuated style, or the salute everlasting, is practised by Sir Courtly Nice with Leonora and her Aunt:

SIR COURTLY. Madam, your most – (*goes to salute Leonora, Aunt steps first*).
AUNT. Sir Courtly, your very humble servant.
SIR COURTLY. Oh! your ladyship's very humble servant – (*salutes Aunt*).
AUNT. Your most humble servant.
SIR COURTLY. Now, madam, your most humble servant (*to Leonora*).
AUNT. An incomparable fine gentleman!

More of these absurd salutations follow, until one wonders who is more exhausted, the actor or the spectator.

Comedy was free to develop the elegant, deadly style of Sir Charles and Lady Graveairs, who '*salute coldly, and trifle some time before they speak*' in *The Careless Husband*, III.1. Or the plain uncouth style of Squire Sullen in *The Beaux' Stratagem*, II.1, who enters with a drunken roar and no courtesies to his lady at all: 'My head aches consumedly!' are his first words. She offers him tea or coffee, but his cry is simply, 'Bring me a dram!' So social forms create the character, but the dramatist presents the actor. In *The Constant Couple* Farquhar achieved a triumph with his charming libertine Sir Harry Wildair, 'an airy gentleman affecting humorous gaiety and freedom in his behaviour'. In the first scene of the play he is given a daring entrance, which sets up all the expectations and leaves them agreeably unsatisfied: Sir Harry '*crosses the stage singing*' with footmen following him. Colonel Standard asks, 'Heyday! who the devil have we here?', and Vizard explains, 'The joy of the playhouse, and life of the Park; Sir Harry Wildair newly come from Paris'; and Sir Harry is not permitted to make a proper entrance until thirteen lines later.

If one door made for a colourful entrance, the use of prompt side and opposite prompt doors simultaneously was doubly effective. '*Several*', '*severally*' and '*at several doors*' were the terms used. In this way Courtall and Freeman meet in the New Spring Garden in *She Would If She Could*, IV.2:

Enter Courtall and Freeman severally.
COURTALL. Freeman!
FREEMAN. Courtall, what the devil's the matter with thee?
COURTALL. What unlucky devil has brought thee hither?

There is just a trace of a *commedia dell'arte* entrance here, and their dialogue continues with such echoing lines until they discover that each has received an identical letter of assignation.

An actor leaving the stage was often also required to perform the courtesies of departure, and on occasion an exit could be elaborately spectacular. When Worthy and Berinthia leave the stage *'several ways'* in *The Relapse*, V.2, their departure on opposite sides would fill the available space. A repeated exit would be equally spacious, as in *The Gentleman Dancing-Master*, act V, when Monsieur de Paris comically returns to speak another line and then repeat his French salute. Wycherley expands this effect into a trick to distract Pinchwife in *The Country Wife*, act III, when his three tormentors, Horner, Harcourt and Dorilant, perform a splendid triple adieu, only to return immediately after Pinchwife has left, in order to catch the ladies without him. There are as many as twelve salutations in this instance, with bows from the three men, and responses from Pinchwife and three women:

HORNER. Goodnight, dear little gentleman; madam, goodnight; farewell, Pinchwife. Did not I tell you, I would raise his jealous gall? (*apart to Harcourt and Dorilant.*)
Exeunt Horner, Harcourt and Dorilant.
PINCHWIFE. So they are gone at last; stay, let me see if the coach be at this door. (*Exit.*)
Horner, Harcourt, Dorilant return.
HORNER. What, not gone yet? Will you be sure to do as I desired you, sweet sir?
MRS PINCHWIFE. Sweet sir, but what will you give me then?
HORNER. Anything. Come away into the next walk.
Exit Horner, haling away Mrs Pinchwife.

The ladies are taken by storm, and a scene of prolonged comic tension is capped by a repeated exit that is dazzling to look at.

In its rejection of all courtesies an 'exit running', familiar in plays from *Marriage à la Mode* to *The Provoked Wife*, would come with all the shock of the unnatural, and in a lady was a direct indication of her loss of decorum. The character of Dryden's Melantha is founded upon the high spirits which propel her into entrances and exits on the run, all the more amusing because neither the female costume nor her head could readily tolerate such treatment without a sweet disorder in the dress. In *The Provoked Wife*, III.1, Lady Brute and Bellinda *'run off'* when Lord Brute

42 La femme coquette et le vieux jaloux

'*rises in a fury, throws his pipe at 'em and drives 'em out*', and Lady Fancyfull, like Melantha, affects a running entrance and a running exit in the same scene. Then, when Lady Brute is hotly pursued by her lover Constant, she must take to her heels again:

CONSTANT (*catching her hand*). By heaven, you shall not stir, till you give me hopes that I shall see you again at some more convenient time and place.

LADY BRUTE. I give you just hopes enough (*breaking from him*) to get loose from you. And that's all I can afford you at this time. (*Exit running.*)

The lady has yet more running to do in IV.4 when she finds herself in Spring Garden. Herrick would have approved a winning wave in the tempestuous petticoat and ribbands flowing confusedly, which add charm to her loss of composure on these occasions.

Entrance and exit were emphatic because the actor was happily dominant on the small non-representational stage. There was no scenic feature other than a door or 'the hangings' behind which an actor could conceal himself, and the term '*at a distance*' is found when it is necessary to separate a character on the same stage. The convention implies that the actor is motionless in an upstage corner of the apron, lurking in the unlit shadows. *The Man of Mode*, III.3, is set in the Mall, where Dorimant is briefly seen '*standing at a distance*' while he watches the attractive ways of Harriet. It is a sure sign that he has been smitten, and so it proves when he speaks, '*coming up gently and bowing to her*'. In *The Gentleman Dancing-Master*, II.1, Hippolita and Gerrard converse '*at a distance*' when the girl sees her father and aunt already there before them. And in *The Plain Dealer*, IV.2, Manly enters '*treading softly, and staying behind at some distance*' in order to judge Olivia's faithlessness when she tries to flirt with Fidelia.

In a comedy of sex, one of deceiving, and being deceived by, husband, wife, mistress or lover, hiding on stage, usually to eavesdrop, was commonplace. It even occurs when there is no apparent need for it other than to add zest to a marital mismatch, like that of the Pinchwifes in *The Country Wife*. In act II the introduction of Margery is made through her highly ambiguous cross-questioning of Alithea, to which Wycherley adds the heightening presence of Pinchwife '*peeping behind at the door*', one of the proscenium doors at Drury Lane. The effect is to accentuate her every innocent impropriety – 'Jealous? What's that?' and 'I was aweary of the play, but I liked hugeously the actors' and 'He says he won't let me go abroad for fear of catching the pox.' The husband exhibits his apoplectic expression at each of Margery's admissions, until he can contain himself no longer and bursts in only to be met with her disarming response, 'O my dear, dear bud, welcome home! Why dost thou look so fropish? Who has nangered thee?'

In D'Urfey's *A Fond Husband*, IV.4, the cuckolding of Peregrine Bubble, 'a credulous fond cuckold', reaches a crisis when Rashley and Ranger invade his wife's room and are forced to seek cover, one *'under a table'* and the other *'in a closet'*, a proscenium door at Dorset Garden. In *The Double Dealer*, IV.6, Congreve (who incidentally prefers the word 'absconding' to 'hiding') arranges it that Mellefont *'goes behind the hangings'* to spy on Lady Touchwood with Maskwell her lover. When the moment is ripe, Mellefont *'leaps out'* and catches them in a cliché scene of an interrupted *amour*:

MELLEFONT. And may all treachery be thus discovered!
LADY TOUCHWOOD (*shrieks*). Ah!

In Farquhar's *The Inconstant*, II.2, Duretete hides in order to observe Bisarre, and here it is interesting that while the dialogue invites him to go 'behind this screen', the stage direction indicates that he actually *'stands peeping behind the curtain'*.

In the corpus of Restoration comedies, Farquhar gets the most comedy from the absconding device from its use in *The Beaux' Stratagem*. He had planted the idea of Archer's ruse by hinting in the fourth act at the convenience of a back door and a closet as a way to come at Mrs Sullen; this act also ends with Mrs Sullen's expression of desire to see Archer as a lover in provocative circumstances – 'If I met him dressed as he should be [i.e., like a gentleman and not a servant], and I undressed as I should be . . .' Thus when in v.2 the scene changes to her bedchamber and the lady is undressed, the audience is all expectancy. Mrs Sullen first discloses her amorous feelings to Dorinda:

MRS SULLEN. Heigh-ho!
DORINDA. That's a desiring sigh, sister.
MRS SULLEN. This is a languishing hour, sister.
DORINDA. And might prove a critical minute if the pretty fellow were here.

Farquhar leaves nothing to chance, and in the ordinary way the line 'if the pretty fellow were here' would be cue enough for Archer to swing out from his closet door on the other side of the stage and give the audience an impertinent little bow which would not be seen by Mrs Sullen and Dorinda.

It has been played like this, but in the text Farquhar plans Archer's entrance to be something wonderfully histrionic. Mrs Sullen is speaking in soliloquy:

Thoughts free! Are they so? Why, then, suppose him here, dressed like a youthful, gay, and burning bridegroom, (*here Archer steals out of the closet*) with tongue enchanting, eyes bewitching, knees imploring. – (*turns a little o' one side, and sees*

Archer in the posture she describes) – Ah! – (*shrieks, and runs to the other side of the stage*). Have my thoughts raised a spirit? – What are you, sir, a man or a devil?

To which he answers, with a wink at the audience, 'A man, a man, madam.' This line is the culmination of the cheeky pantomime he has been performing only for the audience as she is lost in her thoughts. He enacts the reality of an arm outstretched, a flashing smile and a fall upon one knee, but like a caricature of a stage lover; his performance makes her thoughts both comic and larger than life – which perhaps they are. This appearance of Archer to Mrs Sullen at the climax of the play, expected and unexpected, is one of the classic entrances of English comedy.

PATTERNS FOR LOVERS

It was an age rich in reading for those who wished to improve their talents as lovers, and intimate handbooks were published in both Paris and London. In 1676 an anonymous work attracted sales with the irresistible title of *The Art of Making Love: or, Rules for the Conduct of Ladies and Gallants in Their Amours*. It offered the men such advice as:

– A gallant ought always to testify an ardour and impatience: and though he be ice, he ought always to say, he burns. (p. 104)
– Let him show a little melancholy in his eyes and visage; not too much, for fear to alarm her too much. (p. 116)

And the women:

– To render our desires more vigorous and curious . . . she counterfeits always a modest air, and a sober and prudent deportment, and seems to be ignorant in the use of her charms. (p. 50)
– A lady then must not be too disdainful, nor hold a lover too long in her chains: for patience may forsake the inamorato. (pp. 129–30)

She too has work to do with her eyes:

– Observe them first, if her looks be sweet and languishing: for nothing so much manifests the state of a heart, as the languishing of the eyes. (p. 150)

In Behn's *The Dutch Lover*, III.1, Colonel Alonzo and Euphemia '*make signs of love with their eyes*', presumably of the melancholy and languishing variety; but the plays themselves do not always contribute this kind of information. Sometimes an *amour* will prosper merely by the act of 'gazing', as in *The Rover*, I.2, where the 'jilting wench' Lucetta and the 'English country gentleman' Blunt gaze on each other more than enough to convey their intentions:

LUCETTA. This is a stranger, I know by his gazing; if he be brisk he'll venture to follow me, and then, if I understand my trade, he's mine. He's English, too, and they say that's a sort of good-natured loving people, and have generally so kind an opinion of themselves that a woman with any wit may flatter 'em into any sort of fool she pleases.

She often passes by Blunt and gazes on him; he struts and cocks, and walks and gazes on her.

BLUNT. 'Tis so, she is taken; I have beauties which my false glass at home did not discover.

Yet none of this is much different from what goes on in Vanbrugh's *The Confederacy*, V.2, where '*Araminta, Corinna, Gripe and Moneytrap are discovered at a tea-table, very gay and laughing*', with Moneytrap soon '*leering at Corinna*' (Gripe's 16-year-old daughter) and Gripe '*ogling Araminta*' (Moneytrap's wife).

Eyes that gaze, leer and ogle can be hard to distinguish on the stage from those that languish, although the former imply whoring rather than flirting. The difficulty arises because hunting for prey in comedy and farce is a cold-blooded activity. Henshaw points out that in this period 'the unrestrained expression of spontaneous emotion had no place in serious or casual courtship' (p. 395), and there was a severe limitation on passion even in the days before the Commonwealth, as Woodby and Caroline in *Epsom Wells* suggest:

WOODBY. Take your choice. I can make love from the stiff, formal way of the year 42, to the gay, brisk way of this present day and hour.
CAROLINE. . . . I suppose it is for diversion, pray let me see how it is.
WOODBY. Look you, thus (*sings, dances and combs his peruke*).
CAROLINE. Is this it? Why, you don't mind me.
WOODBY. I mind myself though, and make you fall in love with me, after a careless way, by the bye.

(II.1)

An alternative was to play the 'whining' lover who echoed the passionate speeches of heroic tragedy, but since a lover never risked losing his self-control and looking foolish, the result might well take on the air of parody and burlesque, like Bruce's speech and manner in *The Virtuoso*, act III:

BRUCE. Ah, madam, change your cruel intentions, or I shall become the most desolate lover, that ever yet, with arms across, sighed to a murmuring grove or to a purling stream complained. Savage! I'll wander up and down the woods, and carve my passion on the bark of trees and vent my grief to winds that as they fly shall sigh and pity me.
CLARINDA. How now! What foolish fustian's this? You talk like an heroic poet.
BRUCE. Since the common downright way of speaking sense would not please you, I had a mind to try what the romantic way of whining love could do.

Clarinda is rightly suspicious of that 'artifice' which, according to *The Art of Making Love*, was a standard trap for the unpractised lover (p. 121). That good guide invited the use of the sigh instead:

When he has the opportunity to entertain his mistress alone, let him not be too profuse of his talk, but let a few sighs supply the vacancies of discourse. But let him use much caution, lest he be suspected of artifice: let him seem fearful to let 'em escape, and sometimes break 'em in their passage, showing it is some pain and violence to him to suppress them.

Moderation in affairs of the heart, as in other things in the age of reason, was the wisest course.

In *The Rules of Civility* Antoine de Courtin advises against behaviour of another kind, the too enthusiastic approach which might toss or tumble a lady:

In the company of ladies, 'tis too juvenile and light to play with them, to toss or tumble them, to kiss them by surprise, to force away their hoods, their fans, or their muffs. (p. 43)

This more aggressive treatment of the fair sex, however, was fit for the stage in its broader comic moments, as when in *Secret Love*, act V Melissa is 'tousled and mousled' and Celadon *'plucks off her ruff'*. No special rehearsal was needed for tousling and mousling, but this activity, as we shall see, was reversed for particular occasions.

A certain decorum attached to the rules for kissing a lady. Kissing the hand in salutation, one's own or the lady's, was acceptable, but kissing on the face or lips was in real life a personal and private matter, and in public such a greeting even to a close acquaintance of the fair sex was at best a mere gesture of brushing the cheek or the hood without touching her face with the lips. Only in the country might a lady present her face to be kissed. On the stage, therefore, kisses on the lips or cheeks always served a comic purpose – more mousling than tousling here – and each of the following instances occurs in a farcical context.

When sailor Ben makes his first brash appearance in *Love for Love*, act III, Sir Sampson his doting father exchanges three kisses with him, and Ben unused to the ways of polite society, takes his cue from this: 'I'd rather kiss these gentlewomen', he declares, and proceeds to kiss all the women in turn, regardless of rank or favour – Angelica, a lady; Mrs Frail, a harlot; and Miss Prue, the hoyden. It is a kissing game in the same league with the scene in which Prue lands her great smacks on Tattle. Again: Hypolita, who finds herself in breeches for the best part of *She Would and She Would Not*, simply overdoes the kissing of Rosara in act III – 'and there, and there, and there' – to impress the girl's father; but these kisses are a good joke, for in any case the audience knows Hypolita to be a girl herself.

Or else kissing is left to coxcombs who *ipso facto* cannot possibly mean anything by it, like Selfish in *A True Widow*, who demonstrates to Young Maggot how to make love, unwisely choosing as his target the foolish Gartrude:

SELFISH. Ladies, your most humble servant. Now you shall see, Maggot. Dear, pretty creature, let me kiss that nosegay. Well, 'tis a thousand times sweeter in that pretty bosom than in its own bed, though at the sun rising, when the morning dew is in drops upon it. Sweet madam, let me kiss that hand that gathered it.

GARTRUDE. Oh, fine, what rare words are these! He uses me like a princess.

(act II)

He was, of course, doing nothing of the kind – he was tousling and mousling her.

In *Sir Martin Mar-all* Lord Dartmouth attempts to make love to 'pretty Mistress Christian', and because he opens his attack with a smooth tongue and impressive rhetoric, the girl is at first misled about his intentions. When he sits nearer his 'pretty innocence', and then goes to work on her hand and glove, touching, pulling and hugging, he has come close enough to tousling and mousling to reveal his intentions as dishonourable:

LORD DARTMOUTH. What does this white enemy so near me? (*touching her hand gloved.*) Sure 'tis your champion, and you arm it thus to bid defiance to me.

CHRISTIAN. Nay fie my lord, in faith you are to blame (*pulling her hand away*).

LORD DARTMOUTH. But I am for fair wars, an enemy must first be searched for privy armour, e're we do engage (*pulls at her glove*).

CHRISTIAN. What does your lordship mean?

LORD DARTMOUTH. I fear you bear some spells and charms about you, and, madam, that's against the laws of arms.

CHRISTIAN. My aunt charged me not to pull off my glove for fear of sunburning my hand.

LORD DARTMOUTH. She did well to keep it from your eyes, but I will thus preserve it (*hugging her bare hand*).

CHRISTIAN. Why do you crush it so? nay now you hurt me, nay – if you squeeze it ne'er so hard – there's nothing to come out on't – fie – is this loving one? – what makes you take your breath so short?

(II.I)

This is sophisticated, even poetical, tousling, but Lord Dartmouth is not in the best of condition.

The merry encounters of Miss Prue first with Tattle and then with Ben in acts II and III of *Love for Love* are whole-heartedly physical. Prue is the 'silly, awkward country girl', the obvious target for the 'half-witted' Tattle, and they are well matched for a lesson in love in one of the funniest episodes in Restoration comedy. He has persuaded her that a girl's actions should always contradict her words:

TATTLE. Well, my pretty creature, will you make me happy by giving me a kiss?
MISS PRUE. No, indeed; I'm angry with you (*runs and kisses him*).
TATTLE. Hold, hold, that's pretty well, but you should not have given it me, but have suffered me to take it.
MISS PRUE. Well, we'll do it again.
TATTLE. With all my heart. Now, then, my little angel (*kisses her*).
MISS PRUE. Pish.
TATTLE. That's right. Again, my charmer (*kisses again*).
MISS PRUE. O fie, nay, now I can't abide you.
TATTLE. Admirable! That was as well as if you had been born and bred in Covent Garden all the days of your life. And won't you show me, pretty miss, where your bedchamber is?
MISS PRUE. No, indeed, won't I, but I'll run there and hide myself from you behind the curtains.

Prue turns away each time before eagerly accepting the kiss, but the magic of the comedy lies in the repetition, each refusal more vehement, each embrace more enthusiastic than the last, so that the concept of the contradiction between a lady's words and her intentions, taken so literally, grows wildly ridiculous. Nevertheless, Congreve slyly leaves the outcome in Prue's bedchamber to the imagination.

In act III Ben the sailor might have received the same treatment of conflicting signals from Miss Prue, but what is astonishing and yet not astonishing is that her instinct now tells her not to play by Tattle's rules a second time. The love scene is still physical, but it has become a game of musical chairs:

BEN. Come, mistress, will you please to sit down? For an you stand astern a that'n, we shall never grapple together. Come, I'll haul a chair; there, an you please to sit, I'll sit by you.
MISS PRUE. You need not sit so near one; if you have anything to say, I can hear you farther off; I an't deaf.
BEN. Why, that's true, as you say, nor I an't dumb; I can be heard as far as another. I'll have off to please you (*sits farther off*).

Not only will she not allow Ben to get within arm's length of her, but she resolutely chooses to tell him only the truth; she goes on to call him 'you ugly thing', 'you great sea-calf' and 'you stinking tar-barrel'; and she means exactly what she says.

Vanbrugh's management of a love scene for Worthy and Amanda in *The Relapse*, v.4, cannot help but include all the elements of amorous burlesque in its simple structure, and may serve as a compendium of sexual interaction on the comic stage. Worthy first takes and kisses her hand '*eagerly*':

AMANDA. O heavens! Let me go.
WORTHY. Never, whilst I have strength to hold you here (*forcing her to sit down on a couch*).
    My life, my soul, my goddess, oh, forgive me!
AMANDA. Oh, whither am I going? Help, heaven, or I am lost . . . .
WORTHY. Nay, never strive.
AMANDA.   I will, and conquer, too.
    My forces rally bravely to my aid, (*breaking from him*)
    And thus I gain the day.
WORTHY. Then mine as bravely double their attack, (*seizing her again*)
    And thus I wrest it from you. Nay, struggle not,
    For all's in vain: or death or victory,
    I am determined.
AMANDA.   And so am I. (*rushing from him*)
    Now keep your distance, or we part forever.
WORTHY (*offering again*). For heaven's sake –
AMANDA (*going*).   Nay then, farewell.
WORTHY (*kneeling and holding her by her clothes*).
    Oh, stay and see the magic force of love:
    Behold this raging lion at your feet,
    Struck dead with fear, and tame as charms can make him.

Adultery is the ostensible issue here, and Vanbrugh's choice of blank verse to round off a play that is nearly all prose is partly intended to make the issue a serious one. But he is back to tousling and mousling, and the happier effect in this encounter is to set it on the edge of comedy, suppressing any moralistic thrust. The pattern of movement – Worthy's giving chase, the business of taking and kissing an unwilling hand, Amanda's obligatory protests and attempts to break away, the repetitions of this sequence, leaving Worthy at the last upon his knees and pulling at her skirts – is impossible to play in earnest. Moreover, the episode is difficult for the audience to distinguish from the joyful comedy of the parallel scene between Loveless and Berinthia in IV.3 as well as from the attack on Berinthia by the luckless Worthy in v.2. It is not surprising that Farquhar was well able to parody the pattern for his seduction scene between Mrs Sullen and Archer in *The Beaux' Stratagem* ten years later. For the present, Vanbrugh's pattern for making love – seizing and running and seizing again, and doing this two or three times in succes-

sion – provides a satisfying formula and a compromise between the serious
and the slapstick.

This section began by drawing on a book of etiquette, and concludes
with indications from the comic poem published in two books in 1700 by
Charles Hopkins with the title, *The Art of Love: Dedicated to the Ladies.*
Although the poem's intention is gently satirical, it may for that reason
give a fair impression of the amorous activity seen on the comic stage.

Book I offers advice to the man. First he must attract the lady's
attention:

> – With folded arms, pass melancholy by,
> Now softly murmur, and now softly sigh.
> Pass back again, and yet again return,
> And seem the loss of some dear friend to mourn,
> Your languid arms cross your sad breast be thrown,
> You press her heart, whilst thus you press your own.
> Enter at last, made by your passion fleet,
> And throw yourself beneath the charmer's feet. (p. 79)

> – If in the theatre the maid be found,
> Thence may your passion with success be crowned.
> Whist now she mourns the fancy's hero's fate,
> Whilst in her eyes her ready sorrows wait,
> Attend their fall; claim all her tears your due,
> The fancy's lover never loved like you. (p. 95)

Book II offers a word to the girl in the case:

> – Let indifference act the part of pride,
> The easy grant the price of bliss destroys,
> Man ever least esteems what he enjoys. (p. 15)

> – Receive the visit, which the youth shall make,
> Be seen, as if by chance, or by mistake.
> Play with your fan, call for you coach, your chair,
> Be just a-going out to take the air.
> Pretend some visits which must needs be made,
> And his you can't receive till these be paid.
> Business pretend, or sickness, seem in haste,
> Have many things to do, some minutes past,
> 'Tis late you know, you may do none at last.
> You think the weather dull, 'tis cold, if not,
> But you would change it spite of heaven, – 'tis hot . . . .
> Enquire the news; he answers you, 'tis love.
> Say anything impertinence can move.
> Hear all he says, sit in some distant place,
> Whilst his eyes fasten on your charming face. (p. 17)

> – Now pleased, now vexed, now merry and then sad,
> Now very thoughtful, and now very mad,
> A thousand humours move a thousand ways,
> For most of all, variety must please. (p. 29)

The darling object will be at last engaged:

> – Her eyes entreat you, and her melting tongue,
> But all their soft entreaties last not long.
> To her own breasts her wandering hands repair,
> Which when you feel, receive, and press them there;
> Forbear, she cries, but hopes you won't forbear. (I, p. 57)

> – Play with thy fingers twining in her hair,
> Cupid, in every curl has spread his snare. (p. 61)

> – Link her fair fingers in the gentlest bands
> And print soft kisses on her snowy hands. (p. 63)

This is tousling and mousling in the polite manner.

DORIMANT SUFFERS THE RITES OF LOVE

The love game may be played like a protracted stage duel, a series of clashes running through the play. At the end of all in *The Man of Mode*, Dorimant and Harriet outwit everyone – by deciding upon marriage. Harriet is the county heiress from the wilderness of Hampshire, and should have been fair game. Of all the women in the play, however, she is the one who follows her own inclinations and is most herself in so doing. It is she who prefers to toss loose her curls rather than let her maid set them in order – in Etherege's eyes a very straightforward way of demonstrating her independence from the world of the Loveits and Bellindas. Harriet is also the rebel who dares to reject her mother's choice of husband for her ('Shall I be paid down by a covetous parent for a purchase?'), and takes a singular pleasure, with the complicity of Young Bellair himself and the all-seeing audience, in mimicking the performance expected of a young gentlewoman caught in the throes of love, in order to deceive 'their gravities', the father and mother. It is Harriet's unconventional and self-confident attitude which defeats Dorimant in spite of all his experience with the opposite sex. She refuses to play by the rules, and in having as much wit as he, forces him to bow to her every whim.

Harriet and Dorimant have three encounters in their extended duel. They meet first in the Mall, a setting for sometimes more than 'the formal bows, the affected smiles, the silly by-words and amorous tweers in passing'. In this meandering scene (III.3) Etherege's easy action for his characters is one of coming and going, the doors in constant use as the persons of the play pass in review in their walking-clothes, Harriet, Young Bellair, Dorimant, Lady Woodvil, Sir Fopling, Medley, Loveit, Bellinda, all crossing and returning to trace new designs on the stage. The pace of the scene is gentle, that of the leisurely gentlefolk who display themselves.

Dorimant catches a first glimpse of Harriet with Young Bellair, and sets off in casual pursuit; when they return, he watches her, waiting his chance 'at a distance'. Does she observe him out of the corner of her eye as she leaves? At all events, the moment comes when she ventures an opinion that he certainly hears about gambling her reputation, an apt metaphor for her life-style.

HARRIET. Because some who want temper have been undone by gaming, must others who have it wholly deny themselves the pleasure of play?
DORIMANT (*coming up gently and bowing to her*). Trust me, it were unreasonably, madam.
HARRIET (*starts and looks grave*). Lord, who's this?

Young Bellair now plays the role of go-between to Dorimant and Harriet. Dorimant bows low and remarks on her new seriousness; at the same time, she confesses in a quick aside to the audience 'a change within'. Each, then, is interested in the other, but nothing of true feelings yet appear; rather, they test each other with a little jocular sparring. Dorimant impertinently takes up her notion of gambling by asking, 'Pray, what may be your stint [limit]?' She returns his impudence with a cut that forces him to change his tactics: 'You are for masks and private meetings, where women engage for all they are worth, I hear.' Their conversation continues at this light level of repartee, but Dorimant, accustomed to easy victory, scores no points this time. Meanwhile that curt aside has granted the audience the pleasure of perceiving something of the secret Harriet beyond the badinage, so that what she says even seems slightly defensive: 'Mr Bellair! Let us walk, 'tis time to leave him. Men grow dull when they begin to be particular.' She had already turned away.

Dorimant can find only praise for this elusive girl when she has gone, and echoing her own sentiments about him, confesses to the audience that her 'pleasing image . . . wanders in my soul'. So the scene of circling in the Mall gives way to another (IV.1), this time at Lady Townley's ball, although for all practical purposes her house could just as easily have been the Park. Harriet's mother Lady Woodvill believes that Dorimant 'delights in nothing but in rapes and riots', so at Harriet's suggestion (she is always ready with some device of impersonation), he pretends to be a

Mr Courtage in order to see the daughter again. To the older lady he grows exceedingly polite and agreeably flattering, even to the point of dancing with her; but at least he has ensured a second meeting with Harriet.

A 'grave bow' and a 'demure curtsy' start their mocking new beginning, and Harriet is quick to scold Dorimant with 'Affectation is catching, I find.' He accuses her of 'scorn and coldness' in her look, but the audience notes that he is not now able to return her banter in kind. So she is afforded the opportunity of putting him neatly in his place: she is not the one to make fashionable *doux yeux*, will not be 'tied to the rules of charming'. She wins the second argument, a polite exchange of brilliant barbs, and in another aside to the audience he admits not only that he has been smitten, but also that she has 'an ascendant' over him. Fatally, he goes on to give love its name, whereupon she is free to tease him mercilessly. She does it in her characteristic way, by the mockery of pantomime, acting out the demure maiden to excess.

Yet Etherege is resolutely anti-romantic. In the middle of his first real passion, the new Dorimant is careful not to forget his old assignation with Bellinda. The crowded scene of the ball passes to the privacy of Dorimant's rooms, just in time to reveal Bellinda on the point of parting with *her* new lover as the two emerge from the bedchamber. The playwright indicates the cynicism of the moment by offering a glimpse of Handy '*tying up linen*', a dry perspective on the commonplace event this cold affair has been.

However, with Loveit shaken off and Bellinda disabused, the way is finally clear for the third and final meeting of Dorimant and Harriet, and in v.2 Dorimant again attempts a casual entrance with Waller on his lips. But he is not the same man. This time, Harriet, already on stage, coolly completes his couplet:

DORIMANT. 'Music so softens and disarms the mind –'
HARRIET. 'That not one arrow does resistance find.'

Their final scene together is all of aside and innuendo passed through the audience, the tone of voice and the use of the eyes saying everything. Their mutual confession of love is wholly circumscribed by quips: when, for example, Dorimant hears the news of Emilia's impending marriage to Young Bellair, he offers to 'rescue' her with, 'In this sad condition, madam, I can do no less than offer you my service.' But Harriet is quick to interject, 'The obligation is not great: you are the common sanctuary for all young women who run from their relations.' Dorimant turns this thrust with, 'I have always my arms open to receive the distressed', and dares to go on to make a quite unconvincing promise to her: he will forsake all other women. To this she responds with feigned alarm: 'Hold! Though I wish you devout, I would not have you turn fanatic.'

Nevertheless, taking half a leaf from *Le Misanthrope*, she tests his devotion by inviting him to return with her to Hampshire. But Dorimant is no Alceste, nor Harriet a Célimène, and without turning a hair he lightly agrees to any proposal. Again she as good as calls him liar: 'I know all beyond High Park's a desert to you, and that no gallantry can draw you farther', and she will make no promises to him:

DORIMANT. May I not hope?
HARRIET. That depends on you and not on me; and 'tis to no purpose to forbid it.

Dorimant is struggling to regain his former dominance, struggling for his freedom, and if the audience has any doubts about his two faces, it is given two quick reminders. He tries to appease Loveit by telling her he only wants Harriet's money, and he proposes another *rendez-vous* with Bellinda. But neither Loveit nor Bellinda now respond to his blandishments, and the new Dorimant is fast in Harriet's trap.

When Lady Woodvill is persuaded actually to invite him to her house in the country, Harriet is able to tease him for the last time: 'There you'll find my mother, an old lame aunt, and myself, sir, perched up on chairs at a distance in a large parlour, sitting moping like three or four melancholy birds in a spacious volary. Does not this stagger your resolution?' But Dorimant concedes his position without a blush – indeed, he mouths a pretty speech about 'the pangs of love' in the whining vein. 'This is more dismal than the country', is Harriet's tart answer, playing her part to the end. She certainly has the last word, and appears to win the last bout of the wooing game. She keeps him dangling, never for a moment suggesting that she prefers Hampshire to London. Thus all the evasions a man is capable of in his actions, and all a woman's sweet deviousness in her words, inform their final encounter, and while the audience may believe that Harriet loves Dorimant and that he loves her, it will never know for sure. Laughter on the stage, laughter in the house, and no room at all for sentiment.

LOVERS PLAY LOVERS

When Etherege used Harriet and Young Bellair as his puppets in *The Man of Mode*, III.1, for a scene of mock flirtation so that they might deceive their parents, the pantomime became better than the occasion warranted. One generation observes another, and the audience observes both, seeing through old and young eyes simultaneously. Human sexual behaviour is shown twice removed, once for the characters in their situation and once for the players to demonstrate their talents as real or pretended lovers. The greater the distancing device, the more incisive is the comedy. But justly famous as Etherege's scene is, it is not atypical.

Mimicry, especially of lovers and love-making, is a recurring feature in Restoration comedy that is unique to the period and the genre. It is of the theatre theatrical and is not drawn naturally from real life. It is highly self-conscious and partakes fully of the spirit of comic writing, and this alone may account for its inclusion in play after play, often for its own sake. It exhibits the niceties of behaviour, especially sexual behaviour, and it is commonplace in the work of those writers who have a strong visual sense of performance. For the actors it involves an extra dimension of posturing and projection, and demands a conscious sense of style verging on caricature and burlesque. It has no conventional history, although it embodies elements of Elizabethan dumbshow and the pantomime of the French and Italian comedy. It justifies the role of the drama in this period as an indulgent charade.

The Gentleman Dancing-Master affords an early instance in acts II and III. The lovers Hippolita and Gerrard, who till then have been only in the preliminaries of flirtation, must quickly deceive her father Don Diego and her aunt Mrs Caution. The girl, who has been making all the running, proposes that they pretend to be dancing the courante, a stately affair in which the man must take the lead.

HIPPOLITA. What shall I do? stay – nay, pray stir not from me, but lead me about, as if you lead me a courante. (*Leads her about.*)
DON DIEGO. Is this your government, sister, and this your innocent charge, that has not seen the face of a man this twelve-month? *En horâ mala.*
CAUTION. O sure it is not a man, it cannot be a man! (*Puts on her spectacles.*)
DON DIEGO. It cannot be a man! if he be not a man he's a devil; he has her lovingly by the hand too, *valga me el cielo.*
HIPPOLITA. Do not seem to mind them, but dance on, or lead me about still.

The dance itself is a form of flirtation, and the pair are in actuality flirting behind its conventions. In his edition of Wycherley's *Complete Plays* Gerald Weales makes the additional point that the gravity of the courante should heighten the effect of arrogance on the part of the lovers (p. 159), so infuriating Hippolita's father the more. Meanwhile the audience is delighted to watch the love affair impudently in masquerade.

In *Marriage à la Mode*, III.1, husband and wife Rhodophil and Doralice pretend to play the happily married couple in order to deceive the 'court lady' Artemis, a pair of public eyes, and act out the appropriate behaviour to excess.

DORALICE. O dear Rhodophil!
RHODOPHIL. O sweet Doralice! (*embracing each other.*)

ARTEMIS (*aside*). Nay, I am resolved, I'll never interrupt lovers: I'll leave 'em as happy as I found 'em. (*Steals away.*)

At once the play-acting ceases:

RHODOPHIL (*looking up*). What, is she gone?
DORALICE. Yes; and without taking leave.
RHODOPHIL (*parting from her*). Then there's enough for this time.
DORALICE. Yes sure, the scene's done, I take it.
They walk contrary ways on the stage; he, with his hands in his pocket, whistling; she, singing a dull melancholy tune.
RHODOPHIL. Pox o' your dull tune; a man can't think for you.
DORALICE. Pox o' your damned whistling.

The audience is invited to witness the proprieties of marriage, all the while knowing it is only a game to be played for society to see. The comic anticlimax that comes when husband and wife break apart implies that all public displays are false, all marriages a deception.

When later in the same act Melantha rehearses what she will say to her lover Rhodophil in the grotto (see p. 128 above), she has no difficulty in playing both the parts herself, and, what is more, it is the one way of making sure her lover says exactly what she wants him to say. In pantomime she has it all her own way, even to the impropriety of being tousled and mousled, even tossed down. And the audience has the additional pleasure of being privy to this lady's private thoughts. Her solo is rivalled only by Lady Wishfort's determined practice of her 'figures' when she prepares for the arrival of 'Sir Rowland' (see p. 131 above), where the actress is able to demonstrate point by point what her audience would never otherwise see. Meanwhile Wishfort is like an actress herself, making all her gestures to very thin air in the exaggerated way of rehearsal; at the same time the audience sees a wonderful travesty of the pretty motions that would be quite suitable to a young girl if they were not played by an elderly frump.

The playwrights play many variations on the game of amorous pantomime. Coxcomb and coquette are well matched in Brisk and Lady Froth in *The Double Dealer*, IV.6, and by pantomime Congreve superimposes hypocrisy on vanity and pretence on hypocrisy in a sequence which could only belong to the Restoration. Alone, Brisk finds 'an opportunity to practise', so that the audience is secure in the sense that everything that follows will be hollow. To attract the lady, Brisk further pronounces, 'I'll seem not to see her', and so performs a little scene as a heroic lover:

BRISK (*sings, walking about*). 'I'm sick with love,' ha, ha, ha, 'prithee come cure me. I'm sick with, etc.' O ye pow'rs! O my Lady Froth, my Lady Froth!

> My Lady Froth! Heigho! Break heart; Gods I thank you. (*Stands musing with his arms a-cross.*)
>
> LADY FROTH. O heav'ns, Mr Brisk! What's the matter?
>
> BRISK. My Lady Froth! Your ladyship's most humble servant; – The matter, madam? Nothing, madam, nothing at all i'gad. I was fallen into the most agreeable amusement in the whole province of contemplation: that's all – (I'll seem to conceal my passion, and that will look like respect.) (*Aside.*)
>
> LADY FROTH. Bless me, why did you call out upon me so loud? –
>
> BRISK. O Lord, I madam! I beseech your ladyship – when?
>
> LADY FROTH. Just now as I come in, bless me, why don't you know it?
>
> BRISK. Not I, let me perish – But did I! Strange! I confess your ladyship was in my thoughts; and I was in a sort of dream.

Brisk's play-acting is a projection of his empty head, but it succeeds in flattering Lady Froth. Moreover, he is the sort who laughs at his own jokes, so that what he calls his 'new airy invention' is an affectation that turns every sentiment into laughter, and the lady catches the trick herself:

> BRISK. The deuce take me, I can't help laughing at myself, ha, ha, ha; yet by heav'ns I have a violent passion for your ladyship, seriously.
>
> LADY FROTH. Seriously? Ha, ha, ha . . . . Hang me if I have not a violent passion for Mr Brisk, ha, ha, ha.

Their amorous display is licensed behind its screen of laughter, and they embrace – laughing still. Or is it giggling?

The expected happens when the solemn Lord Froth catches them. Without hesitation his wife springs into a country dance – and into another pretence.

> BRISK. Zoons, madam, there's my lord. (*Softly to her.*)
>
> LADY FROTH. Take no notice – but observe me – Now cast off, and meet me at the lower end of the room, and then join hands again; I could teach my lord this dance purely, but I vow, Mr Brisk, I can't tell how to come so near any other man. Oh here's my lord, now you shall see me do it with him.
>
> *They pretend to practise part of a country dance.*

Lady Froth also has the presence of mind to propose doing 'our close dance' with her wooden husband, who retreats immediately from the idea, as she knew he would.

> LADY FROTH. Shall you and I do our close dance, to show Mr Brisk?
>
> LORD FROTH. No, my dear, do it with him.
>
> LADY FROTH. I'll do it with him, my lord, when you are out of the way.

The bawdy *double entendre*, for what it is worth, has to emerge.

Congreve makes his comic stage a pulpit for teaching lessons of honest falseness and frank deception, and in this it echoes the real world, the self-deceiving world where the game of sex is played relentlessly from day to day. The extraordinary recurrence in so many plays of mimic love, play-acting lovers within the given dramatic frame of the play, suggests that the playwrights are taking for granted the complicity of their audience in the games that lovers play. Through such masquerades the comic stage prompts a universal laughter, at the lover, at his mistress, at love itself, and even at the stage that is presenting them.

LOVE IN THE BURLESQUE VEIN

The playworld of Restoration comedy is a mocking one, and the tender passion is rarely allowed to grow maudlin. The devices of play-acting that distance the spectator and undercut any earnest representation of sexual behaviour in the plays repeatedly deny the spirit of representational realism that some have supposed to have overtaken the stage at this time. What the audience sees on the stage is far from being a mirror-image of itself, and the comic stage does not reflect social manners in the way that awkward metaphor suggests. In comedy, the mirror held up to nature is still, and will ever be, a distorting one.

Unfortunately, the language of dramatic criticism is deficient in terms which denote the Restoration mode of distorting ridicule. The scenes cited in the last section are all in various shades of caricature and burlesque, with the emphasis firmly on the actor and his exaggerated style of performance. If the reality would have been sordid or sentimental, the burlesque treatment has the effect of raising the level of comedy to that of the fantastic, and the spectator is no longer distracted by his need to believe in what he sees.

By the time of Congreve and Farquhar many scenes of comic love have fallen into the burlesque mode, and this section will sample three such scenes in order to review their special use of the stage. The first is between Lady Wishfort and the impostor 'Sir Rowland' in *The Way of the World*, an example of fairly 'pure' burlesque, and the second and third are between Archer and Mrs Sullen in *The Beaux' Stratagem* and are examples of 'applied' burlesque. Each masquerade has a rather different impact on the viewer.

Wishfort's love scene in act IV is the simplest. From the beginning it is seen as a mockery because the situation and its setting, together with both of the principals, are all a sham in one way or another, and the audience knows it. Foible has reported that the footmen are wearing their best liveries, and the coachman and the postilion have been 'pulvilled . . . that they may not stink of the stables'. Waitwell has been dressed, probably overdressed, for the role of a brisk lover, and he now speaks with a voice a servant might suppose to belong to a beau. The lady has been preparing her appearance for some time, dressing to kill and practising her 'figures', so that she too is a pretender, about to put on the performance of her life. All the elements of putting on a show are present, and it will be one in which both parties, each playing by different rules, are frauds.

The scene begins as a duet of high-flown words, which come noticeably hard upon the inarticulate lines of a drunken Sir Wilfull, and it is the lady who opens the contest with a curtsy that shivers the image of grace and drops as deep as she dare:

Dear Sir Rowland, I am confounded with confusion at the retrospection of my own rudeness!

The weight of her grandiloquence carries her down to the floor, and the flurry of alliteration that continues with 'I have more pardons to ask than the Pope distributes' matches her immediate loss of decorum before she minces across the stage to greet her visitor. Waitwell at the door looks on, as the audience does, astonished at the sheer abundance of her welcome, if not of her profusely dressed person, before he collects himself to outdo her with a salutation of his own:

My impatience, madam, is the effect of my transport; and till I have the possession of your adorable person, I am tantalized on a rack, and do but hang, madam, on the tenter of expectation.

Playing the imaginary gallant for all he is worth, he too alliterates recklessly ('the possession of your adorable person') and goes one better with a speech made up of highly ironic metaphors – tantalized on a rack and hanging on a tenter embody the rhythm with which his hat sweeps the air and the ground, and at the same time imply the torture that would follow such possession. The ambiguity in the lines is strong enough to warrant a wink to the house.

Yet Wishfort hears only what she wants to hear, and none of the innuendo. She hears the 'brisk man' she hoped for in act III, one who will not fail to 'be importunate and push'. She is overjoyed that Waitwell has allowed her to preserve her 'forms' and save her 'decorums', for now she is able to adopt her simpering posture, that of the demure and reluctant maiden. When the subject of Mirabell's perfidy comes up, Congreve's words grip her ungainly person in a dance that is positively poetical in its sways and loops and the curlicues described by her podgy fingers.

The words are overcharged, the performance extravagantly over-wrought. The preposterous courtship is pure fantasy in both context and content. In Farquhar's scenes hyperbolic speech and gesture are also present, but add an intriguing edge of doubt that the joke is not so much on the characters as on the spectators. As in all good burlesque, the actors themselves have fun at the expense of the whole operation of drama, stage and audience.

Farquhar has sometimes been placed in the camp of the sentimental comedians who arose in the eighteenth century following the strictures of Jeremy Collier and the Lord Chamberlain's warning in 1704 to avoid 'profane and indecent expressions'. Such a judgment misses the subversive power of parodistic speech and burlesque action in the performance, which at once permits and inhibits any easy sympathy and emotion on and off the stage. Such 'applied' burlesque destroys the romantic theatre. Farquhar's verbal exuberance is part of a balancing act which encourages him to write the kind of acid love-scene that looks back to the best of the seventeenth century.

One such scene occurs in Lady Bountiful's gallery when Archer examines Mrs Sullen's portrait. He opens his amorous attack by claiming that he cannot accept it as a sufficient likeness:

Your eyes, indeed, are featured there; but where's the sparkling moisture, shining fluid, in which they swim? The picture, indeed, has your dimples; but where's the swarm of killing Cupids that should ambush there? The lips too are figured out; but where's the carnation dew, the pouting ripeness, that tempts the taste in the original? (IV.I)

Each item of her features in the portrait is found inadequate, and the portrait is berated by an excess of poetical language with which no paint could compete. The words climb to such heights of florid alliteration, from 'sparkling moisture' and 'killing Cupids' to 'pouting ripeness', that they border on the absurd. But Mrs Sullen is well aware that he is flattering her, and loves it ('What a charm is flattery!' she had said a little before). What is more, he is aware that she is aware. Again, the audience also has a strong sense of the truth: in much the same terms Archer enjoyed a flirtation with Cherry, the innkeeper's daughter, in act I, and on that occasion the girl's lips were 'honeycombs' and her face 'a swarm of Cupids'. The audience would get the point immediately if Archer looked at Mrs Sullen's face as he speaks, rather than at the portrait he seems to be speaking of, attempting a kiss on 'tempt the taste of the original'.

The scene of the attempted seduction of Mrs Sullen that follows in V.2 consciously inflates the language to new proportions. She asks how Archer gained access to her chamber, and he replies,

I flew in at the window, madam; your cousin Cupid lent me his wings, and your sister Venus opened the casement.

When she is coy ('What will become of me?'), he resorts to the language of flowers:

The teeming jolly spring smiles in her blooming face, and when she was conceived, her mother smelt to roses, looked on lilies –

    Lilies unfold their white, their fragrant charms,
    When the sun thus darts into their arms.

Farquhar has developed a rhyming couplet of appalling doggerel, and the parody is capped and complete.

It is helpful that the words here have at last taken on a kinetic quality, and their high-flown style smoothly translates into flamboyant movement and gesture. With the line, 'When the warm sun thus darts into their arms', Archer *'runs to her'*, matching the word to the action. Mrs Sullen accordingly *'shrieks'*, but when he *'kneels'*, she returns to words, and her wit, for her defence:

(*Aside*) Now, now, I'm ruined, if he kneels! – Rise, thou prostrate engineer; not all thy undermining skill shall reach my heart. – Rise, and know, I am a woman without my sex; I can love to all the tenderness of wishes, sighs, and tears – but go no further. – Still, to convince you that I'm more than woman, I can speak my frailty, confess my weakness even for you – but –

Each hesitation is constructed as a retreat and an ambiguity ('I am a woman . . . without my sex'; 'wishes, sighs, and tears . . . but go no further'; 'confess my weakness . . . but –'), so that each time he is impelled towards her only to be stopped short. So the episode moves into a final phase, and the stage at last comes alive with Archer giving chase around her bed as her resistance grows weaker:

Then you'll promise –	Anything . . . another time.
When shall I come?	Tomorrow – when you will.
Your lips must seal the promise.	Pshaw!

The comedy explodes into mock ballet, it leaves this earth, but all in the happy, irresponsible vein of burlesque. When he finally kisses her, it is 'Raptures and paradise!'

A STAGE FOR DANCING

The players of Restoration comedy pirouette on the edge of a musical drama in their speech and movement. Performance characteristically aimed at a carefully studied, but apparently effortless, grace of movement and gesture, with feet and legs lightly turned out and arms and hands naturally curving – postures to which every dancing-master subscribed. The dancing style of performance is present in the rhythmical way the lines are phrased and balanced, whereby an inflection of voice or a shift of tone calls for a complementary display of the body. The plays carry a strong suggestion that the mode of comic performance was a balletic one.

When Restoration comedy was revived after its long neglect in the nineteenth century, its impact as theatre was unexpectedly pleasing. *The Double Dealer* had not been played since Kemble adapted it for Drury Lane in 1802, and when the Stage Society produced it at the Queen's Theatre in 1916, A.B. Walkley of *The Times* declared that 'those who still pretend that [Congreve's] comedies are better to read than to act are incorrigible bookworms'. In the same review he drew attention to the unfamiliar and elusive ingredient of the Restoration acting style. When Congreve's plays are presented 'in his stage's fashion', Walkley argued, they are 'far richer in delight than the printed page, rich as that is'. He went on:

How Lady Plyant's coquetries gain from the bodily presence, voice, and air of Miss Helen Haye! How much more droll is the solemn drollery of Lord Froth's utterance when filled out with the absurd person of Mr Ben Field! How much more credible the frenzies and meltings of Lady Touchstone [played by Constance Robertson] when you have a handsome woman before your eyes, cursing or kissing in real earnest!

The simple truth is that you soon give up troubling about the plot and enjoy, as Congreve enjoyed, the moment for moment's sake. A Congreve plot is of no more importance than the plot of a modern revue; it is merely there as a string to hang the 'turns' together. (16 May 1916)

When Walkley saw *The Beaux' Stratagem* done by the Stage Society at the Arts Theatre, he pursued the same point. This time, however, he was more particular about what he perceived as the Society's balletic and fantastic manner of performance:

The personages pirouetted and posed almost as often as they sat or walked . . . . The fantasy of the costumes and the whole mode of performance gives the dialogue a touch of unreality which attenuates and converts almost to elegance much that in a literal, matter-of-fact presentation, could not but seem crude and even brutal . . . . How can you take the rigid view [of the moral critic] when nobody seems for a moment in earnest, and nearly everybody is dancing? (5 February 1919)

When everybody is *dancing*? Perhaps some shadowy region of Lamb's fairyland was here present after all, especially if the mystery of its success lay in the style of Restoration performance.

The period saw the beginning in England of a new age of dance, and dancing served the stage on many occasions. Among the middle and upper classes, court dances grew increasingly popular into the eighteenth century, following the example of France, where Louis XIV himself had a dancing-lesson every day and laid down the rules for those dances he approved. In late seventeenth-century London there were dozens of dancing-masters, and a well-to-do family might well have one in its employ. Handbooks on how to dance were common, and often ran into several editions. Individual dances grew in elaboration, and a difficult dance, like the formal minuet, might take three months to learn. Charles II's favourites were the slow and stately sarabande and the lighter, less formal, gigue (jig), a jolly concoction of gay, hopping steps and little runs. Nell Gwyn's ability and willingness to dance a jig when called upon was doubtless very much in her favour.

In the plays themselves (although not, apparently, in those of Shadwell, Otway, Crowne, D'Urfey and Vanbrugh) it was a practice to bring a comedy to an end by contriving an occasion for music and dance, usually a jig, which was appropriate to comedy. *The Country Wife* was notorious for ending with '*a dance of cuckolds*' (at a guess, a masquerade of men in horns with suitable music), but in mid-course *A True Widow* introduced '*an entry of clowns*' to dance in act IV, and *The Old Bachelor* a '*dance of antics*' in fancy dress in act III. In *The Rehearsal*, III.1, Bayes announces, 'My fancy, in this play, is to end every act with a dance', which tells us plainly enough that it was not uncommon to carry the convention too far.

The court masque declined under Charles II, but a masque of a more occasional sort remained a common feature in many of the comedies throughout the period – yet another opportunity for an exhibition of dancing. In Etherege's first play, *The Comical Revenge*, Sir Frederick Frollick introduces in act III '*six or eight link-boys, dancing and singing*' soon followed by '*a masque of the link-boys, who are dancing-masters disguised as for the frolic*' (a direction which seems to be addressed to the manager rather than the players), and together with fiddlers they perform under the window of the widow Rich. Dryden's *An Evening's Love* sports a masked dance of ladies in III.1, and '*after the dance the cavaliers take the ladies and court them*', Wildblood offering a handsome compliment to Jacinta:

While you have been singing, lady, I have been praying: I mean, that your face and wit may not prove equal to your dancing; for, if they be, there's a heart gone astray to my knowledge.

At the centre of *Marriage à la Mode*, IV.2, Dryden has a court masquerade with two dances performed under torchlight, and, just for the pleasure of it, Behn has a masque of shepherds in *The Dutch Lover*, III.4, which she describes thus: '*Enter swains playing on pipes, after them four shepherds with garlands and flowers, and four nymphs dancing an amorous dance to that music, wherein the shepherds make love to the nymphs, and put garlands on*

43 Fille de qualité aprenant à danser

their heads.' Almost an entr'acte, this episode is apt for the spirit of a play in which several pairs of lovers are manoeuvring for mistresses.

At the end of the seventeenth century the device of the masque was still common in the comedies, although as hard to justify dramatically as a contribution to the narrative line of the play. Cibber's *Love's Last Shift* was a bawdy piece which concluded with the facile reformation of its rakish hero Loveless, as well as with a masque that seems ironically impertinent: '*The scene draws and discovers Love seated on a throne, attended with a chorus.*' The chorus represented Fame, Reason, Honour and Marriage, and Love was played by little Miss Cross, aged twelve. Vanbrugh's sequel to this play, *The Relapse*, also skirts the edge of propriety by pairing the married Loveless with Berinthia and the married Amanda with Worthy, and it too ends cheekily with a masque of Cupid and Hymen, plus chorus.

Thus dancing in one form or another appeared in different ways on the Restoration stage, the dances ranging from those designed for a formal masque to the spirited jigs introduced to bring down the curtain. When these were set among scenes which to modern eyes seem not far removed from those of a dance to begin with, one in which elegance of performance was *de rigueur* for all but the most grotesque characters, it is possible to imagine a style of comedy, choreographic in character, unlike anything before or after on the English stage. The notation for that choreography lay to some degree in the lines and the conventions of speaking them, and to this topic we now turn.

6. A mode of speech

The dramatic virtue of Restoration prose dialogue lies in its fitness for its task. There was no escape for the principals of the comic stage – its norm of speech was excessively polite, and to be 'rustic or clownish' in style of speech, as in behaviour, was a regular target for the rule books. For the coterie of the court it was always a case of art over nature, and Cibber's praise of William Mountfort's manner of speaking confirms that in the mouth of a good actor, the apparently formal lines could spring to life:

> He had a particular talent, in giving life to *bons mots* and *repartees*: the wit of the poet seemed always to come from him extempore, and sharpened into more wit, from his brilliant manner of delivering it; he had himself a good share of it, or what is equal to it, so lively a pleasantness of humour, that when either of these fell into his hands upon the stage, he wantoned with them, to the highest delight of his auditors. (*Apology*, p. 75)

Mountfort's best achievement was as Sir Courtly Nice, in whom 'the insipid, soft civility, the elegant, and formal mien, the drawling delicacy of voice, the stately flatness of his address, and the empty eminence of his attitudes' all came together, words and voice, in performance.

Those who wrote about the twentieth-century revivals were universally impressed by the quality of speech demanded by this kind of comedy. Congreve's lines especially struck the ear as musical, and from listening to the intonations of Helen Haye as Lady Plyant in the Stage Society's production of *The Double Dealer* in 1916, Desmond MacCarthy decided that the interest in Congreve centred in what MacCarthy called 'exhibitions in the art of expression' (*New Statesman*, 20 May). When George Moore saw *Love for Love* done by the Phoenix Society at Hammersmith in 1921, he could think only of music: 'My recollection of *Love for Love* is of voices separating and uniting, an almost musical memory, shall we say, of a very lovely glee' (*Observer*, 27 March). Norman Marshall saw J.B. Fagan's production of the same play at the Oxford Playhouse in 1923, and vividly remembered John Gielgud as Valentine when he answered Angelica's question in act IV, 'Do you know me? . . . Who am I?':

> You're a woman, one to whom heaven gave beauty when it grafted roses on a briar. You are the reflection of heaven in a pond, and he that leaps at you is sunk. You are all white, a sheet of lovely spotless paper, when you first are born, but you are to be

scrawled and blotted by every goose's quill. I know you, for I loved a woman and loved her so long that I found out a strange thing: I found out what a woman was good for.

When Gielgud played the part again in 1943 at the Haymarket, Marshall thought he had improved upon the timing and phrasing of the lines, but not upon his 'gaiety and impudence and high spirits, fresh, ringing tones, a youthful, self-confident dash and swagger' (*The Other Theatre*, p. 22).

A.B. Walkley heard Edith Evans as Millamant and Margaret Yarde as Wishfort in *The Way of the World* in Playfair's production at Hammersmith in 1924, and reported that 'the prose tripped lightly from Millamant, gushed like lava from a volcano from Lady Wishfort' (*The Times*, 8 February). Of the same production James Agate wrote about Evans, 'She has only two scenes, but what scenes they are of unending subtlety and finesse!'; he especially remarked the delicacy of her 'Get up when you will' to Mirabell in the proviso scene of act IV, the delicious mockery of her 'dwindle into a wife', and the way she breathed out her 'adieu – my morning thoughts' as if it were 'early Ronsard or du Bellay'. Of Evans's reading of Millamant's lines 'I nauseate walking' and 'natural, easy Suckling', Agate wrote,

There is a pout of the lips, a jutting forward of the chin to greet the conceit, and a smile of happy deliverance when it is uttered, which defy the chronicler. This face, at such moments, is like a city in illumination, and when it is withdrawn leaves a glow behind. (*Sunday Times*, 10 February)

In her personal memoir Edith Evans's secretary Jean Batters recorded that the actress likened the 'rhythm' of Restoration comedy to 'a ball game with the players tossing the ball back and forth; if a player muffed his catch or dropped it, the rhythm was shattered' (*Edith Evans*, p. 57). However, such rhythm could not have been achieved without a musical text to begin with.

The norm of literary prose in the late seventeenth century possessed a grace and balance of phrasing and emphasis which made it difficult for an actor to slur his lines, even when he played a fop who affected a drawl. The prose is patterned for a crisp precision of diction, although it is deceptively conversational. When Manly in *The Plain Dealer* peremptorily sees off my Lord Plausible from his lodgings in act I, Manly does not say, 'Do not come here and disturb me because you have nothing to do!', but this: 'A pox why should anyone, because he has nothing to do, go and disturb another man's business?' 'A pox' is an explosion of anger, the break after 'anyone' levels that insulting word directly at my lord, and 'nothing to do' sets up 'another man's business' for a second explosion by hitting the end of the line in the equivalent place. It is possible for the actor to say this line forcefully without seeming to lose his temper: the words themselves are arranged to strike home. This controlled elegance of speech varied a good deal as between Wycherley's greater vigour and Congreve's delicacy, Etherege's flow and Farquhar's rounded, billowing lines; but nowhere was the dialogue that of plain speech. Rather, it retained the theatricality necessary for projection on the comic stage, and when the balance of a line or the pointing of a word was accompanied by a gesture of the hand or a movement of the head, well-timed speech became gently physical on the tongue, pleasing the eye as well as it did the ear.

In his letter to John Dennis, 'Concerning Humour in Comedy' (1695), Congreve himself recognized that style could create an exaggerated stage image:

The distance of the stage requires the figure represented to be something larger than life; and sure a picture may have features larger in proportion, and yet be very like the original.

The quality of theatricality in a line provides some clue to the high style of its delivery and the stylization of behaviour that goes with it: it measures the 'aesthetic distance' between stage and audience proposed by each play. It tells us a great deal that Cibber criticized even Mrs Barry's 'defective ear' and 'unskilful dissonance in her manner of pronouncing' at the start of her career, as well as Mrs Oldfield's early weakness as an actress because of the lack of 'propriety' in her diction (*Apology*, p. 91). Eloquent speech and precise diction were of greatest moment on a non-scenic stage where the focus was all on the players and their personal relationships as characters.

When the plays were first revived, the modern actor nurtured on Edwardian drawing-room comedy had difficulty catching the Restoration style of speech. Walkley in *The Times* considered it 'a hard task for our players to master a prose so compact, so precisely expressive that a displacement of a word throws all out of gear' (17 April 1917). If the visual drama was linked to ballet, the aural was likened to an opera full of *bravura* passages. Agate discussed *The Old Bachelor* in exactly these terms in 1924: 'The thing is an opera, with soli, duets, trios, and occasional concert pieces (*Sunday Times*, 8 June), and he particularly remarked the 'duets' of Heartwell and Silvia spoken by William J. Rea and Stella Arbenina, and of the Fondlewifes by Hay Petrie and Isabel Jeans.

The wooing scene of Heartwell and Silvia in act III pleased everyone because it seemed so 'natural', and MacCarthy, reviewing the production for the *New Statesman* on 7 June, dared to attempt an analysis. He cited Heartwell's speech,

Take the symptoms - and ask all the tyrants of thy sex, if their fools are not known by this parti-coloured livery – I am melancholic, when thou art absent; look like an ass, when thou art present; wake for thee, when I should sleep; and even dream of thee, when I am awake; sigh much, drink little, eat less, court solitude, am grown very entertaining to myself, and (as I am informed) very troublesome to everybody else. If this be not love, it is madness, and then it is pardonable.

He then advised his reader to say it aloud:

How easily it runs from the tongue, how naturally it rises to the cynic's climax! The structure of the sentences impels your voice to the right inflexions. And what variety of emotion there is in the whole brief dialogue: the touching simplicity of Silvia's 'I dare not speak till I believe you, and indeed I'm afraid to believe you yet', followed by the arch triumphant irony of that line, 'Must you lie then, if you say you love me?' (Imagine the look, the intonation, with which a real comedy actress, secure in her beauty, would turn upon her elderly adorer.) Her look and her words draw from him a protestation, instantly followed by anger at his weakness. Imagine the painful sincerity which a fine actor would put into those words, 'and tell it for a truth, a *naked* truth' – then, as the old dandy suddenly recollects himself, the husky humiliation in his voice when he adds, 'which I'm ashamed to discover'.

Reviewing *The Country Wife* for the *New Statesman* in 1924, Ralph Wright found the quality of the speaking pleasing because the actors

seemed to be accustomed to being witty, to produce their brightest sayings with a self-confident delight, as in the fact that they knew there were a hundred more left in their brains to pop out as fast as opportunity should offer.   (23 February)

Restoration speech called for a special ear, and the worst that could happen was when, failing this, the modern actor assumed a voice that was consciously quaint – the ladies taking 'tay' while the gentlemen indulged in a little 'rallery'. By contrast, Edith Evans was completely at ease with the wit in her lines, so that T.C. Worsley could write of her, 'When Dame Edith speaks, the words cascade and check, pause and then gush, straight from a living person who has always, you are convinced, spoken just so' (Batters, p. 57).

The necessity of playing out on the apron, together with the intimacy of the Restoration playhouse, not only encouraged a musical range of tone and variety of voice, but it also permitted the speaking to be quicker than was customary in the modern theatre. A well-paced play implies that it is able to slow down as the mood of the drama demands, but this is only possible if the speaking is quick to begin with. In the twenties there was a consensus that a fast pace was necessary if the spirit of these comedies was to be captured. 'Speed is essential to the successful acting of artificial comedy', wrote MacCarthy in the *New Statesman* of 26 December 1925, 'but speed is only attainable by practising often and long together.' In this the Phoenix Society, for all its infrequent productions, achieved a small miracle.

Two reasons were advanced for the necessity of speed, one more questionable than the other. Reporting on *Marriage à la Mode* at Hammersmith in 1920, *The Observer* for 15 February judged that pace solved the problem of obscenity: 'No offence is possible when extravagant comedy is racing along as it raced in last week's performance' – presumably giving the audience no time to reflect. However, any good farce, which in content has often bordered on the bawdy and the amoral, has always worked best when denied any lingering emotionality. A better reason had been offered in *The Observer* following the Stage Society's *Love for Love* at the Aldwych in 1917:

To go slow, to fumble for a second, is to do worse than injure the prose; it is to imply that this or that character was not absolutely and securely himself; and that would be contrary to Congreve's practice in comedy; it is to interrupt the moving dance, which must never threaten for an instant to run down.   (22 April)

The style of the moving dance, and of light operetta, found in Restoration comedy came together in its pace and rhythm of speech, and speaking the lines confidently was as important as wearing the costumes comfortably.

DIFFERENCES IN SPEECH BETWEEN CHARACTERS

'Humour is the ridiculous extravagance of conversation, wherein one man differs from all others,' wrote Dryden in his *Essay of Dramatic Poesy* (p. 72), and within the narrow compass of Restoration stage speech individual differences were marked by a variety of eccentricities of idiom and style. Verbal oddities extended from the reiteration of oaths to all manner of spoken affectations – so many that it would be tiresome to catalogue them all.

Then as now, an oath was good for a laugh. In his *Amusements Serious and Comical* Tom Brown noted the growth of 'new-invented curses' like 'Stap my vitals!', 'Damn my diaphragm!', 'Slit my windpipe!' and 'Sink me ten thousand fathom deep!' (p. 36). Any of these could 'rig up a new beau'. Congreve himself was not past sprinkling the speech of Sir Joseph Wittol in *The Old Bachelor* with a shower of 'agads', until he bursts out with 'Gads daggers, belts, blades and scabbards!', although Sir Joseph was usually in the habit of emphasizing by threes: 'With all my heart, blood and guts, sir', 'He is indeed back, breast and headpiece as it were to me', 'Fighting is meat, drink and cloth to him', and so on. Nor does he hesitate to mix a malapropriate metaphor or two, as in this verbose address to Sharper:

Sir, I most submissively implore your pardon for my transgression of ingratitude and omission; having my entire dependence, sir, upon the superfluity of your goodness, which, like an innundation will, I hope, tótally immerge the recollection of my error, and leave me floating in your sight, upon the full-blown bladders of repentance – by the help of which, I shall once more hope to swim into your favour. (II.I)

Sir Joseph is matched only by Sir Sampson Legend of *Love for Love*, whose favourite oath is 'Body o' me!', and who confronts his son with a unique brand of vituperation: ''Oons whose son are you? How were you engendered, muckworm?' (act II).

Punctuating a character's lines with verbal figures and flourishes was the easy way, and Farquhar, who has more eccentrics to a play than most Restoration playwrights, swiftly creates his 'airy gentleman' Sir Harry Wildair in *The Constant Couple* by a breathless idiom of his own when Angelica asks him if he loves her:

Love you! does fire ascend? do hypocrites dissemble? usurers love gold, or great men flattery? Doubt these, then question that I love .... View your own charms, madam, then judge my passion. Your beauty ravishes my eye, your voice my ear, and your touch has thrilled my melting soul. (III.3)

By the time he wrote *The Recruiting Officer*, Farquhar had freely invented a form of country 'dialect' for Bullock and Rose, his rural lad and lass; when Plume asks how many chickens Rose has to sell, the auditor hears,

ROSE. A dozen, sir, and they are richly worth a crown.
BULLOCK. Come Ruose, Ruose, I sold fifty strack o' barley today in half this time, but you will higgle and higgle. (III.I)

And Farquhar concocted a suitably blunt style for his recruiting sergeant:

Yes, sir, I understand my business, I will say it. You must know, sir, I was born a gypsy and bred among that crew till I was ten year old. There I learned canting and lying. I was bought from my mother, Cleopatra, by a certain nobleman for three pistoles, who, liking my beauty, made me his page. There I learned impudence and pimping. I was turned off for wearing my lord's linen and drinking my lady's brandy, and then turned bailiff's follower. There I learned bullying and swearing. I at last got into the army, and there I learned whoring and drinking. So that if your worship pleases to cast up the whole sum, *viz.*, canting, lying, impudence, pimping, bullying, swearing, whoring, drinking, and a halberd, you will find the sum total will amount to a recruiting sergeant. (III.I)

Kite's brusque logic and rough honesty is well caught in the tidy shape of his lines and their unmistakable tone of authority. One can recognize the authentic man as he speaks.

This air of authenticity is also true of the speech of Farquhar's egotistical officer Brazen in the same play. These are his reasons for thinking himself eligible as Melinda's suitor:

I have had very considerable offers, madam. I might have married a German princess worth fifty thousand crowns a year, but her stove disgusted me. The daughter of Turkish bashaw fell in love with me too, when I was a prisoner among the infidels. She offered to rob her father of his treasure and make her escape with me, but I don't know how, my time was not come. Hanging and marriage, you know, go by destiny. Fate has reserved me for a Shropshire lady with twenty thousand pound. Do you know any such person, madam? (III.1)

It is possible to hear the nonchalance in his voice when he throws away 'but her stove disgusted me', and again in 'my time was not come', just as it is possible to see the impertinent smirk on his face when he bows to Melinda on 'Fate has reserved me for a Shropshire lady with twenty thousand pound.' Yet at the same time Brazen echoes the vanity of the fop whose speech was by now well established as affected, effeminate and high-pitched, with a fastidious manner of selecting and pointing his words.

The speech of languid ladies is also distinctive, often by excessive and weighty diction and the repetition of phrase. In this style Congreve is again notable for his skill in building artifice on artifice. Lady Plyant in *The Double Dealer* attacks Mellefont as much with her exuberant tongue as with her fluttering fan and eyes:

I know love is powerful, and nobody can help his passion: 'tis not your fault; nor I swear it is not mine, – how can I help it, if I have charms? And how can you help it, if you are made a captive? (II.1)

This lady, 'easy to any pretender', also attacks Careless, who remarks that she is 'abounding in all excellence, particularly that of phrase'. She certainly wins any skirmish of words:

You are so obliging, sir . . . So well bred . . . So well dressed, so *bonne mine* [sic], so eloquent, so unaffected, so easy, so free, so particular, so agreeable . . . So gay, so graceful, so good teeth, so fine shape, so fine limbs, so fine linen, and I don't doubt but you have a very good skin, sir. (act III)

Stunned by this avalanche, Careless confesses that he is 'quite out of countenance', although her husband wryly adds that she is 'quite out of breath'.

The Constant Couple presents another of these dangerous coquettes in Lady Lurewell, 'a lady of a jilting temper proceeding from a resentment of her wrongs from men'. She is also a word-monger:

My virgin and unwary innocence was wronged by faithless men, but now glance eyes, plot brain, dissemble face, lie tongue, and be a second Eve to tempt, seduce and damn the treacherous kind . . . . Observe this [she says to her maid] that though a woman swear, forswear, lie, dissemble, backbite, be proud, vain, malicious, anything, if she secures the main chance, she's still virtuous; that's a maxim. (I.2)

Cibber's Lady Easy in *The Careless Husband* is presented in the same spirit:

Was ever woman's spirit, by an injurious husband, broke like mine? A vile, licentious man! Must he bring home his follies too? Wrong me with my very servant? (I.1)

From Lady Easy the audience suffers another verbal bludgeoning.

She speaks here in 'soliloquy', but this convention was different in intention from the solo address to the audience in Elizabethan drama, which was designed variously to introduce a theme, create an atmosphere, push the narrative along, touch in a character. The Restoration solo performance offered the actor a quick, direct opportunity to present an eccentric character with all the fireworks of speech. Maskwell's villainous announcement of his cunning and hypocrisy in *The Double Dealer* is such a piece:

Cynthia, let thy beauty gild my crimes; and whatsoever I commit of treachery or deceit, shall be imputed to me as a merit – treachery, what treachery? Love cancels all the bonds of friendship, and sets men right upon their first foundations. (II.2)

In *The Relapse* Miss Hoyden the country miss makes everything transparent on her first appearance sola:

Sure never nobody was used as I am. I know well enough what other girls do, for all they think to make a fool of me. It's well I have a husband a-coming, or i'cod, I'd marry the baker, I would so. (III.4)

In soliloquy, as we saw (p. 86), Sir John Brute opens *The Provoked Wife* with an explosion of wrath. The attitude of each character – treacherous, silly, sour – is immediately 'given' in the style of speech, unrestricted by the presence of another player, as in a bravura passage in music. The age took enormous pleasure in words, often for their own sake, and sometimes the lines were offered as a particular showpiece. When this happened, it is debatable whether the words are not manipulating the actor, rather than the actor the words. However, when a second actor enters, the dialogue obeys particular rules.

REPARTEE

The element of bravura in Restoration stage speech extended readily to more than one speaker, and the kind of patterned speech in which the playwrights took pride was 'reparty', the word coming into the language at this time. Repartee was a sequence of quick, clever retorts in the form of dialogue, and it could be used to decorate and enliven almost any exchange of lines in comedy. In his 1668 Preface to *An Evening's Love*, Dryden remarked, 'As for reparty in particular, as it is the very soul of conversation, so it is the greatest grace of comedy.' In his *Essay of Dramatic Poesy*, he expanded this: 'As for comedy, repartee is one of its chiefest graces; the greatest pleasure of the audience is a chase of wit, kept up on both sides, and swiftly managed' (p. 59). Such 'brisk writing', as Shadwell called it in *Epsom Wells*, had a parry and thrust which demands of the actor a special skill in stressing and timing the lines.

At its simplest and most effective, an exchange of repartee bounces the ball back and forth, repeating the thought and often repeating the same words with more emphasis. In *She Would If She Could*, IV.2, Courtall and Freeman have separate assignations with Ariana and Gatty in New Spring Garden, and each wants rid of the other:

COURTALL. Why, I have an appointment made me, man, without my seeking, by a woman for whom I would have mortgaged my whole estate to have her abroad but to break a cheese cake.
FREEMAN. And I have an appointment made me without my seeking, too, by such a she, that I will break the whole ten commandments, rather than disappoint her of her breaking one.
COURTALL. Come, you do but jest. Freeman: a forsaken mistress could not be more malicious than thou art. Prithee be gone.
FREEMAN. Prithee do thou be gone.
COURTALL. 'Sdeath! The sight of thee will scare my woman forever.
FREEMAN. 'Sdeath! The sight of thee will make my woman believe me the falsest villain breathing.
COURTALL. We shall stand fooling till we are both undone.

Effective speaking requires Freeman as the 'echo' to hit his pronouns harder ('I . . . me . . . my'; 'thou . . . thee'), and then stress the words capping those uttered in the previous line by Courtall ('break a cheese cake' is capped by 'break the whole ten commandments', and so on). Courtall's last line stops the run before the next sequence begins.

Dialogue grows hot and brisk when a pattern of stichomythic statement and retort shortens the lines. The brothers Worthy are introduced in *Love's Last Shift*, act I, as the younger is trying to persuade his older brother to seek an amour with Hillaria in order that he may advance his own with Narcissa:

ELDER WORTHY. Hillaria has some good qualities, but not enough to make a wife of.
YOUNGER WORTHY. She has beauty!
ELDER WORTHY. Granted.

YOUNGER WORTHY. And money.
ELDER WORTHY. Too much: enough to supply her vanity.
YOUNGER WORTHY. She has sense.
ELDER WORTHY. Not enough to believe I am no fool.
YOUNGER WORTHY. She has wit.
ELDER WORTHY. Not enough to deceive me.
YOUNGER WORTHY. Why then you are happy, if she can't deceive you.

Where nearly every assertion offers a contradiction, this effect, too, counts as repartee, while the staccato phraseology maintains the high level of spirited comedy.

In repartee, the women may be as witty as the men. Farquhar's lively ladies Dorinda and Mrs Sullen in *The Beaux' Stratagem*, IV.1, strike the buoyant note in this classic exchange when they talk about developments with their lovers Aimwell and Archer:

DORINDA. But my lover was upon his knees to me.
MRS SULLEN. And mine was upon his tiptoes to me.
DORINDA. Mine vowed to die for me.
MRS SULLEN. Mine swore to die with me.
DORINDA. Mine spoke the softest moving things.
MRS SULLEN. Mine had his moving things too.
DORINDA. Mine kissed my hand ten thousand times.
MRS SULLEN. Mine has all that pleasure to come.

The repetition of 'Mine . . . Mine', each clipping the last word of the previous line, suggests a pace so fast that the bawdiness in Mrs Sullen's responses is tantalizingly obscured.

In *The Plain Dealer*, act II, Wycherley actually orders a kind of repartee by threes, so inventing an early 'school for scandal' scene. Here Novel is the railer, Olivia matches him in censoriousness and my Lord Plausible is a 'commending' third party. Plausible has dared to raise the subject of the 'glorious superfine beauties of the town':

NOVEL. Very fine ladies! there's first –
OLIVIA. Her honour, as fat as an hostess.
PLAUSIBLE. She is something plump indeed, a goodly, comely, graceful person.
NOVEL. Then there's my Lady Frances, what d'ye call'er? as ugly –
OLIVIA. As a citizen's lawfully begotten daughter.
PLAUSIBLE. She has wit in abundance; and the handsomest heel, elbow, and tip of an ear, you ever saw.
NOVEL. Heel, and elbow! hah, ha! And there's my Lady Betty, you know –
OLIVIA. As sluttish, and slatternly, as an Irishwoman bred in France.
PLAUSIBLE. Ah, all she has hangs with a loose air indeed, and becoming negligence.

The ball is passed twice, in a way which Sheridan perfected a hundred years later. Voices rise in gleeful expectation of a witty corroboration with further evidence, the trio of bodies swaying to the rhythm of the lines. Only Plausible lets the ball drop, so that each time Novel is forced to pick it up again if the sequence is to continue.

The most unusual moment of Restoration repartee is heard, and seen, when Courtall, Freeman, Ariana and Gatty finally arrive on stage together in *She Would If She Could*, II.1. The physical chase ends, but it continues verbally in a fourfold repartee, anticipating by two years Molière's patterned dialogue for Lucile, Nicole, Cléonte and Covielle in his comedy-ballet *Le Bourgeois gentilhomme*, act III:

COURTALL. By your leave, ladies –
GATTY. I perceive you can make bold enough without it.
FREEMAN. Your servant, ladies –
ARIANA. Or any other ladies' that will give themselves the trouble to entertain you.
FREEMAN. 'Slife, their tongues are as nimble as their heels.
COURTALL. Can you have so little good nature to dash a couple of bashful young men out of countenance, who came out of pure love to tender you their service?
GATTY. 'Twere pity to baulk 'em, sister.
ARIANA. Indeed methinks they look as if they never had been slipped before.

The symmetry of the echo matches that of the visual pattern of the two pairs on the stage, but not so formally as to exclude an aside from Freeman (''Slife, their tongues are as nimble as their heels') and an impudent exchange between the girls, back to back as if trapped by the men.

A moment later, it is the men who get their chance to speak to one another, in an 'internal' aside:

ARIANA. The ladies you are going to will not be so hardhearted.
COURTALL (*to Freeman*). On my conscience, they love us, and begin to grow jealous already.
FREEMAN (*to Courtall*). Who knows but this may prove the luckier adventure of the two?
COURTALL. Come, come, we know you have a mind to meet us.

No doubt Courtall's pursuit of Ariana and Freeman's of Gatty have wheeled the girls round gently so that they have been separated, leaving the men back to back centre-stage in a position to toss their remarks to each other over their shoulders. The vocal quartet thus embodies a pretty piece of choreography.

WHINING OF LOVE

On the principle that wit must exclude both what is foolish and affected and what is emotional and passionate, any amorous exchange that falls short may be condemned as maudlin and fit only for ridicule. 'Rant, cant and tone' was the comprehensive label given by J.H. Wilson to characterize the heroic vocalizing that belonged more to the tragedy than to the comedy of the Restoration stage, and he proposed that it was necessary to damn with laughter any sentiment that had to be bellowed ('rant'), whined in rhyme ('cant') or declaimed ('tone') ('Rant, Cant and Tone on the Restoration Stage', p. 592). A comic lover might employ all three.

In the early days the whining tone was an obvious joke. Etherege's Widow in *The Comical Revenge*, III.2, neatly places Sir Frederick Frollick with 'What pitiful rhyming fellow's that?' In Sedley's *The Mulberry Garden*, III.2, Olivia lives 'in most terrible apprehension of a whining copy of verses', so that when Wildish presents her with his song to 'Cloris', she protests in vain, 'I have no more pity on a rhyming lover, than on a beggar that begs in a tone', and must sit through its catalogue of fire and charms, passion and beauty, Cupid and his dart, fate and chains.

A certain amount of suffering necessarily went with the tender passion, but the slightest teardrop is a matter for ridicule, and the treatment of a watery scene can be very dry indeed. In *Epsom Wells*, IV.1, a bawdy drinking-song first prepares the stage for the excessive feelings of Mrs Jilt, who is about to keep her tryst with Rains:

> Her lips are two brimmers of claret,
> Where first I began to miscarry,
> Her breasts of delight
> Are two bottles of white,
> And her eyes are two cups of canary.

And Jilt, who 'thinks most men in love with her', would have been outraged if she had heard Rains's first line, 'Mrs Jilt appointed to meet me here, she's handsome, and I hope sound.' But then he is a man of wit and pleasure who could never do her sufferings justice, and such a prelude to their love scene wholly precludes any romantic flavour in what follows:

JILT. 'Tis no matter what I suffer. Alas! Alas!
RAINS. What's the matter?
JILT. I am the most unhappy lady in the whole world, I'll swear, ah, ha; but 'tis no matter, I may thank myself for't, I vow.
RAINS. What, have you lost friends or money?

JILT. No, no, I have something nearer my heart than all that. 'Tis not money that I
    care for, I'll swear, not I.
RAINS. I find that somebody has catched you, you are in love.

True love and tears, it seems, do not mix in Restoration comedy, and Mrs
Jilt and her feelings are given no quarter.

Florid language betrays the whining lover, and an aside is a quick way to
confirm first impressions. When Careless in *The Double Dealer*, IV.1,
makes a play for Lady Plyant on his knees, he also resorts to the honeyed
tongue, but she enjoys what he is saying so much that he is unfortunately
obliged to keep on and on:

CARELESS (*in a whining tone*). Ah heav'ns, madam, you ruin me with kindness;
    your charming tongue pursues the victory of your eyes, while at your feet
    your poor adorer dies.
LADY PLYANT. Ah! Very fine.
CARELESS (*still whining*). Ah why are you so fair, so bewitching fair? O let me grow
    to the ground here, and feast upon that hand; O let me press it to my heart,
    my trembling heart, the nimble movement shall instruct your pulse, and
    teach it to alarm desire. (*Aside.*) Zoons I'm almost at the end of my cant, if
    she does not yield quickly.

In spite of his physical discomfort and an increasing loss for words, the
lady continues to indulge her ecstatic moment. Still on his knees, he
complains to the audience again, 'I must say the same thing over again,
and can't help it', until the arrival of her husband on the scene relieves
him.

The most ridiculous declamation was reserved for the love between
those who were old enough to know better. Between Lady Faddle and Sir
Thomas Rash in Crowne's *The Country Wit*, I.1, there is so much emotion
that it overflows in flowers of speech, and the lines assume an echoing
pattern which would be repartee were it not devoid of wit:

LADY FADDLE. Oh, Sir Thomas, you over-run me with too great a flood of
    language.
SIR THOMAS. Oh, 'tis your ladyship only is the governess of that province.
LADY FADDLE. Oh, Sir Thomas, it is you are the inheritor; 'tis you have the
    learning, and the parts.
SIR THOMAS. Oh, 'tis your ladyship has the phrase, and the mine.
LADY FADDLE. Oh, Sir Thomas, it is you have all.
SIR THOMAS. Oh, the sovereignty is your ladyship's.
LADY FADDLE. Oh, Sir Thomas, you depose yourself from your rights.
SIR THOMAS. Oh, 'tis your ladyship dethrones yourself.
LADY FADDLE. Oh, Sir Thomas!
SIR THOMAS. Oh, madam!

The lady is finally overwhelmed by a fit of coughing in the ardour of her transport, but not before the chorus of 'Oh's echoes across the stage like a pair of cracked bells.

The dotage of old age introduces another form of cant, and scenes between an old man and his young wife or mistress are regularly marked by a shower of intimate endearments that sound totally incongruous with the dignity of age. Lady Dunce is the young wife of old Sir Davy Dunce in *The Soldier's Fortune*, and, since she has designs on Beaugard, she strings the old cuckold along, knowing that 'his dotage shall blind him', and actually using him as her go-between. There follows a scene in which his senility is indicated by the farmyard menagerie he invokes when he addresses her in III.1: 'my lamb', 'chicken', 'lambkin' and finally 'my dear, my love, my babby'. It is left to the actor playing Sir Davy to invent the absurd behaviour which must accompany such language.

Snarl, the 'old pettish fellow' in *The Virtuoso*, shares a flood of babbling endearments with his mistress Figgup in III.2:

SNARL. How happy I am in thy love! Here I can find retreat when tired with all the rogues and fools in town.
MRS FIGGUP. Ay, dearest, come to thine own miss; she loves thee, buddy, poor buddy. Coachee, coachee.

They proceed to call one another by the doltish expressions 'bird's-nie' and 'pig's-nie', until a discussion of the vices of this 'wicked age' ends with a wicked reference:

MRS FIGGUP. Prithee dear numps, talk no more of 'em. I spit at 'em, but I love n'own buddy man. Perdie, kiss me.
SNARL. Ah poor budd, poor rogue, we are civil now. What harm's in this?
MRS FIGGUP. None, none. Poor dear, kiss again, man . . . .
SNARL. I can bear it no longer, i'faith I cannot. Where are the instruments of our pleasure? Nay, prithee do not frown; by the mass, thou shalt do't now.
MRS FIGGUP. I wonder that should please you so much that pleases me so little.
SNARL. I was so used to't at Westminster School I could never leave it off since.
MRS FIGGUP. Well, look under the carpet [arras] then if I must.

He pulls the carpet and '*three or four great rods fall down*'. So much for Westminster School.

The amorous baby-talk of Fondlewife and his wife Laetitia in *The Old Bachelor*, IV.4, goes as far in this line of cant as Congreve can take it:

FONDLEWIFE. Won't you kiss Nykin?
LAETITIA. Go naughty Nykin, you don't love me.
FONDLEWIFE. Kiss, kiss, ifeck I do.
LAETITIA. No you don't. (*She kisses him.*)

FONDLEWIFE. What not love Cocky!
LAETITIA. No–h. (*Sighs.*)

This and much more like it seems to exceed the excessive, and this gallery of aged Lotharios will close with a remembrance of the way these two say goodbye:

FONDLEWIFE. That's my good dear – Come kiss Nykin once more, and then get
   you in – So – Get you in, get you in. By, by.
LAETITIA. By Nykin.
FONDLEWIFE. By Cocky.
LAETITIA. By Nykin.
FONDLEWIFE. By Cocky, by, by.

Their long-drawn-out parting is a series of excruciating gestures of sighing, ogling and kisses blown into the receiving air.

LOVE ON THE TONGUE

Lovers, not as friends, not as partners, but as tyrants and teases, make the stuff of comedy. Shakespeare knew it, and gave us Rosaline and Biron ('love's whip') and Beatrice and Benedick (who will be 'horribly in love'). Amorous duelling continues in Beaumont and Fletcher (*The Scornful Lady, The Wild Goose Chase*), Shirley (*The Witty Fair One, Hyde Park*) and many others tracked down in John Harrington Smith's *The Gay Couple in Restoration Comedy*. Here the concern is with how witty lovers expressed themselves on the stage.

At bottom it is diverting to hear two attractive young people jeering at love when all the time we know that some sort of sexual chemistry will prove stronger than their clever tongues, and the early Restoration stage dealt in many such couples. Careless and Ruth in Robert Howard's *The Committee*, Loveby and Constance in Dryden's *The Wild Gallant*, Wellbred and Lady Wealthy in James Howard's *The English Monsieur*, Boldman and the Widow Pleasant in Cavendish's *The Humorous Lovers* – these and others established a tradition of love and laughter, and set up a code of rules that made for lively duelling. The gallant speaks for male inconstancy, and his lady for her apparent indifference to him: in Dryden's *An Evening's Love* Wildblood says he usually limits his love to a month, and Jacinta responds by saying she prefers a fortnight. Matrimony is eschewed like the plague by both sexes – or so it seems.

Nevertheless, even in these early comedies, the lady must come to terms with the double standard that is with us still. Whatever she may say, it is only by marrying him that she can have the man she wants, so that

189

marriage remains her ultimate preoccupation. In these circumstances, Smith ventures an interesting opinion:

It may be doubted that any period ever took love more seriously than this one, or thought more seriously about marriage, the degree of its seriousness being measured by the misgivings with which young people in the plays become conscious of their attraction for each other, their struggles to escape the net, and, at the end, the mixture of anxiety and studied insouciance with which they accept the result. (p. 76)

If this is so, on the stage it meant that every witty affair of the heart was founded on the clash of an irresistible force (the male who would stoop to anything to have his way) with an immovable object (the female who could accept him only on her own terms). The best of talking comedy was the result.

Florimell and Celadon set new standards for witty sex in Dryden's *Secret Love*. Celadon boasts his inconstancy and believes himself irresistible to women, represented here in the persons of Olinda and Sabina. Florimell decides to prove that he is not as irresistible as he thinks by disguising herself as a gallant and stealing his girls. Thus they move towards a chastened union, but only after a set of provisos are agreed which all but obliterate the idea of marriage.

In the following banter from II.1 Florimell firmly grasps her initial female advantage. Her lover must prove his passion for her beyond a shadow of doubt, and, with a laugh on her breath, she tells him that he must do nothing less than die for love:

I would have a lover, that if need be, should hang himself, drown himself, break his neck, and poison himself for very despair: he that will scruple this is an impudent fellow if he says he is in love.

Having scored, she walks lightly away. Celadon meanwhile can only answer this sort of challenge by turning it cleverly around, although she manages to throw his riposte back at him again:

CELADON. Pray, madam, which of these four things would you have your lover do? for a man's a man, he cannot hang, and drown, and break his neck, and poison himself, all together.

FLORIMELL. Well then, because you are but a beginner, and I would not discourage you, any one of these shall serve your turn in a fair way.

Eventually she offers to have him if he will wait a year:

FLORIMELL. Shall I make a proposition to you? I will give you a whole year of probation to love me in; to grow reserved, discreet, sober and faithful, and to pay me all the services of a lover. –

CELADON. And at the end of it you'll marry me?
FLORIMELL. If neither of us alter our minds before.

Still not a very satisfying answer, and this arrangement of parry and thrust, in which each party aims to surprise the other (and therefore, of course, the audience), holds the clue to every verbal encounter between the sexes when a balance of equality is struck. The lady especially is not responding as social convention expects, and even if words like 'faithful' and 'marry' are used merely as counters in a game, the resulting dialogue is more substantial than the word-play of repartee.

In act v Celadon attempts a surprise of his own. He asks a favour of the Queen herself in solemn tones. What can it be? She invites him to speak:

CELADON. I beg, madam, you will command Florimell never to be friends with me.
FLORIMELL. Ask again; I grant that without the Queen; but why are you afraid on't?
CELADON. Because I am sure as soon as ever you are, you'll marry me.
FLORIMELL. Do you fear it?

With all his male prerogatives and pretensions, she still has him on the defensive, and at the end he resorts to 'provisos'. At this point the focus shifts from the man to the woman, for while the man agrees merely to be a husband, it is the woman who surrenders her only asset, herself. So Florimell bargains at the last for her liberty:

CELADON. One thing let us be sure to agree on, that is, never to be jealous.
FLORIMELL. No; but e'en love one another as long as we can; and confess the truth when we can love no longer.
CELADON. When I have been at play, you shall never ask me what money I have lost.
FLORIMELL. When I have been abroad you shall never enquire who treated me.

They agree even to abolish the names of husband and wife, and instead adopt 'the more agreeable names of mistress and gallant'. So Florimell again delights the audience by refusing to conform to the requirements of society. Yet she has achieved her primary end, which is to hold Celadon, and she will be married in spite of him. To accomplish all this, to lose her heart and to win his, she has had to hold herself back, put her wits before her feelings, and pick her words with exquisite care and delicacy.

A few of the witty relationships thrown up by the comedy of the sexes invite a second look. In *Marriage à la Mode* Dryden challenges the 'foolish marriage vow' of Doralice's opening song by testing it in action. In act I he turns the indifferent wife Doralice over to a new lover, Palamede, the friend of her husband Rhodophil; this is not a simple case of cuckolding, since Palamede himself is to be married in three days' time – to Melantha, to whom Rhodophil is also paying court. Thus Doralice is married and itches to be free, while Palamede is contracted to be married with no wish to be, so that Doralice may behave according to comic convention and torment her lover:

PALAMEDE. Give me love enough, and life enough, and I defy fortune.
DORALICE. Know then, thou man of vain imagination, know to thy utter
    confusion that I am virtuous.
PALAMEDE. Such another word and I give up the ghost.
DORALICE. Then, to strike you quite dead, know that I am married, too.

When this little game has been played out, neither has any scruples about making a contract – outside marriage:

PALAMEDE. Well, in spite of all that I'll love you. Fortune has cut us out for one
    another, for I am to be married within these three days: married past
    redemption to a young, fair, rich, and virtuous lady. And it shall go hard,
    but I will love my wife as little as I perceive you do your husband.
DORALICE. Remember, I invade no propriety. My servant you are only till you
    you are married.
PALAMEDE. In the meantime, you are to forget you have a husband.
DORALICE. And you, that you are to have a wife.

So this pretty pair parts on her 'Yours for two days, sir' and his 'And nights, I beseech you, madam.' The shocks and surprises in this dialogue are distributed more evenly between the sexes, and the verbal battle is equal. As it happens, Rhodophil and Palamede remain good friends even when each wants the other's lady, although a touch of moral sentiment is felt when the sense of losing what is theirs encourages them to think again about the lady each is neglecting. In *The Gay Couple* Smith considers this development to be 'the perfect balance, in which the absurdity of the antimatrimonial code is delightfully highlighted' (p. 70). If so, it was an absurdity which was thoroughly relished in badinage for four acts, with both lovers confident enough in their marital status to enjoy to the maximum a verbal flirtation.

The effect of sexual stalemate is dramatically deeply satisfying in *Marriage à la Mode*, as it is also in the relationship between Harriet and Dorimant in *The Man of Mode*, and these instances of parity in wit represent peaks in the early comedies. In later years the lady tends perforce to strike the indignant pose when a gallant dares to propose anything less than marriage. How virtue may repel vice too easily becomes a central concern, and the manipulation of sympathy for the vulnerable female dominates the comic process. The need to select the sharpest, the choicest, words for weapons grows less pressing, and smart lines go out with smutty scenes.

In spite of the moralistic tendency, sexual combats of wit nevertheless remained in demand, and the later Restoration stage owed a particular debt to Congreve for his attempts to satisfy it. Bellmour and Belinda first charmed audiences to *The Old Bachelor* in 1693, even though they had to wait until nearly the end of act II for the first of two short skirmishes. In *Love for Love* Congreve succeeded again with Valentine and Angelica, especially in act IV where Valentine pretends madness in order to make Angelica confess her love, only to find that she is too quick-witted for him. When at last he wants to speak sanely of his love, she wins the audience by insisting that he must still be insane:

VALENTINE. Madam, you need not be very much afraid, for I fancy I begin to come to myself.
ANGELICA (*aside*). Aye, but if I don't fit you, I'll be hanged.
VALENTINE. You see what disguises love makes us put on. Gods have been in counterfeited shapes for the same reason, and the divine part of me, my mind, has worn this mask of madness, and this motley livery, only as the slave of love, and menial creature of your beauty.
ANGELICA. Mercy on me, how he talks! Poor Valentine!

With this, he complains of being left in 'this uncertainty' about her feelings, so that she is able to give him the *coup de grâce* with a splendid exit speech in which she tosses his own words back to him, and at the same time defines the philosophy behind the Restoration duel of sex at its best:

Would anything but a madman complain of uncertainty? Uncertainty and expectation are the joys of life. Security is an insipid thing, and the overtaking and possessing of a wish discovers the folly of the chase. Never let us know one another better, for the pleasure of a masquerade is done when we come to show faces. But I'll tell you two things before I leave you: I am not the fool you take me for, and you are mad and don't know it.

This is a world away from the love-talk between characters like Loveless and Amanda in *Love's Last Shift*, which, for all it teeters on the edge of parody, finally focusses on moral right and wrong and not on cheating Hymen. 'Pray, sir, forbear!' cries Amanda in alarm, and Loveless's reply is all words that get him nowhere:

How can I, when my desire's so violent? Oh, let me snatch the rosy dew from those distilling lips; and as you see your power to charm, so chide me with your pity. Why do you thus cruelly turn away your face? I own the blessing's worth an age's expectation; but if refused till merited, 'tis esteemed a debt. Would you oblige your lover, let loose your early kindness.

But the battle is unequal when morality weighs the scales, and Loveless is reclaimed, virtue triumphs and comedy sinks. Amanda dares to ask, 'Can all this heat be real?'

Happily, Farquhar's gift with words will still tantalize the new audiences of the eighteenth century, grateful in *The Beaux' Stratagem* for the presence of an innkeeper's daughter:

CHERRY. Then, friend, goodnight.
ARCHER. I hope not.
CHERRY. You may depend on't.
ARCHER. Upon what?
CHERRY. That you're very impudent.
ARCHER. That you're very handsome.
CHERRY. That you're a footman.
ARCHER. That you're an angel.
CHERRY. I shall be rude.
ARCHER. And so shall I. (act I)

Cherry delightfully holds her own against Archer, but then matrimony with a barmaid was never in contention, and repartee has a free run.

CONTRACTS AND PROVISOS

The formal proviso scene was some years ago traced to a variety of English and French sources by Kathleen Lynch in *The Social Mode of Restoration Comedy*, and in Restoration comedy it emerged fully fledged in the contract made between Celadon and Florimell in *Secret Love*, V.1, as a way of sealing their amorous relationship and helping bring down the curtain. The implied contract is one of an equality of personal rights, which can include almost anything from a choice of partner for a game of ombre to a pact of mutual inconstancy and other outrageous freedoms that go well beyond social propriety.

Nevertheless, if Restoration stage lovers refuse to give ground to one another, the balance of their repartee implies a contract of some kind for as long as they keep talking. Contracts and provisos assume many forms in comic dialogue, and do not necessarily take on a formal, legalistic aspect. Making a quick bargain was part of witty love-making, a casual verbal convention capable of gentle mockery, and another manifestation of the ubiquitous Restoration repartee. In *Marriage à la Mode*, act V, Dryden himself tinkers with the convention when Melantha tries to impose some 'French' conditions on Palamede, who effectively foils her by singing at the top of his voice all through the ceremony. At another extreme, Careless and Hillaria announce conditions in Ravenscroft's *The Careless Lovers*, act V, which are quite shameless: he will keep a mistress and she a lover. The *items* and *imprimises* are simply a joke, a sudden unlikely flash of imagination which no audience need believe for an instant – in contrast with the more realistic set of provisos Congreve invented for Mirabell and Millamant at the end of the century.

The comic convention of provisos is a convenience for adding zest to the relationship between an amorous couple and tickling the imagination with a lightly satirical intent – no offence meant. In *A True Widow*, III.1, Theodosia imposes a frivolous set of conditions on her lover Carlos simply to stop him doing what he likes in the playhouse, a joke clearly levelled at the men in the audience.

THEODOSIA. I must never have you see a play but when I am there.
CARLOS. That is, I must see none at all, for when you are there I can see nothing
    but yourself.
THEODOSIA. Then upon no pretence whatsoever must you go behind the scenes.
CARLOS. That's grown the sign of a fop, and for my own sake I'll avoid it.
THEODOSIA. But the women have beauty and wit enough to hearken to a keeper.
CARLOS. Some of them are so far from having wit of their own that they spoil that
    little the poets put into them by base utterance; and for beauty, they lay it
    on so that 'tis much alike from fifteen to five-and-forty.
THEODOSIA. Item, you must not talk with vizors in the pit, though they look
    never so like women of quality, and are never so coming.

By this Theodosia deprives Carlos of half his pleasure in play-going. It is noticeable, however, that these provisos are lumped in with a variety of derogatory comments on actresses (of whom, of course, she is one), as well as on sundry gallants and ladies in the audience, suggesting that Shadwell had seized an opportunity to draw the spectator into his play.

Farquhar plays a happy variation on the proviso scene at the end of *The Beaux' Stratagem*, v.4, in order to manage a comic separation between husband and wife, the moment when the ill-matched Squire Sullen and Mrs Sullen reach a lively and stichomythic agreement to part:

MRS SULLEN. Is there on earth a thing we could agree in?
SQUIRE SULLEN. Yes – to part.
MRS SULLEN. With all my heart.
SQUIRE SULLEN. Your hand.
MRS SULLEN. Here.
SQUIRE SULLEN. These hands joined us, these shall part us. – Av'ay!
MRS SULLEN. North.
SQUIRE SULLEN. South.
MRS SULLEN. East.
SQUIRE SULLEN. West – far as the poles asunder.

Almost a pattern for dancing, this is too frothy to raise any serious issue of divorce, the lines growing shorter, voices rising, words echoing, feet dancing. When the pair join hands at centre-stage only to break apart and put the width of the stage between them with a joyful skip to the opposite doors, we see a resolution that belongs only to a playworld, that of high comedy.

The proviso scene which has received the most critical attention is that between Mirabell and Millamant in *The Way of the World*, act IV. Yet there is one overriding perception to retain in judging this accomplished exchange of words, that these too are words which belong essentially to the life of the comic stage. Two opposing judgments draw attention to the difference between literature and drama. One is William Archer's in his *Play-making* of 1912, where he chose the proviso scene to criticize Congreve, saying, 'This is very pretty prose, granted; but it is the prose of literature, not of life' (p. 389). Archer is looking for the 'life' of a realistic Nora and Helmer, or Rebecca and Rosmer, and not for stage life. The other opinion is George Meredith's in his *Essay on Comedy and the Uses of*

44 Edith Evans as Millamant and Robert Loraine as Mirabell, *The Way of the World*, Lyric Theatre, Hammersmith, 1924

the Comic Spirit of 1877 (published 1897), which offers the simple judgment that 'It is a piece of genius in a writer to make a woman's manner of speech portray her' (p. 101). Meredith's comment does not waste itself on what is real and unreal, but makes the point that Congreve's words create and embody stage life.

Meredith's comment is justified by performances of the scene in the spirit of its convention. The famous provisos would be a static exchange of impertinences, a mere tit-for-tat, were it not that each condition is a challenge that is passed through the men and women in the audience. Beginning with:

My dear liberty, shall I leave thee? My faithful solitude, my darling contemplation, must I bid thee then adieu? Ay-h adieu – my morning thoughts, agreeable wakings, indolent slumbers, all ye *doucers*, ye *sommeils de matin*, adieu? – I can't do't, 'tis more than impossible.

Congreve is putting his actress on display, and at the same time inviting the sympathy of every lady and entrancing every man in the house.

Millamant's performance implies Mirabell's, and since the audience guesses the outcome of the duel, both players are truly role-playing and have half their attention on the audience. By addressing the audience directly, Millamant first demonstrates how a man may be managed, and how, indeed, to dwindle into a wife with grace. The spectators simultaneously watch and enjoy Mirabell's grimaces as if they were delivering Millamant's conditions for her, until he finally advances the prerogatives of the male sex on the line, 'Well, have I liberty to offer conditions?' At this change in the leadership of the contest, he will step forward, even taking her former position on the stage, and will also address the audience as if the spectators are charged with passing on the conditions. They do so if only with their eyes, now taking them off Mirabell and scrutinizing Millamant, whose turn it is to take the defensive posture. She stands there, half turned away in pretended pain, reacting to his words with little mock expostulations of horror and despair.

Mirabell and Millamant come to rest – 'Then we're agreed' – and a balance is struck. The audience awaits the inevitable submission, although it may not know how this fragile creature will submit: actress, character and role-player have combined to make it believe in her unpredictable reality. She submits by hardly seeming to give way at all, speaking an extraordinarily long-drawn-out, hesitant, reluctant, fastidious, and yet sublimely confident, teasing and provoking affirmative, keeping Mirabell on tenterhooks to the last. She seems to be speaking to Mrs Fainhall as confidante, but she certainly intends Mirabell to hear every word she says, and is actually addressing the house again, as if taking the audience into her confidence:

Fainall, what shall I do? Shall I have him? I think I must have him . . . . Well, then –
I'll take my death I'm in a horrid fright – Fainall, I shall never say it – well – I think
– I'll endure you . . . . Well, you ridiculous thing you, I'll have you – I won't be
kissed, nor I won't be thanked – here, kiss my hand though. – So, hold your tongue
now, and don't say a word.

Her last words are all pretence and performance, fluttering her fan, gently
slapping him with it, frowning, mocking. The audience is to know her true
mind only after Mirabell has departed:

Well, if Mirabell should not make a good husband, I am a lost thing – for I find I
love him violently.

By the end Millamant is arguably too immaculate to be a real woman,
having exhibited everything ideally feminine, but she has come alive on
the stage because the audience has been helping Congreve pull the strings.

A NOTE ON VERSE, SONG AND NON-ILLUSION

Today's playgoer is struck by the casual introduction of couplets and
other gobbets of verse in the comedies. From Dorimant to Mirabell, from
Horner to Harry Wildair, any beau may unexpectedly mouth a lilting line
or two. It was also not uncommon to end an act with a couplet in the
Elizabethan manner, and Farquhar was particularly addicted to inserting
verses at the end of an act, that being the least troublesome place in a scene:
The Constant Couple rounds each act with a few couplets, *The Twin Rivals*
and *The Recruiting Officer* complete their last two acts in this way and *The
Beaux' Stratagem* does it at the end of acts II, III and V.

Within a scene a drift of verse brought an air of parody to a speech and a
quality of travesty to the action. In D'Urfey's *Madam Fickle*, II.2,
Bellamore acquires the tongue of a poet when addressing Madam:

> Mirror of beauty! Abstract of perfection,
> Sweeter than banks of roses . . . !

When Aimwell wakes from his pretended swoon in *The Beaux' Stratagem*, IV.1, he opens his eyes and looks in Dorinda's face to the lines,

> Sure I have passed the gulf of silent death,
> And now I land on the Elysian shore!

This nonsense is spoken with tongue in cheek, as Dorinda well knows,
even if it deceives Lady Bountiful; but it is so thick with mocking
innuendo that it is thoroughly suitable to farcical comedy of this kind.

None of this had anything directly to do with another Restoration
practice, the uncomfortable switching from solemn heroic verse to

conversational prose, from eloquence to wit and back again, found in early examples of double plotting in the plays of Dryden, Etherege, Villiers, Sedley and others. Here the liberty assumed by the poet to manipulate his style of speech in full flight of performance was no doubt intended to signal and control his audience's level of attention. However, this convention, like the other uses of verse in the comedies, is symptomatic of a non-illusory stage.

Not unrelated to a casual use of verse is the equally casual use of song, a detail which again draws attention to the mode of the performance. Restoration comedy was unusually rich in songs, and there was no limit to their number in a play; *She Would If She Could* includes twelve, mostly associated with the singing and dancing of Sir Joslin Jolley, along the lines of

> This is sly and pretty,
> And this is wild and witty;
> If either stayed
> Till she died a maid,
> I'faith 'twould be a great pity. (II.2)

But each comedy enjoys one or more songs of some sort, and the lamest excuse is used to cue them in. It is as if the playhouse was not going to allow the pleasure gardens and other places of entertainment to monopolize so popular an attraction.

- The play might open with a song, as in *Marriage à la Mode*.
- It might close with one, as in *She Would If She Could*. A closing song was often accompanied by a dance, as in *The Beaux' Stratagem*.
- An actress who was a good singer might be cast as a servant in order to sing to her mistress; these actresses are the Bettys and the Busys of the plays.
- Duets also occur for no good dramatic reason, as when Aurelia and her maid sing a part-song in *The Comical Revenge*, II.2; even Sir Courtly Nice sings a duet in his name-play, III.2.
- Supers appear unannounced in order to make up a chorus, as in *The Mulberry Garden*, II.4, where the Widow Brightstone produces three maids for a song and dance, and as in D'Urfey's *The Comical History of Don Quixote*, which suddenly introduces an unlikely group of shepherds and shepherdesses.
- Comic turns were welcome, as when Sergeant Kite in *The Recruiting Officer*, II.3, sings 'Over the hills and far away', with his drunken recruits Costar Pearmain and Thomas Appletree joining him in a lusty chorus.

No great interest has surrounded these songs, unlike that taken in the ways Shakespeare uses songs in his plays as integral ingredients, and it remains at issue whether songs in Restoration comedy were functional – heightening atmosphere, expanding characterization, developing a theme – or were merely decorative. Songs in the comedies were freely introduced without reference to character or situation because the stage was in no way trying to meet the imperatives of the unity of action. They were sung simply because they were in the spirit of the occasion. Nevertheless, a song could not avoid having an intrusive effect in some degree, like one in a play by Brecht which was designed as a device to remind the audience that the theatre is not the real world. In the opinion of Charlene Taylor in her introduction to *She Would If She Could*, by such devices the playwrights 'force the audience to go beyond simple emotional participation to thought and judgment' (p. xx). Thought and judgment may be too great an expectation, but a song can encourage an audience to stay aloof without disturbing its enjoyment of the play.

A prologue and an epilogue was written for every play, and was expected by the audience. The prologue was spoken in front of the curtain, which did not fall until the epilogue had been delivered. These speeches had an importance that is not fully appreciated by today's audiences, and they are usually omitted from modern productions. In their own day they were given judiciously to the central characters or the leading actors, and were much coveted. The epilogue especially served as a comic commentary on a theme in a play, with the actor staying in character in order to speak it: Lady Fidget speaks for *The Country Wife*, Lord Foppington for *The Relapse*, Millamant for *The Way of the World*, Wildair for *The Constant Couple*; and in the case of *The Provoked Wife*, Lady Brute and Bellinda speak a 'duet'.

Montague Summers considered that the prologues and epilogues had a still greater significance, since they were written to meet every theatrical occasion, making the activity of going to a play less a ritual than a special event. In his *Restoration Theatre* he wrote,

Intensely topical and intensely vital, they are indeed a mine of information, not merely with regard to things theatrical but also as indicative of popular feeling and the political currents of the day. In fact it is no exaggeration to say that we have here a body of historical documents.

Summers ventured to add,

So fresh and fadeless is their wit that, as has been proved to be the case, when spoken at performances today even a modern audience has been convulsed by their liveliness and humour. (p. 106)

While such historical values as they contain are now largely dead for performance, it remains true that the frame the prologue and epilogue provide serves to bring their audience into closer touch with the business of the playhouse. In creating the dramatic occasion, the author invites his audience to share his pleasure in play-making as well as distancing it from the action, at once allowing the spectator his freedom to criticize and granting the playwright his freedom to be scandalous. Prologue and epilogue fall into place with verse and song as further marks of a non-realistic stage and drama.

DOUBLE ENTENDRE

In the theatre the term indicates a word, phrase or line which has two meanings, usually for those on stage and the other for the audience. It has no need to be marked 'aside'. As a term, '*double entendre*' actually came into the language during the period of the Restoration, and towards the end of the century Dryden is to be heard comforting the ladies in the audience by explaining in his Prologue to the tragicomedy *Love Triumphant* (1694) that there will be 'No *double entendre*, which you sparks allow, / To make the ladies look – they know not how.' For it works by sly embarrassment, and while ambiguity may be the key to its method, bawdry is often its final intention. Meanwhile its victim in the audience may choose to understand the indelicacy, or not, as it suits him or her. As a form of wit, *double entendre* of course has a longer history, for it sprang up wherever its speaker could rely upon the special knowledge of a homogeneous group; perhaps for this reason it was pervasive throughout the Restoration. In the theatre it gives the actor a curious power, and as a comic device it not only supports the aside, but sometimes outdoes it. Like an aside, it is always addressed to the house, but in performance it also demands that the actor adopt a special look and a special tone of voice, which have the immediate effect of inviting the members of the audience to join in a conspiracy with him. When that happens, the actor is in command.

For an abundance of examples, one may open Wycherley almost at random. From *Love in a Wood*:

– MY LADY FLIPPANT. I never admitted a man to my conversation, but for his punishment certainly.
CHRISTINA. Nobody would doubt that, certainly. (act II)

– GRIPE. Martha, be sure you stay within now; if you go out, you shall never come into my doors again.

MARTHA. No, I will not, sir; I'll ne'er come into your doors again, if once I
should go out. (act IV)

These simple jests just avoid the need to be marked as asides.

The innuendo is such that it is often uncertain whether the character or
the actor is speaking, and then it grows vastly more interesting, as is
appropriate to a non-illusory drama. From *The Gentleman Dancing-
Master*:

– HIPPOLITA. To confine a woman just at her rambling age! take away her
liberty at the very time she should use it! O barbarous aunt! O unnatural
father! to shut up a poor girl at fourteen, and hinder her budding; all things
are ripened by the sun; to shut up a poor girl at fourteen! –
PRUE. 'Tis true, miss, two poor young creatures as we are! (act I)

– PRUE. Indeed, little mistress, like the young kitten, you see, you played with
your prey, till you had almost lost it!
HIPPOLITA. 'Tis true, a good old mouser like you, had taken it up, and run
away with it presently. (act I)

Here the actresses playing Hippolita and Prue may well be including
themselves in the joke, so that the audience is driven to think simultaneously of the play-world and the real world.

A listening character may often contribute greatly to the hidden
implications of the words by reacting with silent glances, again possibly
out of character. From *The Country Wife*:

– MRS PINCHWIFE. Pray, sister, where are the best fields and woods to walk in in
London?
ALITHEA. A pretty question; why, sister! Mulberry Garden, and St James's
Park; and for close walks the New Exchange. (act II)

– MRS PINCHWIFE. Let me alone, I am not well.
PINCHWIFE. O, if that be all – what ails my dearest?
MRS PINCHWIFE. Truly, I don't know; but I have not been well, since you told
me there was a gallant at the play in love with me. (act III)

These references may apply personally to members of the audience, and
inflections of the indicative words conjure up a world more fantastic than
that of either the play or the reality.

Wycherley was an expert in the use of the device, and at the first modern
production of *The Country Wife*, Ralph Wright noted in the *New
Statesman* his 'extraordinary lightness of touch that can give every
sentence a double or treble meaning' (23 February 1924). But no
Restoration comedian entirely dispensed with *double entendre* and
innuendo, and in the following examples Shadwell and Farquhar are also
very free with its use.

In *A True Widow* Lady Cheatly, who intends to make 'a show of fortune to put off herself and her two daughters', in the first scene announces her plan in these terms:

Where is there a better market for beauty, than near the Court? And who will more likely snap at the shadow of a good fortune, than the gentlemen of this end of the town, who are most of 'em in debt?

By this, every man-jack in the audience at Dorset Garden was caught in Shadwell's net, for if he was not actually in debt, then he was certainly in the market for beauty. And in all the plays which are graced with ladies who protest their 'honour', their lines are laden with innuendo, like these of Lady Gimcrack in her relentless affairs of the heart in *The Virtuoso*. Here she speaks to Bruce:

Should we now retire into that cool grotto for refreshment, the censorious world might think it strange. But honour will preserve me. Honour's a rare thing, I swear. I defy temptation . . . . But if you have any wicked intentions, I'll swear you'll move me prodigiously. If your intentions be dishonourable, you'll provoke me strangely. (act III)

A tiny pause, a little quaver in the voice, before words as ambiguous as 'refreshment', 'strange', 'rare', 'temptation', 'move', 'prodigiously', 'provoke', 'strangely' and above all that loaded and disingenuous word 'honour', and out of her own mouth the lady is a whore.

Farquhar managed cunningly to evade much of the criticism that Jeremy Collier brought down upon the Restoration stage by inventing line after line of double meaning. In the scene of Aimwell's swoon in *The Beaux' Stratagem*, act IV, Archer's words are double-edged to a degree hardly known before, having one meaning for the innocent ears of Lady Bountiful and another for the more receptive Mrs Sullen. As the good old lady busies herself about the sick young gentleman, she makes medical enquiries of Archer, disguised as Aimwell's manservant:

LADY BOUNTIFUL. Is your master used to these fits?
ARCHER. O yes, madam, frequently: I have known him have five or six of a night.

Mrs Sullen is no inexperienced quibbler herself:

DORINDA. O sister, my heart flutters about strangely! I can hardly forbear running to his assistance.
MRS SULLEN. And I'll lay my life he deserves your assistance more than he wants it. Did I not tell you that my lord would find a way to come at you? Love's his distemper, and you must be the physician.

The *double entendre* is an incomplete syllogism which the audience must finish, making it as engaging a device as comedy could wish for.

THE GLORIES OF THE ASIDE

The Restoration actor found direct address to the audience as natural and easy as did his Elizabethan predecessor, and in his Epistle Dedicatory to *The Double Dealer* Congreve gave a frank and obvious answer to the apparent absurdity of having a character speak to himself in soliloquy:

We ought not to imagine that this man either talks to us, or to himself; he is only thinking, and thinking such matter as were inexcusable folly in him to speak. But because we are concealed spectators of the plot in agitation, and the poet finds it necessary to let us know the whole mystery of his contrivance, he is willing to inform us of this person's thoughts; and to that end is forced to make use of the expedient of speech, no other better way being yet invented for the communication of thought.

Samuel Johnson was to place his confident finger on the whole issue when he asserted in his *Preface to Shakespeare* that the 'stage is only a stage' and 'the players are only players'.

The force of direct address in performance has to do with the physical relationship between actor and audience, and Cibber was the first to observe how much the quality of stage speech rested upon the intimacy between the two. In chapter 12 of his *Apology* he complained about the foreshortening of the apron as more benches were brought into the pit, because he believed that 'a voice scarce raised above the tone of a whisper' could be as effective as 'the most clamorous passions'. And in chapter 9 he blamed the 'vast, triumphal piece of architecture' of the new Haymarket Theatre of 1705 because it sacrificed subtlety of speech:

The best play . . . could not but be under greater disadvantages, and be less capable of delighting the auditor, here, than it could have been in the plain theatre they came from. For what could their vast columns, their gilded cornices, their immoderate high roofs avail, when scarce one word in ten, could be distinctly heard in it? . . . The tone of a trumpet, or the swell of an eunuch's holding note, 'tis true, might be sweetened by it; but the articulate sounds of a speaking voice were drowned, by the hollow reverberations of one word upon another.

The sorry story is told by the growth of Drury Lane from a capacity of 700 in 1662, to 2,000 in 1772, to a massive 3,611 in 1793.

In the first Restoration playhouses, playing downstage on the apron, with the players in constant facial communication with the house, meant that direct address to the audience was normal. With the small size of the auditorium, the regular use of the downstage doors and the overall illumination, it is not surprising that the dominant and basic speech convention in the comedies was the ubiquitous, the indispensable, aside. In *Sir Harry Wildair*, II.2, a scene of thirty lines, no less than twenty were delivered aside. Not only do the plays bristle with explicit asides used overtly to communicate what the author or his characters are thinking, but sometimes the stage explodes in metatheatrical outbreaks of double asides and runs of asides. In addition, much of the dialogue was spoken to the audience in the form of implicit asides, unmarked as such in the text. The general mode of speech comfortably embraced all these devices and more.

Technically, an aside is a speech spoken as if the other actors cannot hear it. In this simple sense it suspends the explicit action of the play (the 'inner' play or the 'play within') for as long as it is being spoken. However, since the mode of performance excludes the illusion of real life throughout, the aside is an integral part of the whole activity of the play event, and not some awkward interruption. It is as if there are two levels of perception demanded of the spectator as he watches the inner play and hears so many external comments, so that the pace of a scene will seem faster and the comedy more ironic; in this way the action of the scene is actually continuous.

If an aside appears to be spoken out of character, then the actor will also seem to be playing two roles, that of his character and that of the actor creating the part and the play. A sense of the flexibility of the aside, whether explicit or implicit, reveals it as a brilliant effect of a play's style, which encourages the actor to step out of the play repeatedly and so reach out to the spectator, who then becomes something more than a passive observer. The aside may thus become a device for sharing a remark or a whole experience, a quip or a complete choric commentary, and according to its occasion and frequency the audience is less or more active as participants.

The explicit aside can be dull when it merely offers direct information about the plot, but when it speaks what is on a character's mind, comments on another character or reverses a perception already made, it promotes a new ironic interest. In *Love in a Wood*, I.I, Alderman Gripe's daughter Martha uses her asides to show us two faces, one to her father and the other to the audience:

GRIPE. Come hither, child, were you not afraid of Dapperwit?
MARTHA. Yes indeed, sir, he is a terrible man. Yet I durst meet with him in the piazzo at midnight. (*Aside*).

It grows more entertaining in the next scene where a trio of beaux persuades Sir Simon Addleplot, a gentleman looking for a rich wife, to bring on the lady he has found. His 'new rich mistress' turns out to be Lady Flippant, a widow looking for a suitable husband. The young men all know her only too well, and respond immediately on her entrance in a sequence of staccato asides:

DAPPERWIT. How has he got this jilt here? (*Aside*).
RANGER. The widow Flippant! – (*Aside*).
VINCENT. Is this the woman we never saw? (*Aside*).

The three bursts of their explosive reaction perfectly reflect their amazement and the lady's notorious reputation, suggesting that there is more going on offstage than on. As for Flippant, she responds with an aside of her own: 'Does he bring me into company . . .?' In this way the audience is plunged precipitately into the intrigue of the comedy.

The explicit aside is good for marking out an actor's performance in its own right. When the drunken, belching Surly persuades the fastidious Sir Courtly Nice to drink a bumper to his mistress, Sir Courtly, the one who cannot stomach wine after he has discovered that 'the clowns . . . press all the grapes with their filthy naked feet', is granted a series of gestic asides that enable him to play the fop to perfection:

SURLY. Here, Nice, my mistress's health.
SIR COURTLY. What misery is this beast imposing on me! he coughs in the glass too – (*Aside*).
SURLY. Pox on't, a whole gulp went the wrong way. Come, off with it! 'Tis my mistress's health.
SIR COURTLY. This fellow's the devil – (*Aside*).
SURLY. Off with it, man!
SIR COURTLY. I never was so embarrassed since I was born –   (III.2)

With handkerchief to his nose, emitting squeaks and squeals, and pulling wry faces for the audience, his asides are soon lost when he can conceal his revulsion no longer, and in performance it finally hardly matters what is aside and what is not.

A delicious instance of display-by-aside for an actress is provided in *The Provoked Wife*, III.1. Bellinda is determined to make her rival Lady Fancyfull jealous by playing the coquette with Heartfree, the object of the lady's amorous desires. Bellinda does so with no trouble at all, and evinces from Fancyfull the following aside, which exactly demonstrates her vanity and her spite:

I don't like this jesting between 'em. Methinks the fool begins to look as if he were in earnest – but then he must be a fool indeed. Lard, what a difference there is between me and her. (*Looking at Bellinda scornfully*.) How I should despise such a thing if I were a man. What a nose she has! what a chin! what a neck! Then her eyes – and the worst kissing lips in the universe. No, no, he can never like her, that's positive.

As she shows horror at Bellinda's nose, her chin, her neck, her eyes and her lips, she invites comparison with the same features on her own face, and even if she did not move a muscle her tortured expression would be unmistakable. Her eyes follow the hated pair across the stage, and she confides to the audience again:

Very pretty, truly. But how the blockhead went out, languishing at her and not a look toward me. Well, churchmen may talk, but miracles are not ceased. For 'tis more than natural, such a rude fellow as he and such a little impertinent as she should be capable of making a woman of my sphere uneasy. But I can bear her sight no longer; methinks she's grown ten times uglier than Cornet [her maid]. I must go home and study revenge.

The actor or actress perceives and, indeed, feels the wealth of gestures and grimaces in the inflections of such lines.

The versatility of the explicit aside is such that it is doubtful whether there are two exactly alike in function. In the following lines from act I of *The Country Wife*, Sir Jasper Fidget, having heard the story that Horner has circulated about his impotence, immediately upon entrance chooses to test its truth by thrusting his wife at him:

SIR JASPER. My lady, my Lady Fidget, sir.
HORNER. So, sir.
SIR JASPER. Won't you be acquainted with her, sir? (*Aside.*) So, the report is true,
    I find, by his coldness or aversion to the sex; but I'll play the wag with him.

Horner has turned away disdainfully, acting out his pretence to the full, and Jasper is alive with glee, chuckling his aside in order to share his pleasure with the audience at Horner's expense. By his asides he assumes that he is in conspiracy with the house, and yet it is clear that the audience is more in ironic collusion with Horner than with Jasper, who is the deceived and not the deceiver. Inevitably, therefore, the situation ensures that Horner's responses carry the force of *implicit* asides.

SIR JASPER (*aside*). Ha, ha, ha! I'll plague him yet. – Not know my wife, sir?
HORNER. I do know your wife, sir; she's a woman, sir, and consequently a
    monster, sir, a greater monster than a husband, sir.

Peppered with asides and innuendoes, the audience anticipates, shares and enjoys Horner's ruse and the way it works upon his victim, so that Jasper's joke is turned back upon the speaker.

Unnaturally balanced pairs of asides arise naturally in stylized comedy, as they do in *The Sullen Lovers*, II.3, where the morose and melancholy Stanford is set beside his counterpart of the other sex, Emilia, so that together they produce a ridiculous vocal symmetry. Although they will at first have nothing to do with one another, these two echo each other's way of railing against the folly of mankind, and before long they find themselves in polite conversation, while all the time their asides convey how much they are still at loggerheads:

EMILIA. Nay, among the learned themselves, we find many that are great scholars by art, are most abominable fools by nature.

STANFORD (*aside*). This shall not persuade me to believe she is not impertinent.

EMILIA. Now the qualifications of fine gentlemen are to eat à-la-mode, drink champagne, dance jigs, and play at tennis.

STANFORD. To love dogs, horses, hawks, dice, and wenches, scorn wit, break windows, beat a constable, lie with his semptress, and undo his tailor – it distracts me to think on't!

EMILIA (*aside*). Now does he desire to be taken for a discreet fellow, but this will not do.

Their disposition to distrust everyone overrides the fact that they clearly hold the same narrow views, so that their asides are exactly in parallel, and the mere repetition serves to show up their affectation. By III.1 they have been further drawn together, and while they continue uncivil in their speech, their asides now ironically convey their mutual attraction:

STANFORD (*aside*). Why should I be catched thus? But I'll keep my folly to myself. (*To her.*) I can bear this with a little more patience, but if you should grow much impertinent, I should venture to break open the door of my liberty, I can assure you.

EMILIA (*to him*). Pray heaven you don't give me the first occasion. (*Aside.*) Well, I know not what's the matter, but I like this man strangely; but what a fool am I!

Stanford and Emilia finally repair 'to some distant desert' to consummate their love, and there, one imagines, they will continue to enjoy their pretentious duets.

The presence of a foursome of lovers in *Marriage à la Mode* produces an even more artificial bombardment of asides in act II. Doralice is alarmed that her lover Palamede is attracted to Melantha, and Rhodophil is alarmed that Palamede is to be married to her. This situation prompts a convoluted discourse with the audience:

DORALICE (*aside*). I find he has wit; he has gone off so readily; but it would anger me if he should love Melantha.

RHODOPHIL (*aside*). Now I could e'en wish it were my wife he loved; I find he's to be married to my mistress.

It also prompts a corollary from Palamede himself:

PALAMEDE (*aside*). O Jupiter! what a blockhead was I not to find it out! My wife that must be is his mistress.

The convention reaches ridiculous proportions when Rhodophil and Palamede both speak echoing asides, even though they are not supposed to have heard one another:

RHODOPHIL (*aside*). The devil's in me, that I must love this woman.
PALAMEDE (*aside*). The devil's in me, that I must marry this woman.

The echo is so precise that an audience immediately sees the two lovers as puppets of their play, like the lovers in *A Midsummer Night's Dream* when they are manipulated by Puck.

As the asides diminish in number, so the play activity changes in kind. It retreats within the frame of the proscenium and the use of the apron grows less crucial to the effective conduct of the comedy. With the onset of a more realistic performance, the characters begin to speak more on one level, in one mode, and the illusion of the inner play grows apace. With fewer asides punctuating the text, bawdy speech and frank behaviour give place to less explicitness on the stage and more subtextual innuendo in the lines. Nevertheless, the convention was so serviceable that it took a long time to die even when the stage conditions of the Restoration no longer obtained and the theatres had grown in size. We may conclude that, for all the aside is among the most unashamedly theatrical of conventions and devices, in comedy it is possibly the most useful. We may guess how much Shaw would have relished it, and it is not surprising that the contemporary theatre shows many signs of trying to recover it.

7. The spirit of the performance

PLOT OR SITUATION?

Does the stage, like the computer, feed us, or we it? The Restoration comic stage was a reciprocal institution, programmed to return just as much as its audiences brought to it, and while it is never possible to say of its muddled, repetitive situations that they held their audiences in thrall, they worked nevertheless by the essential input of those who went to the playhouse repeatedly and enjoyed what they found. A number of commonplace, formulaic scenes, therefore, made up most the plays, which were written in the knowledge that the audience would be ready with the appropriate responses.

There is a justifiable tradition of finding Restoration comic plots complicated. In his *Essay on Comedy* in 1877 Meredith pronounced that for Congreve a plot was 'an afterthought'. Closer to ritualistic theatre events than to story-telling, the comedies were not constructed like modern well-made plays. The outcome of each play was more or less known for the unexciting thing it was, and there were to be no surprises. In spite of Congreve's assertion that he had made the plot of *The Double Dealer* as strong as he could (meaning as complicated), it is hard to believe that this most accomplished of the Restoration comedians gave the notion of plot (or 'fable', as he called it) much careful thought. Yet his interest in a stageworthy situation never faltered, and it is the Restoration sense of what constitutes a comic situation that makes nonsense of William Archer's criticism in *Play-making*. There he found that *The Double Dealer* did not conform to his principles of a good dramatic plot.

This is, in fact, a powerful drama, somewhat in the Sardou manner; but Congreve had none of Sardou's deftness in manipulating an intrigue. Maskwell is not only a double-dealer, but a triple- or quadruple- dealer; so that the brain soon grows dizzy in the vortex of his villainies. The play, it may be noted, was a failure. (p. 213)

No matter that in his *Restoration Comedy* Bonamy Dobrée expressed 'no doubt about the admirable lucidity of the plot and the ingenuity of the construction' (p. 128), the author of *The Double Dealer* was far less interested in the intrigues of Maskwell than in the salty situations he could concoct for his solemn Lord Froth and his poetical lady, and for his old fool Lord Plyant and his coquette of a wife.

210

It happened that most of the first revivals in the twentieth century were of Congreve, and the new audiences which had been nursed on Ibsen and Galsworthy found the plots to be tortuous. Desmond MacCarthy, however, undeterred by the incomprehensible workings of *The Double Dealer* in 1916, devoted his review in the *New Statesman* to the virtues of the acting, insisting that the interest for Congreve's contemporaries did not lie in the plot, but in his 'exhibitions in the art of expression' (20 May). *The Times* went further:

The simple truth is that you soon give up troubling about the plot and enjoy, as Congreve enjoyed, the moment for moment's sake. A Congreve plot is of no more importance than the plot of a modern *revue*; it is merely there as a string to hang the 'turns' together. (16 May)

This was A.B. Walkley, and reviewing *The Way of the World* in 1924 he again noted the 'labyrinthine tortuosities' of the plot, but said that 'we do not complain' (8 February). In the *Saturday Review* Ivor Brown declared *The Way of the World* to be the work of a lazy man: 'Congreve simply could not be bothered with the stone-breaking and brick-laying which every dramatist must face' (16 February), but also argued that the plotting did not matter. There was a consensus that the stories were unoriginal and loosely narrated, carelessly woven and impossible to keep track of in performance, but that nuggets of pure gold were constantly being struck out of the scenes and incidents to which the productions gave rise.

The other common objection by those who watched the revivals was to the repetition of the same situations. Reviewing *The Assignation* in the *New Statesman* in 1925, Desmond MacCarthy complained that 'the situations are too constantly repeated. The play lacks invention' (31 January), and when he saw *The Gentleman Dancing-Master* later the same year he was annoyed by 'the constant repetition of the same situation with nearly the same dialogue' (26 December). One may as well complain that the Greek tragedians used the same situations over and over again: in the theatre there is strength in repetition itself, and even exhilaration when an audience recognizes a slight variation on some familiar material, as provided by another author or another performer. In this, Restoration comedy also partakes of a theatrical ritualism.

The Restoration audience was programmed by custom and fashion to expect and enjoy familiar material like the conflict of town and country attitudes and ways, the intrigues of the marital triangle, the chase and seduction of the opposite sex, and some few other regular situations. The motto for this chapter must be Bayes's immortal line in Villiers's *The Rehearsal*: 'What the devil does the plot signify except to bring in fine things?'

REAL OR ARTIFICIAL?

The close involvement of the audience with familiar situations does not, however, admit the idea that this drama in any way approached realistic theatre. The conscious element of play-acting at all times eliminated any realistic picture of human behaviour, individual psychology or the working of social forces; the plays are not an authentic portrait of the life of the times. In his introduction to Wycherley's *Complete Plays*, Gerald Weales considered that 'they are artificial in the sense that the characters are stereotypical and the exchanges between them are as set as vaudeville comic turns' (p. xvii).

To say this does not exclude an occasional flash from the seamy side of Restoration life. In its last act *The Country Wit* pulls in 'a beggar-woman with a child begging of Sir Mannerly Shallow' in order to embarrass the foolish knight; *The Man of Mode* makes good use of the Orange-Woman for a bawd, not to mention 'three slovenly bullies'; an interesting wider view is supplied, purely for the purposes of the comedy, by Horner's Quack in *The Country Wife*, the Widow Blackacre's Bailiffs in *The Plain Dealer* and the beggars who plague the Lord Podesta of Naples in *City Politiques*. Appearances by the lower orders increase towards the turn of the century, until Vanbrugh dares to open *The Confederacy* with the unpleasant persons of Mrs Amlet and her neighbour Mrs Cloggit – Mrs Amlet is 'a seller of all sorts of private affairs to the ladies' in Covent Garden, paint, patches, inn-bottles and false teeth. The next year Farquhar began *The Recruiting Officer* with Sergeant Kite and the 'mob' in Shrewsbury's market-place.

Locations are named. Costumes are modern dress and authentic. Movement and gesture are lifelike to match the dress. Stage props are familiar objects. Realistic business like smoking, needlework, card-playing, dressing and drinking adds colour to the life on the stage. Speech is preponderantly in colloquial prose. Character relationships are mostly familial and domestic, those of man and wife, mistress and lover. But there we have it. In spite of all this familiar detail on the stage, the situations in the plays remain resolutely closer to fantasy than to real life, generically more appropriate to farce than to comedy. 'Fantastic concoctions of farcical incident' might well describe the comedies of the Restoration.

Literary criticism is uncomfortable with the term 'farce', beginning with the contempt Dryden expressed in his 1668 preface to *An Evening's Love* for 'those farces which are now the most frequent entertainments of the stage'. Dryden was referring to the form of broad, knock-about entertainment associated with Davenant and Villiers, and with his own play *The Wild Gallant*, then later with Ravenscroft, Duffett and Mrs Behn.

But scenes and incidents that border on farce appear in some measure in all of the comedies, and to invoke the term is to recover their general tenor. A manner of presentation which allowed broader elements to flourish on the same stage with the more subtle affirms that their audiences held out little expectation of realism.

The genre that comes close to the comedy of the Restoration is that of French nineteenth-century 'bedroom' farce, the joyful work of Labiche and Feydeau. In his discussion of farce in *The Life of the Drama*, Eric Bentley argues that 'impropriety was of the essence' (p. 224) and that therefore the institution of marriage and the proprieties of sexual behaviour were its objects of attack. He noted incidentally that 'Restoration comedy was provoked by the Puritans and is forever dedicated to their memory' (p. 229). The style of the French farce was fast, aggressive and without sentimentality, so that matters of adultery and cuckoldry, so serious in real life, are on the Restoration stage, as on the French, exaggerated beyond belief - to the point where there could be no pain for the spectator, and one's own wife or husband could sit beside one in the theatre without embarrassment.

Laughter there must be: 'in a Feydeau play, the careful plan for the husband to be absent when the lover arrives is a gilt-edged guarantee that he will turn up' (Bentley, pp. 245–6). This kind of joke is possible only if the general mode of performance is theatrically unreal, if a substantial aesthetic distance of non-illusion is established between the stage and the audience. The argument bring us back to Lamb, not to the unfortunate notion of fairyland, but to his less-quoted lines:

The Fainalls and the Mirabells, the Dorimants and the Lady Touchwoods, in their own sphere, do not offend my moral sense; in fact they do not appeal to it at all. They seem engaged in their proper element. They break through no laws or conscientious restraints. They know of none. They have got out of Christendom into the land – what shall I call it? – of cuckoldry – the Utopia of gallantry, where pleasure is duty, and the manners perfect freedom.

Later he adds:

No reverend institutions are insulted by their proceedings – for they have none among them. No peace of families is violated – for no family ties exist among them. No purity of the marriage bed is stained – for none is supposed to have a being. No deep affections are disquieted, no holy wedlock bands are snapped asunder – for affection's depth and wedded faith are not of the growth of that soil.

Lamb is at pains to verify the necessary distinction between art and life.

Comedy, almost by definition social in character, trades in the most obvious of social phenomena, the battle of the sexes – the amorous chase, the intricacies of courtship or seduction, intrigues before and after wedlock, the compromises of marriage itself. The more indelicate aspects of the human comedy achieve success in public performance through style, by which a ticklish subject matter is made robust and objective, and thus laughable to an audience. Such objectivity in the theatre calls for the suppression of feeling and emotion and the nice calculation of aesthetic distance: the more *risqué* the situation, the lighter must be the touch, the breezier the playing. The refined rules of farce insist that unwarranted tests of psychological realism are never applied to its dramatis personae, but instead that they are revealed in an extravagant light which cannot offend.

None of this need carry the corrective force of satire. It is possible to ridicule individual behaviour and social convention without suggesting that they are wrong and should be changed. Dorimant's pursuit of three different women one after the other places extraordinary emphasis on social forms, but Etherege is hardly in the business of recommending Dorimant's behaviour as an example to others; nor is he condemning it. Much of the interest in his play lies simply in observing the shifting patterns of relationships between one man and the opposite sex. Congreve's declared intention in the Prologue to *Love for Love* to 'lash this crying age' was followed immediately by his hope that 'there's no ill manners in his play' and that 'he has designed affront to none'. Satire is too starved a theme to carry us far in trying to explain the success of Restoration comedy in its own time.

The few types of scene or incident that make up this last chapter recur in one form or another from play to play, are evidently central to the success of the operation and typically capture the artificial spirit of Restoration performance.

TOWN AND COUNTRY MATTERS

Some of the broadest comic scenes and incidents surround the arrival in London of country cousins and country wives. It is not difficult to see why so many occasions were made in the early years for jokes against the out-of-towners. The coterie audience of the Restoration theatre was preponderantly of the court and the city, and strangers, whether national, religious or social, provided easy butts for a court and city comedy. Etherege's early romp *The Comical Revenge* throws into the pot Dufoy, 'a saucy impertinent Frenchman' and one Sir Nicholas Cully, a puritan knight and fat gentleman from the country. He was played first by the popular comic actor James Nokes as the first of a rich series of foolish knights, Sir Oliver Cockwood, Sir Davy Dunce and Sir Humphrey Noddy. Cully becomes the certain target for the London card-sharpers Wheadle and Palmer; he was 'a country pigeon waiting to be plucked'.

In *She Would If She Could* Sir Oliver and Lady Cockwood, and the foolish Sir Joslin Jolley with his two pretty nieces Ariana and Gatty, are all very happy to escape from the country to learn a little of the liberty of the town: 'Well, faith', says Sir Oliver, 'a man had better be a vagabond in this town, than a Justice of Peace in the country' (i.i). Nevertheless, with all his pretensions, Sir Oliver is not up to it, and in the Bear tavern scene of iii.3, he is dressed in a great peruke and tricked into dancing with his own wife, who is wearing a vizard as if she were a lady of the evening. His country ignorance is not too cruelly lambasted, and the couple come together genially at the end.

Etherege felt no need to introduce a satirical bite into his country jokes; they expect merely an automatic jerk, a shared amusement. Harriet's final test of Dorimant's sincerity in *The Man of Mode*, v.2, is to require him to return to darkest Hampshire with her: 'To a great, rambling, lone house that looks as it were not inhabited, the family's so small'. She has deliberately painted a forbidding scene, yet he answers lightly, 'Not at all, madam.' The audience is left to judge whether or not he will be able to withstand this torture test, although it is hard to believe that he takes Harriet's suggestion seriously.

The differences between Dorimant and Harriet are not at bottom those between town and country, but they may be more so in the case of Horner and Pinchwife. Wycherley's Jack Pinchwife has been a long time absent in the wilderness, and is proud of the fact that he has 'married no London wife'. This sparks several country jokes like this one:

PINCHWIFE. At least we are a little surer of the breed there, know what her keeping has been, whether soiled or unsound.
HORNER. Come, come, I have known a clap gotten in Wales. (act i)

In spite of Pinchwife's repeated assertion, 'I understand the town, sir', *The Country Wife* is devoted to showing how little he does. It also shows how quickly a country wife may become a London wife, for Margery, falling back on her instincts no matter where she was brought up, is set upon securing Horner, a determination that overrides all the differences. At first she too is the occasion for every country joke. When she asks to go 'a-walking', Alithea's laughing response is, 'Lord, a country gentlewoman's leisure is the drudgery of a foot-post; and she requires as much airing as her husband's horses.' But when Pinchwife warns her that she must not like 'the naughty town-women, who only hate their husbands and love every man else, love plays, visits, fine coaches, fine clothes, fiddles, balls, treats, and so lead a wicked town-life', her apt and spontaneous answer is, 'Nay, if to enjoy all these things be a town-life, London is not so bad a place, dear' (ii.i). In the event, Alithea and the Fidgets with all their sophistication are never so successful as country

Margery in her innocent ignorance. Puzzling how to send a love-letter under the nose of her husband, she says, 'Can one have no shift? Ah, a London woman would have had a hundred presently' (v.2), and – lo! – the next minute she has thought of one.

Crowne's unsuccessful comedy *The County Wit* marked a high point in this sort of stage humour. The play deploys many of the tested country jokes, beginning with a raw situation: Sir Thomas Rash has arranged for the marriage of his daughter Christina, a lady with a portion of £5,000, to 'a foolish country knight', Sir Mannerly Shallow, a gentleman blessed with £2,000 a year.

Sir Mannerly will be in town tomorrow, and tomorrow he shall marry you before he sleeps, nay, before his boots are off, nay, before he lights off his horse; he shall marry you a-horseback but he shall marry you tomorrow. (act I)

The problem is that she has never seen her intended, and he comes from Cumberland, which might as well be the antipodes. The *ingénue* Isabella is appalled for her mistress:

ISABELLA. Is it possible for a lady, such a one as my lady, that has never breathed out of the air of the town:
SIR THOMAS. And by consequence never in wholesome air.
ISABELLA. Who has always lived to the height and gallantry of it;
SIR THOMAS. To the height of the foppery of it.
ISABELLA. And conversed with the most refined wits of the times;
SIR THOMAS. With the most debauched rascals of the times.
ISABELLA. Should ever endure a dull country clown, and a melancholy country life? (act I)

Isabella speaks for all.

The audience is compelled to wait until the middle of the play to meet this monster from the country. Sir Mannerly, with, for good measure, his cloddish servant Anthony Booby, at last appears in III.3, and between them they set in train all the expected verbal and visual jests.

SIR MANNERLY. Well, did one ever see the like? What a brave place is this London! It is, as the song says, the finest city town that ever I saw in my life.
BOOBY. Oh 'tis a brave place! 'tis not a city, 'tis a great country all o' houses.

And a porter tells them, 'You must not think you are in the country; people do not know one another here that live in the same street, nay in the same house, nay sometimes that lie in the same bed together.' Comic business follows. Booby has been instructed to observe how his master behaves, and when in act IV Sir Mannerly salutes his aunt Faddle with a kiss, Booby offers to do likewise. The two make a pair, and, on the principle that two of a good thing are twice as good as one, everything is duplicated, even to singing and dancing and amateur theatricals. Then, for his wedding in IV.1, the knight is dressed 'in a fine country-fashioned suit' which challenges the imagination:

SIR MANNERLY. Am I pretty handsome?
BOOBY. I never see a handsomer man peep out of a suit of clothes.

That 'peep out of' invites our speculation. Luckily, he is also a coward, and when Isabella's lover Rambler challenges him to a duel, Mannerly decides that country life is best after all.

The tide of ridicule eventually turns. In *Love for Love* Miss Prue is no substitute for a country wife, and while she is busy un-learning 'our old-fashioned country way of speaking one's mind', seaman Ben manages to be totally honest and returns to his ship with our blessing as soon as he can. Congreve has calculated that an audience may have a good laugh at Prue, but he knows that its heart is with Ben. In *The Way of the World* Sir Wilfull Witwoud serves his turn as choice bait for the wits and for the coquette Millamant, but in his contest with the fop in the 'smoking' scene of act III, his muddy boots are at least honest boots, and the audience is allowed to laugh as much with him as at him (see plate 45). Under Farquhar's broader and more generous pen, the country characters of *The Recruiting Officer* and *The Beaux' Stratagem* have become all but romanticized. The Shropshire ladies Melinda and Silvia are worth the attention of recruiting officers who are rich only in the ways of the city, and the territory marked out by the Lichfield coaching inn, with its genial innkeeper Boniface and his vivacious daughter Cherry, and by the rural household of the charitable Lady Bountiful, has shifted the country to stage centre and into a decidedly sympathetic light. By the time of *She Stoops to Conquer*, the country life that was formerly abhorred supplies the vantage point from which to invite new perceptions of the town.

CHASE AND CAPTURE, SEDUCTION AND CONQUEST

At the heart of the comedy is the game of love, crude or subtle, with many shades between. The audience acknowledges it, knows the rules well, and expects to judge the conduct of the matter in whatever shape it appears. Because love scenes of every kind enliven every play in the prime years of Restoration comedy, no doubt they were anticipated and received with open enthusiasm.

In farce, the salient elements of an amorous exploit could be played as physically as may be. In act III of *City Politiques* the foppish poetaster Craffy makes an inebriated invasion of the chamber of the beauteous

45 Sir Wilfull Witwoud and Lady Wishfort, *The Way of the World*, act III

Rosaura and '*chases her around chairs*'. In IV.2 of *The Comical Revenge* the fat lover Sir Nicholas Cully pursues the inviting Widow into her house, whereupon '*the women shriek within*' to echo Palmer's on-stage comment, 'Hark, he puts them to the squeak.' Less to see, more to imagine, but nothing mysterious in that. However, the manoeuvre may be developed more deviously, suggesting that it is something more than farce. In *The Beaux' Stratagem*, for example, the delicacy of the seduction of Mrs Sullen is in itself of dramatic force and interest, since Archer seems to be deceiving her while all the time she is very far from being deceived; prudently, she pretends to be deceived, but she is not, and, what is more, Archer knows it. The chairs have been removed, the squeaking goes unheard, and the manipulation of the situation is effected by words rather than deeds. We would choose Archer over Craffy and Cully, but the attention excited in the playhouse is only slightly different in kind.

The chase is more stageworthy, certainly, if it involves intrigue, disguise and deception, since the actors' opportunities are stronger, and the inevitable outcome is delayed by shifting the focus from the ends to the means. In *City Politiques* again, Artall is a 'debauch' who discovers in act II that the corrupt old lawyer Bartoline has a young wife, Lucinda, 'an ignorant, wanton country girl'. He promptly assumes 'a nightgown and cap' with 'a patch on his nose' in order to impersonate his counterpart Florio, another debauch who is pretending to die of the pox in order to gain access to Rosaura; Artall's, or Crowne's, assumption appears to be that if a ruse is a good one, repeat it. Artall's performance before Bartoline is outrageous:

I grow weaker and weaker every day, my time draws on. Heaven prepare me for my change, yet I'll use the means to live. Give me my milk.... Is my coffin ready?

Always ready for a quick killing, old Bartoline is immediately drawn to him, and the two strike up a mutually profitable acquaintanceship:

ARTALL. I am glad to know you, sir. I think I see a young woman there, very young. Is she your grandchild, sir?
BARTOLINE. Why, chruly, shir, I am almost ashamed cho chell you she is my wife.
ARTALL. Oh, dear! Would you marry one so young, sir?
BARTOLINE. I wanched a comfort for my age, sir.
ARTALL. And she wants a comfort for her youth. Heaven that made both sexes would have you both provided for.

The old man takes the bait and insists upon leaving Lucinda in Artall's company: 'Wheegle him, d'ee hear? Wheegle him, you may get a good legashy.'

The moment Bartoline has gone, Artall calls for his periwig and 'love equipage'.

LUCINDA. How now! what's this?
ARTALL. An adorer of yours, fair creature, no unsound, false, wicked Florio, but a
    sound, young, vigorous, passionate lover. If you will not believe my
    tongue, believe my nose; the patch covers wholesome flesh. Believe my
    legs, which leap, vault, and run, except from you, sweet creature.
LUCINDA. I am betrayed! drawn into a snare! (*Aside*) But 'tis a sweet one. – Help,
    help, help!
ARTALL. I need no help, my dear.
LUCINDA. But I do. Help, help, help! (*Aside*) Oh, 'tis a lovely gentleman!

Lucinda is a more than willing victim, yet the reference to 'legs, which leap, vault, and run' indicates well enough the physical chase which ensues, while the lady's string of asides, each contradicting her apparent resistance, signals a happy outcome agreeable to all.

The manner of the chase and seduction may seem tantamount to rape, were it not for the farcical spirit of the action and the knowing self-consciousness of the character, and no doubt the actress playing her. Wycherley's first comedy *Love in a Wood* is a collection of lightly woven incidents, one of which has the lecherous old puritan Alderman Gripe entrapped by Miss Lucy, daughter of the bawd Mrs Crossbite working in collusion with another of the same trade, Mrs Joyner the matchmaker. Earlier in act III the audience learned of Lucy's previous employment by her mother at the beneficent hands of Dapperwit. Now Joyner is seen '*leading in Lucy, who hangs backward as she enters*' – clearly acting the innocent:

LUCY. Oh Lord, there's a man, Godmother!
JOYNER. Come in, child, thou art so bashful –
LUCY. My mother is from home too, I dare not.
JOYNER. If she were here, she'd teach you better manners . . . .
GRIPE. Nay, speak to her gently; if you won't, I will.
LUCY. Thank you, sir.
GRIPE. Pretty innocent, there is, I see, one left yet of her age; what hap have I!
    sweet, little gentlewoman, come and sit down by me.
LUCY. I am better bred, I hope, sir.
GRIPE. You must sit down by me.
LUCY. I'd rather stand, if you please . . . .
JOYNER. A poor bashful girl, sir; I'm sorry she is not better taught.
GRIPE. I'm glad she is not taught; I'll teach her myself.

The hypocritical Gripe salivates at the prospect of the lesson, and this would be repulsive were it not for Lucy's awareness of what is happening, and the innuendo in her answers: 'Are you a dancing-master then, sir? but if I should be dull, and not move as you would have me, you would not beat me, sir, I hope? His fate is sealed by the compliant little curtsies that accompany Lucy's lisping of her lines.

The episode ends in a predictable romp. Gripe barricades the door by setting a chair against it, and then seizes Lucy in his arms. The girl responds by crying 'Murder!', whereupon her mother and four men break open the door:

CROSSBITE. What, murder my daughter, villain?
LUCY. I wish he *had* murdered me, oh, oh –

Lucy has slyly changed her cry of 'murder' to suggest that something far worse had been perpetrated, and she persists with her little whinnying noises, 'oh, oh' – 'oh, oh', as her contribution to the chaotic moment. Meanwhile Crossbite gesticulates to her 'all in tears and distraction' and tries to negotiate the damages with the Alderman in hard cash. To the audience bleats and squeals from Lucy sing a song of her happy complicity, while she busily adjusts her dress to look like a girl who has been ravished. So the audience plays out the game of seduction with the actors, as long as winks and asides and innuendoes to the house ensure that there is no doubt about the frivolous intent of the scene.

Vanbrugh and Congreve refined the clichés of seduction by an amusing verbal stagecraft which added a light psychological interest to their characters, who therefore do more talking than sinning. In the case of Young Tom Fashion's attempt on Miss Hoyden in *The Relapse*, IV.I, the scene risks anticlimax, since what begins with gusto dwindles into piety. But in IV.3 of that play the love scene between Loveless and Berinthia is engaging without sacrificing wit for energy, and has been pronounced 'one of the funniest and most lighthearted seductions of the entire period' (Anne Barton, *Times Literary Supplement*, 10 September 1976). Both the seducer and the seduced enjoy the occasion, and it is proper to ask how the audience is invited to share their pleasure. The answer lies first in the way the 'critical moment' is set up, and then in the timing of the action on stage. In mock-medical terms the audience has heard from Berinthia of her willingness to give Loveless 'ease', and of his readiness to lay his 'case' before her (III.2). Thus the usual ingredients of a chase are superseded, and the comedy resides solely in the manner of the seduction.

Phase one begins with Loveless's 'cautious' entrance 'in the dark', the intruder announcing that he is in Berinthia's bedchamber. It is of course 'metaphorical' darkness, since there were no means by which lights could be dimmed, and while Loveless gropes about in pantomime, the audience is privileged to see everything. Even the bed itself is present on the stage, as he reports; it presumably stands there in the discovery space like an expectant altar, for it is not otherwise·used, unless Loveless takes satisfaction in feeling it with his hand. Rather than hide under it, he chooses instead to creep into her closet – one of the stage doors – and so initiates the audience's pleasure of anticipation. His exit also permits Berinthia, '*with candle in her hand*', to remind it again of the darkness, and for an important moment to present herself and her private thoughts in soliloquy: 'I would Loveless were her to *badiner* a little.' She begins a restless circuit of the stage in a titillating delaying action, and perhaps she sits on the guilty bed:

What if I should sit down and think of him till I fall asleep, and dream of the Lord knows what? Oh, but then if I should dream we were married, I should be frightened out of my wits.

The audience again anticipates a tantalizing course of action, until Berinthia spies a book and takes it up to read. With 'Oh, *splénétique*! It's a sermon', she puts it down again, confirming that sin is in the air and awaits only the arrival of the devil's representative.

Phase two may be said to begin when at last she chooses to read an appetizing play, D'Urfey's *The Plotting Sisters*, and to find it she must make for her closet, the very same door behind which Loveless lurks. Opening the doors, she sees his figure in the darkness and shrieks in fright, 'O Lord, a ghost, a ghost, a ghost, a ghost!' No ghost, but the exact fulfilment of her fantasies, Loveless runs out to take her in his arms. However, the shriek was loud enough to bring her maid Abigail to the room, so that Loveless must scurry back into the closet and Berinthia must think up a hurried excuse: ''Twas nothing but the white curtain with a black hood pinned up against it.' Again the house is in suspense until Abigail has gone.

Phase three, and Loveless reappears to a Berinthia more in command of her feelings. She resists him now with words, and throws his married state in his face: 'Some husbands would be of another mind if [Worthy] were at cards with their wives.' All this constitutes a new delaying action, until Loveless offers '*to pull her into the closet*'.

LOVELESS. My dear charming angel, let us make good use of our time.
BERINTHIA. Heavens, what do you mean?
LOVELESS. Pray, what do you think I mean?
BERINTHIA. I don't know.
LOVELESS. I'll show you.
BERINTHIA. You may as well *tell* me.
LOVELESS. No, that would make you blush worse than t'other.
BERINTHIA. Why, do you intend to make me blush?

46 Loveless and Berinthia, *The Relapse*, act IV

LOVELESS. Faith, I can't tell that, but if I do, it shall be in the dark (*pulling her*).
BERINTHIA. O heavens! I would not be in the dark with you for all the world.
LOVELESS. I'll try that (*puts out the candles*).

The audience sees his every bold move, her every coy motion, but now the scene is moving into the shadows of the lurid imagination.

The fourth and final phase achieves a touch of the comical poetic:

BERINTHIA. O Lord! Are you mad? What shall I do for light?
LOVELESS. You'll do as well without it.
BERINTHIA. Why, one can't find a chair to sit down.
LOVELESS. Come into the closet, madam; there's moonshine upon the couch.

The joke about the absence of a chair seems desperate, but when it prompts the mention of a couch, complete with moonshine, we may conclude that she had his very riposte in mind. Each time her pauses and hesitations are harder to justify: 'What shall I do for light?' – 'Why, one can't find a chair.' – 'Nay, never pull, for I will not go.' But the critical moment is upon them, and he lifts her in his arms to carry her off. What should she do now? Should she scream again? Bring Abigail back? Berinthia's lips open to cry out, but the only sound she makes is heard '*very softly*'. She breathes aloud the only words she can muster, absurd as they may be, giving away her most secret thoughts and desires, in a ridiculous but delightful concession to the convention of seduction: 'Help, help, I'm ravished, ruined, undone! O Lord, I shall never be able to bear it.'

When the lady seduces the gentleman, it is another thing, and Congreve's skills never show better than in act III of *The Old Bachelor*, in which the 'surly old bachelor' Heartwell, who has always scorned the snares of the fair sex and berated his juniors for their weakness, is teased by the bewitching Silvia into a promise of marriage. Again, from the beginning the audience knows all there is to know about her; she is not at all the innocent she plays, for she was Bellmour's mistress and has decided to take her maid Lucy's advice and 'strike Heartwell home, before the bait's worn off the hook' (III.I). Besides, when first they are together, Congreve has Heartwell chink his purse at her ('Here are songs and dances, poetry and music'), which impertinent gesture indicates not only that he still believes a woman is an object for sale, but more immediately allows Silvia to show quite clearly that money attracts her.

There follows a brilliant sequence of demands from the old man and tremulous responses from the girl, designed to break down his resistance with each little buttered gesture and syrupy utterance.

HEARTWELL. Speak dear angel, devil, saint, witch; do not rack me with suspense.
SILVIA. Nay don't stare at me so – You make me blush – I cannot look.

HEARTWELL. Oh manhood, where art thou! What am I come to? A woman's toy; at these years! Death, a bearded baby for a girl to dandle.

She has no need to look; he tells her all she wants to know.

HEARTWELL. Can you love me, Silvia? speak.
SILVIA. I dare not speak till I believe you, and indeed I'm afraid to believe you yet.
HEARTWELL. Death, how her innocence torments and pleases me!

She is cunningly coaxing him to yield his ground.

SILVIA. Indeed if I were well assured you loved; but how can I be well assured?
HEARTWELL. Take the symptoms – and ask all the tyrants of thy sex, if their fools are not known by this parti-coloured livery – I am melancholic when thou art absent; look like an ass, when thou art present.

A little smile of triumph is on her lips as she humbles him so thoroughly.

HEARTWELL. Nay yet a more certain sign than all this: I give thee my money.
SILVIA. Ay, but that is no sign; for they say, gentlemen will give money to any naughty woman to come to bed to them – O Gemini, I hope you don't mean so – for I won't be a whore.

A picture of bashful innocence still, she advances relentlessly to her main purpose; but she takes his money nevertheless.

SILVIA. Nay, if you would marry me, you should not come to bed to me – you have such a beard, and would so prickle one. But do you intend to marry me?
HEARTWELL. That a fool should ask such a malicious question! Death, I shall be drawn in, before I know where I am – However, I find I am pretty sure of her consent, if I am put to it. (*Aside.*) Marry you? no, no, I'll love you.
SILVIA. Nay, but if you love me, you must marry me; what don't I know my father loved my mother, and was married to her?

Prickly beards and parental guidance are distracting him and blinding him to the nuptial imperative to which she clings.

HEARTWELL. I'll have my beard shaved, it shan't hurt thee, and we'll go to bed –
SILVIA. No, no, I'm not such a fool neither but I can't keep myself honest; – here, I won't keep anything that's yours, I hate you now, (*throws the purse*) and I'll never see you again, 'cause you'd have me be naught. (*Going*).

She accelerates the inevitable by forcing him to call her back, for she has one last card to play – her tears.

SILVIA. Well – goodbye. (*Turns and weeps.*)
HEARTWELL. Ha! Nay come, we'll kiss at parting (*kisses her*). By heaven, her kiss is sweeter than liberty – I will marry thee – There, thou hast done't. All my resolves melted in that kiss – one more.

'I will marry thee' are the words she has been waiting for. She gently

225

47 Faute de droit a tousjours besoin d'ayde. The verses may be translated:
The beauty possessing such grace
Who's leading the fool in this place
Would merit compassion from all
If, to make the marriage more fair
Of this clearly ill-matched pair
She hadn't this gallant on call.   (trans. Norman Spector)

unfolds herself from his embrace and softly asks the businesslike
question, 'But when?'

The seams in this dialogue are not easy to discern. It drives to a point,
and to Silvia's devastating last line to the house: 'Ha, ha, ha, an old fox

trapped.' In her laugh, Congreve has overturned all conventional expectations about who is seducing whom.

MISMATCHES AND CUCKOLDRY

Cuckolding is a victory by dispossession, of a man and his wife, of his reputation and her virtue. In the plays all old husbands fear it at the hands of young wives, and no device – holding the girl under lock and key, keeping her in ignorance, hiding or disguising her – can prevent the inevitable moment when he is looking the wrong way. Cuckolding scenes harness the forces of nature to defeat the over-possessive husband, but no great insight into nature is needed or demanded to explain why every other Restoration comedy has society's oldest triangular situation as a centrepiece. Jealousy and suspicion await their reward in the only way possible, and intrigue supplies the means. The theme is one which seems not to have lost its comic force for an audience from the beginnings of the Renaissance, and it turns up in play after play from Etherege to Farquhar. Titles like *She Would if She Could, Marriage à la Mode, The Country Wife* and *The Provoked Wife*, to name only a few, tell their own story, and Southerne's *The Wives' Excuse* even carries a subtitle, *Cuckolds Make Themselves*.

Comic cuckolding differs from simple seduction because the husband must actually contribute to his fate. *The Country Wife* is a cuckolding play *par excellence*, not only because it contrives a double triangle, but also because no other attempts a trick quite so preposterous as Horner's pretence of impotence, the open invitation which Sir Jasper Fidget cannot resist. Yet if Lady Fidget is conventionally willing to cuckold her husband, no other play has so possessive a husband as Pinchwife and so endows a young wife with Margery's innocent zest for the wicked life.

Wycherley's plot develops relentlessly to the comic crisis, with all participants contributing to the full by reason of its careful preparation. The measure of theatrical success is the force of the blast at the moment the truth is revealed. Both Jasper and Pinchwife themselves give their wives to the enemy, Jasper actually inviting Horner into his house:

Mr Horner, your servant; I shall be glad to see you at my house. Pray come and dine with me, and play at cards with my wife after dinner; you are fit for women at that game yet, ha, ha! – (*Aside*) 'Tis as much a husband's prudence to provide innocent diversion for a wife as to hinder her unlawful pleasures, and he had better employ her than let her employ herself. (act I)

In Pinchwife's case, he was personally responsible for each step towards Margery's fall from grace:

PINCHWIFE. Come, what's here to do? You are putting the town pleasures in her head, and setting her a-longing.

ALITHEA. Yes, after ninepins; you suffer none to give her those longings, you mean, but yourself.

PINCHWIFE. I tell her of the vanities of the town like a confessor . . . Poor wretch! She desired not to come to London; I would bring her.

ALITHEA. Very well . . . . Was she not at a play yesterday?

PINCHWIFE. Yes, but she never asked me; I was myself the cause of her going.

(act III)

When Pinchwife must take Margery to town again, he rejects the idea of her wearing a mask to conceal her face, for the obvious reason that she will join the ranks of the vizards; instead, he chooses a disguise that only a theatre audience could be sure would prove a greater temptation, having seen breeches parts many times before.

No, I'll not use her to a mask, 'tis dangerous; for masks have made more cuckolds than the best faces that ever were known . . . . So – I have it – I'll dress her up in the suit we are to carry down to her brother, little Sir James; nay, I understand the town tricks.

His fear of what the mask would leave unconcealed ('her shape, stature, habit') is what will now be revealed by breeches, and his fear of what Horner might do if he meets her ('wish her joy, kiss her, talk to her, leer upon her, and the devil and all') is precisely what Horner does.

For a more regular arrangement of the ingredients of cuckoldry, Otway's rollicking entertainment *The Soldier's Fortune* offers a better idea. According to Downes, the play 'took extraordinary well' (p. 36) and remained popular for forty years. This popularity was achieved in spite of the fact that nearly the whole play is given over to the cuckolding of Sir Davy Dunce by the silliest of tricks, with surprisingly little time given to an amorous exchange or two between Lady Dunce and her lover Captain Beaugard. The success may be explained by the simplicity of the formula, and the gratification of the audience by the play's comforting predictability.

The formula begins by emphasizing the mismatch. Sir Davy is all a potential cuckold should be: in Sir Jolly Jumble's words, 'an old, greasy, untoward, ill-natured, slovenly, tobacco-taking cuckold; but plaguy jealous' (1.1). There is more like this from the unmarried Sylvia, who offers this reason for remaining single: ''Tis an unspeakable blessing to lie all night by a horse-load of diseases; a beastly, unsavory, old, groaning, grunting wheezing wretch, that smells of the grave he's going to already.' And Lady Dunce adds to this, 'Bless us, to be yoked in wedlock with a paralytic, coughing, decrepit dotterel; to be dry-nurse all one's lifetime to

228

an old child of sixtyfive; to lie by the image of death a whole night, a dull immoveable, that has no sense of life but through its pains!' (1.2).

Set against this vision is its antithesis, the pretty young wife, and Sir Jolly is again given the task of description. He cannot remember what she says for looking at her lips, which, once the old voyeur begins to speak, chiefly do duty for the rest of her person: 'Such a lip, so red, so hard, so plump, so blub; I fancy I am eating cherries every time I think on't.' He proceeds a little further: 'And for her neck and breasts, and her – odd's life! I'll say no more, not a word more; but I know, I know –' (1.1). It is for the actress playing Lady Dunce to complete the lascivious picture, whether the 'enchanting' Mrs Barry at Dorset Garden in 1680, or the delectable Miss Seyler at the Ambassadors' in 1935, who 'revels in the salacious salad'. So James Agate reported in *The Sunday Times*: 'Miss Seyler keeps it up to the end, and informs the whole character with a perfect sense of its profound enormity' (6 October).

Agate asked, like Claudius, 'Have you heard the argument? Is there no offence in't?' And he answered, 'Of course there is,' adding, 'it is alike in conveying that offence and enjoying its conveyance that the skill of this play's actors and of its audience lies. For not to offend would be to miss its whole point, while not to revel in the offence would be clumsy playgoing!' (*Red Letter Nights*, p. 46). If the plot has no teeth, then the bite must be felt in the way the players comport themselves. The audience has heard the argument and is ready to receive the offence, but it has to wait until nearly the end of the play for the deed to be done, and the rest is slow preparation. To begin with, Sir Davy is blissfully ignorant of his situation, and believes his wife to be all that is virtuous:

Well, of all blessings, a discreet wife is the greatest that can light upon a man of years: had I been married to anything but an angel now, what a beast had I been by this time! Well, I am the happiest old fool! 'Tis a horrid age we live in, so that an honest man can keep nothing to himself. If you have a good estate, every covetous rogue is longing for't (truly I love a good estate dearly myself); if you have a handsome wife, every smooth-faced coxcomb will be combing and cocking at her: flesh-flies are not so troublesome to the shambles as those sort of insects are to the boxes in the playhouse. But virtue is a great blessing, an unvaluable treasure. (II.1)

His complacency is beyond belief, and, so confident is he, he even agrees to carry rings and messages between the lovers. Nevertheless, comes the time when he catches Beaugard in his wife's room, and he makes the mistake of paying two hit-men, Fourbin and Bloody-Bones, to murder him.

This move immediately gives his lady the hold over her husband that she needs. With the help of Sir Jolly, she lays out Beaugard's body as if it were near death, and allows Sir Davy to think he has killed his rival.

SIR DAVY. Bless us! a man! and bloody! what, upon my hall-table! . . . what shall I do? I'll throw myself upon him, kiss his wide wounds, and weep till blind as buzzard.

Just in time, Lady Dunce stops him before he gets too close to the evidence.

LADY DUNCE. Oh, come not near him; there's such horrid antipathy follows all murders, his wounds would stream afresh should you but touch him.
SIR DAVY. Dear neighbour, dearest neighbour, friend, Sir Jolly, as you love charity, pity my wretched case, and give me counsel; I'll give my wife and all my estate to have him live again.

The obligatory line, 'I'll give my wife', justifies whatever may ensue, and it is Sir Jolly, the merry engineer of all illicit deeds in this play, who thinks of a solution: Beaugard should be put into a warm bed to bring him to life again. Sir Davy's next motion is almost predictable.

LADY DUNCE. What would you have me do?
SIR DAVY. Prithee do so much as try thy skill; there may be one dram of life left in him yet. Take him up to thy chamber, put him into thy own bed, and try what thou canst do with him; prithee do: if thou canst but find motion in him, all may be well yet. (IV.3)

Sir Davy actually says his prayers while his wife warms her lover to life in her bed. Thus is the man supremely self-cuckolded, although in the end he is so pleased to find Beaugard alive that he accepts his cuckoldom with joy.

The story of Bellmour and the Fondlewifes in *The Old Bachelor* is confined almost entirely to act IV as if it were an afterthought, and takes a minor place in a play of multiple intrigues. It proceeds upon the principle, 'If the spirit of cuckoldom becomes raised up in a woman, the devil can't lay it, till she has done't.' For an additional irony in this case, the pretty Laetitia Fondlewife is married to so jealous a husband that she must try especially hard to please him before she may deceive him. Indeed, she is so adept at dissembling that Fondlewife grows suspicious. He talks to himself:

Does not thy wife love thee, nay dote upon thee? – Yes – Why then! – Ay, but to say truth, she's fonder of me than she has reason to be; and in the way of trade, we still suspect the smoothest dealers of the deepest designs.

It becomes a contest whether she can manage to please him sufficiently to allay his fears, but not so much that he will not go away. When he suggests that she may be cuckolding him, she resorts, of course, to tears.

LAETITIA (*crying*). Well – Well – you know my fondness, and you love to tyrannize – Go on, cruel man, do, triumph over my poor heart, while it holds; which cannot be long, with this usage of yours – But that's what you want – Well, you will have your ends soon – You will – You will – Yes it will break to oblige you. (*Sighs*).

FONDLEWIFE. Verily I fear I have carried the jest too far – Nay, look you now if she does not weep – 'tis the fondest fool – Nay, Cocky, Cocky, nay, dear Cocky, don't cry, I was but in jest, I was not ifeck . . . . Nay come kiss, buss poor Nykin – and I won't leave thee – I'll lose all first.

LAETITIA (*aside*). How, Heav'n forbid: that will be carrying the jest too far indeed.

When Bellmour succeeds in invading Fondlewife's house disguised as a man of the cloth, one Mr Spintext, and is about to be discovered, Laetitia has to be particularly inventive. She claims to have been ravished by, of all people, the innocent fool Sir Joseph Wittol. As Fondlewife goes to the door behind which Bellmour is hiding, she '*runs to Sir Joseph, almost pushes him down, and cries out,* Stand off rude ruffian. Help me, my dear – O bless me! Why will you leave me alone with such a satyr?' Needless to say, Bellmour is finally discovered *in flagrante delicto*, and it is all Laetitia can do to mollify her husband. At this point, Congreve fixes the stage in a classic tableau: '*She goes and hangs upon his neck, and kisses him. Bellmour kisses her hand behind Fondlewife's back.*'

The cuckoldry in *The Provoked Wife* reflects the sad decline of the convention in theatrical vigour when its basic ingredients are adulterated. In spite of every provocation, Lady Brute remains virtuous to the end, and in any case Sir John does not care whether he is cuckolded or not. Otherwise, the contestants are presented formally at the outset, and a little verbal in-fighting confirms the mismatch, after which the unhappy Lady Brute says her piece:

I was told before I married him that thus 'twould be. But I thought I had charms enough to govern him, and that where there was an estate a woman must needs be happy; so my vanity has deceived me and my ambition has made me uneasy. But some comfort still: if one would be revenged of him, these are good times. A woman may have a gallant and a separate maintenance too.

The speech indicates a nice reversal from her state of being 'uneasy' to her new satisfaction in 'some comfort still', and the subsequent developments are set in motion. She shares her idea with the audience, and for her gallant she proposes Constant, of whom Bellinda remarks, ''Tis well Constant don't know the weakness of the fortifications, for o'my conscience he'd soon come on to the assault.' Unluckily for the play, the sound to arms is false in almost every respect.

From the beginning, the potential victim of her designs, her husband, lacks all interest in the fight. Vanbrugh may have provoked the wife, but had no intention of provoking the husband and was never sure about provoking the audience:

I have never observed anything in my wife's course of love life to back me in my jealousy of her. But jealousy's a mark of love; so she need not trouble her head about it, as long as I make no more words on't. (v.5)

Notwithstanding the element of irony in offering to test so thick-skinned a husband, the anticlimax is complete: Lady Brute keeps her virtue and Sir John is spared his horns. Adultery is nowhere given its name.

A NOTE ON DISGUISING

On 21 February 1665 Pepys wrote about Frances Jennings, who was sister of the Duchess of Marlborough and living in the house of the Duchess of York:

What mad freaks the Maids of Honour at Court have: that Miss Jennings, one of the Duchess's maids, the other day dressed herself like an orange-wench, and went up and down and cried oranges; till, falling down, or by some accident, her fine shoes were discerned, and she put to a great deal of shame.

In his *Memoirs* the Comte de Grammont tells the same story and elaborates on it, adding a second orange-wench, one Miss Price, the Queen's Maid of Honour (p. 259). In his *History of My Own Times* Bishop Burnet reported that in 1668

the Court fell into much extravagance in masquerading; both King and Queen and all the Court went about masked, and came into houses unknown, and danced there, with a good deal of wild frolic. People were so disguised that, without being in the secret, none could distinguish them. (vol. 1, p. 473)

There are other similar reports. The Restoration passion for disguising has no modern equivalent and is not easy to explain. Norman Holland puts it down to 'the almost magical energy of the age', which expressed itself repeatedly, he thinks, in 'disguises and pretences, masks and affectations' (*The First Modern Comedies*, p. 45). The fashion continued well into the next century and even emerged as a convention in the novel.

The comedies take up this pastime, with its delightful propensity for skylarking, like a gift from the Muse. It is not necessary to find some larger, psychological significance in such masquerades; they are natural to the stage, and, indeed, the stage itself is a manifestation of the sport. The playwright's urge to dress up the characters of a social comedy echoes the stage's need to reveal the roles people play.

48 Sir John Brute, *The Provoked Wife*

From the beginning to the end of the period, few comedies do not enjoy some frivolous pretence of this kind. Sir Simon Addleplot becomes Jonas the clerk in *Love in a Wood*, Gerrard pretends to be the gentleman dancing-master, Prig in *A True Widow* is the parson in act v, Lorenzo turns up as the title part in *The Spanish Friar*, Bellmour pretends to be Tribulation Spintext in *The Old Bachelor*, and in *The Double Dealer* Touchwood and Mellefont are a pair of parsons and in *Love for Love* Tattle and Mrs Frail are disguised as a friar and a nun. Clinch is a porter in *The Constant Couple*, Waitwell in *The Way of the World* is the impostor Sir Rowland, Trueman is a constable in the fifth act of *The Twin Rivals* and Octavio of *She Would and She Would Not* becomes a friar again. In *The Provoked Wife* Sir John Brute is disguised as a drunken parson, a satirical effect which Vanbrugh later eliminated by having him dress himself instead in Lady Brute's petticoats and announcing him as Bonduca, Queen of the Welshmen; it was in this manner that Garrick played the scene. There are many other instances of disguise.

SEX AND FARCE: AIMWELL'S SWOON

On occasion a playwright is able to put together the bawdy and the slapstick, the intrigue and the seduction, all in a consummate scene which exploits the Restoration stage and its actors, engages the audience and justifies the liberties it takes with the comic form. Such a scene is that of Aimwell's pretended sickness in Farquhar's *The Beaux' Stratagem*, act IV.

On the surface the episode appears to be one of pure farce. In order to enter the house of Lady Bountiful and gain access to the young women, her daughter and her daughter-in-law, under her roof, the two gentlemen of 'broken fortunes', Aimwell and Archer, devise a preposterous trick: at the lady's gate Aimwell will pretend to fall into a deathlike swoon, and, playing the part of his servant, Archer will beg her familiar benevolence and abuse her country practice of curing the sick who come to her door. Beneath the surface of this decorous masquerade the audience is to perceive that the stratagem is highly ambiguous, for it will induce a seduction scene in which everyone, including the objects of desire, is aware of the gentlemen's intentions except the one person who is in a position to prevent it, Lady Bountiful herself. And beneath this intrigue, Farquhar will pursue his game of *double entendre* and aside in order that the audience may share in the activity of creating the comedy: the viewer is enabled to take the part of the old lady, then of the male deceivers and finally of the young women, the willing victims. Stagecraft, verbal wit and the actors are to unite to create a huge joke and a tidy example of Restoration metatheatre.

234

49 Aimwell's swoon, *The Beaux' Stratagem*, act IV

The setting is a room where the good lady can apply her homely medicinal ministrations, assisted by Mrs Sullen. Suddenly the stage leaps into activity with two running entrances.

Enter Dorinda [who] runs to Mrs Sullen.
DORINDA. News, dear sister! news! news!
Enter Archer, running.
ARCHER. Where, where is my Lady Bountiful? – Pray, which is the old lady of you three?
LADY BOUNTIFUL. I am.

By Archer's charming little impertinence the audience is immediately alerted to the flippant level of deception that is to be perpetrated. But he is already on his knees flattering Lady Bountiful's 'charity, goodness, benevolence, skill, and ability', and rather cheekily praising heaven too. With her 'Quickly, quickly!', the fast pace is seemingly sustained offstage, while Mrs Sullen and Dorinda are left briefly alone for a more sober conference spoken in excited whispers.

Farquhar provides this necessary interlude in order that the girls may show the audience they are conscious of the trick being played. With Mrs Sullen's cynical remark, 'Did not I tell you that my lord would find a way to come at you?', we are to learn that they also intend to deceive their mother. Thus with Lady Bountiful the only honest and unaffected character on the stage, her normality of speech and behaviour will provide the level from which the other characters' voices and gestures must depart, and determines their positions and movements in relation to each other and to the audience. Archer's attempts to win Mrs Sullen and Mrs Sullen's to tease Archer, Aimwell's to deceive Dorinda and Dorinda's to hide the truth from Lady Bountiful, invite every shade of innuendo, asides within asides and sundry styles of gulling.

Aimwell is carried on stage in the chair the old lady provides, and is seen '*counterfeiting a swoon*' for all he is worth, with spasms and moans as excruciating as Lady Bountiful's innocent concern for his well-being permits. Archer becomes his stage-manager, so that when the old lady takes Aimwell's hand on one side, Archer invites Dorinda to take the free hand on the other. The left and right sides of Aimwell's body now behave differently, and Dorinda's side distinctly shows more independent life than Lady Bountiful's.

DORINDA. Poor gentleman! – O! – he has got my hand within his, and squeezes it unmercifully –
LADY BOUNTIFUL. 'Tis the violence of his convulsion, child.
ARCHER. O madam, he's perfectly possessed in these cases – he'll bite if you don't have a care.

DORINDA. O, my hand! my hand!

LADY BOUNTIFUL. What's the matter with the foolish girl? I have got this hand open, you see, with a great deal of ease.

ARCHER. Ay, but, madam, your daughter's hand is somewhat warmer than your ladyship's, and the heat of it draws the force of the spirits that way.

Archer's original law of thermodynamics does not deceive anyone but Lady Bountiful, and the moment is one of pure farce.

At this point in the seduction of Dorinda a remark from Mrs Sullen to Archer suggests that these two are, as it were, outside the inner action of the scene of the sick man, since both speak apart as if from a position of superior observation:

MRS SULLEN. I find, friend, you're very learned in these sorts of fits.

ARCHER. 'Tis no wonder, madam, for I'm often troubled with them myself; I find myself extremely ill at this minute. (*Looking hard at Mrs Sullen*).

And the little aside from Mrs Sullen to the audience, 'I fancy I could find a way to cure you', probably indicates her downstage promixity to the pit. Their tone of voice is here more intimate and ironic, and the dialogue is on the edge of the salacious.

When Lady Bountiful cross-questions Archer about the cause of his master's sickness, the ever-resourceful Archer resorts to a quasi-medical description of *love-sickness*, and in this the play of words speaks, not for Aimwell's, but for Archer's feelings. As he speaks, he continues to 'look hard' at Mrs Sullen, and even to move towards her, so that while the old lady is preoccupied with her remedies, Mrs Sullen and her lover lightly engage in subtly perceptible motions of flirtation. To the delight of the audience, meanwhile, Archer's verbose attempt to explain the effects of love-sickness elicits a simple diagnosis from Lady Bountiful: 'Wind, nothing but wind!'

Archer's more sophisticated word-play is nicely interwoven with the business of Aimwell's roaming arm and hand, so that Dorinda can be in no doubt, if she ever was, that he is conscious and knows what he is doing. This amusing side of the stage action now reaches a peak with a great joke at Aimwell's expense. When Lady Bountiful administers smelling salts to his nose it becomes impossible for him to maintain his pretence, and involuntarily, let us say, he jerks and sneezes.

LADY BOUNTIFUL. O, he recovers! – The lavender water – some feathers to burn under his nose – Hungary water to rub his temples. – O, he comes to himself! – Hem a little, sir, hem. – Gipsy, bring the cordial-water.

At this intelligence, Aimwell takes fright and '*seems to awake in amaze*', no doubt coughing and spluttering. The sprinkling of the lavender water and the burning of feathers under the nose is a treatment which performs an infallible cure even before it is applied.

When Aimwell finally rises and looks about him, Farquhar completes the picture by having him slip into some atrociously well-larded verses after the style of Lovelace, and he speaks them with suitably sweeping gestures and his eyes cast heavenward. Lady Bountiful's innocent comment follows:

LADY BOUNTIFUL. Delirious, poor gentleman!
ARCHER. Very delirious, madam, very delirious.

It is not clear whether their verdict is on the state of Aimwell's health or on his poetry, but Archer's agreement acknowledges that the good lady shall have the last word. Better yet, she also deals the last blow when she makes Aimwell quaff a cordial 'of her own making', which stops the ardent lover in his tracks. In her innocence, paradoxically, Lady Bountiful seems to have won the day, and Dryden's forced humours and unnatural events are arranged at the last for a richly comic irony.

Of Farquhar Hazlitt wrote, 'There is a constant ebullition of gay, laughing invention, cordial good-humour, and fine animal spirits in his writings', and he found that 'he makes us laugh from pleasure oftener than from malice'. Echoing this judgment in *Restoration Comedy*, Bonamy Dobrée decided that Farquhar was not so much critical of manners as he was 'intent upon lively action and the telling of a roguish tale': 'It is all fun and frolic with him, a question of disguises and counterfeits, the gaining of fortunes, and even of burglarious entries . . . . In his dramatic world very little is impossible; it is full of Rabelaisian gaiety touched with a satire that is as light as a feather' (pp. 162–3). On the evidence of this scene from *The Beaux' Stratagem*, one would not wish to change a word of this.

A TEMPLE OF PAGAN DELIGHTS

That the Restoration was a time when libertinism was fashionable and that the stage enjoyed an extraordinary licence is not disputed. 'I fancy poor Congreve's theatre is a temple of pagan delights and mysteries not permitted except among the heathens', wrote Thackeray in his *English Humourists* (p. 38). Yet some distinction between a bawdy comedy and bawdy in comedy should be made. It is a distinction between ends and means, the former intended to debauch, the latter to induce laughter; and while it is impossible to be sure that a bawdy play was written to debase its audience, a proper ridicule is never absent whenever bawdy is used in word or deed.

One reader's list of ribaldries from the unspeakable theatre may be very like another's. Pepys was a representative judge, and when he heard of the excesses in Thomas Killigrew's *The Parson's Wedding*, he mentions it in his diary as 'a bawdy loose play'. But he was far from dismissing it with contempt, and when he reported that it was 'acted by nothing but women at the King's House', he ventured to add, 'I am glad of it' (11 October 1664). Some scenes would not have been acceptable in the next century, as we may judge by their stage directions:

- *The Parson discovered in bed, and the Bawd with him* (IV.1).
- *Enter Wild and Careless in their shirts, with drawers under; nightgowns on, and in slippers* (IV.7).
- *Master Sadd and Constant, undressed, and buttoning themselves as they go* (V.3).

By today's standards none of these samples seems particularly flagrant, and, needless to say, all of these characters are offered as objects of the broadest laughter. With women playing all the parts, the general state of undress was no doubt given an extra edge, but always at the expense of the male sex.

Pepys was less pleased with James Howard's *All Mistaken; or, The Mad Couple*, in spite of the popularity of Charles Hart and Nell Gwyn in the mad parts. Yet Pepys made no accusation of bawdy, even though in act II Philidor is pursued by six jilted mistresses one after another:

So here comes one of my promised virgins,
Nay a second one too – a third – a fourth . . .
A fifth – a sixth – welcome blessed
Half-dozen, now will I go master my
Nurses and children too, and go against the
Great Turk.

Philidor is well matched with Mirida, evidently a tease at a very young age: 'I'm now but five years i'the teens, / And I have fooled five several men.' It is true that Pepys's opinion of the play slipped: from calling it 'a pretty pleasant play' on 20 September 1667, he thought it 'but an ordinary play' on 28 December and 'a mean play altogether' on 29 July 1668; but he saw it three times, and what is more, he took his wife with him.

Dryden's *The Assignation; or, Love in a Nunnery* flaunts a prurient subtitle. It was too late for our weathercock Pepys to have seen it, and from the author all we know is that it 'succeeded ill in the representation'. A little of the dialogue from act I, when the sisters Laura and Violetta introduce themselves, may seem to qualify the play as bawdy, essentially because of their youth:

LAURA. Are you fit at fifteen to be trusted with a maidenhead?
VIOLETTA. How! I a novice, at ripe fifteen? I would have you know that I have
    killed my man before I was fourteen, and now am ready for another
    execution.
LAURA. A very forward rosebud: you open apace, gentlewoman.

Yet those girls are not unusually precocious for the comedy of the day, and
it is necessary to remember that they are stage creatures who will suitably
meet their match in a pair of licentious young men, Aurelium and Camillo.

Shadwell's *Epsom Wells* is numbered among the bawdiest of Restoration comedies, and includes the following titillating by-play between silly
Carolina and the rake Woodly after he offers to kiss her:

CAROLINA. Well, I vow you're a pleasant man, but you go too fast.
WOODLY. For your lover of the last age I grant you; but the world is well mended
    since, fair ladies and fortified towns yield upon easier terms nowadays.
    (*Offers to kiss her again.*) Now I see you dare not stand the trial, 'tis e'en so;
    I'll be hanged if you han't crooked legs too. (*Offers to lift up her coats.*)
CAROLINA. I had rather you should think so than take the pains to satisfy you; but
    I vow you'd make one burst, you have such a way with you, ha, ha, ha.
    (II.1)

Even Carolina has wit enough to take care of herself, and if the episode
seems to contain cause for offence, Montague Summers's word for the
style of this play is 'vivacious'. This example of sexual pantomime is not
isolated among all the boisterous comedies written for the English stage in
the seventeenth century.

Many have decided that the most indecent play of the age is Dryden's
Limberham; or, The Kind Keeper, thought to be a rollicking 'satire' against
keeping, the widespread vice at court. According to Gerard Langbaine in
An Account of the English Dramatick Poets of 1691, it was accorded an
unfavourable reception because of its indelicacy: 'In this play (which I
take to be the best comedy of [Dryden's]) he so much exposed the keeping
part of the town, that the play was stopped when it had but thrice appeared
on the stage.' The immediate cause for concern was the setting of the play
in the pious and hypocritical Mrs Saintly's 'boarding-house', which for all
intents and purposes is a bawdy-house, and the adventures therein which
are of gentlemen, old and young, who are keepers. The action of the play is
otherwise that of farce of the ripest kind, as in III.2 where Dryden has
contrived to bring three women together in young Woodall's chamber.
First Mrs Brainsick, the married gentlewoman, awaits him alone, until
she hears a '*noise*':

Hark, I hear him coming. – Ah me! the steps beat double: he comes not alone. If it
should be my husband with him! where shall I hide myself? I see no other place,

but under his bed: I must lie as silently as my fear will suffer me. Heaven send me safe again to my own chamber!

And as she *'creeps under the bed'*. The girl with Woodall is Mrs Tricksy, the kept mistress of Limberham:

WOODALL. Well, fortune at the last is favourable, and now you are my prisoner.
TRICKSY. After a quarter of an hour, I suppose, I shall have my liberty upon easy
    terms. But pray let us parley a little first.
WOODALL. Let it be upon the bed then. Please you to sit?

On their first kiss, *'Mrs Brainsick pinches him from underneath the bed'*, and then she proceeds to run a pin into them, with predictable results.

But this is not all. Mrs Saintly's voice is heard outside, and in alarm Mrs Tricksy *'gets into the bed, and draws the clothes over her.'* Saintly has come in search of Woodall to tell him that she will betray him – unless he 'atone'. How he might have to satisfy her is left unsaid, for she *'throws herself suddenly down upon the bed; Tricksy shrieks and rises; Mrs Brainsick rises from under the bed in a fright.'* Woodall's comment to the audience is, 'So! here's a fine business! my whole seraglio up in arms!' This bedroom imbroglio would compare favourably with any in Feydeau, and the modern verdict on the play now seems to be beside the point, if Allardyce Nicoll's reaction to reading it for his *History of English Drama* is typical: 'A sickening atmosphere of sex and of animalism hangs over it . . . . There is nothing to atone for the foetid odour that seems to hang about it' (vol. I, p. 230). Of course, in the scene of Woodall's seraglio, as in the 'china' scene in *The Country Wife*, there is little to see and everything to imagine.

Horner's china scene is of special interest because, from the exchange between Olivia and Elizabeth in the second act of *The Plain Dealer*, it is evident that Wycherley himself felt that he may have overstepped the bounds. Yet he undoubtedly gave his delighted audience the riposte it wanted when he had Eliza say, 'You'll pardon me, I cannot think the worse of my china for that of the playhouse.' By implying this distinction between what was less acceptable in real life and more acceptable in the theatre, the playwright was reminding his audience of the abiding principle of excess, exaggeration and licence which finds an appropriate place in the playworld of comedy. When Aphra Behn offered an argument in her own defence in the preface to *The Lucky Chance*, she arrived at the same conclusion: bawdy scenes are not by necessity indecent, they 'so naturally fall into the places they are designed for, and are so proper to the business, that there is not the least fault to be found with them'. 'Bawdy in comedy' was a determination the Restoration stage made for itself when it judged what was a necessary element in sexual farce; whether it was well or badly written or performed was another matter.

The way a bawdy scene should be performed is very much to the point. Summers was untroubled by any suggestion of indecency in the plays he promoted or produced with the Phoenix Society, and observed that in their own time 'even the racier scenes of comedy were given a breadth and vigour which would, I apprehend, be infinitely surprising to a modern audience' (*The Restoration Theatre*, p. 189). And so it proved. When the plays were revived in the twentieth century, at a time when their reputation was still very low, those commentators who feared the worst were in fact disarmed by the style of the playing. In *The Provoked Wife*, III.3, Bellinda says that she always blows her nose rather than be caught laughing at 'a nasty thing in a play': there was no nose-blowing at the unexpurgated and unashamed production of this play at the King's Hall, Covent Garden in 1919, nor any bursting of stays in an attempt to contain the laughter, according to the correspondent for *The Times* on 15 January. There could be a variation on nose-blowing: at *The Country Wife* in 1924, Hubert Griffiths found himself wondering why the lady behind him sighed every time a spade was called a spade (*Observer*, 24 February) – she was of the tribe who contended that sex on the stage was a bore, a view which Kenneth Tynan later considered to be an 'odd defensive reflex' (*Observer*, 16 December 1956).

Not all of Restoration comedy is a comedy of sex, but so much of it is that it is imperative that its rules for performance be observed, and the chief of these is that scenes of seduction, cuckolding and the like must be funny if they are not to be offensive. They are not to trouble the spectator with the state of his immortal soul. Before the Justices of Middlesex considered that the playhouses were nurseries of debauchery and blasphemy, and before Jeremy Collier's word was out that 'the business of plays is to recommend virtue and discountenance vice', sex comedy had to be sport and obey the laws of sport. Any just evaluation turns upon the degree of success or failure in the way the sport is played.

The competitors in the game were to be instantaneously recognizable as such. The ignorance, not the innocence, of country girls and restless wives made them a prime target for seduction, and the jealousy of elderly husbands made them the natural butt for cuckoldry. Outwitting members of the opposite sex carried some of the spice of breaking a social code, and was therefore equivalent to the pleasure of outwitting society itself. For both sexes, the comedy was very much in the business of exploring a degree of sexual freedom outside the bonds and burdens of matrimony, and to ridicule the conventions of marriage struck at the heart of society's most familiar ritual. The playwrights knew all this. The farceur Wycherley has the modern reputation of being the satirical scourge of his generation, but in the light of performance this judgment smacks of an academic fabrication to justify in the good name of *saeva indignatio* and corrective comedy the amorality of the game he played. For in the mode of farce, the operative word is 'ridicule' – as a general rule a ridicule that excluded moralizing and romanticizing. There was much brisk talk of sparks and coquettes, pimps and bawds, whoring and the pox, but almost nothing of faithfulness and sincerity, love and courtship. There was no room for true passion, no time for marital bliss; but then, in the play-world, there were few pregnancies and certainly no babies. When the rules for comedy changed in the eighteenth century, the cold, hard puppetry of the characters and the broad, high style of the action were swept away, and the old, irresponsible theatre game ended rather abruptly.

THE SPIRIT, THE STYLE AND THE REVIVALS

It would be unkind to end on a hint of diminished responsibility in a study which purports to be a celebration of a particular achievement in dramatic art. We should remember, rather, the efforts of Montague Summers with his omnivorous scholarship, and the Stage Society and the Phoenix Society for their insistence upon testing the Restoration plays some 250 years out of their time. We should remember also Nigel Playfair in the heyday of his tenure at the Lyric Theatre, Hammersmith, in the 1920s, with his successors. And we should not forget the actors who taught themselves how to act in a style that was alien to them.

The English-speaking stage owes more than it has acknowledged to the Sunday-night productions of the English Stage Society and the Phoenix Society (and others like the Fellowship Players, the Three Hundred Club and the Renaissance Society). These groups offered to fill the gaps left by the commercial theatre. Partly in imitation of the Russian 'studio' productions, such societies enabled the interested public to see rare full-length plays performed by mostly professional casts for one or two performances at a time. Writing of the Stage Society in the *London Mercury* in November 1929, Clifford Bax recorded that it was 'conducted by enthusiastic amateurs and sustained by the work and goodwill of the profession . . . . I suppose that every actor and actress who has been famous in England during this century must have played for the Society.' The productions were put together on a shoe-string and everything was done in the best sense of the term 'amateur' – for the love of the art. There was no money to experiment with design, and little for costumes, but at least the lost plays were brought out of obscurity and their unfamiliar style tried and tested.

These revivals had everything to do with the change in the critical view of Restoration comedy. There were some who maintained an unshakable attitude, like J.T. Grein, who wrote of the Stage Society's *Love for Love*, 'I do not care for unexpurgated dialogue in the presence of women' (*Sunday Times*, 22 April 1917). 'Tarn' of the *Spectator* reviewed the Phoenix's *Marriage à la Mode* and found it 'exceedingly unedifying', arguing that 'the whole structure of the play is infected with the pestilential morality of the day' (17 January 1920). St John Ervine could see no justification for producing the Phoenix's 'insufferably dull' *Amphitryon* (*Observer*, 4 June 1922). And there were some who hedged their verdicts, like the *Times*'s correspondent who was in two minds in 1915 when he reviewed *The Recruiting Officer*: 'The stuff of the play is fundamental human nature, robust and full-blooded, here and there rather coarse for modern taste, though with no real harm in it' (26 January).

Yet the old comedies enjoyed a striking success, and a variety of explanations were offered for it. One was that it was important to play it in period, and Sydney Carroll wrote of the Stage Society's *The Provoked Wife* of 1919 that those actors 'who conceived their performances in the modern drawing-room spirit, who were hurried in speech, slovenly and undistinguished in manner, consequently created a sense of dullness' (*Sunday Times*, 19 January). Another was that the plays reflected modern taste, and the anonymous reviewer of the Phoenix's *Love for Love* for the *Saturday Review* decided that 'public taste today, so far as indecency is concerned, really seems very much that of 1795' (2 April 1921). In recent years this curious line of argument is still faintly to be heard: Alan Pryce-Jones saw the Old Vic's *The Double Dealer* in 1959 and wrote that 'the society which Congreve depicted was as disillusioned as our own' (30 August).

The general consensus was, however, that this strange material leaped to life when it was performed. From the first revivals was heard the cry that the plays were better to act than to read. Hubert Griffith at the Phoenix's *The Country Wife* in 1924 joined in the chorus of pleased surprise when he wrote, 'There is all the difference in the world between reading such a play as this and seeing it acted' (*Observer*, 24 February), while Edward Shanks at the same production was more specific in saying that 'what offends in the printed page does not necessarily offend in the theatre' (*Outlook*, 23 February). When this production was offered back-to-back with Playfair's *The Way of the World* at Hammersmith, Ralph Wright in the *New Statesman* was impelled to write that 'a revolution is imperceptibly, though not so very slowly, taking place in English taste' (23 February).

Revolution was too strong a word for the rediscovery of Restoration comedy, but the test of the stage – the achievement of an appropriate verve and style – was a revelation. A.B. Walkley of *The Times* led the field in expressions of apparent enlightenment: 'These revivals set one's mouth watering', he wrote on 15 January 1919 after seeing *The Provoked Wife*, and after the success of *The Way of the World* in 1924, he felt that the old prejudice was at an end (13 February). By the 1930s and 40s is heard a new tone of critical confidence. When Ivor Brown reviewed Tyrone Guthrie's *The Country Wife* in 1936, he declared, 'The direct ethical effect of these coarse comedies is probably nothing at all. But what *is* bad for the community is hypocrisy' (11 October), and in 1948 *The Times* opened its review of John Burrell's *The Way of the World* by saying that we no longer reiterate the moral strictures of Jeremy Collier and William Archer, but we instead 'experience the characters in all their glittering absurdity without judging them' (23 October). I like best the possibly unintentional irony of the same reviewer's comment on Anthony Quayle's production of *The Relapse* the year before: 'It makes an unexpectedly good addition', he said, 'to the Christmas entertainments' (18 December 1947).

Summers and the Phoenix Society had wanted to show that the comedies were good and that they acted well. This could only be done by producing them as authentically as possible and without bowdlerizing them: 'not in any spirit of pedantic antiquarianism, but nevertheless with due regard to the actual conditions of the theatre for which [they were] written,' he wrote in his appendix to *The Restoration Theatre*; 'I had always maintained that the drama of the Restoration – and for that matter any other drama too – fully to be appreciated and understood must be seen upon the stage, and the plays moreover must be given as nearly the original production as modern methods and changed conditions will reasonably permit' (p. 324). In practice, Norman Marshall reported in *The Other Theatre*, 'the Phoenix productions had a continuity of style unusual in the work of Sunday societies. This was mainly due to the fact that nearly all the plays were produced by Allan Wade in a setting by Norman Wilkinson.' Marshall goes on to add,

The chief feature of Wade's productions was their simplicity. Nothing was allowed to interfere with continuity of action and swiftness of speech. He reduced furniture and props to a minimum. He seemed at his happiest as a producer with a bare stage which gave him complete freedom to design bold movement and striking pictorial groupings. He never attempted to stunt or fantasticate the plays. He believed in allowing them to stand or fall on their own merits. (p. 77)

In effect Wade was making sure that the Phoenix productions carried no taint of what was called in the profession 'the old *School for Scandal* way' of playing comedy, that is, as picturesque nineteenth-century *divertisse-ments*, in John Gielgud's account, with 'pages, minuets and animals' (*Stage Directions*, p. 64).

Nigel Playfair also dared to revive the old comedy, and for a wider public. He too cherished the ambition of giving his generation 'an opportunity of seeing all the leading classics of the eighteenth century upon the stage within the space of their theatre-going days' (*The Story of the Lyric Theatre*, p. 212). He did not fulfil his ambition, but he managed an unprecedented run of 3½ years with *The Beggar's Opera* (from June 1920 to December 1923) for a start, although, sad to relate, this production failed in America and Australia. The next year (1924) he followed John Gay with Congreve, and risked all he had achieved on the ill-omened *The Way of the World* and made a success of it. Later, but less successfully, he directed *The Beaux' Stratagem* in 1927 and *The Old Bachelor* in 1931.

If a certain lack of faith in his material and in his audience led Playfair, as we saw, to over-decorate his productions with period trimmings and trappings, he managed to attract West End audiences to an important drama they knew little about. Marshall was not alone in finding his way of engaging an audience's interest 'irritatingly obvious': the members of the orchestra were dressed in costume and periwig, and Playfair had 'a maddening fondness for footmen promenading around the stage lighting or extinguishing candles' (*The Other Theatre*, p. 36). James Agate cheekily quoted Jane Austen's Mr Bennet to his daughter Mary: 'That will do, child; you have delighted us sufficiently' (*Red Letter Nights*, p. 44). Nevertheless, even Marshall hastened to add that Playfair's aim was frankly 'to make new entertainments out of old plays' at a time when the English theatre was sadly lacking in style of any sort (p. 37).

More importantly, there were other signs that Playfair was working in the right direction. If his settings were too highly coloured and prettified, he made no attempt to localize them. In Gielgud's words, they 'were merely drop scenes and wings, and served as a background (but not as a home) for the characters in the play' (*Stage Directions*, p. 67). Above all, everyone was impressed by his practice of having his actors deliver their lines directly to the house. Marshall again:

When he began his work at the Lyric the whole technique of acting and production in England was based on a pretence of ignoring the audience and isolating the actors in their own world behind the footlights. Playfair's method was to accept the presence of the audience, to make them a partner in the play, and to establish a feeling of intimacy between the stage and auditorium. It was a method of production ideally suited to the Lyric with its small, friendly auditorium. (p. 41)

There are other contributors to this honourable history. Barry Jackson was 'not over-fond of the Restoration dramatists and their cynical rakes', according to J.C. Trewin (*The Birmingham Repertory Theatre*, p. 184),

50 Edith Evans as Mrs Sullen and Nigel Playfair as Gibbet, *The Beaux' Stratagem*,
Lyric Theatre, Hammersmith, 1927

but he too made it his business to revive the old comedies in the 1920s and
30s. In *The Confederacy* in 1920, *Marriage à la Mode* in 1928 and *She
Would If She Could* at Malvern in 1931, together with several eighteenth-
century plays, he achieved a style which was 'more than costume fidgets'
(p. 61). In 1924 J.B. Fagan directed a joyful *Love for Love* at the Oxford
Playhouse in what he called a 'presentational' production on a virtually
bare apron stage after the manner of Jacques Copeau's *tréteau nu* at the
Vieux Colombier in Paris. John Gielgud played Valentine to Flora

Robson's Angelica in this production, and it was he who carried the banner for Congreve thereafter as both actor and director. A full account of Gielgud's enthusiasm for the Restoration, with that of a few distinguished contemporaries like Alec Clunes, John Clements and Anthony Quayle, would, however, take us too far into the future.

The story must nevertheless acknowledge the work of two actresses. Playfair's productions were blessed with the services of Edith Evans as Millamant, Mrs Sullen and Laetitia Fondlewife; she later played Lady Fidget and Mrs Malaprop. She was an actress with an uncanny sense of period style, and one who also believed in studying the original stage conditions of a play in order to arrive at its proper mode of presentation. Playfair believed that 'the particular method of the delivery of the words' furnished 'a sort of review and criticism – a *parody* if you like, but a parody which expresses admiration and not contempt' (*The Story of the Lyric Theatre*, p. 95), and Evans's concern was very much for the elusive Restoration 'style', in the knowledge that the manner in which the comedies were performed would take their audience to the centre of their meaning and experience. Theory apart, it was she who most seemed to embody the period and work the miracle. In the words of J.C. Trewin from his biography of the actress:

Other players have explored the Restoration. One feels that Edith Evans has always been there before them, eager as a resident to show them around. She can let a sentence stream out upon the air, a silken scarf unfurling in a light wind. She can let the voice crackle exquisitely through an intricate pattern, a mazy damascene, or else flash a speech home with a thrust-and-twist that closes the door and turns the key. It becomes the voice of the period. (p. 61)

With her, the way the words were spoken dictated the spirit of the play, and in James Agate's view, her acting was (echoing Hazlitt on Congreve's style) 'a shower of brilliant conceits, a new triumph of wit, a new conquest over dullness' (*Sunday Times*, 10 February 1924).

For more about such essentials, one turns to another actress who worked with Playfair, Athene Seyler, whose contribution to an understanding of the comedy has been unique. The publication in 1943 of her little collection of letters to Stephen Haggard, *The Craft of Comedy*, was a first attempt to record insights into the art she practised with a sparkling sense of humour. She has told how as a child she danced the hornpipe, 'during which, to the intense pleasure of the audience, my knickers fell down, so I thought perhaps I was in for comedy'. Can we see in this anecdote something of her attitude to portraying Melantha, Mrs Frail and Lady Fidget? In her practical analysis of a scene from *Love for Love* (pp. 67–79), she writes of her belief that comedy is a comment on life from outside, an observation of human nature:

51 Edith Evans as Lady Fidget and Michael Redgrave as Horner, *The Country Wife*, Old Vic, 1936

Comedy seems to be standing outside a character or situation and pointing out one's delight in certain aspects of it. For this reason it demands the cooperation of another mind on which this observation is to be made – the audience . . . . The intention of your job as a comedian is to point out something to an audience, and that the audience's reaction to this makes up an integral part of your job. You must create a delicate thread of understanding of the character you are portraying between yourself and your spectator, so that, in a way, you jointly throw light upon it. I wonder if this strikes you as rather shocking? (pp. 8–9)

She also believes that high comedy is 'technically dependent on accents of emphasis', upsetting proportion, sharpening the angles of character. But comic acting requires that the actor first see the truth of a character before it is possible for him to upset its balance. In this, actor and audience share a secret, and recognition of that secret expresses itself in laughter from the audience. The conspiracy of the stage with the house is a matter of careful planning in style: 'A laugh arises from the quick reaction of one character to another, and it is often like a rally at tennis – the quicker one returns the impact of a remark, the sooner comes the volley of an audience's pleasure' (p. 39). An understanding of the manners and customs of a period, she believes, is inextricably bound up with the rhythm of a play's dialogue and 'the mixture of precision and nonchalance' with which it is delivered, so different from the normal speech of the twentieth century.

Seyler's recognition of the role the *audience* must play in the success of Restoration comedy reinforces the emphasis in this study. For it is true that while the comedy can never be fully recreated in circumstances other than its own, a modern actor or director must have some sense of the first conditions of performance in order to recover its original spirit. Restoration style is not a collection of outmoded period mannerisms imposed upon the lines, but an integrated and harmonious effect of showing and sharing what they stood for. A fastidious speech by a Millamant is to be matched by a hand on a fastidious fan and a glance from a fastidious eye; at that moment, actress and audience are delighted to have the fastidiousness in common. If the scene is rumbustious, then the actors must work to have the stage and audience share alike in the pleasure of rumbustiousness. Therein lies the universal language of good comic theatre, a mysterious infectiousness, by which its common humanity can cross period, and even national, boundaries.

52 Athene Seyler as Melantha, *Marriage à la Mode*, Lyric Theatre, Hammersmith, 1920

A partial list of Restoration comedies revived in the twentieth century

ABBREVIATIONS

after 1660
DG	Duke's Theatre, Dorset Garden
DL	Theatre Royal, Drury Lane
HM	Queen's Theatre, Haymarket
LIF	Duke's Theatre, Lincoln's Inn Fields
TRB	Theatre Royal, Bridges Street

after 1900
Birm	Birmingham Repertory Theatre
Cam	Festival Theatre, Cambridge
Ev	Everyman Theatre, Hampstead
Ham	Lyric Theatre, Hammersmith
NT	National Theatre
OV	Old Vic
Ox	Oxford Playhouse
PS	Phoenix Society
PT	Prospect Theatre Company
RC	Royal Court Theatre
RSC	Royal Shakespeare Company
SS	Stage Society

APHRA BEHN

	IST PROD.		REVIVED		
The Lucky Chance	1686	DL	1984	RC	Jules Wright, dir.
The Rover	1677	DG	1984		Upstream Theatre

COLLEY CIBBER

The Comical Lovers	1707	HM	1963		Questors Theatre
She Would and She Would Not	1702	DL	1955		Salisbury Playhouse

WILLIAM CONGREVE

The Double Dealer	1693	DL	1916	SS	Queens Theatre, 14–15 May
			1948	Birm	
			1959	OV	Michael Benthall, dir. (from Edinburgh Festival)

252

			1969	RC	William Gaskill, dir.
			1978	NT	Peter Wood, dir.
Love for Love	1695	LIF	1917	SS	Aldwych Theatre, 15–16 Apr.
			1921	PS, Ham	20–22 Mar.
			1924	Ox	J.B. Fagan, dir.
			1932	Cam	Norman Marshall, dir. transferred to Arts Theatre
			1934	OV	Tyrone Guthrie, dir.
			1940		New York Players
			1943		Phoenix Theatre/ Haymarket John Gielgud, dir.
			1947		The Royale, New York John Gielgud, dir.
			1965	NT/OV	Peter Wood, dir.
			1985	NT	Peter Wood, dir.
The Old Bachelor	1692	DL	1924	PS	Regents Theatre, 1–2 June
			1931	Ham	Nigel Playfair, dir.
The Way of the World	1700	LIF	1904		Court Theatre
			1918	SS	King's Hall, 12–14 May
			1924	Ham	Nigel Playfair, dir.
			1927		Wyndham's Theatre, Leon M. Leon, dir.
			1948	OV	New Theatre John Burrell, dir.
			1953	Ham	John Gielgud, dir.
			1954		Unnamed Society, Manchester
			1956		Saville Theatre John Clements, dir.
			1969	NT/OV	Michael Langham, dir.
			1976		Stratford, Ontario Robin Phillips, dir.
			1978	RSC	Aldwych Theatre John Barton, dir.
			1984		Chichester Festival Theatre William Gaskill, dir.

JOHN DRYDEN

Amphitryon	1690	DL	1922	PS	Daly's Theatre, 28–30 May

The Assignation   1672 LIF   1925 PS   Aldwych Theatre,
                                                    25–26 Jan.
Marriage à la Mode 1672 LIF   1920 PS, Ham 8–9 Feb.
                                    1928 Birm   W.G. Fay, dir., 14 Apr.
                                    1928 Cam   Terence Gray, dir.,
                                                    3 Dec.
                                    1946   St James Theatre
                                                    John Clements, dir.

SIR GEORGE ETHEREGE

The Man of Mode   1676 DG   1965 PT   Georgian Theatre,
                                                    Richmond
                                                    Toby Robertson, dir.
                                    1971 RSC   Aldwych Theatre
                                                    Terry Hands, dir.
*She Would If She
  Could*   1667 LIF   1931 Birm   Malvern Festival
                                    1979   Greenwich Theatre
                                                    Jonathan Miller, dir.

GEORGE FARQUHAR

*The Beaux'
Stratagem*   1707 HM   1919 SS   Haymarket Theatre,
                                                    4 Feb.
                                    1925   Cambridge ADC
                                    1926   Maddermarket Theatre,
                                                    Norwich
                                    1927 Ham   Nigel Playfair, dir.
                                    1928   Royalty Theatre, New
                                                    York
                                    1949   Phoenix/Lyric Theatres
                                                    John Clements, dir.
                                    1957   Phoenix Company, New
                                                    York
                                    1957 Birm
                                    1963   Ashcroft Theatre,
                                                    Croyden
                                    1970 NT/OV   William Gaskill, dir.
                                    1985   Stratford, Ontario
                                                    Edwin Stephenson, dir.
The Constant Couple 1699 DL   1943   Arts Theatre
                                    1951   Winter Garden,
                                                    New York
                                                    Alec Clunes, dir.

			1967	PT	Arts, Cambridge/ New Theatre Richard Cottrell, dir.
Love and a Bottle	1698	DL	1969		Nottingham Playhouse William Chappell, dir.
The Recruiting Officer	1706	DL	1916	SS	Haymarket Theatre, 24 Jan.
			1941		Garrick Theatre
			1943		Arts Theatre Alec Clunes, dir.
			1956		Bristol Old Vic
			1961		Unity Theatre
			1963	NT/OV	William Gaskill, dir.
			1970	PT	Arts Cambridge Richard Cottrell, dir.
The Twin Rivals	1702	DL	1912/ 13		Bath
			1981	RSC	The Other Place John Caird, dir.

THOMAS OTWAY

The Soldier's Fortune	1680	DG	1926	PS	Renaissance Theatre, Apr.
			1935		Ambassadors Theatre
			1964	PT	Oxford Playhouse Toby Robertson, dir.
			1967	RC	Peter Gill, dir.
			1981	Ham	Sheila Hancock, dir. Phoenix Theatre

EDWARD RAVENSCROFT

| *The London Cuckolds* | 1681 | DG | 1979 | RC | Stuart Burge, dir. |
| | | | 1985 | Ham | Stuart Burge, dir. |

THOMAS SHADWELL

| *Epsom Wells* | 1672 | DG | 1969 | | Thorndike Theatre, Leatherhead Anthony Wiles, dir. |

Appendix A

SIR JOHN VANBRUGH

The Confederacy	1705	HM	1920	Birm	
			1924	Ox	J.B. Fagan, dir.
			1951	Birm/OV	Douglas Seal, dir.
			1964	PT/Ox	Toby Robertson, dir.
			1974		Chichester Festival
					Wendy Toye, dir.
The Provoked Wife	1697	LIF	1919	SS	King's Hall, 12–14 Jan.
			1936		Embassy Theatre
					John Fernald, dir.
			1963	PT	Richmond/Oxford/
					Vaudeville Theatre
					Toby Robertson, dir.
			1967		Stratford East
					Joan Littlewood, dir.
			1973		Greenwich Theatre
					Frank Proud, dir.
			1980	NT	Peter Wood, dir.
The Relapse	1696	DL	1931	Birm	
			1947	Ham	Phoenix Theatre
					Anthony Quayle, dir.
			1950		Theatre Guild, New York
			1954		Richmond Theatre
			1963		Mermaid Theatre
					Wendy Toye, dir.
			1967	RSC	Aldwych Theatre
					Trevor Nunn, dir.
			1983	Ham	William Gaskill, dir.

GEORGE VILLIERS, DUKE OF BUCKINGHAM

The Chances	1666	TRB	1922	PS	Shaftesbury Theatre, 29–30 Jan.
			1962		Chichester Festival Theatre
					Laurence Olivier, dir.
The Rehearsal	1671	TRB	1925	PS	Regent Theatre, 5–6 July
			1959		Hovenden Theatre Club

WILLIAM WYCHERLEY

The Country Wife	1674	DL	1924	PS	Regent Theatre, 17–18 Feb.
			1926	Ev	

			1934		Ambassadors Theatre Baliol Holloway, dir.
			1936	OV	Tyrone Guthrie, dir. (transferred to New York)
			1940		Little Theatre Miles Malleson, dir.
			1955		Theatre Royal, Stratford E. Tony Richardson, dir.
			1956	RC	George Devine, dir.
			1957		New York Playwright's Company
			1963	Birm	
			1965		Lincoln Center, New York
			1966		Nottingham Playhouse Ronald Magill, dir.
			1969		Chichester Festival Theatre Robert Chetwyn, dir.
			1977		Peter Hall and Stewart Trotter, dir.
			1985	Ox	OUDS Richard Williams, dir.
The Gentleman Dancing-Master	1672	DG	1924		Maddermarket Theatre, Norwich
			1925		Renaissance Theatre, Regent Theatre
			1963		New Oxford Playhouse
The Plain Dealer	1676	DL	1925		Renaissance Theatre, Scala Theatre
			1975		LAMDA

APPENDIX B

The comedies in order of popularity

1660–1747

(from George Winchester Stone, Jun., 'The Making of the Repertory' in Robert D. Hume, *The London Theatre World, 1660–1800*, chapter 6.)

Farquhar	*The Recruiting Officer*	164 perfs.
Farquhar	*The Beaux' Stratagem*	145
Rbt. Howard	*The Committee*	131
Dryden	*The Spanish Friar*	128
Congreve	*Love for Love*	127
Congreve	*The Old Bachelor*	120
Cibber	*Love Makes a Man*	119
Cibber	*The Careless Husband*	100
Betterton	*The Amorous Widow*	98
Behn	*The Rover*	93
Farquhar	*The Constant Couple*	89
Vanbrugh	*The Relapse*	87
Cibber	*Love's Last Shift*	83
Shadwell	*The Squire of Alsatia*	81
Crowne	*Sir Courtly Nice*	74

AFTER 1900

Wycherley	*The Country Wife*
Farquhar	*The Beaux' Stratagem*
Congreve	*Love for Love*
Congreve	*The Way of the World*
Farquhar	*The Recruiting Officer*
Vanbrugh	*The Relapse*
Congreve	*The Double Dealer*
Vanbrugh	*The Confederacy*
Vanbrugh	*The Provoked Wife*
Otway	*The Soldier's Fortune*
Wycherley	*The Gentleman Dancing-Master*
Dryden	*Marriage à la Mode*

THEN EQUALLY

Villiers	*The Chances*
Farquhar	*The Constant Couple*
Etherege	*The Man of Mode*
Congreve	*The Old Bachelor*
Wycherley	*The Plain Dealer*
Villiers	*The Rehearsal*
Etherege	*She Would If She Could*
Farquhar	*The Twin Rivals*

Selected bibliography

Adventures of a Rake, The, 1759

Agate, James, *Red Letter Nights,* 1944

Archer, William, *The Old Drama and the New,* 1923

  Play-making: A Manual of Craftsmanship, 1912

Art of Making Love, or, Rules for the Conduct of Ladies and Gallants in Their Amours, The, 1676

Avery, Emmett L., 'The Restoration Audience', *Philosophical Quarterly,* XLV.1, January 1966

  and Arthur H. Scouten, *The London Stage, 1660–1800,* vol. I, 1968

Batters, Jean, *Edith Evans: A Personal Memoir,* 1977

Bayne-Powell, Rosamund, *Eighteenth-Century London Life,* 1937

Bellegarde, Jean-Baptiste Morvan de, *Reflexions upon Ridicule,* 1706

  Reflexions upon the Politeness of Manners, 1707

Bentley, Eric, *The Life of the Drama,* 1965

Bethell, S.L., *Shakespeare and the Popular Dramatic Tradition,* 1944

Betterton, Thomas, *The History of the English Stage,* 1741

Birdsall, Virginia Ogden, *Wild Civility: The English Comic Spirit on the Restoration Stage,* 1970

Boswell, Eleanor, *The Restoration Court Stage, 1660–1702,* 1932

Boucher, François, *A History of Costume in the West,* 1965

Bridges-Adams, W., *Looking at a Play,* 1947

Brooke, Iris, *Dress and Undress: Restoration and Eighteenth Century,* 1958

Brown, John Russell and Bernard Harris (eds.), *Restoration Theatre,* 1965

Brown, Laura, *English Dramatic Form, 1660–1760: An Essay in Generic History,* 1981

Brown, Tom, *Amusements Serious and Comical, and Other Works* (1700), ed. Arthur L. Hayward, 1927

Burnet, Gilbert, *The History of My Own Times,* vol. I, ed. O. Airy, 1724–34

Campbell, Lily B., *Scenes and Machines on the English Stage during the Renaissance,* 1923

Character of the Beaux, The, 1696

Chesterfield, Philip Dormer Stanhope, *Letters,* ed. Bonamy Dobrée, 1932

Chisman, Isabel and H.E. Raven-Hart, *Manners and Movements in Costume Plays,* 1934

Cibber Colley, *An Apology for the Life of Colley Cibber, Comedian,* ed. B.R.S. Fone, 1968

Coffee-House Jests, 1677

Cominges, le Comte Gaston Jean-Baptiste de, *A French Ambassador at the Court of Charles II,* trans. J.J. Jusserand, 1892

Selected bibliography

Congreve, William, *et al., Letters on Several Occasions,* 1696
Cosmo the Third, Grand Duke of Tuscany, *Travels through England during the Reign of Charles the Second,* 1669
Courtin, Antoine de, *Nouveau Traité de la Civilité Française,* 1676
  The Rules of Civility; or, Certain Ways of Deportment Observed amongst All Persons of Quality upon Several Occasions, 1671
Dennis, John, *The Critical Works,* ed. E.N. Hooker, 2 vols., 1939–43
Dobrée, Bonamy, *Restoration Comedy, 1660–1720,* 1924
Donaldson, Ian, *The World Upside-Down,* 1970
Downes, John, *Roscius Anglicanus* (1708), ed. Montague Summers, 1929
Dryden, John, *An Essay of Dramatic Poesy,* ed. Thomas Arnold, 1889
Elwin, Malcolm, *The Playgoers' Handbook to Restoration Drama,* 1928
Essex John, *The Dancing Master; or, The Whole Art and Mastery of Dancing Explained; and the Manner of Performing the Stops in Ball-Dancing Made Short and Easy,* from the French of M. Rameau, 1726
Evelyn, John, *Diary,* ed. E.S. de Beer, 1959
Farquhar, George, *Discourse upon Comedy,* 1702
Fiennes, Celia, *The Journeys of Celia Fiennes,* ed. Christopher Morris, 1949
Flecknoe, Richard, *A Short Discourse on the English Stage,* 1664
Foxon, David Fairweather, *Libertine Literature in England, 1660–1745,* 1965
Fujimura, Thomas H., *The Restoration Comedy of Wit,* 1952
Gaillard, Jean, *The Compleat Gentleman; or, Directions for the Order of Youth as to Their Breeding at Home and Travelling Abroad,* 1678
Gay, John, *Trivia; or, The Art of Walking the Streets of London,* 1716
Genest, John, *Some Account of the English Stage from the Restoration in 1660 to 1830,* vol. I, 1660–90, 1832
Gentleman Instructed in the Conduct of a Virtuous and Happy Life . . . . To which Is Added a Word to the Ladies, The, 1716
Gielgud, John, *Stage Directions,* 1963
Gilder, Rosamund, *Enter the Actress: The First Women in the Theatre,* 1931
Gildon, Charles (supposed author), *A Comparison between Two Stages,* ed. Staring B. Wells, 1942
  The Life of Mr Thomas Betterton, 1710
Gosse, Edmund, *A History of Eighteenth-Century Literature,* 1889
  Seventeenth-Century Studies, 1897
Grammont, Comte de, *Memoirs* (1713), trans. Peter Quennell, 1930
Granville-Barker, Harley, *On Dramatic Method,* 1931
Grotowski, Jerzy, *Towards a Poor Theatre,* ed. Eugenio Barba, 1969
Hawkins, Harriett, *Likenesses of Truth in Elizabethan and Restoration Drama,* 1972
Henshaw, Nancy Wanderlie, 'Graphic Sources for a Modern Approach to the Acting of Restoration Comedy', University of Pittsburgh dissertation, 1967
Highfill, Philip H., Jun., Kalman A. Burnim and Edward A. Langhans, *A Biographical Dictionary of Actors, Actresses, Musicians, Dancers, Managers, and Other Stage Personnel in London, 1660–1800,* 1973–
Holland, Norman N., *The First Modern Comedies,* 1959

Holland, Peter, *The Ornament of Action: Text and Performance in Restoration Comedy*, 1979

Hollar, Wenceslaus, *Ornatus Mulierbris Anglicanus*, 1640

Hopkins, Charles, *The Art of Love: Dedicated to the Ladies*, 1700

Hotson, Leslie, *The Commonwealth and Restoration Stage*, 1928

Hughes, Leo, *A Century of English Farce*, 1956

The Drama's Patrons: A Study of the Eighteenth-Century London Audience, 1971

Hume, Robert D., *The Development of English Drama in the Late Seventeenth Century*, 1976

'The Dorset Garden Theatre: A Review of Facts and Problems', *Theatre Notebook* 33, 1979

(ed.) *The London Theatre World, 1660–1800*, 1980

The Rakish Stage: Studies in English Drama, 1660–1800, 1983

Jerome, Joseph, *Montague Summers: A Memoir*, 1965

Kerr, Walter, *Tragedy and Comedy*, 1967

Krutch, Joseph W., *Comedy and Conscience after the Restoration*, 1949

Langbaine, Gerard, *An Account of the English Dramatick Poets*, 1691

Langhans, Edward A., 'A Conjectural Reconstruction of the Dorset Garden Theatre', *Theatre Survey* 13, November 1972

Restoration Promptbooks, 1981

'Wren's Restoration Playhouse', *Theatre Notebook* 18, 1964

Lanier, Henry Wysham, *The First English Actresses*, 1930

Lauze, F. de, *Apologie de la Danse*, trans. Joan Wildeblood, 1952

Leacroft, Richard, *The Development of the English Playhouse*, 1973

Loftis, John and Richard Southern, Marion Jones and A.H. Scouten, *The Revels History of Drama in English*, vol. v, *1660–1750*, 1976

(ed.) *Restoration Drama: Modern Essays in Criticism*, 1966

Lynch, Kathleen M., *The Social Mode of Restoration Comedy*, 1926

McAfee, Helen, *Pepys on the Restoration Stage*, 1916

Makin, Bathsua, *An Essay to Revive the Ancient Education of Gentlewomen*, 1673

Marshall, Norman, *The Other Theatre*, 1947

Mercure Galant, Le, trans. John Dancer, 1672–8

Meredith, George, *An Essay on Comedy*, ed. Lane Cooper, 1897

Milhous, Judith and Robert D. Hume, *Producible Interpretation: Eight English Plays, 1675–1707*, 1985

Thomas Betterton and the Management of Lincoln's Inn Fields, 1979

Misson, Henri de Valbourg, *Memoirs in His Travels over England, with Some Account of Scotland and Ireland*, trans. John Ozell, 1719

Mitchell, John D., *Theater: The Search for Style*, 1983

Muir, Kenneth, *The Comedy of Manners*, 1970

Mullin, Donald C., *The Development of the Playhouse*, 1970

Muralt, *Letters Describing the Character and Customs of the English and French Nations*, 1726

Nicoll, Allardyce, *A History of English Drama, 1660–1900*, vol. i, revised 1952

Oxenford, Lyn, *Producing Period Plays*, 1957

Paine, Clarence B., *The Comedy of Manners (1660–1700): A Reference Guide to the Comedy of the Restoration*, 1941

Palmer, John, *The Comedy of Manners*, 1913

Pepys, Samuel, *The Diary*, ed. G. Gregory Smith, 1905

Playfair, Nigel, *Hammersmith Hoy: A Book of Minor Revelations*, 1930
The Story of the Lyric Theatre, Hammersmith, 1925

Pope, W. Macqueen, *Ladies First*, 1952

Poulain, F. de la Barre, *The Woman as Good as a Man*, trans. A.L., 1677

Powell, Jocelyn, *Restoration Theatre Production*, 1984

Prynne, William, *Histriomastix, the Players' Scourge*, 1633

Rameau, P., *The Dancing Master* (1725), trans. Cyril W. Beaumont, 1931

Reresby, John, *Memoirs and Travels*, ed. A. Watt, 1904

Sennet, Richard, *The Fall of Public Man*, 1977

Seyler, Athene and Stephen Haggard, *The Craft of Comedy*, 1943
'Fans, Trains and Stays', *Theatre Arts* 31, 1947

Smith, John Harrington, *The Gay Couple in Restoration Comedy*, 1948

Southern, Richard, *Changeable Scenery*, 1952

Southworth, James Granville, *Vauxhall Gardens: A Chapter in the Social History of England*, 1941

Spingard, J.E., *Critical Essays of the Seventeenth Century*, 3 vols., 1907

Staves, Susan, *Players' Scepters: Fictions of Authority in the Restoration*, 1979
'A Few Kind Words for the Fop', *Studies in English Literature* 22, 1982

Summers, Montague, *A Bibliography of the Restoration Drama*, 1934
Essays in Petto, 1928
The Galanty Show: An Autobiography, ed. Brocard Sewell, 1980
The Playhouse of Pepys, 1935
The Restoration Theatre, 1934

Sutherland, James, *English Literature of the Late Seventeenth Century*, 1969

Swinburne, Algernon Charles, *Miscellanies*, 1895

Taney, Retta M., *Restoration Revivals on the British Stage (1944–1979): A Critical Survey*, 1985

Taylor, Charlene M. (ed), *George Etherege, She Would If She Could*, 1972

Thackeray, W.M. *The English Humourists of the Eighteenth Century*, ed. F.E. Bumby, 1911

Thompson, Roger (ed.), *Samuel Pepys' Penny Merriments*, 1977
Unfit for Modest Ears, 1979

Tomlinson, Kellom, *The Art of Dancing Explained by Reading and Figures*, etc., 1735

Trewin, J.C., *The Birmingham Repertory Theatre, 1913–1963*, 1963
Edith Evans, 1954
'A Shining Star' (Edith Evans), *Plays and Players*, December 1976

Underwood, Dale, *Etherege and the Seventeenth-Century Comedy of Manners*, 1957

Vincent, Samuel, *The Young Gallant's Academy*, 1674

Selected bibliography

Ward, Edward (Ned), *The London Spy: The Vanities and Vices of the Town Exposed to View* (1698–1703), ed. Arthur L. Hayward, 1927
   The London Terrefilius, 1707
   A Walk to Islington, 1701
Weales, Gerald, Introduction to Wycherley, *The Complete Plays*, 1966
Wildeblood, Joan and Peter Brinton, *The Polite World: A Guide to English Manners and Deportment from the Thirteenth to the Nineteenth Century*, 1965
Wilson, John Harold, *All the King's Ladies: Actresses of the Restoration*, 1958
   Court Wits of the Restoration, 1948
   A Preface to Restoration Drama, 1965
   'Rant, Cant and Tone on the Restoration Stage', *Studies in Philology* 52, 1955

Index

Index

Index

Davis, Moll, 134
Dekker, Thomas (?1570–1632): *The Gull's Hornbook* (1609), 9
Dennis, John (1657–1734), 7, 54, 84, 177
déshabillé, 99–100, 102ff
dialogue, 175ff
discovery (scene), 16, 27, 28ff
disguising, 232
Dobrée, Bonamy, 210, 238
doors (stage), 22, 23–4, 25, 147, 148, 151, 152, 204
Dorset, Charles Sackville, Earl of (1638–1706), 91
Dorset Garden Theatre, 13, 20, 35, 152, 203, 229
double entendre, 57, 141, 166, 201ff, 234ff
Dover, John (1644–1725): *The Mall: Or, The Modish Lovers*, 29
Downer, Alan, 16
Downes, John (?1662–1710), 26, 91, 228
Drury Lane Theatre Royal, 5, 20–1, 22, 30, 32, 35, 37, 151, 171, 204
Dryden, John (1631–1700), 3, 4, 8, 11, 25, 60, 91, 199; *Amphitryon: Or, The Two Sosia's* (1690), 37, 39, 63, 244; *The Assignation: Or, Love in a Nunnery* (1672), 26, 35, 39, 93, 239–40; *The Conquest of Granada by the Spaniards* (1670), 8; *An Essay of Dramatic Poesy* (1668), 179, 183; *An Evening's Love: Or, The Mock Astrologer* (1668), 25, 26, 143, 172, 183, 189, 212, 238; *The Kind Keeper: Or, Mr Limberham* (1678), 240; *Love Triumphant: Or, Nature Will Prevail* (1694), 201; *Marriage à la Mode* (1672), 4, 37, 63, 94, 123, 127–8, 137, 149, 164–5, 172, 179, 191–2, 194, 199, 208–9, 227, 244, 247, 251; *Secret Love: Or, The Maiden Queen* (1667), 26, 93–4, 106, 115–16, 134, 136–7, 143, 155, 190–1; *Sir Martin Mar-all: Or, The Feigned Innocence* (1667), 15, 26, 125, 156; *The Spanish Friar: Or, The Double Discovery* (1680), 87, 234; *The Wild Gallant* (1663), 24, 37, 93, 189, 212
duet, 199, 200
Duffett, Thomas, 212
Duke's Men, 19, 90
D'Urfey, Thomas (1653–1723), 172; *The Comical History of Don Quixote* (1694), 10, 127, 199; *A Fond Husband: Or, The Plotting Sisters* (1677), 86, 152, 222; *Madam Fickle: Or, The Witty False One* (1676), 25, 86, 103, 198; *The Marriage-Hater Matched* (1692), 10

Elizabethan (stage, theatre), 7, 12, 22, 24, 25, 27, 29, 36, 93, 133, 164, 182, 198, 204
entrance, 16, 23, 147ff
epilogue, 6, 60, 200ff
Ervine, St John (1883–1971), 244
Essex, John: *The Dancing-Master* (1726), 121
Etherege, Sir George (1634–91), 1, 4, 8, 11, 15, 177, 199; *The Comical Revenge: Or, Love in a Tub* (1664), 10, 65, 92, 93, 172, 186, 199, 214, 219; *The Man of Mode: Or, Sir Fopling Flutter* (1676), 15–16, 24, 33, 50, 54–9, 60, 65–6, 69, 70, 71, 72, 75–9, 81–4, 103, 105, 111–12, 118, 125, 145, 151, 160–3, 192, 198, 212, 214, 215; *She Would If She Could* (1668), 4, 15, 23, 24, 31, 32, 33, 37, 46, 60, 62, 116, 148–9, 183, 185, 199, 215, 227, 247
etiquette books, *see* courtesy books
Evans, Dame Edith (1888–1976), 39, 45, 94, 95, 97, 108, 133, 135, 176, 178, 196, 247, 248
Evelyn, John (1620–1706), 16, 45, 91
Everyman Theatre, 42
exit, 16, 147ff

Fagan, J.B. (1873–1933), 175, 247
fan, 107ff
farce, 43, 212ff, 234, 240
Farquhar, George (1678–1707), 1, 59, 167, 177, 180, 202, 238; *The Beaux' Stratagem* (1707), 27–8, 38, 39, 74, 86, 148, 152–3, 167, 168–70, 171, 184, 194, 195–6, 198, 199, 203, 217, 218, 234–8, 246, 247; *The Constant Couple: Or, A Trip to the Jubilee* (1699), 25, 40, 122, 148, 180, 181–2, 198, 200, 234; *Discourse upon Comedy* (1702), 11–12; *The Inconstant: Or, The Way to Win Him* (1702), 145, 152; *Love and a Bottle* (1698), 60; *The Recruiting Officer* (1706), 23, 27, 41, 43, 69, 111, 138, 139, 140, 180–1, 198, 199, 212, 217, 244; *Sir Henry Wildair, Being the Sequel to the Trip to the Jubilee* (1701), 74, 189, 204; *The Twin Rivals* (1702), 27, 50–1, 134, 198, 234
farthingale, 100
Fellowship Players, 243
fencing, 17
Feydeau, Georges (1862–1921), 212, 241
Field, Ben, 171
Flecknoe, Richard: *A Short Discourse on the English Stage* (1664), 45

266

Index

floats, *see* footlights
fontange, 106ff
footlights, 36
fop, 1, 48ff, 62ff, 70ff, 84, 147ff

Gaillard, Jean: *The Compleat Gentleman;
  or, Directions for the Order of Youth as
  to Their Breeding at Home and
  Travelling Abroad* (1678), 17
Galsworthy, John (1867–1933), 111
Garrick, David (1717–79), 86, 234; *The
  Country Girl* (1766), 95
Gay, John (1685–1732), 16; *The Beggar's
  Opera* (1728), 39, 246; *Trivia, or, The
  Art of Walking the Streets of London*
  (1716), 62
*Gentleman Instructed in the Conduct of a
  Virtuous and Happy Life, The* (1716),
  102–3
Gerard, Rolf, 40
gesture, 17, 22, 170, 177, 212
Gibbons's tennis court, 19, 20
Gieldgud, Sir John (1904–   ), 42, 49, 99,
  133, 175–6, 245, 246, 247–8
Gilbert, Sir W.S. (1836–1911): *Patience*
  (1881), 130
Gilder, Rosamund, 90
Gildon, Charles, 65
Goldoni, Carlo (1707–93): *The Servant of
  Two Masters* (1746), 138
Goldsmith, Oliver (1730–74), 44; *She
  Stoops to Conquer* (1773), 217
Gole, I., plate 8
Goodall, Edyth, 94
Gordon, Ruth (1896–1985), 142
Gosse, Sir Edmund (1849–1928), 4
Grammont, Comte de: *Memoirs* (1713),
  93, 232
Grein, J.T. (1862–1935), 244
Griffith, Hubert, 95, 120, 242, 244
Grotowski, Jerzy, 12
Guthrie, Sir Tyrone (1900–71), 245
Gwyn, Nell, 90, 93, 106, 134, 136, 172,
  239

Haggard, Stephen, 79, 248
Hands, Terry, 76
Hart, Charles (?–1683), 90, 93, 239
Haye, Helen (1874–1957), 94, 171, 175
Haymarket, Theatre Royal, 176, 204
Hazlitt, William (1778–1830), 3, 238, 248
head-dress, 106ff
Henrietta Maria, Queen (1609–69), 89
Henshaw, Nancy Wanderlie, 17, 64, 68,
  109, 143, 154
Herrick, Robert (1591–1674), 151

hiding, 151ff
Highfill, Philip H., Jun., 16
Holland, Norman, 272
Hollar, Wenceslas (1607–77), plate 29
Holloway, Baliol, 39, 44
Holey, Iris, 85
Hopkins, Charles: *The Art of Love:
  Dedicated to the Ladies* (1700), 107,
  143–4, 159–60
Howard, Alan, 56
Howard, Hon. James: *All Mistaken: Or,
  The Mad Couple* (1667), 239; *The
  English Monsieur* (1663), 50, 189
Howard, Sir Robert (1626–98), 91; *The
  Committee* (1662), 25, 86, 189
Howard, Trevor, 139
Hughes, Margaret, 90
Hume, Robert, 16, 20
Hunt, Leigh (1784–1859), 3
Hyde Park, 29

Ibsen, Henrik (1828–1906), 5, 211; *A
  Doll's House* (1878), 196; *Rosmersholm*
  (1885), 196
illusion, 5, 11, 12, 27, 198ff
innuendo, 7, 115, 209, 236
Interregnum, *see* Commonwealth
Irishman (stage), 86ff
Irving, Ethel, 94
Islington, 30

jackanapes coat, 46
Jackson, Sir Barry (1869–1961), 246
Jacobean drama, 14
Jeans, Isabel (1891–   ), 94, 95, 96, 177
Jennings, Frances, 93, 232
Jerome, Joseph, 4
Jeu de Paume des Mestayers, 19
jig (gigue), 36, 172
Johnson, Dr Samuel (1709–84): *Preface to
  Shakespeare* (1765), 204
Jolly, George (*fl.* 1640–73), 19
Jones, Inigo (1573–1652), 28
Jones, Marion, 43
Jordan, Thomas: *A Royal Arbour of Loyal
  Poesie* (1664), 90

Kemble, John Philip (1757–1823), 171
Kensington, 30
Kerr, Walter, 4
Killigrew, Thomas (1612–83), 19, 20, 36,
  90; *The Parson's Wedding* (1640, 1664),
  93, 129, 239
King's Hall, 38, 242
King's Men, 19, 89, 90
Kip, John, plate 3

267

Index

268

Strength Training
Past 50

Second Edition

Wayne L. Westcott
Thomas R. Baechle

Human Kinetics

Library of Congress Cataloging-in-Publication Data

ne L., 1949-
ning past 50 / Wayne L. Westcott, Thomas R. Baechle. -- 2nd ed.

ndex.
: 978-0-7360-6771-3 (soft cover)
): 0-7360-6771-X (soft cover)
ght training. 2. Physical fitness for middle-aged persons. I. Baechle, Thomas R., 1943-
. III. Title: Strength training past fifty.
46.W47 2007
.7'130844--dc22   2006037962

N-10: 0-7360-6771-X
BN-13: 978-0-7360-6771-3

Copyright © 2007, 1998 by Wayne L. Westcott and Thomas R. Baechle

This publication is written and published to provide accurate and authoritative information relevant to the subject matter presented. It is published and sold with the understanding that the author and publisher are not engaged in rendering legal, medical, or other professional services by reason of their authorship or publication of this work. If medical or other expert assistance is required, the services of a competent professional person should be sought.

Acquisitions Editor: Jason Muzinic; **Developmental Editor:** Leigh Keylock; **Assistant Editor:** Christine Horger; **Copyeditor:** Annette Pierce; **Proofreader:** Joanna Hatzopoulos Portman; **Indexer:** Betty Frizzéll; **Permission Manager:** Carly Breeding; **Graphic Designer:** Nancy Rasmus; **Graphic Artist:** Kim McFarland; **Photo Manager:** Neil Bernstein; **Cover Designer:** Keith Blomberg; **Photographer (cover):** Neil Bernstein; **Photographer (interior):** Neil Bernstein; **Art Manager:** Kelly Hendren; **Illustrator:** Al Wilborn; **Printer:** United Graphics

Human Kinetics books are available at special discounts for bulk purchase. Special editions or book excerpts can also be created to specification. For details, contact the Special Sales Manager at Human Kinetics.

Printed in the United States of America   10 9 8

The paper in this book is certified under a sustainable forestry program.

Human Kinetics
Web site: www.HumanKinetics.com

United States: Human Kinetics
P.O. Box 5076
Champaign, IL 61825-5076
800-747-4457
e-mail: humank@hkusa.com

Canada: Human Kinetics
475 Devonshire Road, Unit 100
Windsor, ON N8Y 2L5
800-465-7301 (in Canada only)
e-mail: info@hkcanada.com

Europe: Human Kinetics
107 Bradford Road
Stanningley
Leeds LS28 6AT, United Kingdom
+44 (0)113 255 5665
e-mail: hk@hkeurope.com

Australia: Human Kinetics
57A Price Avenue
Lower Mitcham, South Australia 5062
08 8372 0999
e-mail: info@hkaustralia.com

New Zealand: Human Kinetics
P.O. Box 80
Torrens Park, South Australia 5062
0800 222 062
e-mail: info@hknewzealand.com

Contents

Acknowledgments

We gratefully acknowledge the following individuals who graciously gave their time, effort, and expertise to assist us in the publication of this book. We begin with the outstanding editorial staff at Human Kinetics, especially Leigh Keylock, Laurel Plotzke, and Jason Muzinic, as well as our talented photographer Neil Bernstein. We greatly appreciate the manuscript preparation, typing, and editing provided by our administrative associates, Jamie Robinson and Simone Strouble. We are especially pleased with the excellent performance of our exercise models, Rita La Rosa Loud, Dick Raymond, and Roderic Wilmore. In addition, we thank the Executive Directors of the South Shore YMCA, Ralph Yohe, Mary Hurley, and Natalie Sheard, for providing us with the facilities, staff, and support essential for conducting our studies and gaining greater insight into strength training. Finally, we express our most heartfelt appreciation to our wives, Claudia Westcott and Susan Baechle, for their love, prayers, and patience during the many months of manuscript development.

Introduction

You are probably no stranger to strength training. You may have lifted weights in high school or college or the military, and now you are working out with weights again, or at least thinking about it. If you have lifted in the past, you may remember the basic exercises and the standard training protocols for sets and repetitions. You may even subscribe to a fitness magazine that offers information on using a variety of strength training equipment and routines to increase your muscular strength. If you are like many past-50 exercisers, you have discovered that a few of these programs work pretty well, others don't work at all, and some are more harmful than helpful.

If you would like the most up-to-date, research-based information on safe, sensible, and effective strength training specifically for people your age and at your fitness level, then this is the book for you. The primary objective of this book is to provide purposeful and productive programs of resistance exercise that will enable you to achieve your personal training goals.

The first chapter provides information about assessing your current level of muscular fitness. It offers simple assessments to determine the relative strength of your major upper-body, leg, and midsection muscles. Based on the results of these easy-to-perform evaluations, you will select the most appropriate strength training program for maximizing your muscular development. That is, you will know where to start training for best initial results as well as for continued progress in the months ahead.

The second chapter explains the advantages, disadvantages, and key features of different resistance-exercise equipment, with emphasis on free weights and weight-stack machines. After learning more about various strength training tools and exercise biomechanics, you will be able to make equipment selections based on training considerations such as exercise effectiveness, exercise efficiency, emphasis on single or multiple muscle groups, and performance objectives.

The third chapter provides clear illustrations and precise explanations of proper exercise technique for performing more than 60 free weight, machine, and body-weight exercises that include all of the major muscle groups. This information is particularly important for experienced weight trainers, who tend to emphasize exercise weight loads over training technique, which typically produces inferior results and often leads to injuries. Correct exercise technique and practical protocols for optimally increasing the workload (resistance, repetitions, and sets) are key components of successful strength training programs.

Chapter 4 presents the essential strength training principles along with practical applications for designing the most effective exercise program to progressively increase your muscular strength. Included in these research-based recommendations are guidelines for training frequency, number of exercise sets and repetitions, exercise resistance, movement speed, movement range, and training progression. This chapter establishes the foundation for productive strength training sessions. These principles apply to workouts to develop muscular strength in general and to strength training to improve performance in specific sports. It also provides guidelines for increasing training safety and reducing the risk of setbacks, injuries, and strength plateaus.

Chapters 5, 6, and 7 provide specific strength training programs for people at different levels of muscular fitness. Chapter 5 presents resistance training programs for men and women who attained a "base" rating of muscular fitness on their chapter 1 strength assessments. Chapter 6 provides strength training programs for those who achieved an "experienced" rating of muscular fitness on their chapter 1 strength assessments. Chapter 7 offers more advanced strength training protocols for extremely fit exercisers who maxed out their chapter 1 strength assessments.

The eighth chapter addresses more specialized strength training programs for enhancing athletic performance in running, cycling, swimming, skiing, tennis, and golf. The conditioning exercises for these sports serve two purposes: first, to reduce the risk of overuse and imbalance injuries specific to each activity, and second, to improve the musculoskeletal function of the specific sport actions and movement patterns and your overall performance of them.

Chapter 9 includes important nutritional information for 50-plus exercisers who want to experience maximum benefits from their strength training program. Because eating smart is a critical component of energized workout sessions and optimal muscular development, the chapter also explains how to use the United States Department of Agriculture's MyPyramid Plan to make sound food choices. The chapter also provides guidelines for enhancing protein intake, as well as for reducing fat and its associated health-risk factors.

We are pleased that you are interested in starting a strength training program or are already performing regular resistance exercise. Of course, we want you to continue strength training and to exercise even more effectively and efficiently as a result of reading this book. You have undoubtedly discovered that strength training makes you look better, feel better, and function better. However, there are many more health-related reasons for maintaining your muscular fitness, especially after age 50. Consider the following research-based benefits associated with the strength training programs presented in chapters 5, 6, 7, and 8.

1. Strength training will help you avoid the 5 to 7 pounds (2.3 to 3.2 kilograms) per decade of muscle loss typically experienced by adults over the age of 50. In fact, research shows that adults average a 3-pound (1.4-kilogram) increase in muscle tissue after just 10 weeks of sensible strength exercise.

2. Strength training will help you avoid the 3 to 5 percent per decade reduction in resting metabolic rate that adults over the age of 50 typically experience.

In fact, research demonstrates a 7 percent increase in resting metabolism after just three months of sensible strength exercise.

3. Strength training will help you lose fat weight even in the absence of dietary restriction. Research indicates approximately 4 pounds (1.8 kilograms) of fat loss from strength exercise alone after just 10 weeks of training and twice as much fat loss when combined with minor dietary adjustments.

4. Strength training has been shown to significantly increase bone mineral density, thereby reducing the risk of osteoporosis.

5. Strength training has been shown to significantly increase glucose uptake, thereby reducing the risk of type 2 diabetes.

6. Strength training has been shown to significantly increase gastrointestinal transit speed, thereby reducing the risk of colon cancer.

7. Strength training has been shown to significantly reduce resting blood pressure, thereby reducing the risk of cardiovascular disease.

8. Strength training has been shown to significantly improve blood lipid profiles, thereby reducing the risk of cardiovascular disease.

9. Strength training has been shown to significantly increase full-range lower back strength, thereby reducing the risk of low back pain.

10. Strength training has been shown to significantly increase musculoskeletal function and concurrently ease the pain of osteoarthritis and rheumatoid arthritis.

You have made a wise decision to perform regular strength training. As you can see, the benefits of this activity are far greater than most people realize. We trust that the information in this book will help you to experience even more productive exercise sessions and enable you to achieve the many positive health and fitness outcomes that are possible through a well-designed strength training program.

1

Assessing Current Strength

You are ready to begin a productive program of strength training to develop higher levels of muscular ability and physical capacity. However, before you begin training you need to accurately assess your muscular fitness. In this chapter, we present factors that influence your muscular potential, procedures for determining your overall strength level, and suggestions for selecting your initial training program. We recommend that before performing the strength assessments you acquire your physician's approval for performing resistance exercise. Certain conditions may preclude your participation in a strength training program. In addition, the following questionnaire will help you determine if you are physically ready to start strength training.

Factors That Influence Strength Potential

The three most critical characteristics that affect your muscular fitness are your gender, age, and lifestyle. Nonetheless, regardless of your gender, age, or lifestyle, the training programs in this book enable you to gain strength and add muscle for a higher level of physical fitness and functional ability. Let's take a closer look at these factors as they relate to strength development.

Gender

It is no secret that men are stronger than women. For example, in our study of more than 900 middle-aged adults, the men were found to be 50 percent stronger than the women in a standard test of leg strength. Does this mean that males have higher-quality muscle than females? Not at all. It simply means that men, who

Assessing Your Physical Readiness

You should consult a physician before beginning a strength training program if you answer yes to any of the following questions.

Yes   No

____ ____   Are you over age 50 (female) or 40 (male) and not accustomed to exercise?

____ ____   Do you have a history of heart disease?

____ ____   Has a doctor ever said your blood pressure was too high?

____ ____   Are you taking prescription medications, such as those for heart problems or high blood pressure?

____ ____   Have you ever experienced chest pain, spells of severe dizziness, or fainting?

____ ____   Do you have a history of respiratory problems, such as asthma?

____ ____   Have you had surgery or experienced bone, muscle, tendon, or ligament problems (especially in the back or knee) that might be aggravated by an exercise program?

____ ____   Is there a physical or health reason not already mentioned that should keep you from following a weight training program?

Adapted, by permission, from T.R. Baechle and R.W. Earle, 1995, *Fitness weight training* (Champaign, IL: Human Kinetics), 24.

are typically larger, have more muscle mass than women. When compared on a muscle-for-muscle basis, however, the men and women in this study were equally strong. Research also reveals that men and women experience similar rates of improvement in muscular strength and endurance even though women typically use lighter training loads.

So the only real difference between men's and women's approaches to strength training is the amount of weight used. To demonstrate this point we have included table 1.1, which shows training loads used by 134 men and women over age 50. The data in this table show the loads used after two months of training on Nautilus machines.

Age

The loads in table 1.1 clearly show a drop in strength as one gets older. In fact, among adults who do not exercise their muscles, there is a 5 to 10 percent decrease per decade. This is caused by the gradual loss of muscle tissue that accompanies the aging process. Unless you strength train regularly, you lose several pounds of muscle every decade of adult life (typically 5 pounds [2.3 kilograms] for women and 7 pounds [3.1 kilograms] for men), which results in a lower strength level and a slower resting metabolic rate.

Table 1.1   Weight Load After Two Months of Strength Training*

| | Age groups | | | | | |
| | 50-59 | | 60-69 | | 70-79 | |
	Males (lb/kg)	Females (lb/kg)	Males (lb/kg)	Females (lb/kg)	Males (lb/kg)	Females (lb/kg)
Leg extension	90/41	60/27	82.5/37.4	57.5/26.1	75/34	55/25
Leg curl	90/41	60/27	82.5/37.4	57.5/26.1	75/34	55/25
Leg press	180/82	120/54	160/73	110/50	140/63	100/45
Chest crossover	85/38	50/23	80/36	47.5/21.5	70/32	45/20.5
Chest press	87.5/39.6	50/23	80/36	47.5/21.5	72.5/32.9	45/20.5
Compound row	117.5/53.3	77.5/35	110/50	75/34	102.5/46.5	70/32
Shoulder press	82.5/37.4	42.5/19.3	72.5/32.9	40/18	62.5/28.3	37.5/17
Biceps curl	75/34	42.5/19.3	70/32	40/18	60/27	37.5/17
Triceps extension	75/34	42.5/19.3	70/32	40/18	60/27	37.5/17
Back extension	95/43	72.5/32.9	90/41	67.5/30.6	85/38	65/29
Abdominal curl	95/43	57.5/26.1	90/41	55/25	80/36	52.5/24

*There were 134 subjects training on Nautilus machines. Actual weight loads will be different on other resistance machines, but the strength relationships will be similar for men and women across the three age groups.

Fortunately, regular training maintains and increases muscle strength. The 367 men and women represented in figure 1.1 increased muscle strength an average of 22.2 pounds (10 kilograms), or more than 40 percent, during the eight-week training program. Even more impressive was that the rate of strength gain was similar for all age groups (50 years through 80 years).

Average weight load (lb)

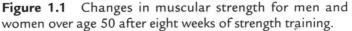

Figure 1.1   Changes in muscular strength for men and women over age 50 after eight weeks of strength training.

Lifestyle

Our research data provide reasonable estimates of average strength levels for men and women of various ages. The estimates do not account for different lifestyle choices, such as physical activity patterns. For example, if you have a physically demanding occupation, such as carpentry, you are likely to be stronger than your neighbor who is an accountant. Likewise, if you enjoy active hobbies, like gardening or hiking, you will probably be stronger than a friend who spends time knitting. It should also be understood that the loads shown in our charts have been established using Nautilus equipment and that using other equipment might result in slightly different results.

Although your lifestyle and activity patterns may influence your current strength level, they will not limit your potential for developing strength if you decide to start strength training. Whatever your entry strength level is, you can become a lot stronger than you are now. And that is what really matters—personal physical improvement that enhances your health, fitness, appearance, daily function, and sports performance.

Assessing Overall Muscular Strength

We recommend three simple assessment procedures for accurately evaluating your current level of muscular fitness. Based on the results of these assessments, you will choose the strength training program most appropriate for maximizing your rate of muscular development and minimizing the risk of unproductive or counterproductive exercise sessions.

Upper-Body Strength Assessment

The first assessment procedure should be somewhat familiar because it involves the traditional push-up exercise. Push-ups, when properly performed, work the muscles of the chest (pectoralis major), back of the arms (triceps), and shoulders (deltoids) and serve as a relatively reliable predictor of upper-body strength. Perform the push-up test in the following manner.

Push-Up Starting Position

- Men: Assume a standard push-up position with toes on floor, knees straight, body straight from heels to shoulders, head up, hands on floor slightly wider than shoulder-width apart, and elbows extended (see figure 1.2*a*).
- Women: Assume a modified push-up position with toes and knees on the floor, body straight from shoulders to hips, head up, hands on floor slightly wider than shoulder-width apart, and elbows extended (see figure 1.3*a*).

Push-Up Exercise Execution

- Lower your body slowly until your elbows form right angles and your upper arms are parallel to the floor (see figures 1.2*b* and 1.3*b*). Keep your body straight, taking one full second for the downward movement.

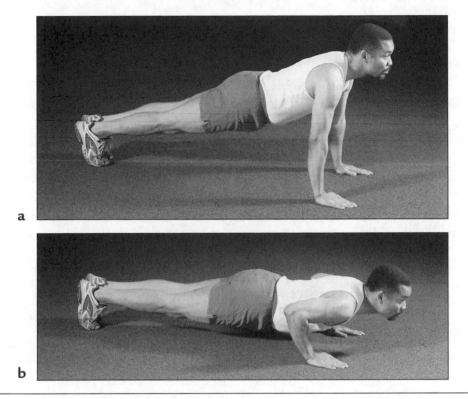

Figure 1.2 Standard push-up: *(a)* starting position and *(b)* execution.

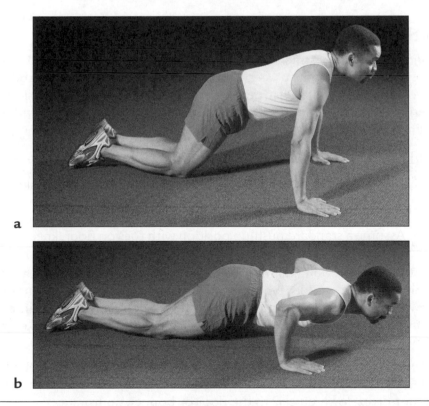

Figure 1.3 Modified push-up: *(a)* starting position and *(b)* execution.

- Push your body upward slowly until your elbows are fully extended. Keep your body straight, taking one full second for the upward movement.
- Inhale during the downward movement; exhale during the upward movement.

Three Steps to Determining Your Upper-Body Strength

1. Perform as many push-ups as possible.
2. Record the number of consecutive push-ups completed with correct technique at the top of table 1.2 where requested.
3. Identify which number range your score falls into in the left column, and circle the corresponding number 5, 6, or 7 in the right column of table 1.2.

Table 1.2   Push-Up Classification Chart for Assessing Upper-Body Strength

Number of push-ups completed ____		Upper-body strength index score (circle a number)
Men	Women	
0-9	0-9	5
10-19	10-19	6
20 or more	20 or more	7

Midsection Strength Assessment

Our second strength assessment also uses a familiar exercise, one that you may perform regularly. The trunk curl is a simple exercise that involves the abdominal muscles (rectus abdominis). When performed correctly, the trunk curl test provides an excellent evaluation of midsection, or core, muscle strength and endurance. Perform the trunk curl test in the following manner.

Trunk Curl Starting Position

- Lie faceup on the floor with your head, upper back, arms, and hips on the floor, your hands next to hips, your knees bent approximately 90 degrees, and your feet flat on the floor (see figure 1.4a).

Trunk Curl Exercise Execution

- Contract your abdominal muscles to lift your upper back and head off the floor as far as possible (typically four to six inches [10 to 15 centimeters] between shoulders and floor). Your lower back should remain in contact with the floor as your hands slide forward (see figure 1.4b). Take one full second for the upward movement.
- Lower your upper back and head to the floor, resuming the starting position. Take one full second for the downward movement.
- Do not drop down quickly to the floor or bounce up from it.
- Exhale during the upward movement; inhale during the downward movement.

Figure 1.4 Trunk curl: *(a)* starting position and *(b)* execution.

Three Steps to Determining Your Midsection Strength

1. Perform as many trunk curls as possible.
2. At the top of table 1.3, where requested, record the number of consecutive trunk curls completed with correct technique.
3. Identify which number range your score falls into in the column on the left, and circle the corresponding number 5, 6, or 7 in the far right column.

Table 1.3   Trunk Curl Classification Chart for Assessing Midsection Strength

Number of trunk curls completed ____		Midsection strength index score (circle a number)
Men	Women	
0-24	0-19	5
25-49	20-39	6
50 or more	40 or more	7

Leg Strength Assessment

Unlike the push-up and trunk curl tests, which involve moving your body weight, the leg strength test uses equipment. The YMCA leg extension test, which calls on strength from the muscles in the front of the thigh (quadriceps), assesses your lower-body strength. The exercise is easy to learn and to perform safely.

To complete the YMCA leg extension test you need access to a leg extension machine. These are available in virtually all fitness clubs and are also common in home gyms.

A unique characteristic of the YMCA leg extension test is that it evaluates muscular strength relative to body weight; the person who weighs more is expected to be able to lift more weight. Because the score is based on the percentage of your body weight that you can lift 10 times rather than on the absolute weight of the load you lift, this test more fairly assesses strength among people of substantially different weights. For example, a 100-pound (45-kilogram) woman who completes 10 repetitions with 50 pounds (23 kilograms) earns the same score as a 150-pound (68-kilogram) woman who completes 10 repetitions with 75 pounds (34 kilograms) because both women perform the exercise with 50 percent of their body weight.

The classification categories established for this test are based on the test results of more than 900 men and women with training experience. This test should give you a good indication of your lower-body strength and help you select your entry-level strength training program. Be sure to follow instructions for the YMCA leg extension test precisely as they are presented.

YMCA Leg Extension Test Starting Position

- Sit on the leg extension machine with your knee joint in line with the machine's axis of rotation (the point around which the movement arm revolves), your back in full contact with the seat back, your hands on the handgrips, and your shins against the movement pad (see figure 1.5a).

YMCA Leg Extension Test Execution

- Lift the movement pad upward until your knees are fully extended (see figure 1.5b). Take two full seconds for the upward movement.
- Pause momentarily with the knees fully extended in the up position.
- Lower the movement pad downward until the weight plate almost, but not quite, touches the remaining weight stack. Allow four full seconds for the downward movement.
- Exhale as you lift the movement pad upward, and inhale as you lower it.

Six Steps to Determining Your Lower-Body Strength

1. Determine a load that is 25 percent of your body weight, insert the weight stack pin closest to that weight, and perform 10 repetitions. Rest two minutes.
2. Increase the load so that it is about 35 percent of your body weight and perform 10 repetitions, followed by two minutes of rest.

Figure 1.5   Leg extension: *(a)* starting position and *(b)* execution.

3. Increase the load so that it is about 45 percent of your body weight and perform 10 repetitions, followed by two minutes of rest.

4. Continue testing in this manner, progressively adding more weight, until you find the heaviest load that you can lift 10 times with correct technique.

5. Divide this load by your body weight to determine your lower-body strength score, and record this number in the blank provided in table 1.4. For example, if you weigh 120 pounds (54 kilograms) and you completed 10 leg extensions with 40 pounds (18 kilograms), then your leg strength score is 33 (40 divided by 120 equals .33, or 33 percent).

6. Identify which range your score falls into in the column on the left, and circle the corresponding number 5, 6, or 7 in the far right column.

Table 1.4   Leg Extension Classification Chart for Assessing Lower-Body Strength

Score for lower-body strength ____		Lower-body strength index score (circle a number)
Men	Women	
0-49%	0-39%	5
50-69%	40-59%	6
70% or higher	60% or higher	7

Determining Overall Strength and Your Strength Training Program

You can now use the strength index numbers circled in the far right-hand columns of tables 1.2, 1.3, and 1.4 to establish your overall strength fitness level. This information will tell you which of the strength training programs presented in chapters 5, 6, and 7 is best suited to your strength level.

Simply add up the three numbers in the far right-hand columns and divide by three. For example, if you scored 5 on all three tests, then your overall strength score is 5 (15 divided by 3 equals 5). If you scored 5, 5, and 6, then your overall strength score is 5.3 (16 divided by 3 equals 5.3). If you scored 7, 7, and 6, then your overall strength score is 6.6 (20 divided by 3 equals 6.6).

If your average score for the three strength tests is 5, 5.3, or 5.6, then you should begin with one of the strength training programs presented in chapter 5, Base Fitness Programs. If your average score for the three strength tests is 6, 6.3, or 6.6, then you should begin with one of the strength training programs presented in chapter 6, Experienced Training Programs. If your score for the three strength tests is 7, then you should begin with one of the recommended strength training programs presented in chapter 7, Advanced Training Programs. Although you may start training at a lower level than indicated by your overall strength score, we advise against beginning at a level higher than indicated by your overall strength assessment.

It is possible that you may not be able to perform one of the strength tests because of injury or inaccessibility to a leg extension machine. If you complete only two tests, add both strength index scores and divide by two to determine your overall strength score. If your average score is 5 or 5.5, then you should begin with one of the strength training programs presented in chapter 5. If your average score for the two strength tests is 6 or 6.5, then you should begin with one of the strength training programs presented in chapter 6. If your average score for the two strength tests is 7, then you may begin with one of the strength training programs presented in chapter 7.

Summary

Like you, we take strength training seriously, and we want an exercise program that is best suited to our current level of muscular fitness. By performing the three assessments presented in this chapter you will acquire knowledge about your upper-body, midsection, and lower-body strength that will help you determine which strength training program in chapters 5, 6, or 7 is best for you. It is well worth the time and effort to evaluate your overall muscular strength because this information will help you to implement the most effective exercise program for further strength development.

2

Selecting Exercise Equipment

The strength training equipment used in the programs in this book includes only a few of the hundreds of equipment options that are available to you. And because there are so many types of exercise equipment, both for home use and use in fitness facilities, this chapter provides relevant information on selecting the best resistance equipment for safe, effective, and efficient strength training. This chapter presents important considerations for evaluating exercise equipment and provides checklists to help you assess the safety and function of free weights and weight-stack machines.

Free Weight Home Equipment

The least expensive and most versatile equipment to purchase are free weights, including barbells and dumbbells. Free weights do not take up much space, and you can use them to perform hundreds of different exercises. The unrestrained movement patterns permitted by free weight equipment allow your joints to move through their full range, both increasing your flexibility and improving your overall muscle coordination. These advantages help explain why 40 million Americans use free weights.

Let's look at the basic free weight equipment you'll need if you choose this equipment option. Typically it will include a set of dumbbells, a barbell, and a bench with supports.

Dumbbells

The adjustable dumbbells shown in figure 2.1*a* enable you to assemble the loads you need by adding weight plates to the dumbbell bar and securing them with locks, which are fasteners that fit on the ends of the bar. Make sure that the locks (figure 2.1*a*) are easy to tighten and loosen and that you can rely on them to keep the weight plates securely on the bar.

What exactly should you look for? Before purchasing locks, determine how much strength it takes to tighten and loosen them. Then, check to see if the weight plates stay on the dumbbell bar when it is tilted to a 45-degree angle. Ask the salesperson to tilt a lightly loaded bar to see if the weight plates stay on the end of the bar. If you do not have the grip strength needed to easily use a particular lock, or if the weight plates slide off when the bar is tilted, seek a different type.

If you are willing to spend a little more money, the premolded, or fixed-weight, solid dumbbells are easier to use than the adjustable dumbbells (see figure 2.1*b*). Because you do not have to assemble or disassemble them between exercises, premolded dumbbells enhance training efficiency. The downside of this type of dumbbell is that you need to purchase quite a few of them if you want to use different weight loads in your workouts, which you probably will. A more economical approach, and one that will equip you with what you need to complete all of the exercises in the program options in chapters 5, 6, 7, and 8, is to purchase two adjustable dumbbells and the weight plates listed in the Basic Dumbbell Set sidebar. Two dumbbells and the 75 pounds (34 kilograms) of weight plates provide 15 different load options, ranging from 2 to 39.5 pounds (.9 to 17.9 kilograms) on each dumbbell, assuming an unloaded bar weighs 2 pounds (.9 kilograms), for approximately $70. (All costs are listed in U.S. dollars.) Please note that the metric conversions listed are exact conversions and do not correspond to standard metric weight plates. The equipment listed will easily accommodate your dumbbell equipment needs.

Figure 2.1   Free weight equipment: *(a)* adjustable dumbbells, *(b)* premolded dumbbells, *(c)* barbell, *(d)* Olympic bar, *(e)* weight plates, and *(f)* locks.

Basic Dumbbell Set

A basic adjustable dumbbell set includes the following:

2 dumbbell bars with locks and

4 of each of the following:
 10-pound (4.5-kilogram) plates
 5-pound (2.3-kilogram) plates
 2.5-pound (1.1-kilogram) plates
 1.25-pound (.6-kilogram) plates

Barbells

The barbell (see figure 2.1c) you select should be five or six feet (1.5 or 1.8 meters) long unless you prefer an Olympic barbell set that features a seven-foot (2.1-meter) bar and revolving sleeves where the weight plates are placed (figure 2.1d). As with dumbbells, easy-to-use but secure locks are essential (figure 2.1f). Therefore, apply the same convenience and safety criteria when selecting barbell locks. The following list specifies the weight plates that compose a basic 100-pound (45-kilogram) barbell set. Most bars weigh 25 to 30 pounds (11.4 to 13.6 kilograms) when unloaded. Adding two 1.25-pound (.6-kilogram) plates to this set will provide more load options. The bar and plates specified create 16 load options at a cost of approximately $70.

Basic Barbell Set

A basic adjustable barbell set includes the following:

1 barbell 5 to 6 feet (1.5 to 1.8 meters) long with locks and

4 of each of the following:
 10-pound (4.5-kilogram) plates
 5-pound (2.3-kilogram) plates
 2.5-pound (1.1-kilogram) plates
 1.25-pound (.6-kilogram) plates

Weight Benches

Weight benches are typically of two types. A flat bench does not have uprights (figure 2.2a), and a bench press bench has uprights that provide a safe place for the barbell to rest (figure 2.2b). Each bench enables you to perform a variety of chest, arm, and shoulder exercises while lying on your back or while sitting. If you intend to use one of the free weight programs in chapter 5, 6, or 7, you'll need a bench press bench to do the chest-pressing exercises with a barbell. A flat bench works fine for the basic free weight workouts performed with dumbbells.

Figure 2.2   Weight benches: *(a)* flat bench, *(b)* bench with uprights, and *(c)* adjustable bench.

Figure 2.3   Squat rack.

For a little more money you can purchase an incline bench that will adjust to different angles as shown in figure 2.2*c*. Because you can change it to various seat positions, it is the most versatile type of bench for pressing exercises.

What else might you need? The squat rack shown in figure 2.3 is a piece of free weight equipment that enables you to safely include excellent exercises for the legs (squats) and shoulders (overhead presses), even without spotters. Unless you have two qualified spotters, you should purchase a squat rack with safety bars if you decide to include the barbell squat exercise in your training programs.

Free Weight Equipment Costs

The equipment requirements and costs associated with performing the free weight exercises in chapters 5, 6, and 7 are presented in the sidebar on the following page. The sidebar also includes costs associated with optional equipment. As indicated, the cost of the dumbbells and bench needed for our free weight programs is approximately $200, and the additional cost for equipment needed to complete the free weight workouts in this book is $650. Purchasing this equipment can provide several training options in your home for a relatively small initial investment. In comparison, a high-quality, easy-to-use, and versatile strength training machine costs $1,500 to $2,500.

Free Weight Equipment Safety

If you decide to purchase and exercise with free weights, use the following checklist to safely achieve the most training benefit from your equipment. Time spent inspecting your equipment is always a good investment for insuring safe and effective exercise sessions.

Basic and Optional Equipment Costs

Basic Equipment
For the free weight exercises in chapters 5, 6, and 7 you'll need the following:

2 adjustable dumbbells with locks and 75 pounds (34 kilograms) of weight plates	$70
1 flat bench	$130
Total	**$200**

1 barbell 5 feet (1.5 meters) long with locks and 87.5 pounds (40 kilograms) of weight plates	$100
1 bench press bench (with uprights)	$130
1 squat rack	$420
Total	**$650**

Optional Equipment

1 set of premolded (solid) dumbbells (5-, 10-, 15-, 20-, 25-pound [2.3-, 4.5-, 6.8-, 9-, 11.4-kilogram] pairs)	$140
1 adjustable bench (substitute for other benches)	$160
Total	**$300**

Free Weight Checklist

Before and During Training Sessions
- Always load each end of the bar evenly.
- Make sure loose locks are secure and tight.
- Store weight plates appropriately so that you don't trip over them.
- Ensure that the bench is stable.
- Lift with your legs, not your back, when moving dumbbells and barbells from the floor to the racks.

Working With a Spotter

Some free weight exercises, such as the barbell bench press, barbell squat, and barbell heel raise increase your risk of injury because of the positioning of the barbell and the movement pattern. For example, if you are unable to complete the last repetition in the barbell bench press exercise and cannot place the barbell back on the standards, the bar may drop onto your chest or face and cause injury. Therefore, you must have a spotter to help you in certain barbell exercises, such as the bench press, in which you hold the weight over your face; the squat, in which you hold the weight on your back; and the standing press, in which you hold the weight over your head.

The spotter can help you lift the bar from the standards to start the exercise, can offer encouragement, and can "catch" a barbell or dumbbell if you lose control of it or lose your balance, thus protecting you from injury. For safety's sake be sure that a competent and attentive spotter helps you whenever you perform over-the-face, on-the-back, and over-the-head exercises with a barbell or dumbbells because these may be difficult and dangerous to perform alone. We have addressed the need for a spotter in every exercise that requires one. It is important that you take this information seriously and use a spotter where we have suggested that you do so.

Weight-Stack Machines

The popularity of strength training among men and women, which now exceeds 60 million participants in the United States, has spawned tremendous development of weight training machines, especially for use in home gyms. Machine exercises have been designed for ease of performance and safety. You can change weight loads quickly, and movement patterns are predetermined, making machine exercises easier to perform than free weight exercises. Machines also provide support for the body, and some models automatically match the resistance to your strength throughout the movement range.

If you have problems with balance or are beginning at a low strength level, start your strength training program using machines and the machine workouts described in chapter 5. Resistance machines allow you to do most of your exercises from a sitting position, usually with back support, or while lying faceup. They generally limit your movements to those actions that are unlikely to result in injury and to movement patterns that are appropriate for the target muscles. They eliminate the possibility of dropping barbells, dumbbells, or weight plates on yourself, and they don't require you to stoop to lift equipment. Once your balance is good and your strength levels are high enough, consider using free weights and following the free weight workouts as well as the more advanced machine workouts presented in chapters 6, 7, and 8, while following the standard safety precautions. Both types of equipment are well suited to bringing about dramatic improvements in your strength fitness level.

Machine Characteristics

Well-designed machines place a consistent stress on the muscles by means of a cam or other device that creates a longer (figure 2.4a) or shorter (figure 2.4b) distance between the pivot point and point where the force is being applied, called the pivot-point distance. The design of the cam or other device is an attempt to match the shortest pivot-point distance with the most difficult range of the exercise and the longest pivot-point distance with the easiest range. Thus, the cam's shape attempts to match the strength curve (variation in strength throughout a range of movement) of the muscles involved in an exercise. In doing so, these machines approximate a muscle's force capability at each angle of movement, enabling it to maintain a more consistent level of effort throughout each repetition.

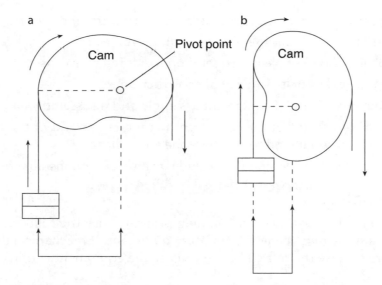

Figure 2.4   As the cam rotates from position *a* to *b*, the distance from the pivot point to the weight plate shortens, which has the effect of reducing the load, thereby resulting in a more uniform muscle effort throughout each repetition.

Reprinted, by permission, from T.R. Baechle and B. Groves, 1992, *Weight training: Steps to success* (Champaign, IL: Human Kinetics), 22.

Free weight exercises involve leverage changes that produce more resistance in some exercise positions and less in other positions. For example, as the dumbbell in figure 2.5 reaches level 3, the distance between the elbow and the dumbbell and the force required to continue the curling movement are at their most challenging position. When fatigue terminates a repetition in this exercise, failure usually occurs at level 3 even though you have sufficient strength to continue curling the dumbbells from points 1 to 2 and 4 to 5. Well-designed machines attempt to accommodate your muscles' force capabilities, enabling them to contract through the most challenging position, referred to as the *sticking point*. When shopping for a machine, keep in mind that devices that use elastic resistance, such as those commonly advertised on television, may not effectively adapt to your muscles' varying capabilities. Their advantages over machines with cams, like those shown in figure 2.4, however, are that they are easy to move and store and are less expensive.

If you prefer to train on a machine in your home, consider the following points:

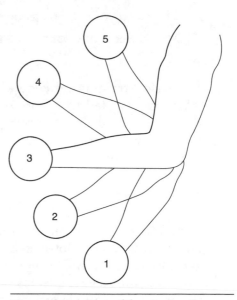

Figure 2.5   At position 3, the distance between your elbow and the dumbbell and the force required to complete the curl are at their greatest.

- Application—how easy the exercises will be to learn and execute
- Versatility—how many exercises you can perform on it
- Simplicity—how simple it is to set it up for different exercises
- Equipment durability—quality of construction
- Convenience—ease of equipment assembly and disassembly
- Reputation—status of the equipment manufacturer and of the distributor from which you intend to purchase the equipment
- Cost—price of the equipment, including shipping and installation

Machine Safety

If you decide to follow a machine training program, use the following checklist to safely attain the most benefit from your equipment. If mechanical deficiencies exist, be sure to have them fixed before you use the equipment.

Machine Checklist

Before and During Training Sessions
- Check for frayed cables, belts, pulleys, worn chains, and loose pads.
- Make sure plates move smoothly on guide rods.
- Adjust levers and seats as needed.
- Insert selector keys all the way into the weight stack.
- Keep your hands away from the chains, belts, pulleys, and cams.
- Never place your fingers or hands between weight stacks.

Develop training procedures that stress caution. Always fasten the seat belt if one is provided to ensure proper body alignment. And develop the habit of double-checking the little things. For example, if you use machines, learn where to properly position your seat and what the correct load is; double check them before each set.

Exercise Balls

Performing exercises on an air-inflated exercise ball typically involves more of the core muscle groups (lower back, abdominals, obliques) than when performing the same exercises on the floor, while standing, or while sitting on a bench. Although exercising on a less stable base generally requires using lighter resistance, involving the stabilizing muscle groups in addition to the target muscles adds a different dimension to standard exercises. When selecting an exercise ball, use table 2.1 to determine the correct size.

Table 2.1   Exercise Ball Selection

Exerciser height	Ball diameter
5'1"-5'7" (155-170 cm)	55 cm (21.6")
5'8"-6'1" (173-185 cm)	65 cm (25.5")
6'2"-6'7" (188-201 cm)	75 cm (29.5")

Fitness Facility or Home Training

You may decide that you need the environment of a fitness facility to enjoy the workouts presented in this book. If so, the key factors to consider when choosing a training center are

- exercise equipment availability,
- qualifications of the fitness staff,
- services offered, and
- membership costs.

Ideally, the facility you choose will be well equipped and will employ qualified professional instructors to develop and implement an individualized training program that meets your needs and fits your abilities.

In addition, an exercise area should be spacious. Accidents are rare among adult strength trainers, but crowded exercise areas can increase the likelihood that they will occur. If you wish to train at a fitness center, choose one that has plenty of space between the strength training machines and free weight equipment. Avoid facilities that have cluttered floors because items underfoot increase the potential for injury. In addition, too many people in the exercise room can hinder your concentration, possibly leading to mishaps.

If you train at home, find a spacious area to set up your exercise equipment and specific places to store your weights. Make sure you have ample lighting and air ventilation. Setting up workout equipment in a corner of a cluttered room can make your training sessions less enjoyable and create safety problems, especially if the exercise area is too small.

Selecting a Personal Trainer

A knowledgeable personal trainer can help you enjoy and benefit the most from the training programs presented in this book. A good personal trainer is capable of individualizing the workouts presented in chapters 5, 6, 7, and 8, showing you how to perform the exercises correctly and motivating you to make each workout most productive. If necessary, he or she can also give you advice about the equipment you need for home use and recommend a reputable retail store, where you can purchase the appropriate equipment at a reasonable price. If you decide to hire a personal trainer to help you with your training, we strongly recommend that you identify one who has the skills just discussed and that you also ask prospective trainers the following questions, then have them provide you with references from their current and previous clients.

- *Describe your academic preparation for personal training.* Look for course work associated with exercise physiology, biomechanics, nutrition, and, ideally, a degree in exercise science, exercise physiology, physical therapy, athletic training, or physical education.

- *What certification credentials directly associated with personal training have you earned?* Look for personal trainers who have earned certifications offered by organizations that are accredited by the National Commission for Certifying Agencies (www.noca.org), such as the National Strength and Conditioning Association (NSCA), the American College of Sports Medicine (ACSM), and the American Council on Exercise (ACE).

- *How long have you been a personal trainer?* Look for someone who has been active in the business of personal training for at least two years. Be cautious about hiring an inexperienced personal trainer.

Before signing a contract with a personal trainer, observe a prospective trainer working with a client. Even if you like what you see, delay signing a contract until you train with him or her for at least one session. Also, consider the cost, which typically ranges from $40 to $90 a session, and ask if the cost per session is less if you commit to a specific number of sessions.

Functional Activity Attire

Strength training is a challenging physical activity and as such requires functional exercise clothes. This begins with supportive athletic shoes that provide good traction to prevent slipping. It also includes a pair of loose-fitting shorts and a T-shirt or a lightweight warm-up suit. Loose and light exercise clothes enable you to easily transfer body heat to the environment, avoiding undesirable rises in body temperature. Proper activity wear also allows freedom of movement, permitting you to move comfortably and without restriction through a full range of exercise actions.

Summary

Using the right equipment can add variety and enjoyment to your strength training as well as provide better results. Whether you decide to use machines or free weights, you should carefully consider the unique characteristics of each, and you should consult qualified professionals before purchasing and using the equipment. Regardless of the training equipment selected, heed the safety checklists provided in this chapter. Finally, we encourage you to secure a qualified professional to help you in the early phases of your strength training program, and be sure to evaluate his or her credentials, services offered, costs, and comments from previous clients before signing a contract.

3

Performing Exercises Correctly

Knowing how much weight to lift is essential, but knowing how to lift that weight is even more important. Exercise technique affects both training response and training safety, which really represent two sides of the same coin. Simply stated, proper exercise technique increases training effectiveness and decreases the risk of injury. In this chapter we describe and illustrate correct training technique for exercises performed with weight-stack machines, free weights, body weight, and exercise balls.

You will note that some exercises are performed with a rotary movement pattern. That is, the exercise action is circular in nature. Rotary movements, such as leg extensions and barbell curls, involve a single joint action that is typically produced by one or sometimes two major muscle groups. For example, the leg extension exercise addresses the quadriceps muscles and activates the knee joints. Similarly, the barbell curl exercise addresses the biceps muscles and activates the elbow joints.

Other exercises are performed with a linear movement pattern. That is, the exercise action is essentially a straight line. Linear movements, such as leg presses and bench presses, involve more than one joint action and are typically produced by two or more major muscle groups. For example, the leg press exercise addresses the quadriceps, hamstrings, and gluteal muscles and activates both the knee and hip joints. Likewise, the bench press exercise addresses the pectoralis major, anterior deltoids, and triceps muscles and activates both the shoulder and elbow joints. We believe that a comprehensive strength training program should include both rotary and linear exercises to maximize overall muscle development. Please read the exercise performance instructions carefully, and practice perfect form on every repetition.

Leg Extension

QUADRICEPS

Beginning Position

1. Adjust seat so that knees are in line with the machine's axis of rotation (where the machine pivots). The axis of rotation is indicated by a red dot on Nautilus machines, which are shown in the following exercise illustrations.

2. Sit with back firmly against seat back.

3. Position ankles behind roller pad, knees flexed about 90 degrees.

4. Grip handles.

Upward Movement Phase

1. Push roller pad slowly upward until knees are extended.

2. Exhale throughout upward movement.

Downward Movement Phase

1. Return roller pad slowly to starting position.

2. Inhale throughout lowering movement.

a

b

Leg Curl

HAMSTRINGS

Beginning Position

1. Lie facedown on a bench, with the head in line with the body.

2. Position ankles under roller pad, with knees in line with the machine's axis of rotation.

3. Grip handles.

Upward Movement Phase

1. Pull roller pad slowly upward until knees are fully flexed.

2. Exhale throughout pulling movement.

Downward Movement Phase

1. Allow roller pad to return slowly to starting position.

2. Inhale throughout return movement.

a

b

Leg Press

QUADRICEPS, HAMSTRINGS, GLUTEALS

Beginning Position

1. Adjust seat so that knees are flexed to 90 degrees or less.

2. Sit with back firmly against seat back.

3. Place feet flat on foot pad, in line with knees.

4. Grip handles.

Forward Movement Phase

1. Push foot pad forward slowly until knees are almost extended, but not locked.

2. Keep feet, knees, and hips aligned.

3. Exhale throughout pushing phase.

Backward Movement Phase

1. Allow foot pad to slowly return to starting position.

2. Inhale throughout return movement.

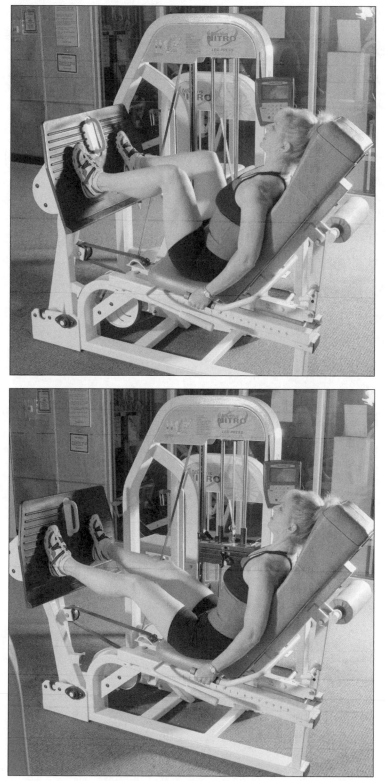

a

b

Hip Adduction

HIP ADDUCTORS

Beginning Position

1. Sit with back firmly against seat pad.

2. Position knees outside of movement pads and feet on supports.

3. Adjust movement lever to starting position with legs comfortably apart.

4. Grip handles.

Inward Movement Phase

1. Pull movement pads together slowly.

2. Exhale throughout pulling movement.

Outward Movement Phase

1. Allow pads to slowly return to starting position with legs apart.

2. Inhale throughout return movement.

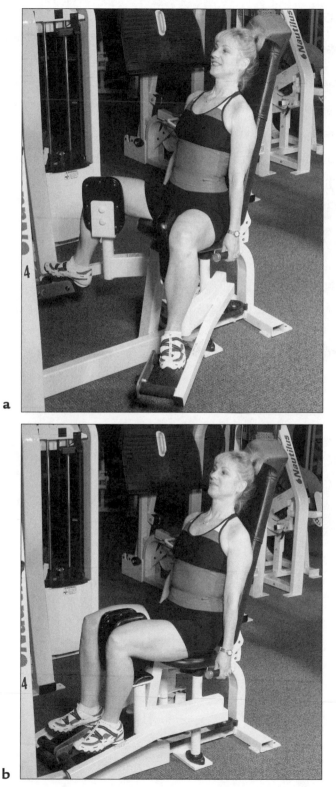

a

b

Hip Abduction

HIP ABDUCTORS

Beginning Position

1. Sit with back firmly against seat pad.

2. Position both knees inside of movement pads and feet on supports with legs together.

3. Grip handles.

Outward Movement Phase

1. Push movement pads apart slowly as far as comfortable.

2. Exhale throughout pushing movement.

Inward Movement Phase

1. Allow movement pads to slowly return to starting position with legs together.

2. Inhale throughout return movement.

a

b

Heel Raise

GASTROCNEMIUS, SOLEUS

Beginning Position

1. Position and secure the resistance belt around waist.

2. Stand with balls of feet on rear edge of step.

3. Place hands on support bar.

4. Allow heels to drop below step as far as comfortable.

Upward Movement Phase

1. Rise slowly on toes to lift heels upward as high as possible.

2. Keep knees straight.

3. Exhale throughout upward movement.

Downward Movement Phase

1. Return slowly to starting position, heels below step.

2. Inhale throughout downward movement.

a

b

Dumbbell Squat

QUADRICEPS, HAMSTRINGS, GLUTEALS

Beginning Position

1. Grasp dumbbells with arms extended, and stand erect with feet about hip-width apart and parallel to each other.

2. Position dumbbells with palms facing the outside surfaces of thighs.

Downward Movement Phase

1. Keep head up, eyes fixed straight ahead, shoulders back, torso erect, and weight on entire foot throughout the upward and downward movement phases of the exercise.

2. Squat slowly until thighs are parallel to floor.

3. Inhale throughout downward movement.

Note: If balance is a problem, try positioning your upper back and buttocks against a wall for support (i.e., slide up and down a wall). Do not allow the knees to move farther forward than the toes.

Upward Movement Phase

1. Begin upward movement by slowly straightening the knees and hips.

2. Exhale throughout upward movement.

a   b

LEG EXERCISES: FREE WEIGHTS

Barbell Squat

QUADRICEPS, HAMSTRINGS, GLUTEALS

Beginning Position

1. Position feet shoulder-width apart or wider and grip the bar overhand while it's on a rack.

2. Position bar on shoulders at base of neck, head up, eyes looking ahead.

3. Stand erect lifting bar out of rack.

Downward Movement Phase

1. Keep head up, eyes fixed straight ahead, shoulders back, torso erect, and weight on entire foot throughout the upward and downward movement phases of the exercise.

2. Squat slowly until thighs are parallel to floor.

3. Inhale throughout downward movement.

Note: Do not allow the knees to move farther forward than the toes. This exercise requires a competent spotter for safe performance.

Upward Movement Phase

1. Begin upward movement by slowly straightening knees and hips.

2. Exhale throughout upward movement.

3. Return bar to rack carefully after completing the set.

a   b

Dumbbell Step-Up

QUADRICEPS, HAMSTRINGS, GLUTEALS

Beginning Position

1. Grasp dumbbells with arms extended, and stand erect with feet about hip-width apart and parallel to each other, directly in front of step (or bench).

2. Position dumbbells with palms facing the outside surfaces of thighs.

Upward Movement Phase

1. Keep head up, eyes fixed straight ahead, shoulders back, and torso erect throughout the exercise.

2. Place right foot on the step, followed by the left foot, so you are standing on the step.

3. Exhale throughout upward movement.

Downward Movement Phase

1. Place the right foot on the floor, followed by the left foot, so you are standing on the floor.

2. Inhale throughout downward movement.

Note: Alternate the lead foot every repetition.

LEG EXERCISES: FREE WEIGHTS

a   b   c

Dumbbell Lunge

QUADRICEPS, HAMSTRINGS, GLUTEALS

Beginning Position

1. Grasp dumbbells with arms extended, and stand erect with feet about hip-width apart and parallel to each other.

2. Position dumbbells with palms facing outside surfaces of thighs.

Downward Movement Phase

1. Keep head up, eyes fixed straight ahead, shoulders back, and torso erect throughout the exercise.

2. Take a long step forward with the right foot and bend the right knee to a 90-degree angle.

3. Step forward far enough that the right knee is directly above (not in front of) the right foot.

4. Inhale throughout downward movement.

Upward Movement Phase

1. Push off right foot and return to standing position with feet parallel to each other.

2. Exhale throughout upward movement.

Note: Alternate the lead foot every repetition.

a   b

Dumbbell Heel Raise

GASTROCNEMIUS, SOLEUS

Beginning Position

1. Grasp dumbbells with arms extended and stand erect.

2. Position dumbbells with palms facing the outside surfaces of the thighs.

3. Place balls of feet on a *stable,* elevated surface (approximately one to two inches [2.5 to 5 centimeters] high) with feet hip-width apart and parallel to each other.

Upward Movement Phase

1. Keep head up, eyes fixed straight ahead, shoulders back, torso erect, and weight on balls of the feet throughout the upward and downward movement phases of the exercise.

2. Rise slowly on the toes while keeping the torso erect and knees straight.

3. Exhale throughout upward movement.

Downward Movement Phase

1. Lower heels as far as comfortable while keeping the torso erect and knees straight.

2. Inhale throughout lowering movement.

a

b

LEG EXERCISES: FREE WEIGHTS

Barbell Heel Raise

GASTROCNEMIUS, SOLEUS

Beginning Position

1. Stand erect, position feet shoulder-width apart, and grasp bar with an overhand grip.

2. Hold bar against thighs with arms straight, head up, and eyes looking ahead. (Another way to perform this exercise is with the bar on shoulders at base of neck. Please note, this variation requires a spotter).

3. Place balls of feet on a *stable,* elevated surface (approximately one to two inches [2.5 to 5 centimeters] high) with feet hip-width apart and parallel to each other.

Upward Movement Phase

1. Keep head up, eyes fixed straight ahead, shoulders back, torso erect, and weight on balls of feet throughout the upward and downward movement phases of the exercise.

2. Rise on toes slowly while keeping torso erect and knees straight.

3. Exhale throughout upward movement.

Downward Movement Phase

1. Lower the heels as far as comfortable while keeping torso erect and knees straight.

2. Inhale throughout lowering movement.

a

b

Exercise Ball Wall Squat

QUADRICEPS, HAMSTRINGS, GLUTEALS

Beginning Position

1. Grasp dumbbells with arms extended, and stand erect with feet about hip-width apart and parallel to each other.

2. Position dumbbells with palms facing outside surfaces of thighs.

3. Place exercise ball between back and wall with feet far enough from the wall that knees are directly over the feet in the down position.

Downward Movement Phase

1. Keep head up, eyes fixed straight ahead, shoulders back, torso erect, and weight on entire foot throughout the exercise.

2. Squat slowly until thighs are parallel to floor, rolling ball between the back and wall as you descend.

3. Inhale throughout downward movement.

Upward Movement Phase

1. Begin upward movement by slowly straightening the knees and hips, rolling ball between the back and wall as you ascend.

2. Exhale throughout upward movement.

a

b

Exercise Ball Heel-Pull

HAMSTRINGS, HIP FLEXORS

Beginning Position

1. Lie faceup on floor with legs extended and heels planted firmly on top of an exercise ball.

2. Place hands on floor next to hips.

Backward Movement Phase

1. Pull ball toward hips slowly by flexing knees toward chest.

2. Exhale throughout backward movement phase.

Forward Movement Phase

1. Return ball slowly until legs are extended.

2. Inhale throughout forward movement phase.

Note: Do not lift hips off the floor during the heel-pull exercise.

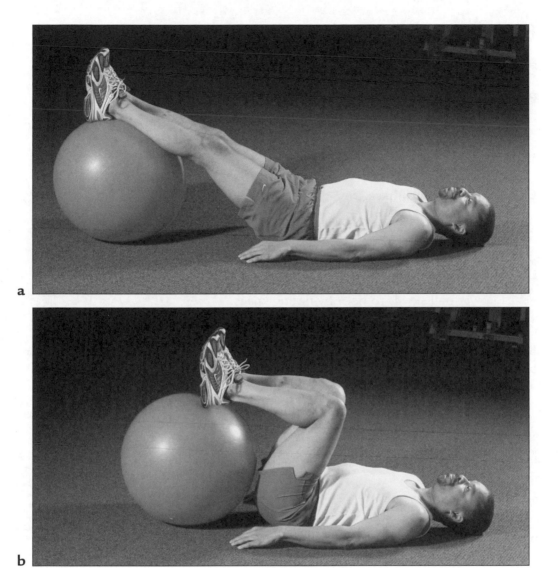

a

b

LEG EXERCISES: EXERCISE BALL

Exercise Ball Leg Lift

QUADRICEPS, HIP FLEXORS, RECTUS ABDOMINIS

Beginning Position

1. Lie faceup on floor with knees bent and feet pressed against the sides of an exercise ball.

2. Place hands on floor next to hips.

Upward Movement Phase

1. Lift ball upward slowly by extending knees until legs are straight.

2. Exhale throughout lifting movement.

Downward Movement Phase

1. Lower ball slowly to floor by flexing knees.

2. Inhale throughout lowering movement.

Note: Try to keep thighs in the same position while you lift and lower the exercise ball.

LEG EXERCISES: EXERCISE BALL

a

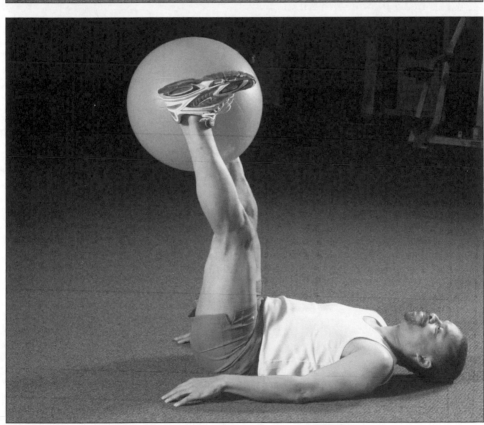

b

Low Back Extension

ERECTOR SPINAE

Beginning Position

1. Sit all the way back on seat and adjust foot pad so that knees are slightly higher than hips.

2. Secure seat belts across thighs and hips.

3. Cross arms on chest.

4. Place upper back firmly against pad with trunk flexed forward.

Backward Movement Phase

1. Push upper back against pad until trunk is fully extended.

2. Keep head in line with torso.

3. Exhale throughout extension movement.

Forward Movement Phase

1. Allow pad to slowly return to starting position.

2. Inhale throughout return movement.

a

b

MIDSECTION EXERCISES: MACHINES

Abdominal Flexion

RECTUS ABDOMINIS

Beginning Position

1. Adjust seat so that navel is aligned with the machine's axis of rotation.

2. Secure seat belt.

3. Sit with upper back firmly against pad.

4. Place elbows on arm pads and hands on handles.

Forward Movement Phase

1. Pull pad forward slowly by contracting abdominal muscles until trunk is fully flexed (tightening abdominal muscles as tight as you can).

2. Keep upper back firmly against pad.

3. Exhale throughout forward movement.

Backward Movement Phase

1. Allow the pad to slowly return to the starting position.

2. Inhale throughout return movement.

a

b

MIDSECTION EXERCISES: MACHINES

Rotary Torso

RECTUS ABDOMINIS, EXTERNAL OBLIQUES, INTERNAL OBLIQUES

Beginning Position

1. Sit all the way back on seat, facing forward with torso erect.

2. Wrap legs around seat extension.

3. Position left upper arm behind arm pad and right upper arm against (in front of) the arm pad.

Rotation Movement Phase

1. Rotate torso slowly to the right, about 45 degrees.

2. Exhale throughout rotation.

Return Movement Phase

1. Allow torso to slowly return to starting position (facing forward).

2. Inhale throughout return movement.

3. Change arm position and repeat exercise to the left.

MIDSECTION EXERCISES: MACHINES

a   b

MIDSECTION EXERCISES: FREE WEIGHTS

Dumbbell Side Bend

RECTUS ABDOMINIS, EXTERNAL OBLIQUES, INTERNAL OBLIQUES

Beginning Position

1. Grasp dumbbell in right hand with arm extended and stand erect with feet about hip-width apart and parallel to each other.

2. Position dumbbell with palm facing the outside surface of right thigh.

3. Keep shoulders square with hips and arms straight throughout the exercise. Do not bend forward or backward.

Upward Movement Phase

1. Lift right dumbbell upward by bending at waist to the left.

2. Exhale throughout upward movement phase.

Downward Movement Phase

1. Lower right dumbbell downward as far as possible by bending at waist to the right.

2. Inhale throughout downward movement phase.

Note: After completing all of the repetitions with the dumbbell in the right hand, switch the dumbbell to the left hand and repeat.

a   b

MIDSECTION EXERCISES: FREE WEIGHTS

Dumbbell Dead Lift

ERECTOR SPINAE, QUADRICEPS, HAMSTRINGS, GLUTEALS

Beginning Position

1. Hold dumbbells on floor with arms straight, feet about hip-width apart, knees flexed, hips flexed, back straight, and head up.

2. Position dumbbells with palms facing outside surfaces of ankles.

Upward Movement Phase

1. Rise slowly to a standing position by extending knees, hips, and trunk.

2. Exhale throughout upward movement phase.

Downward Movement Phase

1. Return slowly to starting position with dumbbells on floor.

2. Inhale throughout downward movement phase.

Note: Your back remains in a relatively stable position throughout the performance of the exercise. Most of the movement is around the hip and knee joints.

a   b

Body-Weight Trunk Extension

ERECTOR SPINAE

Beginning Position

1. Lie facedown on mat or carpeted floor.

2. Place hands under chin to maintain a neutral neck position.

Upward Movement Phase

1. Raise chest slowly off floor about 30 degrees.

2. Exhale throughout upward movement.

Downward Movement Phase

1. Lower chest slowly to floor.

2. Inhale throughout downward movement.

Note: It may be necessary to secure the feet to properly perform this exercise.

MIDSECTION EXERCISES: BODY WEIGHT

a

b

MIDSECTION EXERCISES: BODY WEIGHT

Twisting Trunk Curl

RECTUS ABDOMINIS, RECTUS FEMORIS, HIP FLEXORS, OBLIQUES

Beginning Position

1. Lie faceup on mat or carpeted floor.

2. Place hands behind head to maintain a neutral neck position.

Upward Movement Phase

1. Raise upper back about 30 degrees off floor, and keep the trunk curled throughout the exercise.

2. Lift both legs off floor with right leg straight and left leg bent.

3. Twist torso to left and pull left leg back until right elbow touches left knee.

4. Reverse leg positions and concurrently twist torso to right, pulling right leg back until left elbow touches right knee.

Downward Movement Phase

1. Complete as many twisting trunk curls as possible, then lower legs and upper back to floor.

2. Breathe continuously throughout the exercise.

Note: If you are unable to touch elbow to knee, just twist torso and pull knee back as far as possible on each repetition.

a

b

Exercise Ball Trunk Curl

RECTUS ABDOMINIS

Beginning Position

1. Lie faceup on ball with feet flat on floor and lower back on ball.

2. Place hands behind head to maintain a neutral neck position.

Upward Movement Phase

1. Raise upper back slowly about 30 degrees off exercise ball.

2. Exhale throughout upward movement.

Downward Movement Phase

1. Lower the upper back slowly until it is in full contact with exercise ball.

2. Inhale throughout downward movement.

Note: This exercise is similar to standard trunk curls, but the exercise ball increases the movement range and requires more core stabilization from the midsection muscles.

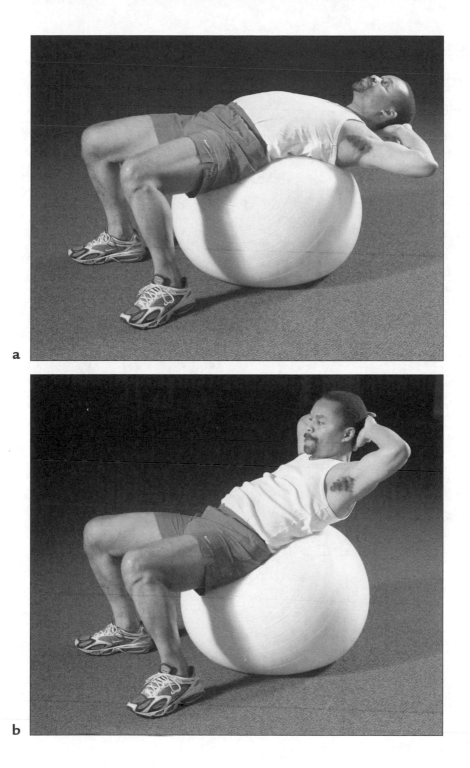

a

b

Chest Crossover

PECTORALIS MAJOR, ANTERIOR DELTOIDS

Beginning Position

1. Adjust seat so that shoulders are in line with the machine's axis of rotation and upper arms are parallel to floor.

2. Sit with head, shoulders, and back firmly against seat back.

3. Position forearms against arm pads and hands on the handles.

Forward Movement Phase

1. Pull arm pads slowly together, exerting more force with the forearms than with the hands.

2. Keep wrists straight.

3. Exhale throughout pulling movement.

Backward Movement Phase

1. Allow arm pads to slowly return to the starting position.

2. Inhale throughout return movement.

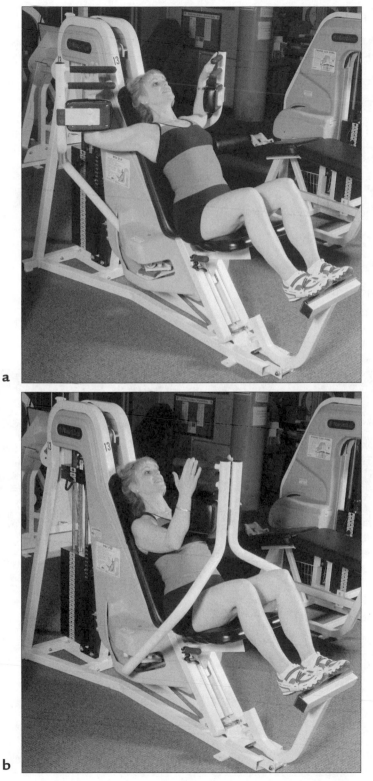

a

b

Chest Press

PECTORALIS MAJOR, ANTERIOR DELTOIDS, TRICEPS

Beginning Position

1. Adjust seat so that handles are in line with middle of chest.

2. Sit with head, shoulders, and back against seat back.

3. Grasp handles with palms facing away.

Forward Movement Phase

1. Push handles forward slowly until arms are fully extended.

2. Keep wrists straight.

3. Exhale throughout pushing movement.

Backward Movement Phase

1. Allow handles to return slowly to the starting position.

2. Inhale throughout the return phase.

 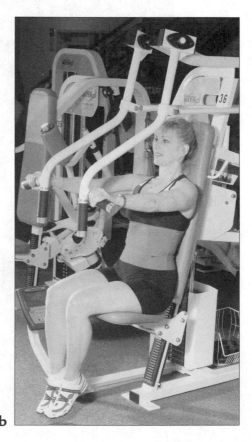

a   b

UPPER-BODY EXERCISES: MACHINES

Incline Press

PECTORALIS MAJOR, ANTERIOR DELTOIDS, TRICEPS

Beginning Position

1. Adjust seat so that handles are below chin level.
2. Sit with head, shoulders, and back against seat pad.
3. Grasp handles with fingers and thumbs, palms facing away.

Upward Movement Phase

1. Push hands upward slowly until arms are fully extended.
2. Keep wrists straight.
3. Exhale throughout pushing movement.

Downward Movement Phase

1. Return handles slowly to starting position.
2. Inhale throughout lowering movement.

a

b

Lateral Raise

DELTOIDS

Beginning Position

1. Adjust seat so that shoulders are in line with the machine's axis of rotation.
2. Sit with head, shoulders, and back firmly against seat pad.
3. Position arms against arm pads and hands on handles, with arms close to sides.

Upward Movement Phase

1. Lift arm pads upward slowly, exerting more pressure with the arms than with the hands.
2. Keep wrists straight.
3. Stop upward movement when arms are parallel to floor.
4. Exhale throughout lifting movement.

Downward Movement Phase

1. Allow pads to slowly return to starting position.
2. Inhale throughout lowering movement.

a   b

UPPER-BODY EXERCISES: MACHINES

Shoulder Press

DELTOIDS, TRICEPS, UPPER TRAPEZIUS

Beginning Position

1. Adjust seat so that handles are below chin level.
2. Sit with head, shoulders, and back against seat pad.
3. Grasp handles with fingers and thumbs, palms facing away.

Upward Movement Phase

1. Push hands upward slowly until arms are fully extended.
2. Keep wrists straight.
3. Exhale throughout pushing movement.

Downward Movement Phase

1. Return handles slowly to starting position.
2. Inhale throughout lowering movement.

a

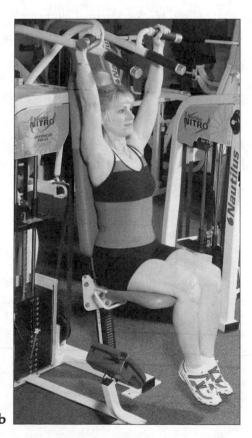
b

UPPER-BODY EXERCISES: MACHINES

Pullover

LATISSIMUS DORSI

Beginning Position

1. Adjust seat so that shoulders are in line with the machine's axis of rotation.

2. Sit with back firmly against seat pad, seat belt secured.

3. Place feet on foot lever and press forward to bring arm pads into starting position near face.

4. Position arms against arm pads and hands on bar.

5. Release foot pad.

Downward Movement Phase

1. Pull arm pads downward slowly, leading with elbows until bar touches body.

2. Keep wrists straight.

3. Allow back to round slightly during downward movement.

4. Exhale throughout downward movement.

Upward Movement Phase

1. Allow arm pads to slowly return to starting position.

2. Inhale throughout return movement.

Note: After completing the final repetition, place feet on foot lever, press forward to hold weight stack, remove arms from arm pads, and lower weight stack slowly.

a

b

Lat Pull-Down

LATISSIMUS DORSI, BICEPS

Beginning Position

1. Place knees under restraining pads, keeping torso upright.

2. Grip the handles with arms fully extended overhead.

Downward Movement Phase

1. Pull handles downward slowly below chin.

2. Exhale throughout pulling movement.

Upward Movement Phase

1. Return slowly to starting position with arms fully extended.

2. Inhale throughout the upward movement.

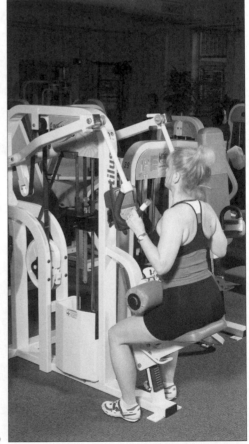

a   b

UPPER-BODY EXERCISES: MACHINES

Seated Row

LATISSIMUS DORSI, BICEPS

Beginning Position

1. Adjust seat so that handles are at shoulder level.
2. Sit with chest against chest pad and torso erect.
3. Place feet flat on floor.
4. Grasp each handle, with arms fully extended.

Backward Movement Phase

1. Pull handles slowly back toward chest.
2. Keep wrists straight.
3. Exhale throughout pulling movement.

Forward Movement Phase

1. Allow handles to return slowly until arms are fully extended.
2. Inhale throughout return movement.

a　　　　　　　　　　b

Weight-Assisted Chin-Up

LATISSIMUS DORSI, BICEPS

Beginning Position

1. Keep in mind that adding weights makes this exercise easier because they counterbalance your body weight.

2. Climb steps and grasp chin bar with an underhand grip.

3. Place knees on platform and descend until arms are fully extended.

Upward Movement Phase

1. Pull body upward until chin is above chin bar.

2. Keep wrists straight.

3. Keep back straight.

4. Exhale throughout pulling movement.

Downward Movement Phase

1. Return slowly to starting position (until arms are fully extended).

2. Inhale throughout return movement.

a

b

Weight-Assisted Bar Dip

PECTORALIS MAJOR, TRICEPS

Beginning Position

1. Keep in mind that adding weights makes this exercise easier because they counterbalance your body weight.

2. Climb steps and grasp dip bars with hands evenly spaced.

3. Place knees on platform and descend until elbows are flexed about 90 degrees.

Upward Movement Phase

1. Push body upward slowly until arms are fully extended.

2. Keep wrists straight.

3. Keep back straight.

4. Exhale throughout pushing movement.

Downward Movement Phase

1. Return slowly to starting position (until elbows are flexed about 90 degrees).

2. Inhale throughout return movement.

UPPER-BODY EXERCISES: MACHINES

a   b

UPPER-BODY EXERCISES: MACHINES

Rowing Back

LATISSIMUS DORSI, POSTERIOR DELTOIDS, RHOMBOIDS

Beginning Position

1. Adjust seat so that upper arms contact center of movement pads when parallel to floor.

2. Sit with head, shoulders, and back against seat pad, and feet on foot bar.

Backward Movement Phase

1. Push movement pads backward as far as possible, maintaining an erect torso.

2. Exhale throughout the backward movement phase.

Forward Movement Phase

1. Return movement pads slowly to starting position.

2. Inhale throughout return movement phase.

a

b

UPPER-BODY EXERCISES: FREE WEIGHTS

Dumbbell Chest Fly

PECTORALIS MAJOR, ANTERIOR DELTOIDS

Beginning Position

1. Lie faceup on bench with legs straddling bench and knees flexed at 90 degrees, feet flat on floor.

2. Keep head, shoulders, and buttocks in contact with the bench, and feet in contact with the floor throughout the exercise.

3. Grasp dumbbells so palms face each other.

4. Push dumbbells in unison to a position over chest with elbows slightly flexed.

Downward Movement Phase

1. Lower dumbbells slowly and in unison, keeping elbows slightly flexed and perpendicular to torso, until upper arms are parallel to floor.

2. Inhale throughout lowering movement.

Upward Movement Phase

1. Lift dumbbells upward in unison to the starting position, with elbows slightly flexed.

2. Exhale throughout upward movement.

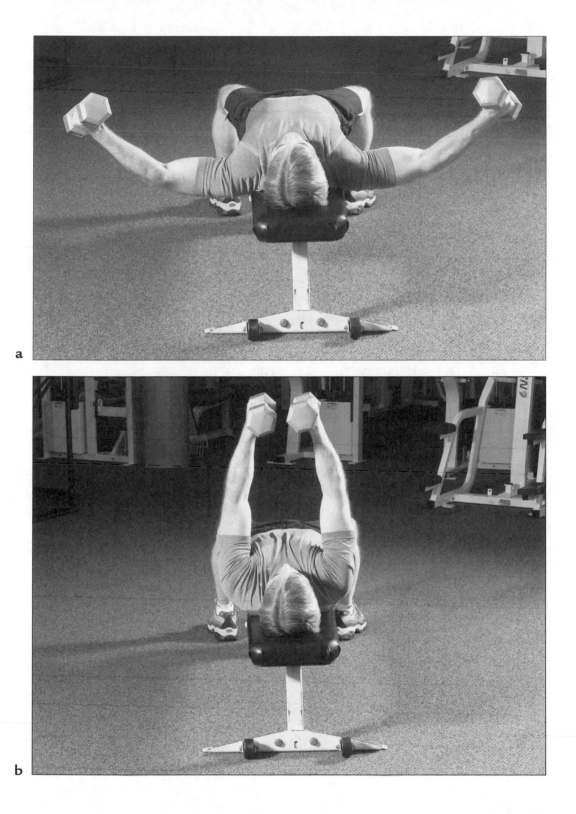

a

b

Dumbbell Bench Press

PECTORALIS MAJOR, ANTERIOR DELTOIDS, TRICEPS

Beginning Position

1. Lie on back with legs straddling bench, knees flexed at 90 degrees, feet flat on floor.

2. Keep head, shoulders, and buttocks in contact with the bench, and feet in contact with the floor throughout the exercise.

3. Grasp dumbbells so palms face away and push upward until arms are fully extended above chest.

Downward Movement Phase

1. Lower dumbbells slowly and evenly to chest.

2. Inhale throughout lowering movement.

Upward Movement Phase

1. Press dumbbells upward in unison until arms are fully extended.

2. Exhale throughout upward movement.

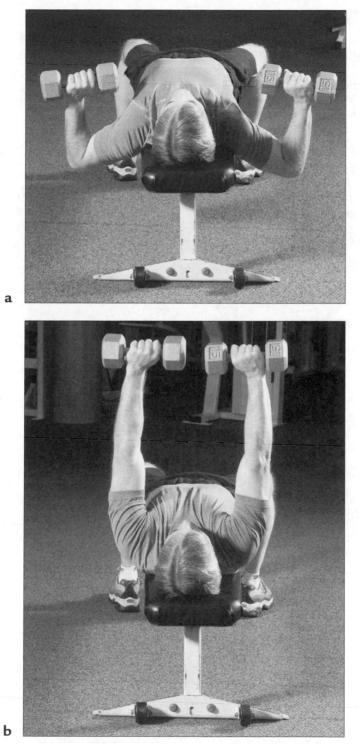

a

b

UPPER-BODY EXERCISES: FREE WEIGHTS

Barbell Bench Press

PECTORALIS MAJOR, ANTERIOR DELTOIDS, TRICEPS

Beginning Position

1. Lie on back with legs straddling bench, knees flexed at 90 degrees, feet flat on floor.

2. Keep head, shoulders, and buttocks in contact with the bench and feet in contact with the floor throughout the exercise.

3. Grasp barbell so that palms face away, and push upward until arms are fully extended above chest.

Downward Movement Phase

1. Lower bar slowly and evenly to chest.

2. Inhale throughout the lowering movement.

Upward Movement Phase

1. Press bar upward evenly until arms are fully extended.

2. Exhale throughout pressing movement.

Note: This exercise requires a competent spotter for safe performance.

a

b

Dumbbell One-Arm Row

LATISSIMUS DORSI, BICEPS

Beginning Position

1. Grasp dumbbell with right hand and support weight by placing left hand and knee on the bench, keeping the right leg straight, and right foot flat on the floor.

2. Position dumbbell so that palm faces bench, keeping arm straight.

3. Keep back flat throughout exercise.

Upward Movement Phase

1. Pull dumbbell slowly to chest.

2. Exhale throughout pulling movement.

Downward Movement Phase

1. Lower dumbbell slowly to starting position.

2. Inhale throughout lowering movement.

Note: Repeat exercise from the beginning position with left arm and reversed leg positions.

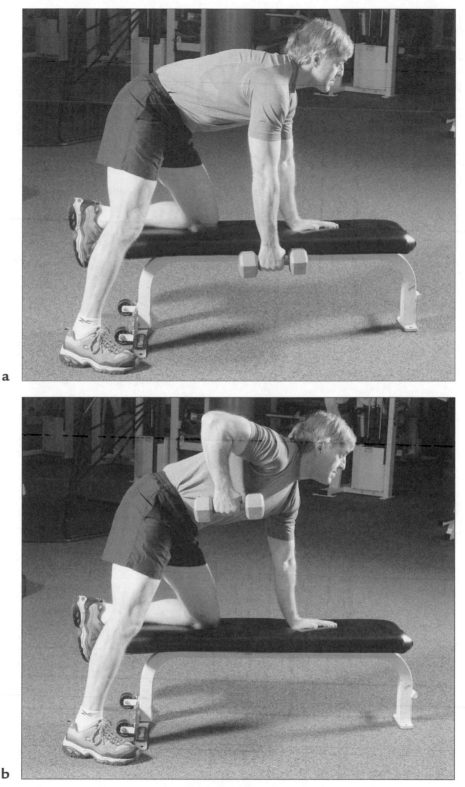

a

b

Dumbbell Pullover

LATISSIMUS DORSI, TRICEPS

Beginning Position

1. Lie faceup on bench with feet flat on floor.
2. Hold dumbbell with both hands behind head.

Upward Movement Phase

1. Lift dumbbell upward and forward until it is just above the chest.
2. Exhale throughout upward movement.

Downward Movement Phase

1. Return dumbbell slowly to starting position.
2. Inhale throughout return movement.

Note: Keep elbows flexed and close to head throughout the exercise.

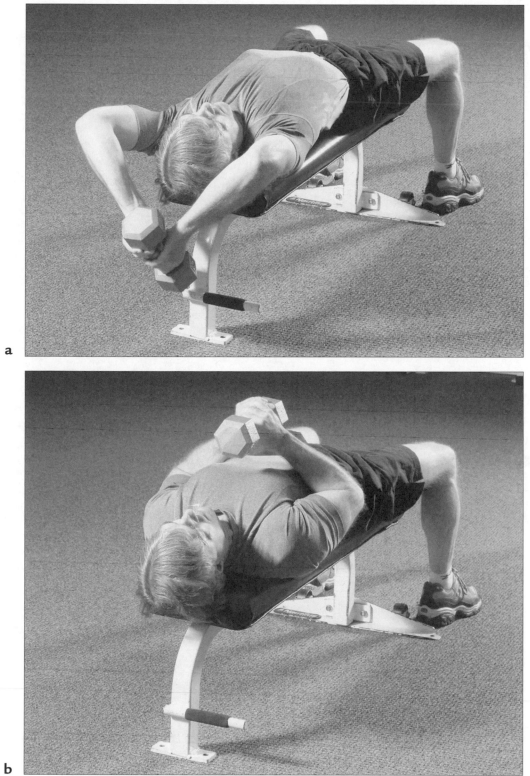

a

b

UPPER-BODY EXERCISES: FREE WEIGHTS

Dumbbell Lateral Raise

DELTOIDS

Beginning Position

1. Grasp dumbbells with palms facing the outside surfaces of thighs and elbows slightly flexed.

2. Stand erect with feet hip-width apart.

Upward Movement Phase

1. Lift dumbbells upward slowly and in unison until level with shoulders, arms parallel to floor.

2. Exhale throughout the upward movement.

Downward Movement Phase

1. Lower dumbbells slowly and in unison to starting position.

2. Inhale throughout lowering movement.

UPPER-BODY EXERCISES: FREE WEIGHTS

a   b

Barbell Incline Press

PECTORALIS MAJOR, ANTERIOR DELTOIDS, TRICEPS

Beginning Position

1. Sit with head, shoulders, and back in contact with incline bench, and feet flat on floor throughout the exercise.

2. Grasp barbell with an overhand grip slightly wider than shoulders, and push upward until arms are fully extended above shoulders.

Downward Movement Phase

1. Lower bar below chin level slowly and evenly.

2. Inhale throughout lowering movement.

Upward Movement Phase

1. Press bar upward evenly until arms are fully extended above shoulders.

2. Exhale throughout pressing movement.

Note: The barbell incline press exercise requires a competent spotter for performance safety.

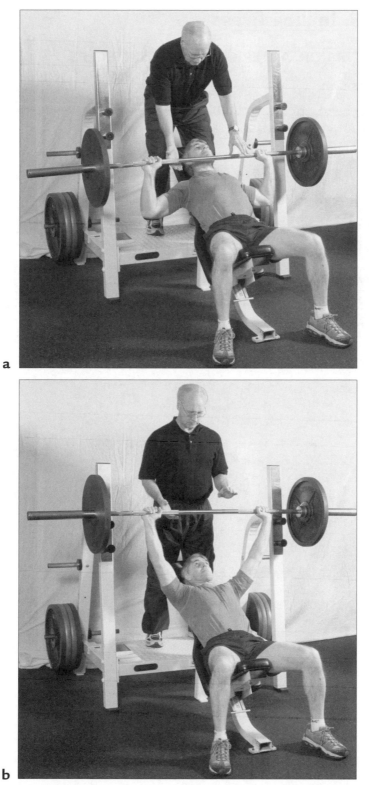

a

b

Dumbbell Incline Press

PECTORALIS MAJOR, ANTERIOR DELTOIDS, TRICEPS

Beginning Position

1. Sit with head, shoulders, and back against incline bench, and feet flat on floor throughout exercise.

2. Grasp dumbbells with overhand grip and hold directly above shoulders with arms fully extended.

Downward Movement Phase

1. Lower dumbbells slowly and evenly to chin level.

2. Inhale throughout lowering movement.

Upward Movement Phase

1. Press dumbbells upward evenly until arms are fully extended above the shoulders.

2. Exhale throughout pressing movement.

a

b

Dumbbell Seated Press

DELTOIDS, TRICEPS, UPPER TRAPEZIUS

Beginning Position

1. Sit with legs straddling bench and feet in contact with floor at all times.

2. Grasp dumbbells with palms turned forward, positioned at shoulder height.

Note: If you're using an upright or adjustable bench, keep head and entire back in contact with it.

Upward Movement Phase

1. Push dumbbells upward slowly and in unison until arms are fully extended over the shoulders.

2. Exhale throughout pushing movement.

Downward Movement Phase

1. Lower dumbbells slowly and in unison to shoulder level.

2. Inhale throughout lowering movement.

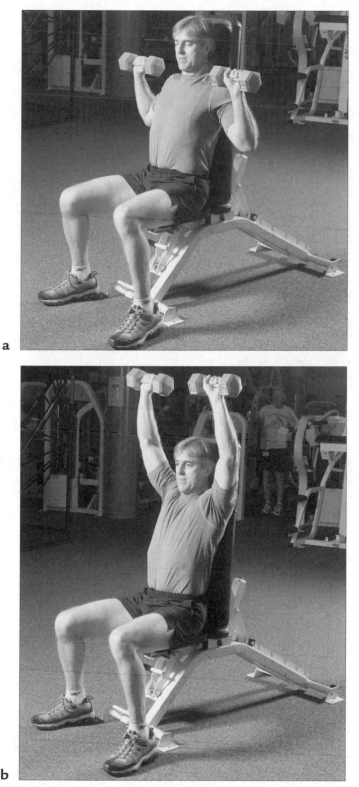

a

b

Dumbbell Alternating Shoulder Press

DELTOIDS, TRICEPS, UPPER TRAPEZIUS

Beginning Position

1. Stand with feet about shoulder-width apart and with torso erect.

2. Grasp dumbbells with an overhand grip and hold just above shoulders.

Upward and Downward Movement Phases

1. Extend left arm overhead slowly without moving right arm.

2. Lower left arm slowly to starting position.

3. Extend right arm overhead slowly without moving left arm.

4. Lower right arm slowly to starting position.

5. Continue alternating pressing movements with left arm and right arm.

6. Exhale during each pressing action, and then inhale during each lowering movement.

Note: Maintain erect posture throughout the dumbbell alternating shoulder press exercise, making certain not to lean backward at any time.

UPPER-BODY EXERCISES: FREE WEIGHTS

a

b

Exercise Ball Push-Up

PECTORALIS MAJOR, DELTOIDS, TRICEPS, RECTUS ABDOMINIS

Beginning Position

1. Assume standard push-up position with hands on floor, slightly wider than shoulder-width apart.

2. Place ankles on top of exercise ball with a straight body position.

Downward Movement Phase

1. Lower chest toward floor, while maintaining a straight body position.

2. Inhale throughout the lowering movement.

Upward Movement Phase

1. Press body upward until arms are fully extended. ·

2. Exhale throughout the pressing movement.

Note: This exercise is similar to a standard push-up, but use of the exercise ball requires additional core stabilization from the midsection muscles.

a

b

Body-Weight Chin-Up

LATISSIMUS DORSI, BICEPS

Beginning Position

1. Grasp chin bar with underhand grip, hands shoulder-width apart, arms fully extended.

2. Maintain a straight body position throughout the exercise.

Upward Movement Phase

1. Lift body upward until chin is above chin bar.

2. Exhale throughout upward movement phase.

Downward Movement Phase

1. Lower body slowly until arms are fully extended.

2. Inhale throughout downward movement phase.

a

b

Body-Weight Dip

PECTORALIS MAJOR, ANTERIOR DELTOIDS, TRICEPS

Beginning Position

1. Grasp dip bars with an overhand grip, arms fully extended.
2. Maintain a straight body position throughout the exercise.

Downward Movement Phase

1. Lower body slowly until elbows are flexed to 90 degrees.
2. Inhale throughout downward movement phase.

Upward Movement Phase

1. Press body upward until arms are extended.
2. Exhale throughout upward movement phase.

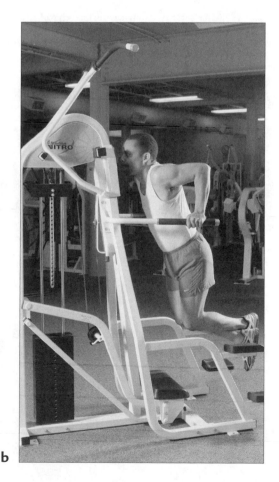

a   b

Biceps Curl

BICEPS

Beginning Position

1. Adjust seat so that elbows are in line with the machine's axis of rotation and upper arms are angled slightly upward.

2. Grasp handles with underhand grip and with elbows slightly flexed.

3. Sit with head in neutral position and torso erect.

Upward Movement Phase

1. Curl handles upward slowly until elbows are fully flexed.

2. Keep wrists straight.

3. Exhale throughout lifting movement.

Downward Movement Phase

1. Allow handles to return slowly to starting position.

2. Inhale throughout lowering movement.

a   b

Triceps Extension

TRICEPS

Beginning Position

1. Adjust seat so that elbows are in line with the machine's axis of rotation.

2. Sit with back firmly against seat pad.

3. Place sides of hands against hand pads and allow pads to move close to shoulders.

Forward Movement Phase

1. Push handles forward slowly until arms are fully extended.

2. Keep wrists straight.

3. Exhale throughout forward movement.

Backward Movement Phase

1. Allow handles to return slowly to the starting position.

2. Inhale throughout return movement.

a

b

Triceps Press

TRICEPS, PECTORALIS MAJOR, ANTERIOR DELTOIDS

Beginning Position

1. Adjust seat so that elbows are at 90-degree angles when hands are grasping handles.

2. Sit with erect torso and hands grasping handles directly below shoulders.

3. Secure seat belt.

Downward Movement Phase

1. Push handles downward until arms are fully extended.

2. Keep wrists straight.

3. Exhale throughout pushing movement.

Upward Movement Phase

1. Return handles slowly to starting position.

2. Inhale throughout return movement.

a

b

Triceps Press-Down

TRICEPS

Beginning Position

1. Stand erect with feet hip-width apart and knees slightly flexed.

2. Grasp bar with an overhand grip.

3. Pull bar down until upper arms are perpendicular with floor and touching sides, with elbows flexed.

Downward Movement Phase

1. Push bar downward until arms are fully extended.

2. Exhale throughout pushing movement.

Upward Movement Phase

1. Return bar slowly to starting position.

2. Inhale throughout upward movement.

Note: Prepare for an unexpected upward pull from the bar during the upward movement phase!

a

b

Barbell Curl

BICEPS

Beginning Position

1. Grasp bar with an underhand grip with upper arms against sides. Ensure that upper arms remain perpendicular to floor and against sides throughout this exercise.

2. Stand erect with feet hip-width apart and parallel to each other.

Upward Movement Phase

1. Curl barbell upward slowly toward shoulders.

2. Exhale throughout curling movement.

Downward Movement Phase

1. Lower barbell slowly until arms are fully extended.

2. Inhale throughout lowering movement.

a   b

Dumbbell Standing Curl

BICEPS

Beginning Position

1. Grasp dumbbells with an underhand grip, arms straight. Ensure that upper arms remain perpendicular to floor and against sides throughout this exercise.

2. Stand erect with feet about hip-width apart and parallel to each other.

Upward Movement Phase

1. Curl dumbbells upward slowly and in unison toward shoulders by flexing elbows until palms face the chest.

2. Exhale throughout upward movement.

Downward Movement Phase

1. Lower dumbbells slowly and in unison to starting position.

2. Inhale throughout lowering movement.

a

b

Dumbbell Incline Curl

BICEPS

Beginning Position

1. Sit on an incline bench with shoulders and back against seat pad and feet on floor.

2. Grasp dumbbells with an underhand grip, arms perpendicular to floor.

Upward Movement Phase

1. Curl dumbbells upward slowly until elbows are fully flexed, keeping upper arms stationary.

2. Exhale throughout upward movement.

Downward Movement Phase

1. Lower dumbbells slowly to starting position.

2. Inhale throughout lowering movement.

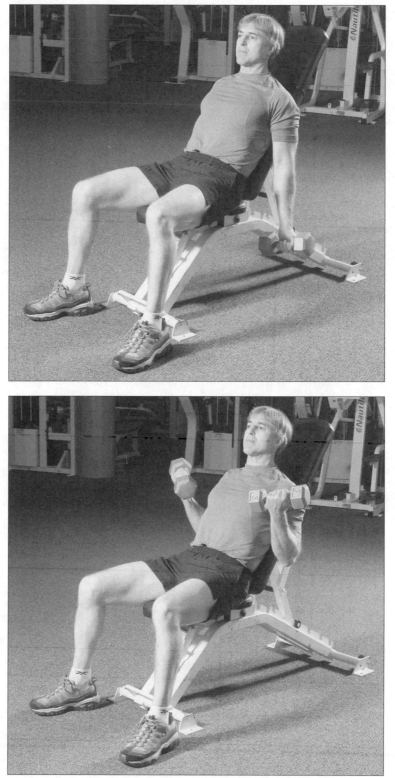

a

b

Dumbbell Preacher Curl

BICEPS

Beginning Position

1. Sit on preacher bench with upper arms supported on diagonal arm pad and with feet on floor.

2. Grasp dumbbells with an underhand grip and arms nearly extended.

Upward Movement Phase

1. Curl dumbbells upward slowly until elbows are fully flexed.

2. Exhale throughout upward movement.

Downward Movement Phase

1. Lower dumbbells slowly to starting position.

2. Inhale throughout lowering movement.

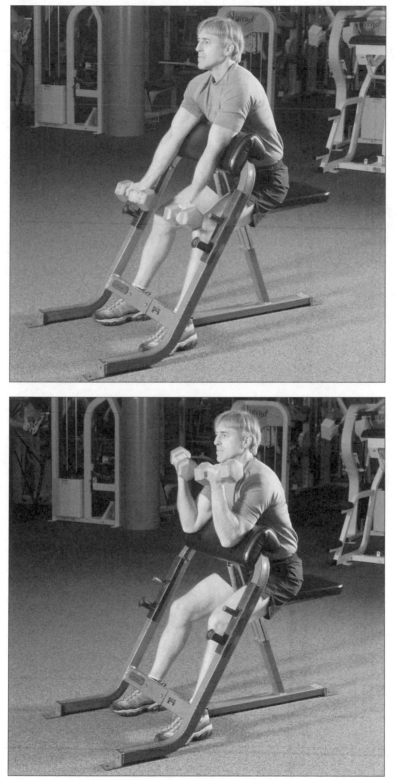

a

b

Dumbbell Concentration Curl

BICEPS

Beginning Position

1. Sit on a bench and grasp dumbbell in right hand with right elbow braced against right thigh, feet shoulder-width apart, and upper body leaning slightly forward. Right elbow should remain firmly braced against thigh throughout the exercise.

2. Begin with arm straight and palm facing away from the body.

Upward Movement Phase

1. Curl dumbbell slowly toward chin.

2. Exhale throughout curling movement.

Downward Movement Phase

1. Lower dumbbell slowly back to starting position.

2. Inhale throughout lowering movement.

3. Repeat from beginning position with left arm (left elbow on left thigh).

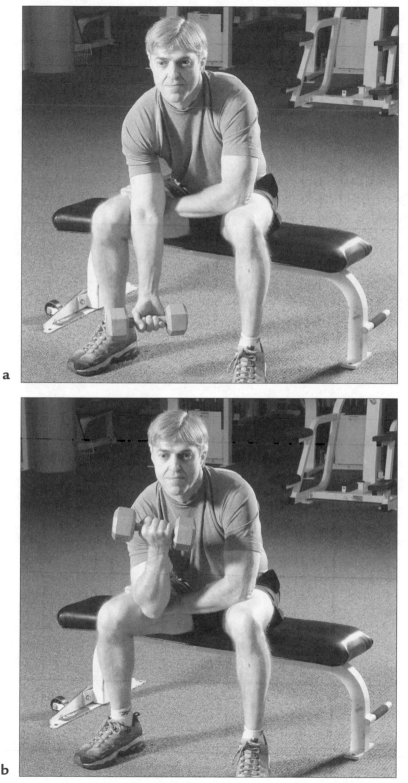

a

b

Dumbbell Overhead Triceps Extension

TRICEPS

Beginning Position

1. Grasp one dumbbell with both hands and stand erect with feet about hip-width apart.

2. Lift dumbbell upward until arms are fully extended, directly above head. Keep upper arms perpendicular to floor throughout exercise.

Downward Movement Phase

1. Lower dumbbell slowly toward base of neck.

2. Inhale throughout lowering movement.

Upward Movement Phase

1. Lift dumbbell upward slowly until arms are fully extended.

2. Exhale throughout lifting movement.

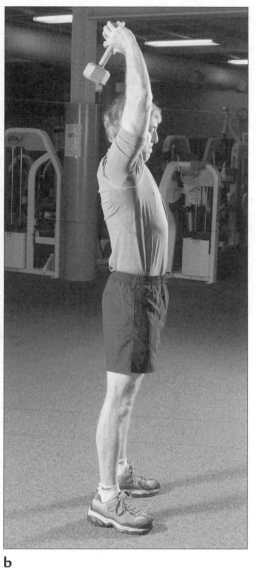

a

b

Dumbbell Lying Triceps Extension

TRICEPS

Beginning Position

1. Lie faceup on flat bench with feet on floor.

2. Grasp dumbbells with palms facing each other.

3. Lift dumbbells upward until the arms are fully extended directly above shoulders.

Note: Keep upper arms perpendicular to floor throughout exercise.

Downward Movement Phase

1. Lower dumbbells slowly until they are next to ears.

2. Inhale throughout lowering movement.

Upward Movement Phase

1. Lift dumbbells upward slowly until arms are fully extended directly above shoulders.

2. Exhale throughout upward movement.

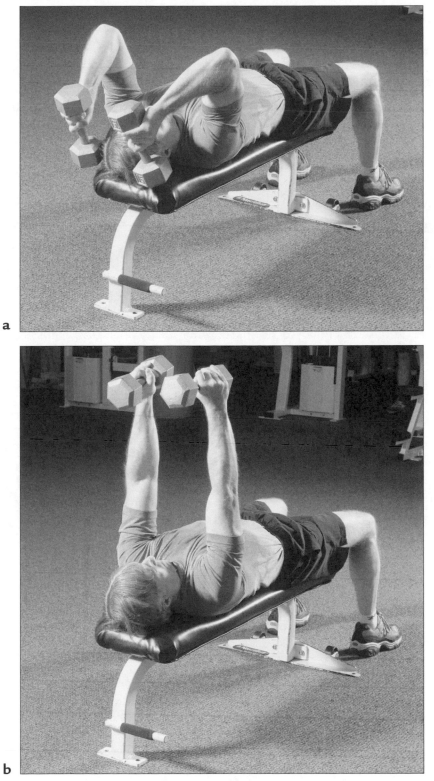

a

b

Exercise Ball Bench Dip

TRICEPS, PECTORALIS MAJOR, ANTERIOR DELTOIDS

Beginning Position

1. Place heels of hands on bench with arms extended and heels of feet on exercise ball with legs extended so that hips are in front of bench.

2. Maintain an L body position throughout the exercise.

Downward Movement Phase

1. Lower hips slowly toward floor until elbows are bent to 90 degrees.

2. Inhale throughout downward movement.

Upward Movement Phase

1. Press body upward slowly until arms are fully extended.

2. Exhale throughout upward movement.

Note: This exercise is similar to standard bench dips, but using the exercise ball requires additional core stabilization from the midsection.

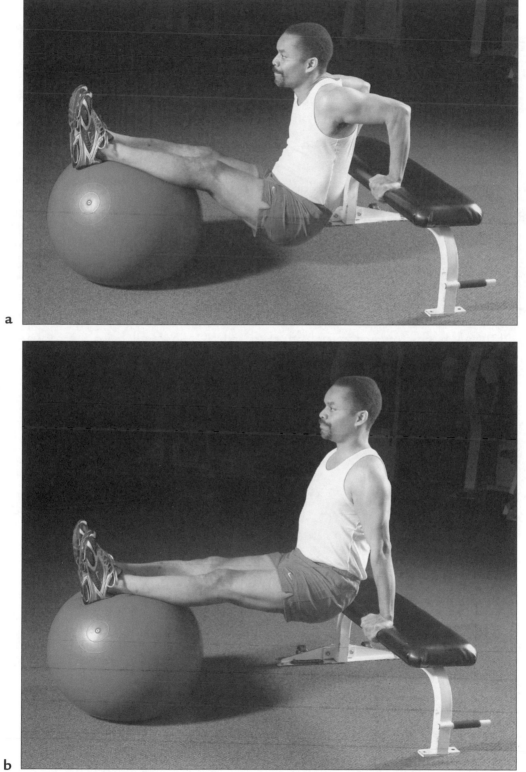

a

b

ARM EXERCISES: EXERCISE BALL

Exercise Ball Walk-Out

TRICEPS, PECTORALIS MAJOR, ANTERIOR DELTOIDS

Beginning Position

1. Assume standard push-up position with hands on floor, slightly wider than shoulder-width apart.

2. Place ankles on top of exercise ball, and maintain a straight body position parallel to floor.

Note: Maintain straight body position throughout the exercise.

Backward Movement Phase

1. Walk hands backward toward exercise ball, allowing legs to roll backward over ball.

2. Breathe continuously throughout backward movement.

Forward Movement Phase

1. Walk hands forward away from exercise ball, allowing legs to roll forward over ball.

2. Breathe continuously throughout forward movement.

a

b

Neck Extension

NECK EXTENSORS

Beginning Position

1. Adjust seat so that back of head fits comfortably in head pad.

2. Adjust torso pad for an erect posture.

3. Place back of head against head pad, with head angled slightly forward.

4. Grip handles.

Backward Movement Phase

1. Push head pad backward slowly until neck is comfortably extended.

2. Keep torso straight.

3. Exhale throughout backward movement.

Forward Movement Phase

1. Allow head pad to slowly return to starting position, with head angled slightly forward.

2. Inhale throughout return movement.

a

b

NECK EXERCISES: MACHINES

Neck Flexion

NECK FLEXORS

Beginning Position

1. Adjust seat so that face will fit comfortably against head pad with nose parallel to crossbar.

2. Adjust torso pad for erect posture.

3. Place forehead and cheeks against head pad, with head angled slightly backward.

4. Grip handles.

Forward Movement Phase

1. Push head pad forward slowly until the neck is fully flexed.

2. Keep torso straight.

3. Exhale throughout forward movement.

Backward Movement Phase

1. Allow head pad to return slowly to starting position, with head angled slightly backward.

2. Inhale throughout return movement.

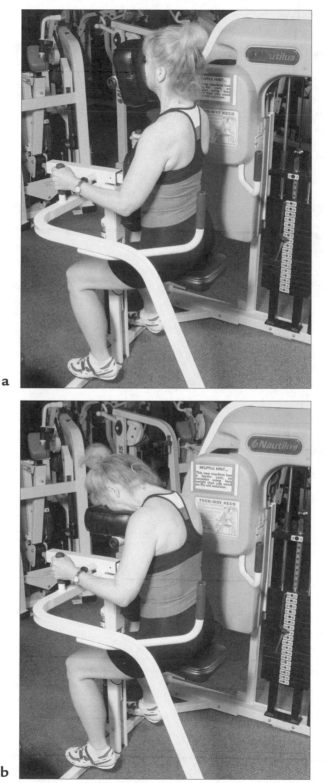

a

b

Dumbbell Shrug

UPPER TRAPEZIUS

Beginning Position

1. Grasp dumbbells with palms facing thighs, arms at sides and fully extended. Keep arms straight throughout the exercise.

2. Stand erect with feet hip-width apart.

Upward Movement Phase

1. Elevate (shrug) the shoulders in unison toward ears as high as possible.

2. Exhale throughout shrugging movement.

Downward Movement Phase

1. Lower dumbbells slowly and in unison to starting position.

2. Inhale throughout lowering movement.

a   b

Barbell Shrug

UPPER TRAPEZIUS

Beginning Position

1. Grasp barbell with an overhand grip, arms at sides and fully extended. Keep arms straight throughout the exercise.

2. Stand erect with feet hip-width apart.

Upward Movement Phase

1. Elevate (shrug) the shoulders toward the ears as high as possible.

2. Exhale throughout shrugging movement.

Downward Movement Phase

1. Lower barbell slowly to starting position.

2. Inhale throughout lowering movement.

a   b

4

Practical Strength Training Principles

In this chapter, we present research-based guidelines that are essential for maximizing strength development and ensuring safe training experiences. These guidelines are discussed in the following order: program design variables, exercise techniques, and workout organization.

The need to address program design should be obvious, and this section carefully examines all of the essential training factors. However, it is equally important to address proper exercise technique because it is closely related to your training effectiveness and risk of injury. Finally, you should find the information on workout organization helpful, especially if you perform both strength training and aerobic activity.

Program Design Variables

This chapter provides guidelines for selecting and organizing exercises and for determining the training frequency, the weight loads to use, the number of repetitions and sets to perform, and the length of rest periods. The chapter also explains how to maximize your training effort and outcome. Adhering to these guidelines results in safe and successful strength training.

Exercise Selection

Hundreds of different strength training exercises can be performed with free weights, weight-stack machines, and body-weight resistance. It is therefore important to carefully select exercises that provide the best balance of exercise effectiveness, training efficiency, and workout safety. This section presents the rationale for designing a purposeful and practical program of strength exercises that provides comprehensive muscle development in accordance with sensible training principles.

Perform One Exercise for Each Major Muscle Group   One the most important guidelines for choosing exercises to include in your program is to perform at least one exercise for each major muscle group. This ensures that your workouts will result in symmetrical muscular development. The major muscle groups include the chest, shoulders, back, arms, midsection, and legs. As you can see in the far left column in table 4.1, there is at least one exercise for each major muscle group.

Select Exercises for Opposing Muscle Groups   Many people select certain exercises because they are more popular, more convenient, or more satisfying to perform than others. For example, most strength training programs feature bench presses for upper-body development. It is true that the bench press strengthens the chest, front shoulder, and rear arm muscles (triceps). However, if you do not give equal attention to the *opposing muscles* of the upper back, rear shoulder, and front of the arms (biceps), you may develop a *strength imbalance* that leads to poor posture and a greater susceptibility to joint injuries.

Opposing muscles—Muscles that produce opposing movements around a joint (e.g., biceps that bend the elbow and triceps that straighten it).

Strength imbalance—Disproportionate strength on one side of a joint or muscle area as a result of overemphasizing the training on one side.

Exercise Order

There seems to be general confusion about the order in which strength exercises should be performed. Some people prefer to begin with their stronger muscle groups, and others choose to start with their weaker muscle groups when they are fresh. Because larger muscle groups (e.g., quadriceps) use more energy, produce more fatigue by-products, and elicit higher blood pressure responses than smaller muscle groups (e.g., biceps), most strength training authorities recommend an exercise order that progresses from larger to smaller muscle groups.

We prefer to train larger muscle groups before smaller muscle groups. Table 4.1 lists the major muscle groups from largest (thigh) to smallest (forearms) and suggests an order for performing exercises that develop each of these muscle groups: lower-body exercises, followed by upper-body exercises, followed by those for the midsection and neck. Some refer to this as priority training because it prioritizes exercises that work the larger muscles before the smaller muscles. Arranging the order of exercises in this manner ensures that you train the larger muscles while you are fresh, enabling you to emphasize their development over smaller groups.

Of course, you do not have to use this recommended sequence for training. For example, you may occasionally want to work your weaker muscle groups first while you are fresh. Keep in mind though, that when you vary the exercise order, the number of repetitions you can perform will change accordingly. You should be able to perform more repetitions of an exercise if you move it from the end to the beginning of your training session, because you will be less fatigued in the early stages of your workout.

Table 4.1   Suggested Exercises For Major Muscle Groups

Muscle group	Machine exercise	Free weight exercise
Front thigh (quadriceps)	Leg extension	Dumbbell squat or barbell squat
Rear thigh (hamstrings)	Leg curl	Dumbbell squat or barbell squat
Inner thigh (hip adductors)	Hip adduction	—
Outer thigh (hip abductors)	Hip abduction	—
Lower leg (gastrocnemius)	Heel raise	Dumbbell heel raise
Chest (pectoralis major)	Chest crossover	Dumbbell or barbell bench press
Upper back (latissimus dorsi)	Pullover	Dumbbell one-arm row
Shoulders (deltoids)	Lateral raise	Dumbbell seated press
Front arm (biceps)	Biceps curl	Dumbbell standing curl
Rear arm (triceps)	Triceps extension	Dumbbell overhead triceps extension
Low back (erector spinae)	Low back extension	Body-weight trunk extension
Abdominals (rectus abdominis)	Abdominal flexion	Body-weight trunk curl
Sides (external and internal obliques)	Rotary torso	Twisting trunk curl
Front neck (sterno-cleidomastoids)	Neck flexion	—
Rear neck (upper trapezius)	Neck extension	Dumbbell or barbell shrug
Forearms (wrist flexors and extensors)	Forearm flexion and extension	Wrist curl and extension

Training Frequency

Regular strength training stresses your muscles and produces some degree of *tissue microtrauma*. After each workout, the exercised tissues respond to the training stimulus by rebuilding tissue, resulting in larger and stronger muscles. These tissue-building processes typically take 48 to 96 hours. Although your training frequency may vary, most people make consistent strength improvements with two or three exercise sessions per week.

An every-other-day program of strength training ensures consistency and produces excellent results. But two strength workouts a week produce nearly

Tissue microtrauma—Temporary weakening of muscle cells that stimulates tissue-building processes and strength development.

as much muscle development as three strength workouts a week. As shown in figure 4.1, in our 8-week study of 1,132 subjects, those who trained two days a week experienced almost 90 percent as much muscle development as those who trained three days a week. Our follow-up 10-week study, also shown in figure 4.1, involving 1,644 subjects revealed equal gains in muscle weight for those who trained two days a week and those who trained three days a week. The average age of the trainees in both of these studies was over 50, so these findings are applicable to our recommended training protocols.

Based on these studies, we recommend two or three strength training sessions a week. Your rate of muscle development should be about the same whether you do two or three weekly workouts. Although you can gain strength by training only one day a week, your rate of muscle development will be reduced by about 50 percent, based on our studies.

Another key fact to remember is that training consistency is as important as exercise frequency. Missing scheduled training sessions is unproductive, and working your muscles two days in a row to make up a missed session is counterproductive. Therefore, you should establish a regular strength training workout schedule that is compatible with your lifestyle, either two or three nonconsecutive days each week.

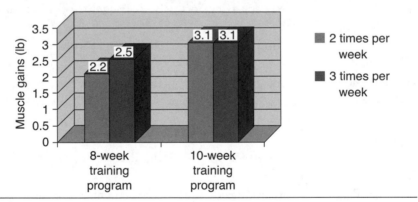

Figure 4.1   Changes in lean (muscle) weight for men and women performing two or three strength training sessions a week (2,776 subjects).

Exercise Sets

An exercise set refers to a group of consecutive repetitions that you perform in a given exercise. For example, if you pick up the dumbbells and perform 10 biceps curls, then return the dumbbells to the rack, you have completed one set of 10 repetitions. If you rest, then repeat this procedure, you have completed two sets of 10 repetitions. People starting a strength training program should perform one set of each exercise.

One set of an exercise is the minimum required for strength improvement, and single-set strength training is an efficient and effective means of muscle development. One research study on upper-body strength gains—measured by increases in repetitions performed—showed similar results among groups of participants who did one, two, or three sets of chin-ups and bar dips over a 10-week training period (see figure 4.2).

Figure 4.2 Comparison of one-, two-, and three-set strength training (77 subjects).

Figure 4.3 Comparison of one- and three-set strength training (38 subjects).

A University of Florida study compared lower-body strength gains—measured by percentage of increase in the load lifted—for participants who performed one or three sets of leg extensions and leg curls. As illustrated in figure 4.3, both training groups made almost equal gains in lower-body strength during the 14-week training period. Based on the results of these studies, it seems both prudent and productive to begin strength training with one set of each exercise, then progress to two or three exercise sets if you have the time and motivation to do so.

Rest Periods Between Sets and Exercises

When performing two or more sets of the same exercise, allow your muscles to recover for one to two minutes between sets. This is sufficient time to rest your muscles and restore most of your anaerobic energy supply. Also take a brief rest between successive exercises to reduce the general effects of fatigue on subsequent muscular performance. Resting about one minute between different exercises as you progress through your workout is sufficient.

Exercise Load

The first safety concern for anyone participating in strength training is to select an appropriate exercise resistance. The most important consideration is making sure your beginning weight loads are not too heavy. Of course, the weight, or load, you use largely determines the number of repetitions that you can perform in an exercise set.

For example, if your strength assessment in chapter 1 places you in the chapter 5 training programs, then you will use loads that enable you to complete 12 to 16 repetitions of the exercises listed. If you begin with chapter 6 training programs, then you will use heavier loads that enable you to complete 8 to 12 repetitions of the exercises. If you select workouts from chapter 7, your training loads should be heavy enough to fatigue your muscles in 4 to 8 repetitions.

Generally speaking, most people can complete 16 repetitions with approximately 60 percent of their maximal load, 12 repetitions with approximately 70 percent of their maximal load, 8 repetitions with approximately 80 percent of their maximal load, and 4 repetitions with approximately 90 percent of their maximal load. For example, if your exercise range is 8 to 12 repetitions, start with a load that enables you to comfortably perform 8 to 10 repetitions. Continue training with this load until you can complete 12 repetitions using proper technique, then increase the resistance in accordance with the overload principle.

For decades, successful strength training programs have been built on the overload principle. Overload means using progressively heavier loads to stimulate further strength development. For example, if you can complete 10 bench presses with 100 pounds (45 kilograms), you could experience an overload by simply increasing the weight by 5 pounds (2.3 kilograms) and performing as many repetitions as you can with this slightly heavier load.

It is possible to apply the overload principle by performing low repetitions with relatively heavy loads or by performing a high number of repetitions with relatively light loads. Therefore guidelines are necessary. These guidelines are based on the percentage of the maximum amount of weight that you can lift in an exercise one time, referred to as percentage of maximum resistance. Because of the stable relationship between resistance and repetitions presented in the following list, it is not necessary for you to determine your maximum weight loads. Charts are also provided in each of the program chapters (5, 6, and 7) to help you select the appropriate exercise resistance. For most training purposes, you should use loads that allow you to perform 4 to 16 repetitions, which equals 90 to 60 percent, respectively, of the maximum load you can lift one time.

Relationships Between Resistance and Repetitions

Maximum resistance, generally referred to as the repetition maximum or 1RM weight load, is the heaviest resistance that you can lift one time. Loads that are less than 100 percent of 1RM will permit the number of repetitions shown in the following list.

   95 percent 1RM = 2 repetitions

   90 percent 1RM = 4 repetitions

   85 percent 1RM = 6 repetitions

   80 percent 1RM = 8 repetitions

   75 percent 1RM = 10 repetitions

   70 percent 1RM = 12 repetitions

   65 percent 1RM = 14 repetitions

   60 percent 1RM = 16 repetitions

Exercise Repetitions

The key to developing stronger muscles is using a progressive training system that gradually increases the loads used in each exercise. Loads that allow you to perform 4 to 16 reps using your best effort are considered ideal. If you select a load that is too heavy, you will not be able to complete 4 reps. If it is too light, you will be able to perform more than 16 reps. As muscles become stronger in response to training, using the same load will result in more repetitions. When this occurs, it is important to increase the load, which creates the *overload* that is needed to stimulate further strength increases.

If you perform repetitions in a controlled manner, it will take about 6 seconds (2-second lifting phase and 4-second lowering phase) to complete each repetition. At a 6-second repetition speed, a set of 4 reps requires about 25 seconds, and a set of 16 reps requires about 95 seconds. Performing repetitions in this manner will maximize muscle tension and strength development and minimize movement momentum, which will reduce the risk of training injuries.

In a study examining resistance–repetitions relationships, 141 subjects were tested to determine how many repetitions they could complete with 75 percent of their maximum resistance. As illustrated in figure 4.4, the average number of repetitions performed was 10.5. However, some people performed fewer repetitions and some performed more repetitions using the same relative load. These differences are caused by genetic variations in muscle fiber makeup, and they explain in part why some people prefer lower-repetition training and others prefer higher-repetition training.

Generally speaking, it is advisable to periodically progress from higher-repetition training with lighter loads to lower-repetition training with heavier loads, and then repeat the process as your training becomes more advanced. As an example, the sample base training programs in chapter 5 use 12 to 16 repetitions, the experienced training programs in chapter 6 use 8 to 12 repetitions, and the advanced programs in chapter 7 use 4 to 8 repetitions. After several weeks using 4- to 8-repetition training, you should reduce the weight loads and switch to higher repetition sets (12 to 16 reps or 8 to 12 reps) for a couple of months before progressing again to fewer repetitions with heavier loads.

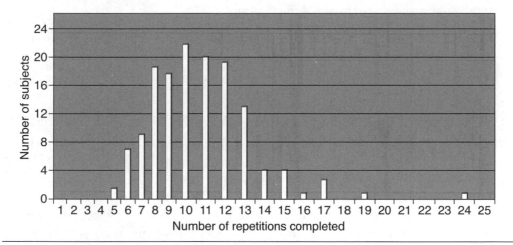

Figure 4.4   Distribution of repetitions completed with 75 percent of maximum weight load (141 subjects).

Training Progression

As you continue training, you will increase your muscle strength and want to use heavier weight loads. Progression is the key to continued strength development, but you must approach it gradually and systematically for best results. Keep in mind that strength training is a lifetime activity, and there is no reason to do too much too soon, which can lead to injury and setback.

Double-Progressive System

We recommend the 5 percent rule, which you can easily apply to any of the strength training protocols in this book, for safe and successful strength training progression. The 5 percent rule dictates that whenever you reach the end of your repetition range for two workouts in succession, you increase the resistance by 5 percent (or less) for your next workout. For example, if you are using a protocol of 12 to 16 repetitions, and you complete 16 leg extensions with 100 pounds (45 kilograms) in two successive workouts, you should raise the resistance to 105 pounds (47.25 kilograms) for your next training session. Likewise, if you are using a protocol of 8 to 12 repetitions, and you complete 12 bench presses with 50 pounds (23 kilograms) twice in a row, you should raise the resistance by 2.5 pounds (1.15 kilograms) for your next workout.

This is a double-progressive system in which you first add repetitions (within your training range), and then add resistance (by 5 percent or less). Although relatively simple in application, this double-progressive exercise approach has an outstanding safety record and typically enables beginning participants to attain more than 40 percent strength gains after just two months of training.

Multiple-Set Training

Another strategy for progressively increasing the workout intensity is the use of multiple-set training. Multiple-set training offers a greater volume of muscular work for each exercise and may be performed by people who prefer a longer training session. Within this approach are three standard options.

Protocol 1: Use the same training load in all sets, and perform the same number of repetitions.

Protocol 2: Increase the training load in each set, and perform the same number of repetitions.

Protocol 3: Increase the load in each set, and reduce the number of repetitions.

In the first approach, you perform multiple exercise sets with the same training load, such as completing three sets of 10 leg extensions, using 100 pounds (45 kilograms) for each set. This exercise protocol provides both a relatively high training volume and a relatively high training effort on each exercise set, making it a challenging workout when using appropriate resistance. In the second example, you follow an exercise protocol that features multiple-set training with increasingly greater loads, such as a set of 10 leg extensions with 60 pounds (27 kilograms), a second set of 10 leg extensions with 80 pounds (36 kilograms), and a third set of 10 leg extensions with 100 pounds (45 kilograms). This training method provides a progressive warm-up before performing the heaviest set, but it requires a relatively high training effort on only the final exercise set. In the third option, you follow a training method, sometimes referred to as the pyramid approach, which involves using heavier loads and fewer repetitions in successive sets. For example, you perform 10 leg extensions with 100 pounds (45 kilograms), 8 leg extensions with 115 pounds (52 kilograms), and 6 repetitions with 130 pounds (59 kilograms). A well-designed pyramid protocol requires a relatively high training effort on each exercise set, and it permits performance with relatively heavier weight loads than the other training methods. Less experienced exercisers should probably begin multiple-set training with protocol 2, because it provides progressive warm-up sets and only one high-effort set. More experienced exercisers may choose either protocol 1 or protocol 3, depending on whether they prefer to perform high-effort sets with the same resistance or high-effort sets with progressively heavier weight loads and correspondingly fewer repetitions.

Because a wide range of exercise loads can produce excellent strength gains, periodically train with different percentages of your maximum load. For example, the sample programs in chapter 5 use 60 to 70 percent of maximum resistance (12 to 16 reps), those in chapter 6 use 70 to 80 percent of maximum resistance (8 to 12 reps), and those in chapter 7 use 80 to 90 percent of maximum resistance (4 to 8 reps). Systematically changing your exercise resistance offers both physiological and psychological benefits. Keep in mind that strength training with loads of 60 to 90 percent of maximum are highly effective for gaining strength and building muscle.

Training Effort

Exercise physiologists agree that training at a high level of muscular effort enhances strength development. You'll get the best results when your exercise intensity is high enough to fatigue the target muscles. This level of fatigue will occur if you train to muscle failure in each set. Following this guideline and performing 4 to 16 repetitions with 90 to 60 percent of your maximum load will provide an ideal training effect. As your strength fitness improves, you should also consider ways to increase your exercise effort.

For example, you may perform a set of leg extensions, rest two minutes, and complete another set of leg extensions. As a more time-efficient alternative, you may perform a set of leg extensions followed closely by a set of leg presses. Both of these exercises target your quadriceps muscles but involve different movement patterns to provide an additional training stimulus. Of course, you should only follow this more challenging type of workout if you want to put greater effort into your exercise program.

Exercise Technique Guidelines

Inexperienced exercisers tend to use momentum-assisted repetitions with accelerated movement speed and abbreviated movement range, both of which decrease training effectiveness and increase injury risk. Beginners also tend to hold their breath as they lift the weight loads, which results in higher blood pressure responses. The three technique guidelines presented next for repetition speed, range of motion, and breathing patterns are all important for maximizing the training effect and making your workouts safer.

Movement Speed

Movement speed refers to the time required to perform each exercise repetition. This includes the total time you use to lift and lower the load (note that *lift* refers to the upward direction that the weight stack, barbell, or dumbbell moves, regardless of the direction your body moves). Although your training speed during repetitions is partly a matter of personal preference, it is important to perform all exercise repetitions under control. Under control generally refers to repetitions that take at least four seconds. These slow movement speeds involve more muscle tension and less momentum, which should increase your training stimulus and decrease your injury risk. But it is difficult to determine an ideal movement speed for performing strength training exercises.

For example, a recent study examined the effects of 4-, 6-, 8-, and 14-second repetitions on strength development in 198 men and women (see table 4.2). All four exercise groups made excellent strength gains over an eight-week training period. Repetition speeds of 4 to 14 seconds were all effective for improving strength across 13 major muscle groups. So there is clearly a range of controlled movement speeds that are safe and productive for muscle development.

You can exert more muscle force lowering the weight load than lifting the weight load. Therefore, to challenge your muscles during the lowering part of the exercise, slow your movement speed. For example, a popular and time-tested training protocol is 2 seconds for the more difficult lifting phase and 4 seconds for the easier lowering phase of each repetition. The training protocols in our program chapters use lifting speeds of 1.5 to 2 seconds and lowering speeds of 2.5 to 4 seconds.

One means for assessing your movement speed is the stop test. If you can stop the repetition at any point in the movement range during a repetition, you are using the right speed. Try this test during workouts to see if you are performing repetitions at the proper speed.

Table 4.2   Movement Speed and Strength Improvement

Training protocol (8 weeks)	Reps per set	Time per set (in seconds)	Mean weight increase (on 13 Nautilus machines in pounds/kilograms)
4 sec/rep	10	40	+22/10
6 sec/rep	10	60	+22/10
8 sec/rep	10	80	+23/10.4
14 sec/rep	5	70	+27/12

Movement Range

We recommend exercising through the *full range of joint movement* for two reasons. First, research indicates that full-range strength training enhances joint flexibility. Second, studies show that full-range exercise movements are necessary for developing full-range muscle strength.

Full range of joint movement— Exercising the muscle from the fully stretched position to the completely contracted position.

The importance of full-range muscle strength is underscored by extensive research on patients with low back pain at the University of Florida College of Medicine. The researchers discovered that people with weak low back muscles were more likely to experience low back pain than people with strong low back muscles. They also determined that exercising the low back muscles through their full movement range was necessary for developing strength in all positions between full trunk flexion and complete trunk extension. This was an important finding because about 80 percent of the patients who increased their full-range back strength experienced less low back discomfort.

Although some people believe that strength training reduces joint flexibility, our research with golfers over age 50 showed that eight weeks of full-range strength training exercises did not decrease their movement range. In fact, the golfers significantly improved their club-head speed and driving power as a result of the strength training program.

So what exactly is full-range strength training exercise? Full-range strength training exercise means training from the position of full muscle stretch to the position of full muscle contraction. See an example in figure 4.5. Note that when the target muscle group (e.g., biceps) is fully contracted, the opposing muscle group (e.g., triceps) is fully stretched, and vice versa.

Figure 4.5   Moving through a full range of motion is important in exercises such as the pullover.

Of course, you should not exceed normal joint limits or experience pain in any portion of the exercise movement. Eliminate or abbreviate exercises that cause joint discomfort, training only in the pain-free movement range.

Breathing Pattern

Regardless of the exercise, never hold your breath when strength training. Holding your breath may cause excessive internal pressure that restricts blood flow, resulting in lightheadedness and high blood pressure responses. Prevent these undesirable occurrences by breathing continuously during every exercise set. Breathe out during the more difficult lifting phase, sometimes referred to as the sticking point, and inhale during the easier lowering phase of each repetition.

Breathing out when you lift the weight load and breathing in when you lower the weight load maintains a more desirable internal pressure response. Because continuous breathing is a critical component of safe strength training exercise, be sure to practice proper breathing on every repetition.

Workout Organization

Now that you understand how to choose and sequence exercises and how to determine weight loads and repetitions, let's examine how to best organize your workout. This section presents information about performing aerobic (cardiorespiratory) exercise in the same workout as strength training. It also provides guidelines for warming up and cooling down.

Order of Strength and Aerobic Workouts

Strength training is best for improving muscular fitness, and aerobic exercise is best for improving cardiorespiratory fitness. But if you want to include both activities in the same training session, is it better to begin with strength training or endurance exercise?

In one of our studies, 205 adults performed identical programs of strength training (10 machines) and endurance exercise (25 minutes of cycling, walking, or stepping) three days a week for 10 weeks. Half of the subjects always did the strength training first, and half of the subjects always did the endurance exercise first. As presented in table 4.3, both training groups experienced essentially equal strength increases after two months of exercise. Therefore, the order that you do strength training and aerobic exercise is largely a matter of personal preference. Of course, if your primary goal is better strength fitness, it makes sense to perform strength training first. If your main objective is better cardiovascular fitness, it is logical to perform endurance exercise first.

Whichever activity order you choose, be sure to begin each training session with a few minutes of warm-up exercise and conclude each training session with a few minutes of cool-down exercise. These transition phases between rest and vigorous physical activity provide important physiological and psychological benefits.

Table 4.3   Strength Gain and Workout Order

Training protocol (10 weeks)	Mean weight increase for 10 Nautilus machines (in pounds/kilograms)
Strength exercise first	+16/7.3
Endurance exercise first	+15/6.8

Warm-Ups and Cool-Downs

Strength training is high-effort training that places relatively heavy demands on your musculoskeletal system. Therefore, you should not jump right into a strength workout, nor should you abruptly end a strength workout. Warm-ups and cool-downs should involve large-muscle activity such as cycling, walking, or stepping. They may also include a few body-weight exercises such as knee bends, side bends, or trunk curls. To warm up for the strength training programs in this text, perform one set of 10 repetitions of each exercise using approximately half of the training load.

After strenuous activity, blood tends to accumulate in the lower legs, which can cause undesirable changes in blood pressure and stress your cardiovascular system. Cool-downs facilitate blood flow to your heart and a smooth return to resting circulation. Recommended cool-down activities include easy cycling and walking, followed by gentle stretching exercises. It is usually sufficient to warm up and cool down for 5 to 10 minutes.

Summary

This chapter should help you design safe and productive strength training programs, with a practical understanding and appreciation of the basic strength training principles. The key components of your strength training program are exercise selection, exercise order, training frequency, exercise sets, rest periods, exercise loads, exercise repetitions, training progression, and training effort. The most important exercise technique factors are your movement speed, movement range, and breathing pattern. Training intensity is most affected by loads, reps, and sets. The major aspects of your workout organization are activity order and warm-ups and cool-downs. All of these strength training considerations are presented in the following summary table with recommendations for successful exercise performance and program implementation.

Summary of Strength Training Principles and Practices

To derive the benefits of strength training while reducing the likelihood of injury, we recommend that you adhere to the following guidelines.

Program Design Variables

Exercise Selection

Select at least one exercise for each major muscle group to create symmetrical muscular development. Choose exercises that train opposing muscles groups to ensure a strength balance across joints and muscle areas.

Exercise Order

Train your lower body first, then your upper body, followed by midsection and neck exercises; work the larger muscles within these body areas first.

Training Frequency

Train on two or three nonconsecutive days each week.

Exercise Sets

Begin your strength training program with one set of each exercise. As you become more advanced, consider adding a second or third set of exercise if you so desire.

Rest Periods Between Sets and Exercises

Rest one to two minutes between sets of the same exercise, and rest one minute between different exercises.

(continued)

(continued)

Exercise Load

For most training purposes, use a load that allows you to lift 4 to 16 repetitions. This corresponds to 90 to 60 percent of your maximum resistance, respectively.

Exercise Repetitions

Depending on the training loads used, perform 4 to 16 repetitions in each set of exercises.

Training Progression

Raise training loads about 5 percent whenever you complete the prescribed number of repetitions with proper form during two successive workouts. Progress from more repetitions with lighter loads to fewer repetitions with heavier loads—then repeat the process. You may increase your training effort by performing more sets of exercises or by increasing the number of exercises for a given muscle or muscle group.

Training Effort

Train to the point of momentary muscle failure in each set to derive maximum benefits, and consider making the workouts more challenging by adding more sets.

Exercise Technique Factors

Movement Speed

You should perform all strength training exercises at moderate to slow speeds, and always under control. A good guideline is to use six seconds for each repetition (two seconds lifting and four seconds lowering).

Movement Range

Whenever possible, perform exercises through a full range of joint movement, from a position of full muscle stretch to a position of complete muscle contraction.

Breathing Pattern

Breathe continuously during each repetition, exhaling through the more difficult (lifting) movement phase and inhaling during the easier (lowering) movement phase.

Workout Organization

Order of Strength and Aerobic Workouts

Perform strength training and aerobic exercise in the order you prefer.

Warm-Ups and Cool-Downs

Precede strength training sessions with 5 to 10 minutes of warm-up activity to gradually shift from rest to vigorous exercise. Conclude workouts with 5 to 10 minutes of cool-down activity.

5

Base Fitness Programs

Based on the results of your strength fitness assessments in chapter 1, the training programs in this chapter are best suited to your current level of muscular fitness. In addition to the general information on base fitness training, we provide two sample exercise programs for training with weight-stack machines and two sample exercise programs for working with free weights. We suggest starting with the shorter programs (5A or 5C) and then progressing to the longer programs (5B or 5D).

Training Loads and Repetitions

Regardless of the sample program you select, use a training load that is 60 to 70 percent of the weight (or load) you can lift for one repetition (1RM). Because a fairly predictable relationship exists between the resistance you use and the number of repetitions you are able to perform, it is not necessary to determine your maximum load for each exercise. The list that follows outlines the relationship between the number of repetitions possible when using loads that equal 60 to 100 percent of the maximum load in an exercise.

Relationships Between Resistance and Repetitions

Maximum resistance = heaviest weight load you can lift one time (1RM)

95 percent 1RM = 2 repetitions

90 percent 1RM = 4 repetitions

85 percent 1RM = 6 repetitions

80 percent 1RM = 8 repetitions

75 percent 1RM = 10 repetitions

70 percent 1RM = 12 repetitions

65 percent 1RM = 14 repetitions

60 percent 1RM = 16 repetitions

Although variations occur among different people and in different exercises, typically you can count on completing about 12 repetitions with 70 percent of your maximum load and about 16 repetitions with 60 percent of maximum. With this in mind, experiment with each exercise to determine the load that will result in 12 repetitions when giving a good effort. The load determined will serve as your temporary training load.

Progression

Once you find the load that allows you to perform 12 repetitions, you are in the recommended training-load range. Continue training with this load until you can complete 16 repetitions. When you can perform 16 or more repetitions with proper technique during two consecutive workouts, you are ready to progress to a heavier training load. As a general rule, increase the resistance by approximately 5 percent. By first increasing the number of repetitions from 12 to 16 and then increasing the weight load by about 5 percent, you are incorporating the double-progressive training system, which is highly effective for stimulating strength gains and muscle development.

Warm-Up

The base fitness training program is predicated on performing one hard set of each exercise. If time is not a limiting factor, perform a warm-up set of each exercise using 50 to 60 percent of the training load. For example, if you can complete 12 dumbbell bench presses with 30-pound (13.6-kilogram) dumbbells, your warm-up load would be 15- to 20-pound (6.8- to 9-kilogram) dumbbells in the bench press. Although it is not essential to do a warm-up set, many exercisers feel that a warm-up set enhances their training performance. Perform the same number of repetitions in both your warm-up set and training set.

Rest Periods

The base fitness training program includes just one set (plus a warm-up set if desired) of one exercise for each major muscle group. Therefore, taking one minute of rest between exercises to reduce the cumulative effects of muscle fatigue as you perform your workout should be sufficient. You can take more time if necessary to set up the next exercise (load the barbell, replace and select dumbbells, and so on). In addition, the rest period between your warm-up and training sets should not exceed one minute. This relatively short recovery time should be sufficient because of the low muscular effort required to perform the warm-up repetitions.

Movement Speed

The suggested speed for performing exercise sets is 4 to 6 seconds per repetition. At an average repetition speed of 5 seconds, 12 repetitions require about 60 seconds of continuous muscle-force output and 16 repetitions require about 80 seconds of continuous muscle tension.

Of course, some exercises use shorter movement ranges than others (e.g., lateral raise vs. back pullover), and some exercises are naturally performed more quickly than others (e.g., dumbbell lunge vs. dumbbell squat). That is why we recommend a range for the repetition speed.

Because people are stronger during lowering movements (eccentric muscle actions) than during lifting movements (concentric muscle actions), it is advisable to lower the weight loads at a slower pace. As a rule of thumb, take 1.5 to 2 seconds for lifting movements and 2.5 to 4 seconds for lowering movements.

Movement Range

It is advantageous to exercise through as much of the range of motion permitted by a joint as you can, as long as you can do so without discomfort or risk of injury. Most machine exercises have predetermined ranges of movement, whereas free weight exercises offer considerable freedom of movement. When using either type of training equipment, strive for a relatively complete muscle contraction at the end of each lifting movement. Although it is best to perform exercises through a full range of motion, do not overstretch your muscles and connective tissues at the start of your exercise movements. For example, in the machine chest press, adjust the seat back so that your hands are even with or slightly ahead of your chest in the starting (chest stretched) position. Allowing the hands to go farther back can place considerable stress on your shoulder joints and increase the risk of injury. Lowering the dumbbells below chest level in the dumbbell bench press creates the same stress on the shoulders and increases the risk of injury.

Training Frequency

Our studies on strength training frequency show similar results for two and three exercise sessions per week when using the base fitness training program. Keep in mind that it is counterproductive to strength train the same muscles on successive days. Therefore, if you want to schedule three weekly workouts, consider training on Monday, Wednesday, and Friday. If two days fit your schedule better, space workouts so that you rest 72 to 96 hours between workouts. A common approach to two-day-a-week training is to schedule workouts on Mondays and Thursdays or Wednesdays and Saturdays.

Training Intensity

You may have heard that you must perform each exercise set to the point of muscle failure (inability of the muscle to continue contraction) to experience strength gains. Although training to muscle failure may be necessary for maximizing strength development in competitive athletes, it is not recommended for the base fitness exercise protocols. You should train reasonably hard, but the final repetition in your exercise set should not be at a do-or-die level of difficulty. Simply train to the point of momentary muscle fatigue, which means you would be unlikely to complete another repetition with proper technique if you tried to do so.

Exercise Spotters

Train with a partner whenever possible, and always use a spotter when one is recommended. None of the exercises in the base fitness training program require a spotter. However, if for some reason you decide to include exercises that do, such as the barbell squat, barbell bench press, or barbell incline press, be sure to train with a spotter. Doing so can prevent injuries caused by being pinned under a heavy barbell. Spotters should stand behind the exerciser, ready to assist in a failed lifting attempt by helping lift the bar to the standards in a bench press or incline press, or helping the exerciser to a standing position during a squat.

Summary of Base Fitness Program Exercise Guidelines

Training loads and repetitions	Use a training load that is 60 to 70 percent of your maximum resistance for one repetition. This should result in momentary muscle fatigue after 12 to 16 repetitions.
Progression	Increase the training load by approximately 5 percent when you can complete 16 repetitions with correct technique in two successive workouts.

Sets	Complete one set of each exercise to the point of momentary muscle fatigue.
Warm-up	Perform one warm-up set with a load that is approximately half of the training load, if desired.
Rest	Take approximately one minute of rest between exercises.
Movement speed	Perform each repetition in 4 to 6 seconds, taking about 1.5 to 2 seconds for lifting actions and about 2.5 to 4 seconds for lowering actions.
Movement range	Perform each exercise through a relatively full movement range that does not cause discomfort or overstretching.
Training frequency	Train on two or three nonconsecutive days per week.
Training intensity	Continue each exercise set to the point of momentary muscle fatigue.
Exercise spotters	Use a spotter if you perform the barbell squat or free weight bench press or incline press.

Protocols for Base Fitness Strength Training

The base fitness protocols are presented for both machine training and free weight training. Programs 5A and 5C include fewer exercises and require less training time, which make them more appropriate for beginning and time-pressured exercisers. Programs 5B and 5D involve more exercises and require more training time, but provide a more comprehensive exercise experience. If you are just starting to strength train or aren't sure which program to choose, begin with the shorter training protocol and progress to the longer training protocol when you are ready to do so.

MACHINE TRAINING

Program 5A—Machine Training

Program 5A is a machine workout that uses seven basic exercises to collectively work the most important major muscle groups. The single leg exercise involves the key muscles of the hips and thighs. The four upper-body exercises address the prominent muscles in the chest, upper back, shoulders, and arms. The two trunk exercises target the lower back and midsection muscles. The first five exercises are linear actions (straight movements) that work at least two major muscle groups simultaneously. The last two exercises are rotary actions (curved movements) that focus on specific muscle groups.

You will note that the seven basic strength training exercises in this program are sequenced to alternately address opposing muscle groups. For example, the chest press (an upper-body pushing exercise) is followed by the seated row (an upper-body pulling exercise). Next, the shoulder press (another upper-body pushing exercise) is followed by the lat pull-down (another upper-body pulling exercise). Finally, the abdominal flexion exercise is followed by the low back extension exercise to work both the front and rear midsection muscles. By training in this exercise pattern, you will obtain overall muscular conditioning in a time-efficient manner.

Program 5A should take only 15 minutes if you perform one set of each exercise. If you perform a preliminary warm-up set, the workout will last approximately 30 minutes. Perform the exercises in the order listed, progressing from larger to smaller muscle groups. The table presents the exercises for program 5A as well as general guidelines for the loads and repetitions to use, sets to perform, and recommendations for repetition speed and recovery periods.

MACHINE TRAINING

Program 5A—Machine Training

Exercise	Muscle group
1. Leg press	Quadriceps, hamstrings, gluteals
2. Chest press	Pectoralis major, triceps
3. Seated row	Latissimus dorsi, middle trapezius, rhomboids, biceps
4. Shoulder press	Deltoids, triceps
5. Lat pull-down	Latissimus dorsi, biceps
6. Abdominal flexion	Rectus abdominis
7. Low back extension	Erector spinae

For each exercise:

Training load	Repetitions	Sets	Repetition speed	Recovery time
60-70% max	12-16	1	4-6 sec	1 min

Program 5B—Machine Training

Program 5B is a machine workout that uses 14 standard exercises to collectively work all of the major muscle groups. The four leg exercises are rotary actions (curved movements) that target all four of the thigh muscle groups. Likewise, the four upper-body exercises are rotary actions that individually address the muscles in the chest, upper back, and shoulders. This program includes two rotary exercises for a more isolated action of the upper-arm muscles. In addition to two rotary exercises for the major trunk muscles (lower back and midsection), program 5B offers two rotary exercises for the muscles that flex and extend the neck.

The 14 selected exercises that compose this more comprehensive strength training program are sequenced specifically to pair opposing muscle groups. These paired exercises include the leg extension and leg curl for the front and rear thighs, the hip adduction and hip abduction for the inner and outer thighs, the chest crossover and seated row for the front and rear torso, the biceps curl and triceps extension for the front and rear arms, the abdominal flexion and low back extension for the front and rear midsection, and the neck flexion and neck extension for the front and rear neck muscles.

If you do a single set of each exercise, you should complete this workout in approximately 30 minutes; it will take twice as long if you perform a preliminary warm-up set. Perform the exercises in the recommended order for best results. The table presents the program 5B exercises along with general guidelines for resistance, repetitions, sets, repetition speed, and recovery time.

MACHINE TRAINING

Program 5B—Machine Training

Exercise	Muscle group
1. Leg extension	Quadriceps
2. Leg curl	Hamstrings
3. Hip adduction	Hip adductors
4. Hip abduction	Hip abductors
5. Chest crossover	Pectoralis major
6. Seated row	Latissimus dorsi, middle trapezius, rhomboids, biceps
7. Lateral raise	Deltoids
8. Back pullover	Latissimus dorsi
9. Biceps curl	Biceps
10. Triceps extension	Triceps
11. Abdominal flexion	Rectus abdominis
12. Low back extension	Erector spinae
13. Neck flexion	Sternocleidomastoids
14. Neck extension	Upper trapezius

For each exercise:

Training load	Repetitions	Sets	Repetition speed	Recovery time
60-70% max	12-16	1	4-6 sec	1 min

Program 5C—Free Weight Training

Program 5C is a free weight workout that features seven basic exercises to collectively train the most important major muscle groups; it is similar to program 5A. The single leg exercise involves the key muscles of the hips and thighs. The four upper-body exercises address the prominent muscles in the chest, upper back, shoulders, and arms. The two trunk exercises target the lower back and midsection muscles. The first five exercises are linear actions (straight movements) that work at least two major muscle groups simultaneously. The last two exercises are rotary actions (curved movements) that focus on specific muscle groups.

You will note that the seven basic strength training exercises in this program are sequenced to alternately address opposing muscle groups. For example, the dumbbell bench press (an upper-body pushing exercise) is followed by the dumbbell one-arm row (an upper-body pulling exercise). Next, the dumbbell seated press (another upper-body pushing exercise) is followed by the lat pull-down (another upper-body pulling exercise). Finally, the twisting trunk curl is followed by the body-weight trunk extension to work the front and rear midsection muscles. By training in this exercise pattern, you obtain overall muscular conditioning in a time-efficient manner.

Program 5C should take about 15 minutes if you perform one set of each exercise. If you perform a preliminary warm-up set, the workout will take approximately 30 minutes. Although we prefer dumbbell training, you may substitute barbells for the squat and bench press exercises if you so desire and if you have a competent spotter. You should experience best results by performing the exercises in the sequence listed. The program 5C exercises and general training guidelines for resistance, repetitions, sets, repetition speed, and recovery time are presented in the following table.

FREE WEIGHT TRAINING

Program 5C—Free Weight Training

Exercise	Muscle group
1. Dumbbell squat	Quadriceps, hamstrings, gluteals
2. Dumbbell bench press	Pectoralis major, triceps
3. Dumbbell one-arm row	Latissimus dorsi, middle trapezius, rhomboids, biceps
4. Dumbbell seated press	Deltoids, triceps
5. Lat pull-down	Latissimus dorsi, biceps
6. Twisting trunk curl	Rectus abdominis
7. Body-weight trunk extension	Erector spinae

For each exercise:

Training load	Repetitions	Sets	Repetition speed	Recovery time
60-70% max	12-16	1	4-6 sec	1 min

Note: The lat pull-down in this program is the same as the machine lat pull-down described on page 76.

FREE WEIGHT TRAINING

Program 5D—Free Weight Training

Program 5D is a free weight workout that uses 11 standard exercises to collectively train all of the major muscle groups. The two leg exercises are linear actions (straight movements) that involve the key muscles of the hips and thighs. The four upper-body exercises include both rotary actions (curved movements) and linear actions for comprehensive conditioning of the chest, upper back, and shoulder muscles. There are two rotary exercises for a more isolated action of the upper-arm muscles, two rotary exercises for the major trunk muscles (lower back and midsection), and one rotary exercise for the neck extension and shoulder elevation muscles. Because it is difficult to isolate individual leg muscles with free weights, this program offers only two leg exercises compared to six upper-body and arm exercises.

The 11 selected exercises that compose this more comprehensive strength training program are sequenced specifically to pair opposing muscle groups. These paired exercises include the dumbbell chest fly and dumbbell one-arm row for the front and rear torso, the dumbbell lateral raise and lat pull-down for the top and rear torso, the dumbbell overhead triceps extension and dumbbell standing curl for the rear and front arms, and the twisting trunk curl and body-weight trunk extension for the front and rear midsection muscles.

You should be able to complete the workout in 20 to 25 minutes if you perform one set of each exercise. The workout should take about twice as long if you perform a preliminary warm-up set. If you have a spotter, you may substitute the barbell squat for the dumbbell squat. Follow the recommended exercise sequence as closely as possible. The table presents the program 5D exercises and general training guidelines for resistance, repetitions, sets, repetition speed, and recovery time.

FREE WEIGHT TRAINING

Program 5D—Free Weight Training

Exercise	Muscle group
1. Dumbbell squat	Quadriceps, hamstrings, gluteals
2. Dumbbell lunge	Quadriceps, hamstrings, gluteals
3. Dumbbell chest fly	Pectoralis major
4. Dumbbell one-arm row	Latissimus dorsi, trapezius, rhomboids, biceps
5. Dumbbell lateral raise	Deltoids
6. Lat pull-down	Latissimus dorsi, biceps
7. Dumbbell overhead triceps extension	Triceps
8. Dumbbell standing curl	Biceps
9. Twisting trunk curl	Rectus abdominis
10. Body-weight trunk extension	Erector spinae
11. Dumbbell shrug	Upper trapezius

For each exercise:

Training load	Repetitions	Sets	Repetition speed	Recovery time
60-70% max	12-16	1	4-6 sec	1 min

Training Program Progression

If you begin with machine training program 5A, the logical progression is to proceed to machine training program 5B if you can add 15 more minutes to your exercise session. Likewise, if you start with the free weight training program 5C, it makes sense to progress to free weight program 5D, unless you have time limitations. Continue training with base fitness programs 5B (machine) and 5D (free weight) until you experience a strength plateau. We define a strength plateau as three weeks of training in which you experience no increase in the number of repetitions completed in your exercise set. For example, you consistently complete 13 leg extensions with 80 pounds (36 kilograms), but you cannot perform 14 repetitions even though you have been at this level for three weeks. Once you have reached a plateau, consider taking a week off (if you feel you have been working too hard) or starting one of the experienced training programs presented in the next chapter (if you feel you have not been working hard enough). Although somewhat more time consuming, the experienced training programs provide more comprehensive workouts that should stimulate further strength gains and muscle development.

6

Experienced Training Programs

Either your chapter 1 assessment of strength fitness has placed you in the experienced training program, or you have progressed to this training category by completing the base fitness program or programs. Whichever the case, you should adhere closely to the experienced training protocols described in this chapter. You will find two sample exercise programs for training with machines and two using free weight equipment. If you prefer machine training, start with program 6A before progressing to program 6B. Start with program 6C before progressing to program 6D if you intend to use free weight equipment.

Training Loads and Repetitions

Regardless of the sample program you select, use a training load of 70 to 80 percent of the weight (or load) you can lift for one repetition. Because a fairly predictable relationship exists between the resistance you use and the number of repetitions you are able to perform, it is not necessary to determine your maximum load for each exercise. The list that follows outlines the relationship between the number of repetitions normally possible when using loads that equal 60 to 100 percent of the maximum load in an exercise.

Relationships Between Resistance and Repetitions

Maximum resistance = heaviest weight load you can lift one time (1RM)

95 percent 1RM = 2 repetitions

90 percent 1RM = 4 repetitions

85 percent 1RM = 6 repetitions

80 percent 1RM = 8 repetitions

75 percent 1RM = 10 repetitions

70 percent 1RM = 12 repetitions

65 percent 1RM = 14 repetitions

60 percent 1RM = 16 repetitions

Although variation occurs among different people and in different exercises, typically you can count on completing about 8 repetitions with 80 percent of your maximum load and about 12 repetitions with 70 percent. With this in mind, experiment with each exercise to determine the load that will result in 8 repetitions when giving a good effort. The load determined will serve as your temporary training load.

Progression

Use the double-progressive approach for safe and successful strength training. The double-progressive system requires that you first increase the number of repetitions, and then increase the load used in the set. For example (keeping in mind the desired repetition range of 8 to 12), if you can perform 9 leg presses with 100 pounds (45 kilograms), continue training with this load until you can complete 12 repetitions. When you reach the end of the repetition range (12 reps) in two consecutive workouts, add approximately 5 percent to the training load for the next workout. Increasing the load in this manner reduces the number of repetitions by 2 or 3 reps, so you may complete 9 or 10 repetitions with the new load (105 pounds [48 kilograms]). Continue to train with 105 pounds (48 kilograms) until you increase the number of reps to 12 in two consecutive workouts, then add another 5 pounds (2.3 kilograms), or 5 percent, to the weight load for your next workout. Training in this double-progressive manner reduces the risk of doing too much too soon and provides regular positive reinforcement for your exercise efforts.

Sets

Try performing two sets of each exercise in the experienced training programs A and C if you have the energy and time to do so. Performing two sets will double the training volume, the amount of time needed to complete workouts, and the energy requirements.

Experienced training programs B and D include exercises that work the same muscle group two or three times in succession, thus dramatically increasing the stress on the muscles involved. Therefore, you should begin with one set of each exercise in experienced training programs B and D, and as your fitness level improves, try to perform a second set of each exercise.

Warm-Up

If you have time, you may perform a warm-up set of each exercise. Your warm-up set should equal 50 to 60 percent of your training weight load. For example, if you can perform 10 leg extensions with 60 pounds (27 kilograms), a warm-up set for this exercise would be 30 to 35 pounds (13.6 to 15.9 kilograms). Warm-ups increase muscle temperature, which helps the neuromuscular system respond more effectively to the stresses of training. Perform the same number of repetitions in both your warm-up sets and training sets: 8 to 12 reps.

Rest Periods

The rest period between your warm-up and training sets should not exceed one minute. The relatively short recovery time should be sufficient because of the low muscular effort required to perform the warm-up repetitions.

If you perform two sets of the exercises in the experienced training program, you will normally need to take a longer recovery interval between sets. We recommend one to two minutes rest between successive sets of the same exercise because this is the approximate time required to replace muscle energy stores after a hard bout of strength training. The rest period between different exercises should be about one minute. This applies even when successive exercises involve the same muscle groups, as in programs 6B and 6D.

Movement Speed

The standard movement speed for performing exercise sets is four to six seconds per repetition. Assuming an average repetition speed of five seconds, 8 repetitions can be performed in approximately 40 seconds, and 12 repetitions can be completed in about 60 seconds. This moderate and controlled pace for performing repetitions permits a relatively continuous and consistent application of muscle force throughout each repetition, thereby limiting the role of momentum and reducing the risk of injury.

Because some exercises use relatively long ranges of movement (e.g., back pullovers, pull-downs), and other exercises have relatively short movement ranges (e.g., lateral raises, trunk curls), the repetition time for different exercises varies. Nonetheless, you should be able to stay within the four-to-six-second time frame for most exercises.

As you may have discovered, you can perform lowering movements (eccentric muscle actions) more easily than you can perform lifting movements (concentric muscle actions). Consequently, we recommend a lifting action that takes 1.5 to 2 seconds and a lowering action that requires 2.5 to 4 seconds for every repetition. This makes your lowering movements more challenging and your eccentric muscle actions more effective for strength development.

Movement Range

Be sure to perform each exercise through a complete range of joint movement, as long as you can do so without experiencing discomfort. Although most machine exercises provide predetermined movement ranges and pathways, free weight exercises typically offer many movement options. Whichever training equipment you use, attempt to attain relatively complete muscle contraction at the conclusion of each lifting action (concentric contraction). On the other hand, do not overstretch your muscles and connective tissues in the starting positions. As an example, when performing the back pullover machine exercise, your starting position should place only a gentle stretch through your latissimus dorsi and triceps muscles. Do not move the arm-placement apparatus into a position that causes discomfort.

Training Frequency

Experienced training exercise protocols are typically more productive when performed just two days per week. Although training on three nonconsecutive days a week is effective, the more demanding experienced training exercise programs may require more than 48 hours for complete muscle recovery and rebuilding. We, therefore, recommend twice-a-week strength training, spacing the exercise sessions throughout the week as evenly as possible, for example, Tuesdays and Fridays or Wednesdays and Saturdays.

Training Intensity

Although it is not necessary to train to the point of muscle failure (inability of the muscle to continue contraction), your exercise sets should not terminate before reaching momentary muscle fatigue. Generally, you should continue exercising until you are certain that you cannot complete another repetition with correct technique. If your muscles fatigue in the middle of a repetition, simply stop. Do not compromise correct lifting technique in an effort to complete an additional repetition after experiencing momentary muscle fatigue.

Exercise Spotters

It is always advisable to train with a partner who can provide encouragement, performance feedback, and positive reinforcement. However, it is essential to work with a spotter when performing the barbell squat, barbell bench press, and incline press. A failed repetition in any of these exercises can result in serious injury if you are pinned under a heavy barbell. Regardless of the weight used, be sure to use a competent spotter when performing these barbell exercises. Spotters should stand behind the exerciser, ready to assist in a failed lifting attempt by helping lift the bar to the standards during a bench press or incline press, or helping the exerciser to a standing position during a squat.

Summary of Experienced Training Program Exercise Guidelines

Training loads and repetitions	Use a training load that is 70 to 80 percent of your maximum resistance for one repetition. This should result in momentary muscle fatigue after 8 to 12 repetitions.
Progression	Increase the training load by approximately 5 percent when you can complete 12 repetitions with correct technique in two successive workouts.
Sets	Complete one or two sets of each exercise in program 6A or 6C, and complete one set of each exercise in program 6B or 6D.
Warm-up	Perform one warm-up set with a load approximately half of the training load.
Rest periods	Take approximately one minute of rest between exercises. Rest one to two minutes between sets of the same exercise.
Movement speed	Perform each repetition in 4 to 6 seconds, taking about 1.5 to 2 seconds for lifting actions and about 2.5 to 4 seconds for lowering actions.
Movement range	Perform each exercise through a relatively full movement range that does not cause discomfort or overstretching.
Training frequency	Train twice a week, spacing the workouts evenly throughout the week.
Training intensity	Continue each exercise set to the point of momentary muscle fatigue.
Exercise spotters	Use a spotter if you perform the free weight barbell squat, bench press, or incline press.

Protocols for Experienced Strength Training

The protocols for experienced strength training are presented for both machine training and free weight training. Programs 6A and 6C include fewer exercises and require less training time, which make them better suited to time-pressured exercisers. Programs 6B and 6D involve more exercises and require more training time, but provide a more comprehensive exercise experience. If you are uncertain about the training program you should follow, begin with the shorter exercise protocol and progress to the longer one when you are ready to do so.

Program 6A—Machine Training

Program 6A is a machine workout that uses 11 basic exercises to collectively train the most important major muscle groups. The first leg exercise is a linear action (straight movement) that works the front thigh, rear thigh, and hip muscles. The next two leg exercises are rotary actions (curved movements) that target the inner and outer thigh muscles. All six upper-body exercises are linear actions that involve two or more major muscle groups simultaneously, and are arranged in an alternating push–pull sequence. The last two exercises are rotary actions that focus on the muscles of the lower back and midsection. You will note that the chest press (an upper-body pushing exercise) is followed by the seated row (an upper-body pulling exercise); the shoulder press (an upper-body pushing exercise) is paired with the lat pull-down (an upper-body pulling exercise); and the weight-assisted bar dip (an upper-body pushing exercise) is followed by the weight-assisted chin-up (an upper-body pulling exercise). Alternating exercises for opposing muscle groups is an effective means for obtaining balanced strength development

If you perform one set of each exercise, program 6A should take about 25 minutes. Performing two sets of these exercises will increase your training time to approximately 50 minutes, assuming a 90-second rest between successive sets. The table presents the program 6A exercise sequence and performance information.

MACHINE TRAINING

Program 6A—Machine Training

Exercise	Muscle group
1. Leg press	Quadriceps, hamstrings, gluteals
2. Hip adduction	Hip adductors
3. Hip abduction	Hip abductors
4. Chest press	Pectoralis major, triceps
5. Seated row	Latissimus dorsi, middle trapezius, rhomboids, biceps
6. Shoulder press	Deltoids, triceps
7. Lat pull-down	Latissimus dorsi, biceps
8. Weight-assisted bar dip	Pectoralis major, triceps
9. Weight-assisted chin-up	Latissimus dorsi, biceps
10. Abdominal flexion	Rectus abdominis
11. Low back extension	Erector spinae

For each exercise:

Training load	Repetitions	Sets	Repetition speed	Recovery time
70-80% max	8-12	1-2	4-6 sec	Between exercises: 1 min Between sets: 1-2 min

Program 6B—Machine Training

Program 6B provides a longer workout, with 17 exercises that collectively address all of the major muscle groups. This comprehensive strength training program includes 4 linear-action (straight-movement) exercises that work two or more muscle groups together, as well as 13 rotary-action (curved-movement) exercises that address specific muscles of the legs, upper body, midsection, and neck. To make this workout even more challenging, it requires that you perform paired exercises for the chest, upper-back, and shoulder muscles. In the paired chest exercises, the first exercise is a rotary movement (chest crossover) that addresses the target muscle group (pectoralis major). The second exercise is a linear movement (chest press) that challenges the same (prefatigued) pectoralis major muscles with assistance from fresh (nonfatigued) triceps muscles. In the upper-back paired exercises, the first exercise is a rotary movement (pullover) that works the target muscle group (latissimus dorsi). The second exercise is a linear movement (lat pull-down) that challenges the same (prefatigued) latissimus dorsi muscles with assistance from fresh (nonfatigued) biceps muscles. In the shoulder paired exercises, the first exercise is a rotary movement (lateral raise) that addresses the target muscle group (deltoids). The second exercise is a linear exercise (shoulder press) that impacts the same (prefatigued) deltoid muscles with help from fresh (nonfatigued) triceps muscles.

This type of training, referred to as preexhaustion training, is most effective with relatively short rests (no more than 30 seconds) between the paired exercises. Perform the exercises in the recommended order for best results. Performed properly, this training protocol should take less than 30 minutes. The table presents the program 6B exercises, along with general guidelines for resistance, repetitions, sets, repetition speed, and recovery time.

MACHINE TRAINING

Program 6B—Machine Training

Exercise	Muscle group
1. Hip adduction	Hip adductors
2. Hip abduction	Hip abductors
3. Leg extension	Quadriceps
4. Leg curl	Hamstrings
5. Leg press	Quadriceps, hamstrings, gluteals
6. Chest crossover	Pectoralis major
7. Chest press	Pectoralis major, triceps
8. Pullover	Latissimus dorsi
9. Lat pull-down	Latissimus dorsi, biceps
10. Lateral raise	Deltoids
11. Shoulder press	Deltoids, triceps
12. Biceps curl	Biceps
13. Triceps extension	Triceps
14. Abdominal flexion	Rectus abdominis
15. Low back extension	Erector spinae
16. Neck flexion	Sternocleidomastoids
17. Neck extension	Upper trapezius

For each exercise:

Training load	Repetitions	Sets	Repetition speed	Recovery time
70-80% max	8-12	1	4-6 sec	Between exercises for different muscles: 1 min. Between paired exercises for the same muscles: 30 sec*

*Paired exercises: Chest crossover and chest press, pullover and lat pull-down, lateral raise and shoulder press

FREE WEIGHT TRAINING

Program 6C—Free Weight Training

Program 6C is a free weight workout that features 12 basic exercises that collectively train the most important muscle groups. It is similar to the program 6A machine workout. The two leg exercises are linear actions (straight movements) that simultaneously work the front thigh, rear thigh, and hip muscles. The five upper-body exercises are also linear actions that involve two or more muscle groups on every repetition. The last five exercises are rotary actions (curved movements) that focus on specific muscles.

You will note that we have sequenced the upper-body exercises in a push–pull pattern to alternately address opposing muscle groups. For example, the barbell bench press (an upper-body pushing exercise) is paired with the dumbbell one-arm row (an upper-body pulling exercise). Likewise, the barbell incline press (another upper-body pushing exercise) is followed by the lat pull-down (another upper-body pulling exercise). In a similar manner, the dumbbell incline curl (an elbow flexion exercise) is paired with the dumbbell overhead triceps extension (an elbow extension exercise), and the twisting trunk curl (a midsection flexion exercise) is paired with the body-weight trunk extension (a midsection extension exercise).

If you perform one set of each exercise, your training duration should be about 25 minutes. If you perform two sets of each exercise, your workout should take approximately 55 minutes, assuming 90-second recovery periods between successive sets. You may substitute barbells for the squat and shrug exercises, and you may substitute dumbbells for the bench press and incline press exercises. Be sure to train with a spotter if you perform the barbell squat, bench press, or incline press. You should experience best results by performing the exercises in the sequence presented. The program 6C exercises and general training guidelines for resistance, repetitions, sets, repetition speed, and recovery time are presented in the table.

FREE WEIGHT TRAINING

Program 6C—Free Weight Training

Exercise	Muscle group
1. Dumbbell squat	Quadriceps, hamstrings, gluteals
2. Dumbbell lunge	Quadriceps, hamstrings, gluteals
3. Barbell bench press	Pectoralis major, triceps
4. Dumbbell one-arm row	Latissimus dorsi, middle trapezius, rhomboids, biceps
5. Barbell incline press	Upper pectoralis major, triceps, anterior deltoids
6. Lat pull-down	Latissimus dorsi, biceps
7. Dumbbell alternating shoulder press	Deltoids, triceps
8. Dumbbell incline curl	Biceps
9. Dumbbell overhead triceps extension	Triceps
10. Twisting trunk curl	Rectus abdominis
11. Body-weight trunk extension	Erector spinae
12. Dumbbell shrug	Upper trapezius

For each exercise:

Training load	Repetitions	Sets	Repetition speed	Recovery time
70-80% max	8-12	1-2	4-6 sec	Between exercises: 1 min Between sets: 1-2 min

Program 6D—Free Weight Training

Program 6D is a comprehensive free weight workout that addresses the major muscle groups in a more challenging manner. This is accomplished by performing two or three successive exercises for the same muscles before moving to a different muscle group. For example, you will perform three consecutive linear-action leg exercises, each of which work the quadriceps, hamstrings, and gluteal muscles concurrently. You will then perform paired exercises for the chest, upper back, and shoulder muscles. In the paired exercises for the chest, the first exercise is a rotary movement (dumbbell chest fly) that addresses the target muscle group (pectoralis major). The second exercise is a linear movement (barbell bench press) that challenges the same (prefatigued) pectoralis major muscles with assistance from fresh (nonfatigued) triceps muscles. In the paired exercises for the upper back, both the dumbbell one-arm row and lat pull-down work the target muscles (latissimus dorsi) but with different assisting muscle groups. In the paired exercises for the shoulders, the first exercise is a rotary movement (dumbbell lateral raise) that addresses the target muscle group (deltoids). The second exercise is a linear movement (dumbbell seated press) that challenges the same (prefatigued) deltoid muscles with assistance from fresh (nonfatigued) triceps muscles.

This type of training, referred to as preexhaustion training, is most effective with relatively short rests (30 seconds or less) between the paired exercises. For best results, perform the exercises in the recommended order. If you complete one set of each exercise, this strength training program should take less than 30 minutes. If you complete two sets of the nonpaired exercises, the total training time should be about 45 minutes, assuming you rest 90 seconds between successive sets. We suggest that you perform the exercises in the order presented. The table provides general training guidelines for exercise resistance, repetitions, sets, repetition speed, and recovery time.

FREE WEIGHT TRAINING

Program 6D—Free Weight Training

Exercise	Muscle group
1. Barbell squat	Quadriceps, hamstrings, gluteals
2. Dumbbell lunge	Quadriceps, hamstrings, gluteals
3. Dumbbell step-up	Quadriceps, hamstrings, gluteals
4. Dumbbell chest fly	Pectoralis major
5. Barbell bench press	Pectoralis major, triceps
6. Dumbbell one-arm row	Latissimus dorsi, middle trapezius, rhomboids, biceps
7. Lat pull-down	Latissimus dorsi, biceps
8. Dumbbell lateral raise	Deltoids
9. Dumbbell seated press	Deltoids, triceps
10. Dumbbell incline curl	Biceps
11. Dumbbell lying triceps extension	Triceps
12. Twisting trunk curl	Rectus abdominis, internal obliques, external obliques
13. Body-weight trunk extension	Erector spinae
14. Barbell shrug	Upper trapezius

For each exercise:

Training load	Repetitions	Sets	Repetition speed	Recovery time
70-80% max	8-12	1 set for exercises 4-9 1 or 2 sets for all other exercises	4-6 sec	Between sets: 1-2 min Between exercises for different muscles: 1 min Between paired exercises for the same muscles: 30 sec*

*Paired exercises: Dumbbell chest fly and barbell bench press, dumbbell one-arm row and lat pull-down, dumbbell lateral raise and dumbbell seated press

Training Program Progression

If you start with machine program 6A, you should logically progress to machine program 6B, assuming you have time to perform the additional six exercises. Similarly, if you begin with free weight program 6C, a sensible progression would be to free weight program 6D, which requires a similar amount of time but is structured differently and is more difficult. Continue training with level 6 programs until you encounter a strength plateau (a three-week period with no improvement). When your exercise efforts no longer elicit a training effect (e.g., more reps with the same load), it is time to change to a workout program that will stimulate more muscle development and improve strength.

When progress in the experienced training programs in this chapter stagnates, switch to one of the advanced training programs presented in the next chapter. In addition to the option of following separate exercise programs for the upper-body and lower-body muscles, you will also have an opportunity to perform a more demanding workout technique known as breakdown training. You should find the advanced training programs highly effective for maximizing your muscular fitness.

7

Advanced Training Programs

Congratulations on attaining a high level of muscular fitness. Either you scored very well on your chapter 1 strength assessments, or you have progressed from the basic or experienced protocols to the more challenging strength training programs in this chapter. As with the basic and experienced training programs, this program includes machine and free weight exercise workouts. Both programs are more specialized and intense than the workouts in chapters 5 and 6 and, therefore, should help you attain even greater strength gains and muscular development. To achieve the best results and to avoid overtraining, comply as closely as possible to the training guidelines provided. Keep in mind that halfhearted training will not produce desired results and that training too hard may result in injury.

In addition to the machine and free weight training options, you may also choose between programs that emphasize the upper body or lower body or choose a full-body workout. You also may increase the intensity of the training program by 1) increasing the loads used, 2) increasing the training volume, or 3) performing additional reps with a lighter load at the end of a set.

Training Loads and Repetitions

At this level of training, you are encouraged to use heavier loads than those recommended in chapter 6 (8 to 12 repetitions with 70 to 80 percent of the maximum weight load). For the workouts in this chapter you should use training loads that are 80 to 90 percent of your maximum resistance. Your higher level of musculoskeletal conditioning should enable you to exercise safely and successfully with heavier loads. On the list that follows, you can see that you should be able to perform four to eight reps when lifting 80 to 90 percent of your maximum resistance.

Relationships Between Resistance and Repetitions

Maximum resistance = heaviest weight load you can lift one time (1RM)

95 percent 1RM = 2 repetitions

90 percent 1RM = 4 repetitions

85 percent 1RM = 6 repetitions

80 percent 1RM = 8 repetitions

75 percent 1RM = 10 repetitions

70 percent 1RM = 12 repetitions

65 percent 1RM = 14 repetitions

60 percent 1RM = 16 repetitions

Load Adjustments

If you cannot perform at least four repetitions with the load you have selected for an exercise or you are able to complete more than eight repetitions with it, you need to change the load. Refer to table 7.1 and make the suggested load changes if this occurs. Even with the use of table 7.1, you may find that you need additional trials before determining a load that produces four to eight repetitions. While trying to identify correct loads, refrain from using loads that result in fewer than four repetitions. If you cannot perform four repetitions, you are using loads that are too heavy, and training with loads that are too heavy increases the possibility of injury. At the same time, loads that are too light (you are able to perform more than eight reps) may not provide a sufficient stimulus to take you to the next level of muscular strength and fitness. A good starting load is one that enables you to perform six reps with a good effort.

Table 7.1   Load Adjustments

		Repetitions completed with the trial load								
		≥18	16-17	14-15	12-13	10-11	8-9	6-7	4-5	2-3	<2
Goal reps	**14-15**	+10	+5		–5	–10	–15	–15	–20	–25	–30
	12-13	+15	+10	+5		–5	–10	–15	–15	–20	–25
	10-11	+15	+15	+10	+5		–5	–10	–15	–15	–20
	8-9	+20	+15	+15	+10	+5		–5	–10	–15	–15
	6-7	+25	+20	+15	+15	+10	+5		–5	–10	–15
	4-5	+30	+25	+20	+15	+15	+10	+5		–5	–10
	2-3	+35	+30	+25	+20	+15	+15	+10	+5		–5
		Load increase (+) or decrease (–)									

Reprinted, by permission, from T.R. Baechle and R.W. Earle, 2005, *Fitness weight training*, 2nd ed. (Champaign, IL: Human Kinetics), 38.

Progression

Even at the advanced training level, you will use the double-progressive approach for consistent strength gains. First, progress by increasing the number of repetitions, then progress by increasing the exercise weight load. For example, train with the resistance that you currently use until you can complete eight repetitions. When you can perform eight good repetitions in two consecutive workouts, add approximately 5 percent more resistance for your next training session.

Increase the Number of Sets   At this level of training, if you have the time and desire to do so, you should perform more than one set of an exercise in a workout *after completing four weeks of training at one set.* Completing more training sets translates into more training volume (volume = sets × reps), and therefore, more work completed during a given exercise session. Consequently, the advanced programs described in this chapter direct you to complete two or three sets of an exercise. Because of the additional intensity created by adding training sets, you should complete one set of each exercise for one month before increasing to two. When increasing the number of sets, do not add sets of all of the exercises at the same time. Instead, perform two sets of no more than four exercises initially, adding a couple more after each subsequent week of training. Follow this approach in all of the workouts presented in programs 7A through 7F (pages 190-201).

Compound Sets   This chapter includes protocols that train the same muscle group back-to-back. Two or three exercises that work the same muscle group, and thus fatigue these muscles, are performed one after the other. Training in this manner forces fatigued muscles to continue to produce muscular force. This training approach simulates the effect of performing two or three successive sets of the same exercise, which increases the intensity of the training. It also works the muscles involved at different angles, thereby providing a more comprehensive training effect and enhancing functional strength. For example, in machine exercise program 7A (pages 190-191), you will perform the pullover exercise, followed by the lat pull-down exercise, followed by the seated row exercise. All three of these exercises work the latissimus dorsi muscles of the upper back. Although you are encouraged to complete two or more sets in the advanced programs, realize that if you perform two sets of these exercises, you will perform six exercises in a row that work the upper-back muscles. If you perform the machine training in program 7A, be sure that you do not increase to two sets until you have completed at least four weeks of training. The same recommendation applies to programs 7B through 7D because the exercises are arranged in a similar fashion.

Use the Breakdown Method   An excellent method for increasing the workout intensity and experiencing greater strength gains is to incorporate the breakdown training method shown in program 7C. This method of training requires you to perform additional reps with a lighter load at the end of a set in which momentary muscular fatigue has occurred.

Use the Double-Progressive System   As training continues, improvements typically occur less frequently and in smaller increments than those experienced in the earlier stages of your exercise program. To prompt continued improvements, follow a double-progressive approach for reaching higher levels of muscular fitness. The double-progressive system requires that you first work to increase the number of repetitions to eight in two consecutive workouts, then increase the load by 5 percent or less. Continue to train with a new load until you can again complete eight reps with correct form in two consecutive workouts; then increase the load again by about 5 percent. The double-progressive method is beneficial in two ways. First, the systematic approach of introducing heavier loads reduces the risk of lifting too much too soon and getting injured. Second, seeing improvements in reps performed and loads lifted provides regular positive reinforcement for your exercise efforts.

Warm-Up

Because you will use relatively heavy loads for the workouts in this chapter, it is important that you perform preliminary warm-up sets. Perform one warm-up set with 50 to 60 percent of your training weight load. For example, if you will perform the barbell squat with 200 pounds (90 kilograms), warm up with 100 to 120 pounds (45 to 54 kilograms) for a set of eight reps, then rest about a minute before doing your first set. Warm-up reps prepare your neuromuscular system to perform better and also appear to reduce the risk of injury.

Although it is essential for advanced exercisers to train hard, you should never sacrifice proper technique to use heavier weights or perform more repetitions. As a rule, muscle fatigue is the point where movement stops, and this signifies the end of the exercise set. An exception to this rule is the breakdown training technique that features a few postfatigue repetitions with reduced resistance (see program 7C for a more detailed explanation and the training protocol).

Rest Periods

The advanced programs in this chapter involve heavier loads, back-to-back sets, multiple exercise sets, and use of breakdown procedures, which all impose a significant training stress. A key factor in your body's ability to tolerate more stress is providing rest periods between sets so that the muscles have the time to recharge their energy stores. That recovery period will permit your muscles to produce high-quality reps set after set. Rest periods of at least two minutes enable fatigued muscles to almost completely recover; therefore, you should take two minutes of rest between sets of the same exercises and at least one minute between different exercises for the same muscle groups.

Movement Speed

A movement speed of four to six seconds per repetition produces properly performed reps. You are undoubtedly aware that it is easier to perform lowering movements (eccentric muscle actions) than it is to perform lifting movements (concentric muscle actions). To make each exercise repetition as productive as possible, move more slowly during the lowering phase. This increases the difficulty of your lowering movements and makes the eccentric muscle actions almost as challenging as the concentric muscle actions. Take 1.5 to 2 seconds to lift the load and 2.5 to 4 seconds to lower the load. If you average 5 seconds for each repetition, a set of four repetitions will take about 20 seconds, and a set of eight repetitions will require approximately 40 seconds. By performing reps in a slow and controlled manner, you will be able to apply a relatively consistent muscular force throughout the lifting and lowering action of each rep, thereby minimizing the role of momentum and reducing the risk of injury. Of course, exercises that have relatively long movement ranges, such as the pullover and lat pull-down, may require more time per repetition, and exercises that have relatively short movement ranges, such as the lateral raise and trunk curl, may take less time per repetition. However, one rep of most of the exercises can be comfortably performed in four to six seconds.

Movement Range

As you become stronger and use heavier training loads, it is easy to inadvertently reduce your movement range on some exercises. Be aware of this tendency and avoid abbreviated exercise movements. Although you should not move into painful positions, it is important to develop full-range muscle strength by performing full-range exercise movements. Whether you use machines that feature predetermined pathways and movement ranges or free weights that offer many movement options, try to achieve relatively complete muscle contraction in each exercise repetition. Conversely, at the starting point of each exercise repetition, be careful not to overstretch your muscles and connective tissue. For example, when performing the barbell incline press, it is not necessary to touch the bar to your chest if this position causes discomfort in your shoulder joints. Simply lower the bar until you feel a gentle stretch in your chest and shoulder muscles, then begin your upward movement.

Training Frequency

As in other workouts described in this text, take at least 48 hours of rest between training sessions to provide time for muscles to recover, rebuild, and become stronger. In most cases, men and women over age 50 attain greater benefit from training programs that provide 72 to 96 hours (three or four days) of recovery between training sessions than from every-other-day workout protocols. But because recovery capabilities from strength training sessions vary widely, we have presented different workout options with various recovery periods. This chapter includes workouts that can be performed two, three, and four days a week, so you can select from programs that allow varying amounts of rest between training sessions. Consider the number of days and the amount of time that you have for strength training, then select from the programs described on pages 190 through 201. Once you begin using one of the programs, note how well your muscles respond to the number of rest days between training sessions. If your strength seems to plateau, consider adding an extra day of rest between these more demanding workouts. This is a simple change and might accelerate training outcomes; sometimes less (training) is better.

Split-Routine Training

Some of the advanced programs described in this chapter include a large number of exercises, and to complete all of them in a single training session would take a considerable amount of time. To keep the amount of time spent working out reasonable, consider *split-routine* training. Split-routine training involves grouping exercises by the body area that they work. A common way to split the training routine is to perform all upper-body exercises in one workout and all lower-body exercises in another workout. Splitting up exercises in workouts this way significantly reduces the amount of training time spent in each workout, because about half of the exercises are performed on different training days. For instance, program 7D presents free weight exercises for the upper body and program 7E presents free weight exercises for the lower body. We recommend doing the upper-body split routine twice a week (e.g., Mondays and Thursdays), and doing the lower-body split routine twice a week (e.g., Wednesdays and Saturdays). Although you will do four weekly workouts, you will train the same muscles only twice a week, with 72 to 96 hours of rest between repeat sessions. The only downside to split training is that it requires more training days compared to two or three total-body workouts per week.

Total-Body Workouts

The split training routines presented in programs 7A, 7B, 7D, and 7E address roughly half of your major muscle groups each workout. The advanced training programs presented in programs 7C and 7F are total-body workouts that should be spaced as evenly as possible, two or three days per week. These total-body workouts are more challenging than those presented in chapters 5 and 6, so consider two-day training protocols for sufficient rest, recovery, and muscle rebuilding. When performed properly, these total-body training programs, which implement postfatigue repetitions, should be highly effective for attaining greater strength and muscle development.

Exercise Spotters

Most people find it difficult to train hard on their own, and this is particularly true when you have already attained a high level of strength fitness. Training with a partner is advantageous, and we recommend doing so whenever possible. When doing some exercises, namely the barbell squat, barbell bench press, and barbell incline press, spotters are essential rather than optional. Because a failed repetition in any of these exercises can cause serious injury, never perform the barbell squat, bench press, or incline press without a competent spotter standing behind you.

Summary of Advanced Exercise Guidelines

Training loads and repetitions	Use a training load that is 80 to 90 percent of the maximum amount of weight you can lift for one repetition. This should result in momentary muscle fatigue after four to eight repetitions.

Progression	Increase the training load by about 5 percent when you can complete eight repetitions with the proper form in two consecutive workouts.
Sets	Complete at least four weeks of workouts performing one set of each exercise before adding a second set of any exercise. This applies to all programs. When adding a second set, add to no more than four exercises initially, and then add to a couple more on successive weeks of training.
Warm-up	Perform one warm-up set of each exercise with about half of the training load.
Rest periods	Rest approximately one minute between exercises. Rest one to two minutes between successive sets of the same exercise. The exception is with breakdown training, which will be described later in the chapter.
Movement speed	Complete each repetition in 4 to 6 seconds, taking about 1.5 to 2 seconds for lifting actions and 2.5 to 4 seconds for lowering actions.
Movement range	Perform each exercise through a relatively full movement range, one that does not cause discomfort or overstretching.
Training frequency	Train on two or three days spaced evenly throughout the week, unless you follow a split routine (perform each split twice a week). If you reach a strength plateau, add an extra day of rest between training sessions.
Training intensity	Continue performing repetitions until reaching the point of momentary muscle fatigue.
Exercise spotters	Use a spotter if you perform the barbell squat, barbell bench press, or barbell incline press.

Protocols for Advanced Strength Training

Congratulations again on achieving advanced strength training status. Most likely, you have progressed in a purposeful and productive manner through the base fitness programs in chapter 5 or the experienced fitness programs in chapter 6 or both. You will find that the advanced strength training exercise protocols are structured differently and are considerably more challenging than the programs in chapters 5 and 6. We present split training routines (upper-body exercises in one session, lower-body exercises in another session) for both machines (programs 7A and 7B) and free weights (programs 7D and 7E). Sample programs 7C and 7F are total-body workouts that conclude each exercise set with a high-intensity training technique using breakdown repetitions. Whichever programs you choose, adhere closely to the training guidelines and performance procedures.

MACHINE SPLIT, UPPER BODY

Program 7A—Machine Split Training, Upper Body

This training program provides 12 machine exercises for the muscles of the chest, back, shoulders, and arms. It should be performed twice a week (e.g., Mondays and Thursdays) in combination with program 7B, which addresses the leg and spinal column muscles.

Because program 7A includes two or three successive exercises for the same muscle groups, a single set of each exercise is sufficient when starting out. When performing a single set, you should be able to complete the 12 exercises in this workout in about 25 minutes. If you perform warm-up sets, or if you complete two training sets, your workout will take longer.

Cumulatively, this training program presents four exercises that work the pectoralis major muscles, four exercises that address the latissimus dorsi muscles, five exercises that work the triceps muscles, four exercises that address the biceps muscles, and four exercises that work the deltoid muscles. The first exercise for each muscle group is a rotary action (curved movement), and the following exercise or exercises use a linear action (straight movement). This training sequence uses the prefatigue principle to enhance the strength-building effect of the exercises. Because of the large number of upper-body exercises, take a one-minute rest between exercises, and a one- to two-minute rest between sets if you progress to multiset training. Perform the exercises in the sequence presented in the table. This chart also provides general guidelines for loads to use, repetitions to perform, number of sets to complete, exercise speed, and recovery time.

MACHINE SPLIT, UPPER BODY

Program 7A—Machine Split Training, Upper Body

Exercise	Muscle group
1. Chest crossover	Pectoralis major
2. Chest press	Pectoralis major, triceps, deltoids
3. Incline press	Upper pectoralis major, triceps, deltoids
4. Pullover	Latissimus dorsi
5. Lat pull-down	Latissimus dorsi, biceps
6. Seated row	Latissimus dorsi, middle trapezius, rhomboids, biceps
7. Lateral raise	Deltoids
8. Shoulder press	Deltoids, triceps
9. Biceps curl	Biceps
10. Weight-assisted chin-up	Latissimus dorsi, biceps
11. Triceps extension	Triceps
12. Weight-assisted bar dip	Pectoralis major, triceps

For each exercise:

Training load	Repetitions	Sets	Repetition speed	Recovery time
80-90% max	4-8	1-2	4-6 sec	Between exercises: 1 min Between sets: 1-2 min

MACHINE SPLIT, LOWER BODY

Program 7B—Machine Split Training, Lower Body

Program 7B complements program 7A by addressing the other muscle groups, specifically lower-body muscles, such as the those in the hips and legs (hamstrings, quadriceps, gluteals, hip adductors, hip abductors) and the muscles of the spinal column (rectus abdominis, erector spinae, internal obliques, external obliques, neck flexors, neck extensors). Like program 7A, this routine should be performed twice a week (e.g., Tuesdays and Fridays), with 72 to 96 hours recovery time between lower-body workouts. If you perform one set of each exercise, you should complete this workout in about 20 minutes.

The program 7B training protocol includes only two paired exercises (for the quadriceps), but provides a concentrated and comprehensive workout for the leg and spinal column muscles. Begin with one set of each exercise, and progress to double sets if you decide to do so. Consider warm-up sets, using 50 to 60 percent of your training load, especially for the spinal column muscles.

Nine of the 10 exercises in program 7B address specific muscle groups; for example, the leg curl focuses on the hamstrings, and the leg extension targets the quadriceps. These exercises are followed by the leg press, which concurrently works the quadriceps and hamstrings as well as the gluteals. The position of the leg press in the workout (after the leg curl and leg extension and before the hip adduction and hip abduction), makes this sequence of leg exercises challenging and productive.

You will achieve the best results by performing the exercises in program 7B in the order listed. The table provides general guidelines for loads to use, repetitions to perform, number of sets to complete, exercise speed, and recovery time.

MACHINE SPLIT, LOWER BODY

Program 7B—Machine Split Training, Lower Body

Exercise	Muscle group
1. Leg curl	Hamstrings
2. Leg extension	Quadriceps
3. Leg press	Quadriceps, hamstrings, gluteals
4. Hip adduction	Hip adductors
5. Hip abduction	Hip abductors
6. Abdominal flexion	Rectus abdominis
7. Low back extension	Erector spinae
8. Rotary torso	Internal obliques, external obliques
9. Neck flexion	Sternocleidomastoids
10. Neck extension	Upper trapezius

For each exercise:

Training load	Repetitions	Sets	Repetition speed	Recovery time
80-90% max	4-8	1-2	4-6 sec	Between exercises: 1 min Between sets: 1-2 min

MACHINE TOTAL-BODY TRAINING

Program 7C—Machine Total-Body Training

Program 7C is a full-body exercise program using machines. This program includes 12 exercises; half address the upper-body muscles, and the other half work the leg and spinal column muscles.

Performing one set of each exercise in program 7C requires less than 25 minutes. However, this training program makes each exercise set more demanding by means of postfatigue *breakdown repetitions*. In breakdown training, perform an exercise to the point of momentary muscle fatigue with a training load that allows you to complete about eight repetitions. When you cannot complete another repetition with correct technique, immediately reduce the load by 10 to 20 percent and do as many additional (postfatigue) repetitions as you can (typically two to four reps) with the lighter resistance. Here's an example: Assume that you can complete eight leg curls with proper technique with 100 pounds (45 kilograms). You may, therefore, begin by performing eight leg curls with 50 pounds (23 kilograms) for a warm-up set. After a one-minute rest, perform eight leg curls to the point of momentary muscle fatigue with 100 pounds (45 kilograms). Immediately lower the weight to 85 pounds (38 kilograms), and complete as many breakdown repetitions as you can until you reach muscle fatigue again (postfatigue set). You should find that one extended set of breakdown training is sufficient for stimulating further strength gains and muscle development.

You will need 72 to 96 hours for complete muscle recovery and rebuilding after your breakdown training sessions. Therefore two evenly spaced workouts per week are recommended, such as Mondays and Fridays. If you choose to perform two sets, do not do so until you have completed four weeks of breakdown training. The table presents the training exercises for program 7C, and provides general guidelines for loads to use, repetitions to perform, number of sets to complete, exercise speed, and recovery time.

MACHINE TOTAL-BODY TRAINING

Program 7C—Machine Total-Body Training

Exercise	Muscle group
1. Leg press	Quadriceps, hamstrings, gluteals
2. Hip adduction	Hip adductors
3. Hip abduction	Hip abductors
4. Chest press	Pectoralis major, triceps, anterior deltoids
5. Seated row	Latissimus dorsi, middle trapezius, rhomboids, biceps
6. Shoulder press	Deltoids, triceps
7. Lat pull-down	Latissimus dorsi, biceps
8. Triceps press	Triceps, pectoralis major
9. Biceps curl	Biceps
10. Abdominal flexion	Rectus abdominis
11. Low back extension	Erector spinae
12. Rotary torso	Internal obliques, external obliques

For each exercise:

Training load	Repetitions	Sets	Repetition speed	Recovery time
80% max	8 + 3	1	4-6 sec	Between exercises: 1 min Between standard reps and breakdown reps: less than 5 sec

FREE WEIGHT SPLIT, UPPER BODY

Program 7D—Free Weight Split Training, Upper Body

If you prefer training with dumbbells and barbells, you may choose from several advanced exercise programs. Programs 7D and 7E are complementary exercise protocols presented in a split-routine format. Program 7D works the muscles of the chest, back, shoulders, and arms, whereas program 7E trains the muscles of the legs and spinal column. Each split program should be performed twice a week, with at least 72 hours of rest between training sessions. For example, you can perform program 7D on Mondays and Thursdays, and program 7E on Tuesdays and Fridays.

Program 7D includes 11 exercises, sequenced to work the target muscles two to four times in succession. For example, the first three exercises (dumbbell chest fly, barbell bench press, dumbbell incline press) all emphasize the pectoralis major muscles. Because of the more challenging exercise format, you should start with just one set of each exercise. If you believe that more sets would be advantageous, perform a second set of each exercise, but wait until you have completed four weeks of single-set training before doing so. When increasing the number of sets, do so for no more than four exercises initially, and then add a second set to other exercises in subsequent training weeks.

Like program 7A, program 7D features a preexhaustion exercise pattern that works targeted muscle groups, such as the deltoids, in succession during the dumbbell lateral raise and dumbbell press exercises. This unique arrangement prefatigues the deltoids with a set of dumbbell lateral raises and works them again in the dumbbell press with assistance from fresh triceps muscles, which were not involved in the dumbbell lateral raise. This exercise sequence enhances the strength-building effect. Because of the large number of upper-body exercises, take a one-minute rest between exercises and a one- to two-minute rest between sets if you progress to multiset training. If you perform one set of each exercise, you should be able to complete this program in less than 25 minutes. A warm-up set will double the training time.

The table presents the recommended exercise sequence and provides general guidelines for loads to use, repetitions to perform, number of sets to complete, exercise speed, and recovery time. Try to follow the workout as it is described as closely as possible.

FREE WEIGHT SPLIT, UPPER BODY

Program 7D—Free Weight Split Training, Upper Body

Exercise	Muscle group
1. Dumbbell chest fly	Pectoralis major
2. Barbell bench press	Pectoralis major, triceps, deltoids
3. Dumbbell incline press	Upper pectoralis major, triceps, deltoids
4. Dumbbell one-arm row	Latissimus dorsi, middle trapezius, rhomboids, biceps
5. Lat pull-down	Latissimus dorsi, biceps
6. Dumbbell lateral raise	Deltoids
7. Dumbbell seated press	Deltoids, triceps
8. Dumbbell overhead triceps extension	Triceps
9. Dumbbell incline curl	Biceps
10. Body-weight dip	Pectoralis major, triceps
11. Body-weight chin-up	Latissimus dorsi, biceps

For each exercise:

Training load	Repetitions	Sets	Repetition speed	Recovery time
80-90% max	4-8	1-2	4-6 sec	Between exercises: 1 min Between sets: 1-2 min

FREE WEIGHT SPLIT, LOWER BODY

Program 7E—Free Weight Split Training, Lower Body

Program 7E, the counterpart to program 7D, works the muscles of the legs and spinal column. Although this program is limited to seven exercises, the initial sequence of barbell squat, dumbbell lunge, and dumbbell step-up provides a challenging workout for the quadriceps, hamstrings, and gluteal muscles.

If you perform one set of each exercise, this workout should take less than 15 minutes. Double sets of each exercise will increase the training duration to about 30 minutes, more or less, depending on your recovery time between successive sets (one to two minutes). Although preliminary sets increase workout length, you should include a warm-up set with about half of the training load before performing barbell squats. Remember to complete four weeks of training with one set before adding a second set, and when doing so, increase the number of sets for no more than four exercises initially.

Perform the workout described in program 7E no more than twice a week, and rest at least 72 hours between training sessions. Closely adhere to the exercise sequence and general training guidelines for resistance, repetitions, sets, repetition speed, and recovery time presented in the table.

FREE WEIGHT SPLIT, LOWER BODY

Program 7E—Free Weight Split Training, Lower Body

Exercise	Muscle group
1. Barbell squat	Quadriceps, hamstrings, gluteals
2. Dumbbell lunge	Quadriceps, hamstrings, gluteals
3. Dumbbell step-up	Quadriceps, hamstrings, gluteals
4. Barbell heel raise	Gastrocnemius, soleus
5. Twisting trunk curl	Rectus abdominis, internal obliques, external obliques
6. Body-weight trunk extension	Erector spinae
7. Barbell shrug	Upper trapezius

For each exercise:

Training load	Repetitions	Sets	Repetition speed	Recovery time
80-90% max	4-8	1-2	4-6 sec	Between exercises: 1 min Between sets: 1-2 min

Program 7F—Free Weight Total-Body Training

Program 7F is a full-body exercise package using barbells and dumbbells. The 13 exercises address all of the major muscle groups, and you should be able to complete them in about 30 minutes if you perform one set of each exercise. Although program 7F begins with two successive exercises for the quadriceps, hamstrings, and gluteal muscles, the remaining exercises alternate opposing muscle groups (e.g., body-weight dip for the pectoralis major and triceps muscles followed by chin-up for the latissimus dorsi and biceps muscles).

Like program 7C, this workout is designed to make each exercise set more demanding by means of postfatigue breakdown repetitions. You train to the point of momentary muscle fatigue with a training load that allows you to complete about eight repetitions. When you cannot complete another repetition with correct technique, immediately reduce the load by 10 to 20 percent and do as many additional (postfatigue) repetitions as you can (typically two to four reps) with the lighter resistance. For example, you are able to do eight dumbbell presses with 50-pound (23-kilogram) dumbbells. You may, therefore, begin by performing eight dumbbell presses with 25-pound dumbbells for a warm-up set. After a one-minute rest, perform eight dumbbell presses to the point of momentary muscle fatigue with 50-pound dumbbells. Immediately lower the weight to 40-pound (18-kilogram) dumbbells and complete as many breakdown repetitions as you can until you reach muscle fatigue again (postfatigue set). You should find that one extended set of of breakdown training is sufficient for stimulating further strength gains and muscle development.

You will need 72 to 96 hours for complete muscle recovery and rebuilding following your breakdown training sessions. We therefore recommend two evenly-spaced workouts per week, such as Mondays and Fridays. If you choose to perform two sets, do not do so until you have first completed four weeks of breakdown training.

The table presents the recommended exercise sequence and provides general guidelines for loads to use, repetitions to perform, number of sets to complete, exercise speed, and recovery time. Please follow this training protocol as closely as possible.

FREE WEIGHT TOTAL-BODY TRAINING

Program 7F—Free Weight Total-Body Training

Exercise	Muscle group
1. Barbell squat	Quadriceps, hamstrings, gluteals
2. Dumbbell lunge	Quadriceps, hamstrings, gluteals
3. Barbell bench press	Pectoralis major, triceps, anterior deltoids
4. Dumbbell one-arm row	Latissimus dorsi, middle trapezius, rhomboids, biceps
5. Barbell incline press	Upper pectoralis major, triceps, anterior deltoids
6. Lat pull-down	Latissimus dorsi, biceps
7. Dumbbell seated press	Deltoids, triceps
8. Dumbbell incline curl	Biceps
9. Body-weight dip	Pectoralis major, triceps
10. Body-weight chin-up	Latissimus dorsi, biceps
11. Twisting trunk curl	Rectus abdominis, internal obliques, external obliques
12. Body-weight trunk extension	Erector spinae
13. Barbell shrug	Upper trapezius

For each exercise:

Training load	Repetitions	Sets	Repetition speed	Recovery time
80-90% max	4-8	1-3	4-6 sec	Between exercises: 1 min Between sets: 1-2 min

Further Training

The sample exercise programs (four in chapter 5, four in chapter 6, six in chapter 7) should be effective for enhancing your strength and muscular fitness. Feel free to follow any of these programs, interchanging them periodically to experience a different training stimulus. By frequently varying the exercise programs and training protocols you should experience more physiological responsiveness and less mental monotony as you make regular strength training a lifetime activity.

Of course, based on your experience with the sample programs, you may design individualized workouts that you find more purposeful and productive for achieving your personal fitness goals. Just be sure to apply the training principles presented in chapter 4 and use correct exercise technique in every strength workout.

8

Sports Performance Programs

Many past-50 exercisers, including the authors, participate in a variety of sports and athletic activities. If you are like us, you take sports performance seriously and strive to do your best in every athletic endeavor. Although some senior athletes still compete in team sports such as soccer, ice hockey, basketball, and softball, most pursue individual or partner activities. This chapter presents specific strength training programs for enhancing your performance in the recreational physical activities that we believe are the most popular—running, cycling, swimming, skiing, tennis, and golf.

We take a twofold approach to strength training for improved sports conditioning. The first is to help you avoid the sports-related injuries typically associated with disproportionate strength and muscle imbalances, and the second is to provide you with exercises that will strengthen the muscles that are most involved in your sport. Concerning this first objective, which is our primary focus, sprinting tends to strengthen the quadriceps muscles of the front of the thigh more than the hamstring muscles of the rear thigh. If the quadriceps muscles become disproportionately stronger than the opposing hamstring muscles, the chances of injuring the hamstrings increase. Conversely, distance running tends to strengthen the hamstring muscles more than the quadriceps muscles, increasing the likelihood that the quadriceps will become injured. We, therefore, encourage sprinters to include hamstring-strengthening exercises in their workouts to reduce the risk of hamstring injuries, and encourage distance runners to perform quadriceps-strengthening exercises to lower the risk of injuring these muscles.

The calf muscles (gastrocnemius and soleus) are used extensively in running, too. Because of their involvement in every running stride, many people think that runners should focus their training on strengthening their calf muscles. Indeed they should, but it is also important to strengthen their weaker counterpart, the shin muscles (anterior tibialis). If you strengthen only the larger and stronger calf muscles, they will eventually overpower the smaller and weaker shin muscles, which may lead to shin splints, stress fractures, and Achilles tendon problems. With this in mind, we recommend that runners always conclude their strength training workouts with a set of weighted toe raises to strengthen the shin muscles and maintain muscular balance in the lower-leg musculature.

Training the muscles that are most prominent (prime movers) in a sport is important because it strengthens these muscles and increases performance power. Success in every sport is ultimately related to performance power, which is the product of muscle force and movement speed.

$$\text{Performance power} = \text{muscle force} \times \text{movement speed}$$

Increasing your movement speed involves complex neuromuscular phenomena and technical training programs that are beyond the scope of this book. Increasing your muscles' force, on the other hand, is a relatively simple process that is best accomplished by implementing the strength training principles, protocols, and procedures presented in the previous chapters. As you increase your muscle strength, you automatically develop the tools to improve your ability to produce performance power.

Because it is necessary to strengthen and stretch the muscles that are less involved in a sport in order to reduce the risk of injury and it is also necessary to strengthen and stretch the prime movers in order to increase power production, a sensible strength training program will work all of your major muscle groups. This will help you avoid injury and improve your overall sports performance.

For example, in our golf studies, our relatively brief but comprehensive approach to overall muscle conditioning produced many positive outcomes, both expected and unexpected. In addition to increasing muscular strength, performance power, and club-head speed, the golfers found that they could play golf more frequently and for longer durations without fatigue. Best of all, none of the golf conditioning participants (including those who had been injured previously) reported a golf-related injury as long as they continued their strength training program.

In this chapter we present specific strength training programs for the sports of running, cycling, swimming, skiing, tennis, and golf. Although the exercises and training protocols are different for each activity, you will work all of your major muscle groups in the manner most appropriate for ensuring overall muscle strength, muscle balance, and power enhancement. You will learn how the major muscles are involved in each athletic event and how to train them properly for integrated strength development and improved sports performance.

Strength Training for Runners

Distance running is a great sport that millions of competitive and recreational athletes enjoy at a variety of levels. Whether you prefer to jog a couple of miles through the neighborhood or are training to complete a marathon, distance running is a highly effective and efficient means of aerobic conditioning. Unfortunately, distance running is considerably less beneficial for your musculoskeletal system, and injury rates among runners are extremely high. In fact, at the high school level, cross country runners experience more injuries than athletes in any other sport, including football and gymnastics.

Why is a noncontact sport like running such a high-risk activity? Actually, running involves an incredible amount of contact, but it is with road surfaces rather than other athletes. Every running stride places about three times the weight of your body on your feet, ankles, knees, and hip joints. These landing forces also add stress to your lower back.

The repetitive pounding encountered mile after mile causes microtrauma to the shock-absorbing tissues. Under ideal conditions, these tissues recover completely within 24 hours. However, numerous factors may interfere with normal recovery processes, eventually resulting in weakened and injury-prone tissues. Factors such as longer running sessions, faster running paces, shorter recovery periods between workouts, downhill running, running on hard surfaces, frequent racing, poor nutritional habits, undesirable changes in sleeping patterns, and poor-quality shoes may singularly, or in combination, compromise your recovery from training and may lead to injury.

Of course, you can take steps to reduce the amount of tissue trauma and decrease your risk of running-related injuries. Such precautions include gradually increasing training paces and distances, selecting running routes or courses on soft surfaces and level terrain, competing in fewer races, and paying careful attention to proper nutrition and sleep. The importance of obtaining guidance when selecting running shoes cannot be overemphasized.

However, one of the most effective means for minimizing tissue trauma is to develop stronger muscles, tendons, fascia, ligaments, and bones. This is the primary reason that every runner should perform a regular strength training program. Consider the results of our four-year strength training project with the Notre Dame High School (Hingham, Massachusetts) girls' cross country and track teams.

For four consecutive years, 30 distance runners from Notre Dame High School participated in a basic and brief strength training program during the summer and winter months between their cross country and track seasons. Every Monday, Wednesday, and Friday, they performed a 30-minute strength training program that included exercises for each major muscle group. During each of these years, the cross country team won both the Massachusetts and New England championships. More important, during the same four years, only one runner experienced an injury that resulted in a missed practice session or meet.

Strength Training Benefits

The Notre Dame runners realized that a sensible strength training program provided many benefits, including the following:

- Greater muscular strength
- Greater muscular endurance

- Greater joint flexibility
- Better body composition
- Reduced injury risk
- Improved self-confidence
- Improved running economy

Although the first six strength training benefits should be self-explanatory, you may be intrigued by improved running economy. In a 1995 study at the University of New Hampshire, the female cross country runners who had participated in a strength training program experienced a significantly greater improvement in their running economy. They required 4 percent less oxygen at submaximal running speeds (7:30-, 7:00-, and 6:30-minute mile paces), meaning that they could run more efficiently and race faster than before.

Runner Concerns

With so many advantages, why so few runners regularly include strength training as a part of their training continues to be a mystery. Perhaps the four following concerns keep runners from strength training: increased body weight, decreased movement speed, less fluid running form, and fatigued muscles. Let's take a closer look at each of these issues.

Increased Body Weight   Very few people who regularly follow a strength training program have the genetic potential to develop large muscles. This is especially true for distance runners, who typically have ectomorphic (thin) physiques. Strength training will increase muscle strength and endurance, but rarely will result in significant weight gain or muscle enlargement.

Decreased Movement Speed   With respect to running speed, our studies and those of many others have shown that greater strength results in faster movement speeds. We need only look at sprinters and middle-distance runners to realize that strength training has a positive impact on running speed, because nearly all of these athletes perform regular strength training exercises.

Less Fluid Running Form   Running involves coordinated actions of the legs and the arms, and one cannot function without the other. Your right arm moves in opposition of your left leg, and your left arm moves in opposition of your right leg, each perfectly counterbalancing the other. That is why it is almost impossible to run fast and move your arms slowly or to move your arms fast and run slowly. By strengthening the upper-body muscles, you more effectively share the running effort between your arms and legs, resulting in more fluid running form.

Fatigued Muscles   Strenuous strength training sessions can cause a considerable amount of muscle fatigue that could adversely affect the quality and quantity of your runs. Therefore brief strength workouts that do not leave you exhausted are recommended. Remember that you are strength training to enhance your running performance, not to become a successful competitive weightlifter. Our program of strength training for runners requires just one set of an exercise for each major muscle group, which does not take much time and does not produce much lasting fatigue, nor will it result in large muscle gains. You may also choose to strength train only one or two days per week, which should make muscle fatigue issues even less likely.

Program Design for Runners

The strength training protocol followed by the Notre Dame athletes described earlier is a comprehensive conditioning program that addresses all of the major muscle groups. This program does not attempt to imitate specific running movements or emphasize specific running muscles, but rather focuses on exercises that will increase strength in the muscle groups relied on in running. The program establishes training frequencies that reduce the possibility of overtraining, muscle imbalances, and injury.

Some people believe that runners should complete numerous sets and many repetitions with light resistance to enhance their endurance capacity. However, this is not the purpose of strength training. Remember that running is best for improving cardiorespiratory endurance and that strength training is best for increasing musculoskeletal strength.

Muscle strength is best developed by training with heavy loads and 1 to 6 repetitions, the type of loads that are used by competitive weightlifters who typically possess a high percentage of fast-twitch muscle fibers. Heavy loads are not recommended for distance runners. Instead distance runners, who usually possess a higher percentage of slow-twitch muscle fibers, will benefit more using lighter loads (60 to 70 percent of maximum resistance) that permit 12 to 16 repetitions per set. Whenever you can complete 16 repetitions using proper form in two successive workouts, increase the exercise load by 1 to 5 pounds (.45 to 2.3 kilograms). One set of each exercise is sufficient for strength development.

Perform repetitions in a slow and controlled manner. Exercising in a controlled manner maximizes muscle tension and minimizes momentum, resulting in a better training effect and reducing the likelihood of injury. Each repetition should take 4 to 6 seconds, 1.5 to 2 seconds for each lifting movement and 2.5 to 4 seconds for each lowering movement. We suggest that you train two or three times a week on nonconsecutive days. Also, it is essential to breathe on every repetition, because holding your breath can lead to undesirable increases in blood pressure and can restrict blood flow. The recommended breathing pattern is to exhale during each lifting movement and to inhale during each lowering movement.

Strength Exercises for Runners

Runners can develop muscle strength by performing a variety of exercises using free weights or machines. The following sections recommend strength training exercises for the major muscle groups, and these are listed in table 8.1 on page 210.

Leg Muscles

Although the barbell squat is the traditional leg exercise, many runners find that placing the barbell on the shoulders is uncomfortable. The dumbbell squat provides

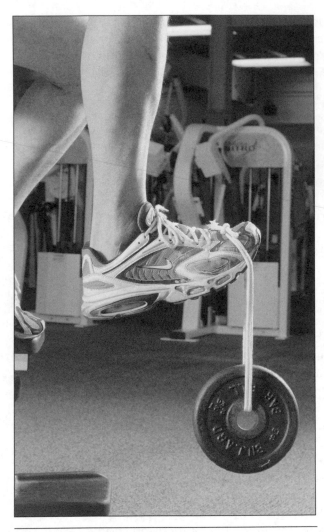

Figure 8.1   Weighted toe raises.

an option; however, some people may find it difficult to balance well enough to perform the exercise properly or may lack the strength to hold heavy dumbbells.

If you decide not to do barbell or dumbbell squats, you can strengthen your hamstrings, quadriceps, and gluteals by doing the leg press on a machine that offers a full movement range and back support. It may be advisable to precede the leg press exercises with leg extension exercises, which target the quadriceps and with leg curl exercises, which target the hamstrings. By prefatiguing these muscle groups, you will use less resistance in the more challenging leg press exercise to achieve the same conditioning effect. One set of each exercise is sufficient, but you may perform an additional set if you desire.

Runners should conclude their strength training workouts with a set of weighted toe raises, as shown in figure 8.1, to strengthen the shin muscles (anterior tibialis) and maintain muscular balance in the lower-leg musculature (gastrocnemius, soleus, plantaris).

Upper-Body Muscles

Popular exercises for developing the upper body are bench press for the chest muscles, bent-over row for the mid- and upper-back muscles, and overhead press for the shoulder muscles. If you lack experience in performing these upper-body exercises with a barbell, dumbbell training is a good alternative. Regardless of which type of equipment you use, how you use it is very important. For instance, performing a standing bent-over row exercise, with the body from the hips to the shoulders parallel with the floor, increases stress on the low back 10 times the weight of the dumbbells or barbell. However, by using one dumbbell, and placing your other hand on a bench for back support, you can greatly reduce the stress on the lower back, thus making the exercise safer and more effective for the upper back.

If you have access to machines, do the chest crossover for the chest muscles, the pullover for the mid- and upper-back muscles, and the lateral raise for the shoulder muscles. These machines effectively isolate the target muscle groups. If you prefer exercises that involve more arm work, the chest press, seated row, and shoulder press machines are excellent choices.

Arm Muscles

The basic exercise for the biceps muscles is the arm curl performed with barbells, dumbbells, or machines. Training the triceps involves some form of arm extension, either with free weights or machines.

A good means for working the biceps and upper-back muscles together is the chin-up with body weight or on a weight-assisted chin-up machine. A good means for working the triceps and chest muscles together is the bar dip with body weight or on a weight-assisted bar dip machine.

Midsection Muscles

Machines provide a safe method for progressively strengthening and conditioning the muscles of the midsection. Key exercises for accomplishing this outcome can be performed on the abdominal and low back machines. These exercises also develop an injury-resistant midsection. The rotary torso machine strengthens the oblique muscles surrounding the midsection.

If you don't have access to machines, the twisting trunk curl is your best alternative for abdominal conditioning. The counterpart for the low back muscles is the body-weight trunk extension. Although both of these exercises are performed with body-weight resistance, they are reasonably effective for strengthening the midsection muscles, especially when you execute them in a controlled manner.

Neck Muscles

The head, which weighs approximately 15 pounds (6.8 kilograms), is held in position throughout each run by the neck muscles. For this reason, many runners experience fatigue in the neck and shoulder muscles. The neck extension and flexion machine, listed in table 8.2, will help runners strengthen these muscles. If you do not have access to this machine, the best approach is to exercise against manual resistance: Place your hands against your forehead and resist slow neck-flexion movements as you press your head forward, and place your hands against the back of your head and resist slow neck-extension movements as you press your head backward.

Table 8.1 presents the strength training exercises for an overall conditioning program for runners. Once you have mastered the basic exercise program, you may want to add some of the complementary exercises presented in table 8.2. To perform the barbell quarter squat listed in the complementary exercises, simply reduce the depth of the barbell or dumbbell squat listed in table 8.1 by performing just one-quarter of the range of motion.

Summary for Running

The main objectives of a strength training program for runners are to decrease injuries while increasing muscular strength and running performance. To obtain these results, the workout should be short, but strenuous. One set of 12 to 16

Table 8.1   Basic Strength Training Exercises for Runners

Targeted muscle groups	Machine exercises	Free weight exercises
Quadriceps, hamstrings, gluteals	Leg press	Barbell or dumbbell squat
Gastrocnemius, soleus	Heel raise	Barbell or dumbbell heel raise
Pectoralis major	Chest crossover	Barbell or dumbbell bench press
Latissimus dorsi	Pullover	Dumbbell one-arm row
Deltoids	Lateral raise	Dumbbell seated press
Biceps	Biceps curl	Barbell or dumbbell curl
Triceps	Triceps extension	Dumbbell lying triceps extension
Erector spinae	Low back extension	Body-weight trunk extension
Rectus abdominis	Abdominal flexion	Twisting trunk curl

Table 8.2   Complementary Strength Training Exercises for Runners

Targeted muscle groups	Machine exercises	Free weight exercises
Quadriceps	Leg extension	Dumbbell lunge
Hamstrings	Leg curl	Barbell quarter squat
Pectoralis major, triceps	Weight-assisted bar dip	Body-weight dip
Latissiums dorsi, biceps	Weight-assisted chin-up	Body-weight chin-up
Internal and external obliques	Rotary torso	Twisting trunk curl
Sternocleidomastoids and upper trapezius	Neck flexion and extension	Manual resistance neck flexion and extension
Anterior tibialis	—	Weighted toe raise

repetitions for each major muscle group will provide a safe, effective, and efficient exercise experience. Two or three training sessions per week are sufficient. Each workout should take no more than 30 minutes, depending on the number of exercises you perform. The key to productive strength training is proper exercise technique, which includes performing the exercises through the full movement range and in a controlled manner. Be sure to eat enough calories to fuel your combined physical activities, including a little more protein and lots of water. Finally, try to sleep at least eight hours nightly so that you enter every exercise session with energy and enthusiasm. After following these training recommendations for a couple of months, you could see your strength increase 40 to 60 percent and your running performance improve, too.

Exercise selection	Include at least one exercise for each major muscle group.
Training load	Use a training load that is 60 to 70 percent of maximum resistance.
Repetitions	Complete 12 to 16 controlled repetitions.
Progression	Increase the resistance by 5 percent when you can complete 16 repetitions during two successive sessions. After two months, consider adding several of the exercises listed in table 8.2.
Sets	Complete one set of each exercise.
Movement speed	Complete each movement at a moderate speed, taking 1.5 to 2 seconds to lift and 2.5 to 4 seconds to lower.
Movement range	Perform each exercise through a relatively full movement range. Avoid a locked-out position on pressing exercises.
Training frequency	Complete two or three exercise sessions per week.

Strength Training for Cyclists

The bicycle is an extremely energy-efficient machine, and cycling is an excellent exercise for enhancing cardiorespiratory endurance. Like running, cycling uses the leg muscles to generate power. Unlike running, cycling does not generate landing forces to the feet, legs, and back, which reduces the risk of impact injuries. Nonetheless, cycling, like any repetitive-movement activity, stresses some muscles more than others, which may lead to overuse injuries.

Let's examine the major muscles involved in cycling. The power stroke in cycling is produced primarily by knee extension from contraction of the quadriceps muscles, and hip extension from contraction of the hamstring muscles, with some assistance from the gluteal muscles of the buttocks. Lower-leg muscles also contribute.

Cyclists use their calf muscles while pushing on the pedals during ankle extension (gastrocnemius, soleus, plantaris) and engage the shin muscles when they pull against the toe clips during ankle flexion (anterior tibialis).

Although the involvement of the thigh and lower-leg muscles in cycling is quite apparent, the role of the triceps, front of the shoulders, and lower back muscles in maintaining the torso position is not. In addition, the upper-back and chest muscles provide stability for the upper-arm position, and forearm strength allows a firm grip on the handlebars. Proper positioning of the handlebars helps to evenly distribute the muscular requirements for maintaining the upper-body posture and delaying the onset of fatigue. The neck extensors help maintain the head position. All of these muscles, therefore, require consideration when designing a strength training program for cyclists.

Like other athletes, cyclists should strengthen all major muscle groups through a comprehensive strength training program. They should train both the primary muscle groups and their opposing muscles in order to achieve balanced strength and muscular development across the joint structures. Training only the primary muscles typically leads to overuse injuries, because muscles on one side of a joint become much stronger than those on the other side, and the weaker musculature is eventually overpowered and damaged.

This does not imply that you should train opposing muscle groups to equal strength levels. For example, the neck extensor muscles are inherently larger and stronger than the neck flexor muscles, so it would be nearly impossible to train both muscle groups to lift the same amount. The same is true of the muscles of the lower leg: The ankle extensor muscles in the calves are larger and stronger than the ankle flexor muscles in the shins; therefore you should not try to train the extensor and flexor muscles to the same strength level. However, both sets of muscles should be addressed in a sensible strength training program.

Strength Exercises for Cyclists

Usually it is advisable to work the larger muscle groups of the legs and then the torso before training the smaller muscles of the arms and neck. However, performing single-joint upper-body exercises with lighter loads before training multiple-joint lower-body exercises with heavier loads is also an option. Table 8.3 presents the basic strength training exercises for cyclists.

Program Design for Cyclists

The exercises in the strength training program for cyclists do not attempt to imitate specific movements or emphasize specific muscle groups, but rather focus on the inclusion of exercises that will strengthen the muscle groups relied on in cycling. Discussed next are our recommendations for exercise execution, loads to use, number of repetitions and sets to perform, and training frequency.

Movement Range

Although cycling involves movements that take the legs through only the middle of the range of motion and requires static contractions of the upper-body muscles,

Table 8.3   Basic Strength Training Exercises for Cyclists

Targeted muscle groups	Machine exercises	Free weight exercises
Quadriceps	Leg extension	Barbell or dumbbell squat
Hamstrings	Leg curl	Barbell or dumbbell squat
Quadriceps, hamstrings, gluteals	Leg press	Barbell or dumbbell squat
Pectoralis major	Chest crossover	Dumbbell chest fly
Pectoralis major, triceps	Chest press	Barbell or dumbbell bench press
Latissimus dorsi	Pullover	Dumbbell pullover
Latissimus dorsi, biceps	Seated row	Dumbbell one-arm row
Deltoids	Lateral raise	Dumbbell lateral raise
Deltoids, triceps	Shoulder press	Dumbbell seated press
Biceps	Biceps curl	Barbell or dumbbell curl
Triceps	Triceps extension	Dumbbell lying triceps extension
Erector spinae	Low back extension	Body-weight trunk extension
Rectus abdominis	Abdominal flexion	Twisting trunk curl
Sternocleidomastoids, upper trapezius	Neck flexion and extension	Barbell or dumbbell shrug

you should perform strength exercises through the full range of motion. To improve cycling performance, it may be acceptable to perform part-range movements, but for safety purposes, you should perform full-range movements. Weakness at the ends of the movement range may reduce joint integrity and increase the risk of injury.

Cyclists should perform rotary exercises, such as the leg extension, from the fully stretched position to the fully contracted position. However, pressing movements, such as the leg press, should end just short of the locked-out position. Locking the knee joint against heavy resistance increases the potential for injury and should be avoided.

Movement Speed

How fast should you execute the strength training exercises recommended in table 8.3? Because the exercises in the strength training program for cyclists do not try to simulate cycling movements and because it would be difficult to perform leg-strengthening exercises at the same rate you can pedal a bicycle—about 90 repetitions per minute—you should complete the exercises in a controlled manner at a moderate speed. This maximizes strength development and minimizes the risk of injury. Research has demonstrated excellent strength gains from exercising at moderate movement speeds.

Loads, Repetitions, and Sets

To effectively increase strength, the exercise resistance should be sufficient to fatigue the target muscles. For most purposes, this means that the loads used in training should equal approximately 75 percent of the maximum load that you can lift one time, using your best effort.

Research demonstrates that most people can complete 8 to 12 repetitions with 75 percent of their maximum load. However, when using 75 percent of their maximum resistance, people with more fast-twitch muscle fibers (sprinters) typically perform fewer than 8 repetitions, and people with more slow-twitch muscle fibers (marathoners) typically perform more than 12 repetitions. Because cycling is an endurance activity, most cyclists should attain excellent strength gains by training with loads that result in 12 to 16 repetitions (equivalent to 60 to 70 percent of maximum load). Of course, this assumes training to the point of muscle fatigue on each exercise set.

Cyclists require considerable time and energy to perform their daily training miles. It is, therefore, not advisable for cyclists to spend unnecessary time and energy in strength training. Fortunately, building muscular endurance and building muscular strength are complementary activities. That is, the same exercise program that develops muscle strength also increases muscle endurance. Research indicates that one set of properly performed strength training exercise is sufficient for stimulating gains in muscle strength and endurance. Therefore, you should start with one set of each exercise. Each exercise set should take 60 to 90 seconds, and by allowing for half a minute of recovery between exercises, the training program in table 8.3 should take just a little more than 30 minutes to complete.

For maximum benefit, you should perform each set of exercises to muscle fatigue, or temporary muscle failure. This means that you exercise until your muscles can no longer complete the repetition.

Frequency

Research shows that two or three properly spaced training sessions per week are effective for improving muscular strength. Cyclists who schedule two strength workouts per week invest only one hour of time for significant improvements in muscular strength. Research with both older and younger people reveals an increase in muscular strength of approximately 50 percent after just two months of twice-a-week resistance training.

Progression

We prefer a double-progressive system of strength development. Begin with a load that you can lift 12 times, and continue training with it until you can complete 16 repetitions. When you perform 16 repetitions on two successive occasions, increase the resistance by about 5 percent. Stay with this load until you can complete 16 repetitions, and then again increase the resistance by about 5 percent. After two months of training, consider adding one more lower-body and one upper-body exercise.

Summary for Cycling

In our experience with cyclists and triathletes, stronger muscles lead to better cycling performance. Because every pedal revolution requires a certain percentage of maximum leg strength, more strength is of considerable advantage. After strength training, many cyclists are able to use higher gears at the same pedal frequency, thereby increasing their road speed. Be sure to eat enough calories to fuel your combined physical activities and to add a little more protein and lots of water. Finally, try to sleep at least eight hours nightly so that you enter every exercise session with energy and enthusiasm.

When developing a sensible strength training program, carefully consider the following exercise guidelines:

Exercise selection	Include at least one exercise for each major muscle group.
Training load	Use a training load that is 60 to 70 percent of maximum resistance.
Repetitions	Complete 12 to 16 controlled repetitions.
Progression	Increase the resistance by 5 percent when you can complete 16 repetitions during two successive sessions. After two months, consider adding a set of lower-body and upper-body exercises.
Sets	Complete one set of each exercise.
Movement speed	Complete each movement at a moderate speed, taking 1.5 to 2 seconds to lift and 2.5 to 4 seconds to lower.
Movement range	Perform each exercise through a relatively full movement range. Avoid a locked-out position during pressing exercises.
Training frequency	Complete two or three exercise sessions per week.

Strength Training for Swimmers

Swimming has been called the perfect physical activity because it appears to address all of the body's major muscle groups. Indeed, swimming involves both the upper body and lower body through pulling movements of the arms and kicking actions of the legs. Nonetheless, some of the major muscle groups are used much more than others, thereby increasing the risk of overuse and imbalance injuries. For example, the upper-body muscles that pull the arms through the water work considerably harder than the opposing muscles that recover the arms through the air. Also, the leg muscles, which are continuously active, move through a relatively short and repetitive range of motion. This can lead to muscle imbalances. Because swimming is an aerobic activity, it is not a particularly good activity for developing strength. However, increasing strength will significantly contribute to your success in swimming. Let's examine how strength training can enhance swimming performance as well as reduce injury potential.

Swimming Actions and Muscle Involvement

The primary muscles used during various phases of the front crawl stroke are shown in table 8.4. Most well-designed strength training programs, including the one shown in table 8.5, include exercises for these muscles as well as exercises for the lower body and midsection.

Table 8.4   Contribution of Upper-Body Muscles to Swimming Strokes

Muscle group	Contribution to stroke
Pectoralis major	Pulls arm back through water
Latissimus dorsi	Pulls arm back through water
Triceps	Extends elbow at end of arm stroke

Table 8.5   Basic Strength Training Exercises for Swimmers

Targeted muscle groups	Machine exercises	Free weight exercises
Pectoralis major, triceps	Chest press	Barbell or dumbbell bench press
Latissimus dorsi, biceps	Lat pull-down	Dumbbell pullover
Deltoids, triceps, upper trapezius	Shoulder press	Dumbbell alternating shoulder press
Latissimus dorsi, biceps, rear deltoids, rhomboids, trapezius,	Seated row	Dumbbell one-arm row
Pectoralis major, triceps, anterior deltoids	Incline press	Barbell or dumbbell incline press
Quadriceps	Leg extension	Dumbbell step-up
Hamstrings	Leg curl	Dumbbell step-up
Quadriceps, hamstrings, gluteals	Leg press	Barbell or dumbbell squat

Upper-Body Exercises

Although it is important to strengthen the primary muscles to improve swimming performance, it is just as important to include exercises for the opposing muscles. This will reduce the risk of injury in the shoulder joint by maintaining muscle balance and joint integrity. Performing the exercises will develop overall musculoskeletal strength in the upper body. You may be tempted to add specific biceps and triceps exercises; however, these muscles are addressed in the five basic upper-body exercises, and adding exercises will increase the risk of overtraining.

Lower-Body Exercises

In addition to balancing primary and opposing muscles, it is also important to balance the development of the upper body and lower body. Therefore a comprehensive strength training program for swimmers includes exercises for the kicking muscles of the lower body. These include leg extension, leg curl, and leg press. If you swim the breaststroke, you may want to add the hip adductor and hip abductor exercises for the inner and outer thigh muscles.

Midsection and Neck Exercises

If time permits, complement your strength training program with the exercises listed in table 8.6, which work the midsection and neck muscles. These muscles are responsible for torso alignment and head positioning, so strengthening them will contribute to your overall swimming success and reduce the likelihood of overuse and imbalance injuries.

Table 8.6   Complementary Strength Exercises for Swimmers

Targeted muscle groups	Machine exercises	Free weight exercises
Internal and external obliques, erector spinae, rectus abdominis	Rotary torso	Twisting trunk curl (body weight)
Sternocleidomastoid	Neck flexion	—
Upper trapezius	Neck extension	Barbell or dumbbell shrug

Program Design for Swimmers

The 11 strength exercises for swimmers address the major muscle groups. Next we discuss recommendations regarding exercise execution, loads to use, number of sets and repetitions to perform, and training frequency.

Movement Range and Speed

Although standard swimming strokes work the upper-body muscles through a fairly full range of motion, the kicking action of the legs uses only midrange movements. To avoid creating a muscular imbalance, perform exercises through a full movement range, but never to the point of discomfort. Also, move through a full range of motion in a slow and controlled manner. Quickly performed repetitions create momentum that may place excessive stress on muscles and joint structures; this should be avoided.

Loads and Repetitions

Muscle strength is best developed by fatiguing the target muscles within the time boundaries of the anaerobic energy system, which typically requires 30 to 90 seconds. At a controlled movement speed of four to six seconds per repetition, a set of 8 to 12 repetitions can be completed within this time frame. Most people can perform 8 to 12 repetitions with 70 to 80 percent of their maximum resistance, which is a safe and productive load. Although periodically you may want to train with more or fewer repetitions, 8 to 12 repetitions are appropriate for most practical purposes.

Exercise Sets

Many studies show that the strength-building benefits that are achieved in single-set training are similar to those achieved in multiple-set training. The number of sets you perform is largely a matter of personal preference and time availability. You can achieve significant results by doing a warm-up set with 50 percent of the training load, resting 60 seconds, then performing one set of the exercise to momentary muscle fatigue with the training load. This training protocol is effective yet time efficient.

Training Frequency

Research reveals that two training sessions per week produce about the same strength development as three training sessions per week, and for some, two days a week is preferable because it allows more time for recovery and muscle rebuilding. Begin your workout with exercises for the larger muscle groups of the legs, followed by the upper-body muscles, and finish with the muscles of the midsection and neck. Like the number of sets, the frequency of strength training is largely a matter of personal preference and time availability.

Exercise Progression

If you perform 8 to 12 repetitions per set, then you need a sensible progression policy. Because muscle strength develops gradually, you should not increase the resistance more than 5 percent at a time. Continue lifting a given load until you can complete 12 repetitions with good form during two successive workouts. Then you can increase the resistance by 5 percent (usually 1 to 5 pounds [.45 to 2.3 kilograms]) in your next workout. This double-progressive system—first adding more repetitions, then adding a heavier load—is a safe and sound method for stimulating consistent strength gains.

Summary for Swimming

In our experience with swimmers, stronger muscles lead to better swimming performances. Because every swimming stroke and push off the wall requires a certain

Table 8.7   Basic Strength Training Exercises For Skiers

Targeted muscle groups	Ski position or action	Machine exercises	Free weight exercises
Quadriceps	Power position	Leg extension	Barbell or dumbbell squat
Hamstrings	Power position	Leg curl	Barbell or dumbbell squat
Hip adductors	Turns	Hip adduction	Dumbbell step-up
Hip abductors	Turns	Hip abduction	Dumbbell step-up
Pectoralis major	Pole action	Chest crossover	Barbell or dumbbell bench press
Latissimus dorsi	Pole action	Pullover	Dumbbell one-arm row
Deltoids	Pole action	Lateral raise	Dumbbell seated press
Biceps	Pole action	Biceps curl	Barbell or dumbbell curl
Triceps	Pole action	Triceps extension	Dumbbell lying triceps extension
Erector spinae	Posture support	Low back extension	Body-weight trunk extension
Rectus abdominis	Posture support	Abdominal flexion	Exercise ball trunk curl
Internal and external obliques	Turns and posture support	Rotary torso	Twisting trunk curl
Sternocleidomastoids and upper trapezius	Posture support	Neck flexion and extension	Barbell or dumbbell shrug
Anterior tibialis	Ankle function	—	Weighted toe raise
Gastrocnemius, soleus	Ankle function	Heel raise	Barbell or dumbbell heel raise

Full Movement Range   Strength is developed by exercising against resistance. Therefore, to develop strength throughout the entire range of a joint's movement, you must apply resistance during the full movement range, working the target muscle from the fully stretched position to the fully contracted position.

Table 8.8   Big-Six Strength Training Exercises for Skiers

Targeted muscle groups	Machine exercises	Free weight exercises
Quadriceps, hamstrings, gluteals	Leg press	Barbell or dumbbell squat
Hip adductors	Hip adduction	Dumbbell step-up
Hip abductors	Hip abduction	Dumbbell step-up
Pectoralis major, deltoids, triceps	Chest press	Barbell or dumbbell bench press
Latissimus dorsi, biceps, rear deltoids, rhomboids, trapezius	Seated row	Dumbbell one-arm row
Internal and external obliques, lower back, rectus abdominis	Rotary torso	Twisting trunk curl

Moderate Movement Speed   Slow strength training movements are more productive than fast strength training movements. This is because slow movement speeds produce more muscle force and muscle tension than fast movement speeds. Slower movement speeds also create less momentum, which focuses the effort on the target muscles. Because downhill skiing involves mostly eccentric muscle contractions, you should emphasize the lowering phase of each repetition. Our recommendation is 4- to 6-second repetitions with 1.5 to 2 seconds for each lifting movement and 2.5 to 4 seconds for each lowering movement.

Breathing   It is essential to breathe on every repetition, because holding your breath can lead to undesirable increases in blood pressure and restricted blood flow. Exhale during each lifting movement, and inhale during each lowering movement.

Program Design for Skiers

A well-designed strength training program for skiers takes into consideration the number of repetitions to perform with a specific load, the number of training sessions per week, and guidelines for progressing to heavier loads. Because strength development is more closely related to training intensity than to training duration, excellent results may be attained using relatively short workouts.

Loads, Repetitions, and Sets

Muscle strength is best developed by fatiguing the target muscles, which in a typical strength training workout, takes 30 to 90 seconds. At a controlled movement speed of four to six seconds per repetition, a set of 8 to 12 repetitions takes 30 to 70 seconds. Most people can perform 8 to 12 repetitions with 70 to 80 percent percentage of maximum arm and leg strength, more strength is a considerable advantage. After strength training, many swimmers are able to perform at a higher percentage of their maximum strength for a longer period of time. When developing a sensible strength training program, consider the following exercise guidelines:

Exercise selection	Include at least one exercise for each major muscle group.
Training load	Use a training load that is about 70 to 80 percent of the maximum resistance.
Repetitions	Complete 8 to 12 controlled repetitions.
Progression	Increase the resistance by 5 percent when you can lift 12 repetitions during two successive sessions. After two months, consider adding a set of a lower- and upper-body exercise listed in table 8.5.
Sets	Complete one set of each exercise.
Movement speed	Complete each movement at a moderate speed, taking 1.5 to 2 seconds to lift and 2.5 to 4 seconds to lower.
Movement range	Perform each exercise through a relatively full movement range. Avoid a locked-out position during pressing exercises.
Training frequency	Complete two or three exercise sessions per week.

The strength training program for swimmers requires approximately 20 minutes to complete (one set of 11 exercises with about one minute between exercises). Although strength training should not interfere with swimming practice, it is probably best to schedule workouts on nonswimming days if possible. Be sure to eat enough calories to fuel your combined physical activities, including a little more protein and lots of water. Finally, try to sleep at least eight hours nightly so that you enter every exercise session with energy and enthusiasm.

Strength Training for Skiers

In spite of the fact that chairlifts take you up the mountain, downhill skiing is a physically demanding activity. The body positions that provide the best combination of balance, stability, control, and speed are those that require relatively high levels of muscular strength. In addition to enhanced skiing performance, a strong musculoskeletal system is your best protection against the acute and overuse injuries that are all too common in this sport.

Although no one would argue the value of cardiorespiratory conditioning, clearly it is not the limiting factor in downhill skiing. And although a lack of joint flexibility may lead to performance limitations, excessive joint mobility is typically more harmful than helpful. The key to better skiing is greater muscular strength, pure and simple. For overall health and fitness, do your favorite endurance activities and stretching exercises. But for confidence and competence on the black diamond trails, do your strength training.

Downhill skiing is a power activity that emphasizes the anaerobic energy system. Forceful contractions of the quadriceps and hamstring muscles position the body to use the snow and gravity to best advantage. Be thankful for turns, because they offer both challenge and change of position. You can't hold the power position for very long during a turn without causing formidable muscle fatigue; therefore, you must change your posture. This brief unloading phase provides momentary release and relief for the hard-working quadriceps and hamstrings. The turning action also activates the rotational muscles of the midsection and the lateral-movement muscles of the thighs. More specifically, smooth turns are closely related to strong external and internal oblique muscles that control midsection rotation, and to strong hip abductor and adductor muscles that shift the hips from side to side.

Although not as important for power production, the muscles of the shoulders, torso, and arms are responsible for effective pole plants and for safely absorbing impact during a fall. Other muscles that provide postural support and play a role in injury prevention are the low back and neck muscles.

Finally, the anterior tibial muscles of the shin largely control the ankle joint during skiing movements. Although modern ski boots reduce ankle injuries, strong anterior tibial muscles certainly enhance foot action and functional ability for downhill skiing.

Strength Exercises for Skiers

To ensure muscle balance and reduce injury potential, downhill skiers should train opposing muscle groups. For example, you should work both the shin muscles and the calf muscles for balanced development in the lower leg. Generally speaking, it is best to begin with exercises for the larger muscle groups of the legs, and then proceed to other muscle groups of the torso, arms, midsection, and neck. Table 8.7 lists the muscles that are called on in the various positions and actions that occur in skiing. It also lists exercises that strengthen those muscles.

The exercises presented in table 8.7 provide an ideal training program for skiers. However, during in-season training, reduce the number of exercises to provide more time for recovery and reduce the likelihood of developing overuse injuries. For in-season training and for skiers who do not have time during the off-season to complete all of the exercises in table 8.7, we recommend the big-six ski strengthening exercises shown in table 8.8 on page 222.

Exercise Technique

It is important to strength train in a safe, effective, and efficient manner. This means using a full movement range and moderate movement speed on every repetition.

Table 8.9   Basic Strength Training Exercises for Tennis

Targeted muscle groups	Machine exercises	Free weight exercises
Quadriceps	Leg extension	Dumbbell step-up or squat
Hamstrings	Leg curl	Barbell or dumbbell squat
Pectoralis major	Chest crossover	Dumbbell chest fly or bench press
Latissimus dorsi	Pullover	Dumbbell pullover
Deltoids	Lateral raise	Dumbbell lateral raise
Teres minor, infraspinatus, supraspinatus, subscapularis	Rotary shoulder	Weight plate or resistance-band rotator cuff lift
Biceps	Biceps curl	Dumbbell curl
Triceps	Triceps extension	Dumbbell overhead triceps extension
Erector spinae	Low back extension	Body-weight trunk extension
Rectus abdominis	Abdominal flexion	Twisting trunk curl
Sternocleidomastoids, upper trapezius	Neck flexion and extension	Barbell or dumbbell shrug

rotator muscles lie beneath the large deltoid muscles and allow the arms to rotate into various positions. Rotating an arm backward, called external shoulder rotation, uses the teres minor and infraspinatus muscles. Rotating an arm forward, called internal shoulder rotation, involves the subscapularis muscles. Keeping the arm within the shoulder joint structure is the primary function of the supraspinatus muscle. Together, these four muscles surround the shoulder joint, providing both structural stability and the ability to produce forehand, backhand, and serving movements.

The good news is that these four relatively small muscles respond well to strength training. The bad news is that most people do not perform specific exercises for their rotator cuff muscles. This is unfortunate, because rotator cuff injuries occur frequently in tennis players and typically require a long recovery period. A well-designed strength training program should include at least one workout per week for the shoulder rotator muscles.

One way to specifically train the rotator cuff muscles is on the rotary shoulder machine, a dual-action exercise that provides full-range rotational resistance for both the external and internal shoulder rotator muscles. If a machine is not available or you prefer not to train on machines, you may also strengthen these important muscles with a dumbbell (or weight plate) or resistance bands (figures 8.2 and 8.3). When using a dumbbell or weight plate, position the upper arm so that it is horizontal to the floor and maintain this upper-arm position throughout the exercise. Next position the forearm perpendicular to the floor and then slowly lift the dumbbell upward while maintaining the 90-degree elbow position (figure 8.2). Lower the dumbbell back to the starting position.

When using resistance bands, attach one to a door at waist level, stand with your left side toward the door, keep your right elbow against your right side, and pull the band across your midsection using your right hand as shown in figure 8.3. Next, keep your left elbow against your left side and pull the band away from your midsection using your left hand. Repeat the exercises standing with your right side toward the door and using the opposite hands. Tennis players should include rotator cuff exercises in their basic and advanced training programs.

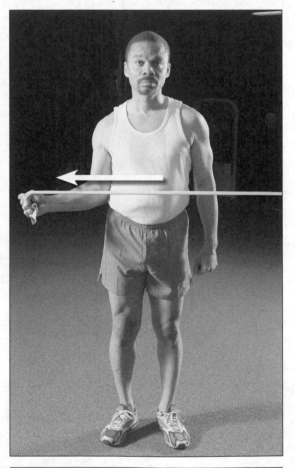

Figure 8.2   Strengthening the rotator cuff muscles with a dumbbell or weight plate.

Figure 8.3   Using resistance bands to strengthen the rotator cuff muscles.

of their maximum resistance, which is a safe and productive load. Although you may periodically want to train with more or fewer repetitions, 8 to 12 repetitions are appropriate for most purposes.

Many studies show that the strength-building benefits achieved in single-set training are similar to those achieved in multiple-set training. The number of sets you perform is largely a matter of personal preference and time availability. Our ski-conditioning program participants have experienced excellent results by doing a warm-up set with 50 percent of their training load, resting 60 seconds, and then performing one set to momentary muscle fatigue with their training load. This training protocol is effective and time efficient.

Training Frequency

Research reveals that two training sessions per week produce about the same strength development as three training sessions per week, and for some, two days a week is preferable because it allows more time for recovery and muscle rebuilding. Because gradual strength gain is the major training objective, resist the temptation to do too much too soon. As with the number of sets, the frequency of strength training is largely a matter of personal preference and time availability.

Exercise Progression

If you perform 8 to 12 repetitions per set, you need a sensible progression plan. Because muscle strength develops gradually, you should not increase the resistance more than 5 percent in any training session. Continue lifting a given load until you can complete 12 repetitions with good form for two successive workouts. Then increase the resistance by 5 percent (usually 1 to 5 pounds [.45 to 2.3 kilograms]) during your next workout. This double-progressive system—first adding more repetitions, then adding a heavier load—is a safe and sound method for stimulating consistent strength gains.

Summary for Skiing

Strength training is an effective conditioning activity for downhill skiing. Table 8.7 on page 221 provides a comprehensive off-season training program that takes about 40 minutes to complete. The shorter big-six strength training program (table 8.8) should take about 15 minutes to complete. Be sure to eat enough calories to fuel your combined physical activities, including a little more protein and lots of water. Finally, try to obtain at least eight hours of sleep nightly so that you enter every exercise session with energy and enthusiasm.

When developing a sensible strength training program, carefully consider the following exercise guidelines:

Exercise selection	Include at least one exercise for each major muscle group.
Training load	Use a training load that is 70 to 80 percent of maximum resistance.
Repetitions	Complete 8 to 12 controlled repetitions.

Progression	Increase the resistance by 5 percent when you can complete 12 repetitions in two successive sessions. After two months of following the big-six program, consider adding exercises listed in table 8.7.
Sets	Complete one set of each exercise.
Movement speed	Complete each movement at a moderate speed, taking 1.5 to 2 seconds to lift and 2.5 to 4 seconds to lower.
Movement range	Perform each exercise through a relatively full movement range. Avoid a locked-out position on pressing exercises.
Training frequency	Complete two or three exercise sessions per week.

Strength Training for Tennis Players

Tennis is a superb sport. It requires excellent eye–hand coordination and agility and keen spatial awareness. In addition to the physical and mental challenge, a good singles match provides both anaerobic and aerobic conditioning. Although skill is essential for top-level tennis, technique development is easier if you are fit—which is also the critical factor for staying power during the second and third sets.

Fitness comes in many forms, and conditioning is specific to the type of training program you follow. For example, stretching exercise enhances joint flexibility, aerobic activity improves cardiorespiratory endurance, and strength training increases muscular strength. Certainly, all of these fitness components contribute to better tennis performance. However, if you choose to focus on one area of physical conditioning for tennis, it should be strength training.

Strength Exercises for Tennis Players

Because playing tennis involves strenuous musculoskeletal activity in the legs, midsection, upper-body, and arms, you should train all of the major muscle groups to ensure overall strength and balanced muscular development. This will enhance performance power and reduce the risk of injuries. The machine and free weight exercises presented in table 8.9 provide a solid conditioning base from which to progress into more advanced training when you are ready. Performing these basic exercises as well as the advanced exercises in table 8.10, which are described later, will produce excellent conditioning for tennis. They will also provide reasonable injury protection when complemented by exercises for the shoulder rotator cuff and forearm muscles discussed next.

Shoulder Rotator Muscles

The rotator cuff consists of a group of muscles (supraspinatus, infraspinatus, teres minor, subscapularis) that surround and stabilize the shoulder joint. The shoulder

Forearm Muscles

Because of the extensive wrist action required for tennis play, the forearm muscles (forearm flexors and extensors) can be easily overstressed, leading to injury at the elbow or wrist joints. The forearm machine provides five separate wrist movements to condition all of the forearm muscles. Few exercises are better suited to tennis players, especially for increasing grip strength and reducing injury potential.

If you don't have access to this training device, an excellent alternative is the wrist roller exercise shown in figure 8.4. Simply attach a 5-pound (2.3-kilogram) weight plate to one end of a 2-foot (61-centimeter) rope and tie the other end to a round wooden dowel. Holding the dowel in both hands, repeatedly flex your wrists clockwise to wind the rope around the dowel and lift the weight. When the weight touches the dowel, extend your wrists counterclockwise to unwind the rope and lower the weight. The clockwise wrist motion strengthens the forearm flexors, and counterclockwise wrist motions strengthen the forearm extensors. These forearm exercises are included in the advanced tennis training exercises listed in table 8.10, but they could also be included in the basic program.

Figure 8.4   Wrist roller.

Program Design for Tennis Players

The exercises in the strength training program for tennis players shown previously in table 8.9 do not attempt to imitate specific movements or emphasize particular muscles, but rather focus on the exercises that will strengthen all of the muscle groups used in tennis. The next section discusses exercise execution, loads to use, number of repetitions and sets to perform, and training frequency.

Movement Speed

Each repetition should take 4 to 6 seconds: 1.5 to 2 seconds for the lifting movement and 2.5 to 4 seconds for the lowering movement. Slowing the lowering phase emphasizes the stronger negative muscle contraction and should increase the productivity of each exercise set. It is also important to perform each repetition through a full range of motion. This enhances both joint integrity and flexibility. It is also essential to breathe on every repetition, because holding your breath can lead to undesirable increases in blood pressure and restricted blood flow. Exhale during each lifting movement, and inhale during each lowering movement.

Loads, Repetitions, and Sets

The exercises in table 8.9 on page 225 are listed from the larger muscles of the legs to the smaller muscles of the neck and should be performed in this order. One set of each exercise is sufficient, as long as you train using good form to the point of muscle fatigue. Because intensity is the key to strength development, use enough resistance to fatigue the target muscle groups in about 50 to 70 seconds. In general, this is achieved with a weight load that you can lift for 8 to 12 controlled repetitions.

Training Frequency

If you play tennis three or four days per week, it is probably best to strength train on two nontennis days. If you practice tennis every day, perform strength training about four hours after your tennis training for best overall results. For example, if you play tennis every morning from 9 a.m. to 11 a.m., schedule your strength exercise for 3 p.m. Strength training once a week or on two days spaced evenly through the week is sufficient for building strength that will improve your tennis game.

Progression

As your muscles become stronger, it is essential to progressively increase the work effort. This is best accomplished by gradually increasing the exercise resistance. Once you complete 12 repetitions, the weight load is no longer heavy enough to produce maximum strength benefits. By increasing the resistance about 5 percent (typically 1 to 5 pounds [.45 to 2.3 kilograms]), you can continue to stimulate strength development.

Advanced Strength Training Program for Tennis Players

After two months of basic training, you should be ready for more advanced strength exercises. Some of the exercises described next and listed in table 8.10 can replace the introductory exercises listed table 8.9. Others provide supplementary training to further improve your tennis performance.

Legs

Let's begin with the powerful leg muscles that generate the force for your ground strokes and your movements across the court. Instead of training the quadriceps and hamstrings separately, replace the leg extension and leg curl with the leg press, which works both of these muscle groups and the gluteals simultaneously. The leg press permits the use of heavier loads and is an excellent exercise for developing functional leg strength. Equally effective free weight exercises are the lunge and squat, performed with dumbbells or barbells. In addition to the quadriceps and hamstrings, the hip adductors and hip abductors play a major role in weight shifts and lateral movements. These opposing muscle groups on the inner and outer thighs are best trained with the hip adductor and hip abductor machines, which you should add to your strength exercise program.

While playing tennis you execute repeated stop-and-go movements. These require the lower-leg muscles to alternately produce great force and then absorb

Table 8.10 Advanced Strength Training Exercises for Tennis

Targeted muscle groups	Machine exercises	Free weight exercises
Quadriceps, hamstrings, gluteals	Leg press	Barbell or dumbbell lunge or squat
Hip adductors	Hip adduction	Dumbbell step-up
Hip abductors	Hip abduction	Dumbbell step-up
Gastrocnemius, soleus	Heel raise	Barbell or dumbbell heel raise
Pectoralis major, triceps	Chest press	Barbell or dumbbell bench press
Latissimus dorsi, biceps, rear deltoids, rhomboids, trapezius	Seated row	Dumbbell one-arm row
Deltoids, triceps	Shoulder press	Dumbbell alternating shoulder press
Latissimus dorsi, biceps	Lat pull-down	Lat pull-down
Erector spinae	Low back extension	Body-weight trunk extension
Rectus abdominis	Abdominal flexion	Exercise ball trunk curl
External and internal obliques	Rotary torso	Twisting trunk curl
Sternocleidomastoids, upper trapezius	Neck flexion and extension	Barbell or dumbbell shrug
Teres minor, infraspinatus, supra-spinatus, subscapularis	Rotary shoulder	Weight plate or resistance band rotator cuff lift
Forearms	Forearm flexion and extension	Wrist roller

great shock. Therefore, it is important to perform calf-strengthening exercises. The dumbbell or barbell heel raise targets the gastrocnemius and soleus muscles of the lower leg, and serves as an excellent supplement to upper-leg exercises.

Midsection

The power generated by the large leg muscles is transferred to the upper body through the muscles of the midsection. Swinging movements (ground strokes and serves) involve the internal and external oblique muscles on both sides of the midsection. You may strengthen these important muscles on the dual-action rotary torso machine, which works the right internal and left external obliques on clockwise movements, and the left internal and right external obliques on counter-clockwise movements. Add the rotary torso exercise to the low back and abdominal machines for comprehensive midsection conditioning. If machine exercises are not a possibility, the twisting trunk curl may be the best alternative for abdominal conditioning.

Upper Body

The major upper-body muscles involved in swinging a tennis racket are the pectoralis major and latissimus dorsi, of the torso; the biceps and triceps, of the arms; and the deltoids, of the shoulders. Although the basic strength training program addresses these muscles individually, it may be advantageous to work some of the groups together. You can accomplish this by doing pushing and pulling exercises such as the bench press, seated row, shoulder press, and lat pull-down.

The chest press and bench press are popular pushing exercises that strengthen the pectoralis major and triceps muscles at the same time. Conversely, the seated row and one-arm row are effective pulling exercises that work the opposing latissimus dorsi and biceps muscles simultaneously.

One of the best means for training the shoulder and triceps muscles together is the shoulder press. The counterpart to this exercise is the lat pull-down, which involves both the latissimus dorsi and biceps muscles.

Summary for Tennis

Remember that skill training is the most important factor in improving your tennis game. However, physical conditioning can certainly enhance your tennis playing efforts and outcomes. The cornerstone of physical conditioning is muscular strength, and a stronger tennis player should always be a better tennis player. Be sure to eat enough calories to fuel your combined physical activities, including adding a little more protein and lots of water. Finally, try to sleep at least eight hours nightly so that you enter every exercise session with energy and enthusiasm.

Exercise Selection	Include at least one exercise for each major muscle group.
Training load	Use a training load that is 70 to 80 percent of maximum resistance.
Repetitions	Complete 8 to 12 controlled repetitions.
Progression	Increase the resistance by 5 percent when you can complete 12 repetitions in two successive sessions. After two months of following the basic program in table 8.9, consider adding one or more of the exercises listed in table 8.10. If you are following the advanced program in table 8.10, consider adding a set to some of the lower-body and upper-body exercises.

Sets	Complete one set of each exercise.
Movement speed	Complete each movement at a moderate speed, taking 1.5 to 2 seconds to lift and 2.5 to 4 seconds to lower.
Movement range	Perform each movement through a relatively full movement range. Avoid a locked-out position during pressing exercises.
Training frequency	Complete two or three exercise sessions per week.

Strength Training for Golfers

You, like 50 million Americans, enjoy playing the great game of golf. If you are like most golfers, you want to play more golf, at a higher level, with no injuries. We refer to this as playing stronger and driving longer, both of which can be accomplished through a well-designed strength training program.

Our approach to golf conditioning involves two brief exercise sessions a week, leaving plenty of time for practicing and playing your sport. Each workout includes strength training, stretching exercises, and optional aerobic activity. Golfers have traditionally avoided strength training for fear of adding body weight, developing large muscles, feeling tight, losing speed, compromising coordination, developing errant drives, and posting higher scores. However, our research has shown significant benefits to golfers who perform regular strength training. As you can see in table 8.11, the 77 adult golfers who completed just two months of our strength training program made impressive improvements in their health, fitness, and driving power.

Table 8.11   Results of an Eight-Week Strength Training Program for Golfers

	Change	Amount
Mean resting blood pressure	Decrease	4.5 mm Hg
Muscle strength	Increase	56%
Body weight	Decrease	.2 lb (.9 kg)
Percent fat	Decrease	2%
Fat weight	Decrease	4.1 lb (1.9 kg)
Muscle weight	Increase	3.9 lb (1.8 kg)
Club-head speed	Increase	6.1%

Golfers who followed our program reduced their resting blood pressure by almost 5 mm Hg, increased their muscle strength by more than 50 percent, lost 4 pounds (1.8 kilograms) of fat, added 4 pounds (1.8 kilograms) of muscle, and increased their club-head speed (driving power) by 6 percent.

Flexibility Exercises

Our golf conditioning participants attained greater increases in club-head speed when they combined stretching exercise with the strength training program. They performed six basic stretches for the major muscle groups, including the thighs, hips, lower back, upper back, chest, and shoulders. They performed each stretch slowly, with a 20-second stationary hold in the fully stretched position. If you have time, stretch after each strength training session to develop the flexibility that will contribute to improved club-head speed.

Performance Power

In simple terms, performance power is muscle force multiplied by movement distance, divided by movement time. You may recall reading about this in the first part of this chapter. You can improve your driving power by increasing your muscle force, increasing your swing distance, decreasing your swing time, or a combination of any of these. Strength training is the best means for increasing your muscular force, and the inclusion of stretching exercises is the best means for increasing your swing distance. Decreasing your swing time is a more complex task, involving practice and coordination; however, stronger muscles and more flexible joints will also help you increase the speed of your swing.

$$\text{Performance power} = \text{muscle force} \times \text{swing speed}$$

Endurance Exercise

Although we did not measure cardiorespiratory conditioning in our golf research studies, we asked the golfers in the program to choose their favorite endurance exercise (walking, jogging, cycling, stepping) or a combination of these to promote a cross-training effect. We encourage you to include regular aerobic activity in your golf training program. This aerobic activity should last about 30 minutes, including a few minutes for warming up and cooling down, and take place on three nonconsecutive days each week. Using an effort scale of 1 to 10, perform the warm-up and cool-down segments at a low intensity (level 3 to 4) and the conditioning segment at a moderate intensity (level 6 to 7). Although improved cardiorespiratory fitness has little direct impact on your golf driving power, it may enable you to play stronger and longer by increasing your resistance to fatigue and your ability to concentrate.

Strength Exercises for Golfers

The following sections present the recommended exercises, training principles, and workout progressions for improving your muscular strength. Let's begin with the muscles of the trunk. They are important for two reasons. First, many golfers experience low back problems caused largely by weak trunk muscles, particularly the erector spinae muscles in the low back. Second, the trunk muscles play a key role in transferring the power produced by the large hip and thigh muscles to the club-swinging muscles of the upper body and arms.

The second group of muscles golfers should strengthen are those of the thighs and hips. The front thigh muscles (quadriceps) and rear thigh muscles (hamstrings) are major generators of force, especially in conjunction with the gluteal muscles of the hips. The leg press and squat exercises are ideal for strengthening these large muscle groups. Because weight transfer and hip thrust are critical components of powerful golf drives, we also recommend specific strength exercises for the inner thigh muscles (hip adductors) and outer thigh muscles (hip abductors).

The third group of muscles that contributes to driving power includes the chest muscles (pectoralis major), upper-back muscles (latissimus dorsi), and shoulder muscles (deltoids). These muscles produce the swinging action of the arms and also control shoulder joint movements. It is, therefore, important to maintain balanced strength in these muscles in order to reduce the risk of shoulder joint injuries.

Finally, if time permits, perform specific strength training exercises for the muscles of the arms and neck. The muscles of the front of the arm (biceps) and rear of the arm (triceps) are involved in club control, which is a key component of the swinging action. Various exercises are included in table 8.12 to work these muscles, either in combination with other muscle groups or in isolation. Because making contact with the ball requires that you keep your head stable, we have included exercises that strengthen the neck.

Program Design for Golfers

The exercises in the strength training program for golfers do not attempt to imitate specific movements or emphasize specific muscles, but rather focus on the exercises that will strengthen all of the muscle groups used in golf. The following sections outline exercise execution, loads to use, number of repetitions and sets to perform, and training frequency.

Movement Speed

Perform each repetition at a moderate speed of 4 to 6 seconds, taking 1.5 to 2 seconds to lift the resistance and 2.5 to 4 seconds to lower it. Perform each repetition through a full range of joint movement if you can do so without discomfort. Breathe during each repetition, because holding your breath can lead to undesirable increases in blood pressure and restricted blood flow. Exhale during each lifting movement, and inhale during each lowering movement.

Table 8.12   Basic Strength Training Exercises for Golfers

Targeted muscle groups	Machine exercises	Free weight exercises
Quadriceps, hamstrings, gluteals	Leg press	Barbell or dumbbell squat
Hip adductors	Hip adduction	Dumbbell step-up
Hip abductors	Hip abduction	Dumbbell step-up
Pectoralis major, triceps	Chest press	Barbell or dumbbell bench press
Latissimus dorsi, biceps	Lat pull-down	Dumbbell one-arm row
Deltoids	Lateral raise	Dumbbell lateral raise
Biceps	Biceps curl	Barbell or dumbbell curl
Triceps	Triceps extension	Dumbbell overhead triceps extension
Erector spinae	Low back extension	Body-weight trunk extension
Rectus abdominis	Abdominal flexion	Exercise ball trunk curl
External and internal obliques	Rotary torso	Twisting trunk curl
Sternocleidomastoids, upper trapezius	Neck flexion and extension	Barbell or dumbbell shrug

Loads, Repetitions, and Sets

Train with an exercise resistance that enables you to complete 8 to 12 repetitions to the point of momentary muscle fatigue. Perform the 12 resistance exercises (using either machines or free weights) during each workout and in the order presented in table 8.12.

Training Frequency

Although one weekly workout is sufficient, you will improve your physical fitness and increase your driving power more quickly by training on two or three nonconsecutive days each week. However, if your time is limited, one session a week will produce results.

Progression

When you can complete 12 repetitions using correct technique during two successive workouts, increase the training load by approximately 5 percent (typically 1 to 5 pounds [.45 to 2.3 kilograms]).

Summary for Golf

Keep accurate records of your workouts, and watch how your driving power correlates to your strength development. Be sure to eat enough calories to fuel your combined physical activities, including the addition of a little more protein and lots of water. Finally, try to sleep at least eight hours nightly so that you enter every exercise session with energy and enthusiasm.

Exercise selection	Include at least one exercise for each major muscle group.
Training load	Use a training load that is approximately 70 to 80 percent of maximum resistance.
Repetitions	Complete 8 to 12 controlled repetitions.
Progression	Increase the resistance by 5 percent when you can lift 12 repetitions in two successive sessions. After two months of training, consider adding a set of lower-body and upper-body exercises.
Sets	Complete one set of each exercise.
Movement speed	Complete each movement at a moderate speed, taking 1.5 to 2 seconds to lift and 2.5 to 4 seconds to lower.
Movement range	Perform each exercise through a relatively full movement range. Avoid a locked-out position on pressing exercises.
Training frequency	Complete at least one, but preferably two or three, exercise sessions per week.

9

Eating for Strength Gains

Your dietary habits have a major impact on your body weight, body composition, and physical health. Unfortunately, most Americans consume too many calories for the amount of activity they perform. As a result, about three out of every four adults in the United States are overweight, which predisposes them to increased risk of heart disease, joint problems, diabetes, and many types of cancer. At the same time, consuming too little protein, calcium, or vitamin D can lead to a weakening of the musculoskeletal system and to osteoporosis; insufficient iron in your diet may cause you to become anemic; and excessive sodium intake may contribute to hypertension.

Eating foods high in fiber, low in fat, and rich in vitamins and minerals is essential for optimal health and for disease prevention. For example, vitamins A and C, found in many fruits and vegetables, are considered important antioxidants (nutritional bodyguards) that protect us from potentially harmful chemical reactions in body cells. Potassium, found in bananas and cantaloupe, is involved in every muscle contraction and, therefore, is especially important for people participating in strength training.

Although you can consume vitamins and minerals through nutritional supplements, do not be tempted to substitute supplements for a well-balanced diet that includes a variety of vegetables, fruits, and whole grains, as well as lean meats and low-fat dairy products. Human nutrient requirements are too complex (and too poorly understood) to be adequately supported by pills, and only a varied (well-rounded) diet can provide the proper foundation for optimal nutrition. We recommend following the guidelines for daily food choices set forth by the United States Department of Agriculture in the MyPyramid Plan (see figure 9.1 on page 240).

And remember, a well-balanced diet is not the same as a low-calorie diet designed for losing weight. Reduced-calorie diets should be approved by your physician or a registered dietitian, especially when you are following the strength training programs presented in this text.

Although we advocate a sensible nutrition plan similar to that recommended for younger adults, everyone over age 50 should consume larger amounts of protein, especially people who perform regular resistance exercise. Why is that? Because older adults do not assimilate protein nearly as well as they did earlier in life. A recent study conducted at the University of Texas revealed that the older subjects (average age of 68 years) assimilated 61 percent fewer amino acids from the protein they ate compared to the younger subjects (average age of 31 years). Because amino acids are the building blocks for muscle tissue, these research results have important implications for all of us who want to attain and maintain muscular fitness as we age.

Consider the following points. First, because we synthesize amino acids less efficiently, senior men and women should eat more protein-rich foods (e.g., low-fat milk, low-fat yogurt, fish, chicken). Unfortunately, most older adults eat fewer protein-rich foods, which leads to insufficient amino acid synthesis and results in muscle loss. Second, the strength training programs presented in chapters 5, 6, 7, and 8 produce various levels of muscle microtrauma that stimulate the tissue rebuilding processes for developing larger and stronger muscles. Of course, the physiological process of muscle synthesis requires sufficient supplies of the amino acid building blocks contained in protein-rich foods. Based on the work of researchers at the University of Texas, we estimate, therefore, that strength exercisers between the ages of 50 and 80 years old may need 50 to 70 percent more protein daily than the minimum levels proposed in the new recommendations. Table 9.1 presents the recommended daily protein intake for men and women over age 50, along with our suggested daily protein consumption guidelines for those in their 50s, 60s, and 70s who perform regular strength training. Table 9.2 lists the grams of protein found in a variety of protein-rich foods. It also lists standard portion sizes.

Table 9.1   Adjusted Minimum Daily Protein Recommendations

Age ranges in years	Recommended daily protein intake	Percent increase for strength trainers	Adjusted daily protein intake for strength trainers
50-59	Men: 56 grams	Men: 50%	Men: 85 grams
	Women: 46 grams	Women: 50%	Women: 70 grams
60-69	Men: 56 grams	Men: 60%	Men: 90 grams
	Women: 46 grams	Women: 60%	Women: 75 grams
70-79	Men: 56 grams	Men: 70%	Men: 95 grams
	Women: 46 grams	Women: 70%	Women: 80 grams

Table 9.2   Grams of Protein Found in Common Protein-Rich Foods

Food	Portion size	Protein grams per serving
Tuna	6 oz (175 g)	45
Chicken (white meat)	6 oz (175 g)	45
Protein powder	6 tbsp in 8 oz (250 ml) of milk	36
Yogurt smoothie	20 oz (600ml)	20
Milk (low fat)	16 oz (500 ml)	16
Peanut butter	4 tbsp	14
Egg whites	2 eggs	12

In addition to consuming sufficient protein for tissue building and muscle development, senior strength trainers should pay close attention to the timing of their protein ingestion. Rather than eating all of your protein-rich foods at one meal, it is better to distribute your protein intake throughout the day. More specifically, recent research reveals that muscle rebuilding processes are enhanced when you ingest protein within one hour of completing your strength workout. The researchers observed excellent results when subjects drank a postexercise glass of milk, but similar protein sources should provide the same muscle-building benefits. For example, you could enjoy a yogurt smoothie; a protein shake; a hard-boiled egg; half a tuna, turkey, or peanut butter sandwich; or another favorite high-protein snack. Just remember to consume the extra protein within an hour after finishing your strength training session.

Certainly, protein is a key nutrient for optimal development of your musculoskeletal system. However, it is essential to design a well-balanced nutrition plan that includes all of the basic nutrients in appropriate amounts for overall physiological function and performance power. Please read and apply the nutritional information in the following sections to maximize the effectiveness of your strength training program. When it comes to food, it is always best to begin with the basics.

Basic Nutrients

As shown in figure 9.1, the MyPyramid Plan is high in carbohydrate, moderate in protein, and low in fat. The carbohydrate choices are divided into grains, vegetables, and fruits. The suggested protein sources are low-fat milk products and lean meats, and the recommended fat-rich foods are vegetable oils used sparingly. Let's consider each of the food categories more carefully.

Grains

Grains include all kinds of foods made from wheat, oats, corn, rice, and the like. Examples of grain foods are cereals, breads, pasta, pancakes, rice cakes, tortillas, bagels, muffins, cornbread, rice pudding, and chocolate cake. Obviously, some grain-based foods, such as cakes, cookies, and pastries, contain a lot of fat, so you should eat them sparingly.

All grains are high in carbohydrate, and some grains or parts of grains, such as wheat germ, are also good sources of protein. Whole grains are typically rich in B vitamins and fiber. Grains are plentiful and inexpensive and should be part of every meal. In fact, the MyPyramid Plan recommends six ounces (180 grams) of grains every day. A serving is equivalent to a slice of bread or a half cup of cooked pasta, so achieving the six ounces (180 grams) is not difficult.

Refer to the following sidebar for sample exchange units for popular food choices within the grains category.

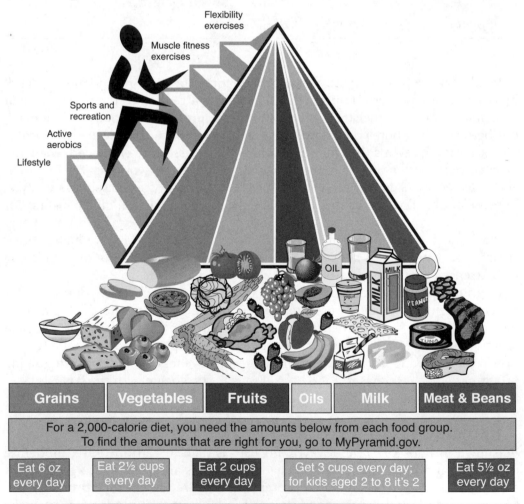

Figure 9.1   United States Department of Agriculture MyPyramid Plan.

From the United States Department of Agriculture (USDA). Available: www.MyPyramid.gov.

Vegetables

Like grains, vegetables are excellent sources of carbohydrate, vitamins, and fiber. Vegetables come in all sizes, shapes, colors, and nutritional characteristics, and they are relatively low in calories. Orange vegetables are typically good sources of vitamin A and beta-carotene. This category includes carrots, sweet potatoes, and winter squash.

Green vegetables are characteristically high in vitamin B_2 and folic acid. Some of the many green vegetables are peas, beans, broccoli, asparagus, spinach, and lettuce.

Red vegetables generally provide ample amounts of vitamin C. The best known vegetables in this category are tomatoes and red peppers.

Other vegetables are essentially white, at least under the skin. These include cauliflower, summer squash, potatoes, and radishes, many of which are good sources of vitamin C.

Sample Exchange Units Equivalent to One Grain Serving

Cereals

1/4 cup nugget cereal (Grape-Nuts)
1/3 cup concentrated bran cereal
1/2 cup cooked hot cereal (oatmeal or Cream of Wheat)
3/4 cup flaked cereal
1 1/2 cups puffed cereal

Breads

1/2 bagel or English muffin
1 slice bread
1 piece of pita bread
1 tortilla

Grains

1/4 cup wheat germ
1/3 cup brown or white rice
1/2 cup pasta, macaroni, or noodles
1/2 cup hominy, barley, or grits

Snacks

3/4 oz (22.5 grams) pretzels
3/4 oz (22.5 grams) rice cakes
4 crackers (1 oz [30 grams])
3 cups air-popped popcorn
Note: 1 cup (imperial)=.946 cup (metric)=1.041 cup (Canada)

The MyPyramid Plan recommends two and a half cups of vegetables. One serving is one-half cup of any raw vegetable, except for lettuce and sprouts, which require one cup per serving. Because heating reduces water content, cooked vegetables require less space than uncooked vegetables and serving sizes may be smaller. Likewise, vegetable juices are more concentrated and require only one-half cup per serving.

It is a good idea to eat some of your vegetables raw and to steam or microwave other vegetables for nutrient retention. In addition, fresh or frozen vegetables have more nutritional value and are lower in sodium than canned vegetables.

Fruit

Fruit is the counterpart to vegetables: relatively low in calories, with as much variety and nutritional value. Essentially all fruit choices are high in carbohydrate and vitamins, and many provide excellent sources of fiber.

As you probably know, citrus fruit, such as oranges, grapefruit, and lemons, are loaded with vitamin C. Like orange-colored vegetables, orange-colored fruit, including cantaloupe, apricots, and papaya, are rich in vitamin A and beta-carotene.

Both green fruit, such as honeydew melon and kiwi, and red fruit, such as strawberries and cherries, are high in vitamin C.

Yellow fruit include peaches, mangos, and pineapples, all of which are good sources of vitamin C. Fruit that are white, at least on the inside, include apples, pears, and bananas, all of which are high in potassium.

Dried fruit are particularly nutrient dense, and the natural sweetness makes them healthy substitutes for high-fat snacks such as candy bars. Raisins, dates, figs, and prunes are all superb energy sources, and prunes are the single best source of dietary fiber.

The MyPyramid Plan recommends two cups of fruit every day. The following list presents sample exchange quantities for a variety of fruit. You will notice that one serving varies considerably, depending on the type of fruit you eat. For example, it takes one-quarter of a melon or one-half of a grapefruit to equal three dates or two tablespoons of raisins. The difference is water content. Fresh fruit contain lots of water, whereas dried fruit are essentially high-density carbohydrate. If you prefer your fruit in liquid form, one-half cup (125 ml) of fruit juice equals one serving, but has less fiber than whole fruit.

Milk Products

The MyPyramid Plan recommends three cups daily of low-fat dairy products, including milk, yogurt, and cheese. These foods are excellent sources of protein and calcium. Because whole milk products are high in fat, you should be selective at the dairy counter. For example, 1 percent milk, low-fat yogurt, and nonfat cottage cheese offer heart-healthy alternatives to higher-fat dairy selections.

Refer to the list on page 243 for exchange units equivalent to one dairy serving. Notice that one-quarter cup of low-fat cottage cheese and one cup (250 ml) of 1 percent milk have similar nutritional values. Although there are many sources of dietary protein, you may have difficulty obtaining sufficient calcium unless

Sample Exchange Units Equivalent to One Fruit Serving

2 tbsp (18 grams) raisins	3/4 cup pineapple
3 dates	2 kiwi
3 prunes	1/2 pomegranate
1/2 cup grapes	1/4 cantaloupe
3/4 cup berries	1/4 papaya
1 apple	1/4 melon
1 banana	1/2 mango
1 peach	5 kumquats
1 pear	1 cup honeydew
3 apricots	1 1/4 cups strawberries
1/2 grapefruit	1 1/4 cups watermelon

Sample Exchange Units Equivalent to One Dairy Serving

1 oz (30 grams) low-fat cheese

1/4 cup low-fat or nonfat cottage cheese

1/4 cup part-skim ricotta cheese

1/4 cup Parmesan cheese

1/2 cup evaporated skim milk

1 cup nonfat or 1 percent milk

1 cup low-fat or nonfat yogurt

1 cup low-fat buttermilk

you regularly consume milk products. If you have problems digesting milk, try to regularly consume other foods that are high in calcium, such as tofu, leafy greens, beans, broccoli, and sesame seeds.

Meat and Beans

According to the MyPyramid Plan, this category includes meat, poultry, fish, eggs, nuts, and dry beans. All these foods are good sources of protein, although some also contain significant amounts of fat. Table 9.3 lists foods in the meat category according to their fat content. Note that how the meat is prepared often affects its fat content. We'll look at this aspect in more detail in the food preparation section.

Although there are differences in fat content, protein exchange units are consistent among the foods in the meat category. As you can see from the following list, three ounces (90 grams) of meat, poultry, and fish (about the size of a deck of cards) have equal exchange values, as do one-quarter cup of dry beans and one-quarter cup of tuna. Try to consume about five and a half ounces (165 grams) from the meat and bean group daily.

Sample Exchange Units Equivalent to One Meat Serving

3 oz (90 grams) fish

3 oz (90 grams) poultry

3 oz (90 grams) meat (e.g., beef, poultry, lamb)

1 egg or 2 egg whites

4 tbsp peanut butter

1/2 cup cooked dry beans

1/2 cup tuna

1/2 cup tofu

6 tbsp (53 grams) nuts

Table 9.3   Meat and Bean Group Foods Categorized By Fat Content

Low fat	Medium fat	High fat
Most fish	Chicken with skin	Beef ribs
Egg whites	Turkey with skin	Pork ribs
Chicken without skin	Roast beef	Corned beef
Turkey without skin	Roast pork	Sausage
Venison	Roast lamb	Lunch meat
Rabbit	Veal cutlet	Ground pork
Top round	Ground beef	Hot dogs
Eye of round	Steaks	Fried chicken
Sirloin tenderloin	Canned salmon	Fried fish
Flank steak	Oil-packed tuna	Nuts
Veal	Whole eggs	Peanuts
Dry beans	Pork chops	Peanut butter

Oils

The smallest section of the MyPyramid Plan represents the oil group, which you should consume sparingly. Although all oils and fats contain more than nine calories per gram,* some oils and fats are more desirable than others from a health perspective. For example, the frequent consumption of saturated fats (such as those found in mayonnaise, butter, and sour cream) increases your risk for developing heart disease more so than consuming monounsaturated fats (such as those found in olive oils and canola oil) and polyunsaturated fats (such as those found in margarine and corn oil). Use the following list to determine serving equivalents for foods in the fat group. Trans fats (such as those found in many commercially baked goods) pose a significant health risk and should be avoided as much as possible.

*1 calorie = .004184 kilojoule; you can also use the Internet to convert values. Many sites exist that convert standard measurements.

Sample Exchange Units Equivalent to One Fat Serving

1 tsp butter	2 tbsp diet salad dressing
1 tsp margarine	1 tbsp cream cheese
1 tbsp diet margarine	2 tbsp light cream cheese
1 tsp mayonnaise	2 tbsp sour cream
1 tbsp diet mayonnaise	4 tbsp light sour cream
1 tsp oil	2 tbsp coffee creamer (liquid)
1 tbsp salad dressing	

Note: 1 U.S. tsp = 5 ml; 1 U.S. tbsp = 15 ml

Water

Water is not included in the MyPyramid Plan because it contains no calories and is not technically a food. Nonetheless, it is far and away the most important nutrient for your body. Your body is mostly water (even your muscles are about 75 percent water), and you can live only a few days without taking in water.

The standard recommendation is to drink eight 8-ounce (250-milliliter) glasses of water daily, and even more water is desirable when you exercise. Unfortunately, our natural thirst mechanism declines with age, so active adults should monitor their water consumption to make sure they drink at least eight glasses every day. Drink a glass of water before and after each strength training session, as well as throughout your workout. Remember that muscle tissue is more than 75 percent water.

Because coffee, tea, diet drinks, and alcoholic beverages act as diuretics, which have a dehydrating effect, do not count them in your daily water supply. But you may substitute other beverages for water, such as seltzer and fruit juices. Apple juice is an excellent source of potassium, and, of course, orange juice is high in vitamin C. Cranberry juice is close to orange juice in vitamin C content and may help prevent bladder infections. Carrot juice is high in vitamin A, vitamin C, potassium, and fiber. Pomegranate juice is reported to be the highest in antioxidants. Low-fat milk is mostly water and an excellent source of both protein and calcium. Sports drinks are also acceptable substitutes for water, but like fruit juices and low-fat milk, contain relatively large numbers of calories.

Three Steps to Better Nutrition

An eating program that provides all your essential nutrients while limiting fat consumption requires careful food selection, substitution, and preparation. The following suggestions should help you implement your best dietary intentions.

Food Selection

If you use the MyPyramid Plan guidelines, emphasizing grains, vegetables, and fruit, along with moderate amounts of milk and meat products, your diet will be generally high in nutrition and low in fat. You should, however, select carefully in the fat category. Because saturated fats such as those found in butter, cream, egg yolks, palm oil, and coconut oil raise blood cholesterol levels, you should consume these foods sparingly. Instead, choose monounsaturated fats, such as olive and peanut oils, or polyunsaturated fats, such as safflower, sunflower, and corn oils. Mono- and polyunsaturated oils tend to lower blood cholesterol levels and may therefore help reduce the risk of heart disease.

The foods listed here contain less saturated fat than other choices in their category, so select them whenever possible:

- Fish
- Poultry without skin
- Low-fat milk, yogurt, cottage cheese
- Olive, peanut, sunflower, safflower, corn, canola oils

Note: Avoid prepared foods that contain saturated fats such as palm and coconut oils as well as hydrogenated products. The container label will indicate if a food is high in saturated fats or trans fats.

Food Substitution

You undoubtedly have certain favorite foods that you do not want to give up even though they are rich in fat. You may be surprised to discover that simple substitutions can reduce the fat content without detracting from the taste. For example, using evaporated skim milk in place of cream cuts the fat and cholesterol content by more than 65 percent. Another practical substitution is to use plain nonfat yogurt or nonfat sour cream in place of standard sour cream on baked potatoes. Doing so reduces the cholesterol content by 90 percent and supplies your body with twice as much beneficial calcium.

Other useful substitutes are two egg whites in place of a whole egg, herbs rather than table salt, low-fat frozen yogurt instead of ice cream, cocoa powder in place of chocolate squares in baked goods, and lemon juice or vinegar instead of high-fat salad dressings.

If you have a sweet tooth, try eating dried fruit (raisins, dates, figs, prunes, dried apricots) in place of candy, cookies, and fat-rich baked goods. If you prefer crunchy snacks like potato chips, you may appreciate lower-fat alternatives such as pretzels (watch the sodium, though), baked chips, or carrot sticks.

Food Preparation

How you prepare your food may increase or decrease the fat content. For example, frying can double and triple the calories in some foods. By using a nonfat vegetable spray or a nonstick skillet you can eliminate the fats and oils typically necessary for frying. It is also better to cook vegetables separate from meat so that they don't absorb fats from the meat. Baked or broiled meats are recommended, and steamed or microwaved vegetables are suggested for nutrient retention. Avoid adding butter and salt to vegetables during the cooking process. If you prefer, apply these sparingly to suit individual taste once the servings are on your plate. This is because it takes less salt and fat to enhance the taste of food after cooking than during cooking.

Sample Daily Menu Plans

Pages 248 to 250 present three sample daily menu plans based on the MyPyramid recommendations for balanced meals and healthy eating. These sample menu plans provide approximately 2,000 calories daily. You will note that the sample menu plans may include a mid-morning, mid-afternoon, and mid-evening snack, in addition to three balanced meals at breakfast, lunch, and dinner. Although these are typically low-calorie mini-meals, many of the suggested snacks provide extra protein that may be beneficial for optimum muscle development. Of course, the sample menu plans are merely models that may be modified as you desire. Just try to maintain an appropriate daily calorie total and a balanced nutrient intake consistent with the MyPyramid dietary guidelines.

Summary

Healthy eating is not the same thing as dieting. Dieting implies a significant reduction in calories for the purpose of losing weight, usually in a short period of time. Most weight-loss diets involve unnatural eating patterns and too few nutrients for optimal physical function. Because such diets deprive you of important nutritional elements, most people cannot maintain diets very long, and they typically regain the weight they have lost soon after they discontinue the diet.

The eating pattern recommended in the United States Department of Agriculture MyPyramid Plan is heart healthy and nutritious and can easily become part of a lifestyle that leads to improved physical well-being. You should find that a sound eating program provides plenty of energy for your strength training workouts and essential nutrients to enhance your muscular development.

Once you have established a sensible nutrition plan, consider increasing your protein consumption for better muscle development. Also, try to ingest protein (e.g., milk, yogurt) within one hour after your strength workout to enhance tissue building and muscle remodeling processes. In addition to eating plenty of protein-rich foods (because muscle is about 25 percent protein), be sure to drink 8 glasses of water daily, and 10 glasses of water on workout days (because muscle is about 75 percent water).

Menu 1

Food	Portion/Calories
Breakfast	
Waffles	2/174
Butter	1 tbsp/102
Peanut butter	2 tbsp/188
Banana	1 small/93
Skim milk	8 oz (250 ml)/86
Snack	
Fat-free wheat crackers	16/160
Lunch	
Tuna	3 oz (90 g)/110
Mayonnaise	1 tbsp/100
Wheat bread	2 slices/130
Lettuce and tomato	1/2 cup/10
Skim milk	8 oz (250 ml)/86
Apple	1/80
Snack	
Pear	1/100
Dinner	
Skim milk	8 oz (250 ml)/86
Pasta	1 cup/197
Tomato sauce	1/2 cup/71
Zucchini	1/2 cup/14
Ground turkey	2 oz (60 g) /84
Garlic bread	1 slice/82
with butter	1 tbsp/102
Snack	
Celery sticks	1/2 cup/10

Menu 2

Food	Portion/Calories
Breakfast	
Orange juice	6 oz (175 ml)/86
Honey Bunches of Oats cereal	2 oz (60 g)/223
Skim milk	8 oz (250 ml)/86
Lunch	
Turkey	3 oz (90 g)/161
Swiss cheese	1 oz (30 g)/95
Tomato	1/4 cup/9
Roll	1/152
Mayonnaise	1 tbsp/100
Grapes	1/2 cup/30
Vegetable juice	12 oz (355 ml)/68
Carrot sticks	1/2 cup/28
Ranch dressing	1 tbsp/60
Snack	
Fat-free vanilla yogurt	1 cup/206
Low-fat granola	2 oz (57 g)/220
Dinner	
Chicken breast	3 oz (90 g)/168
Salsa	1/4 cup/18
Cheddar cheese	1 oz (30 g)/114
Spanish rice	1 1/2 cups/324
Snack	
Apple	1/80

Menu 3

Food	Portion/Calories
Breakfast	
Grape-Nuts	2 oz (60 g)/204
Cheerios	2 oz (60 g)/207
Skim milk	8 oz (250 ml)/86
Orange	1/70
Lunch	
Wheat bread	2 slices/130
Tuna	2 oz (60 g)/73
Mayonnaise	1 tbsp/100
Celery (chopped)	1/4 cup/5
Lettuce	1/2 cup/3
Apple juice	6 oz (175 ml)/87
Snack	
Fat-free crackers	12/120
Peanut butter	2 tbsp/188
Dinner	
Salmon (grilled)	3 oz (90 g)/118
Tossed salad	1 cup/22
Olive oil	1 tbsp (15 ml)/119
Broccoli	1 cup/52
Dinner roll	1/107
Vanilla ice cream	1/2 cup/133
Snack	
Fat-free vanilla yogurt	1 cup/206
Apple	1/80

Index

About the Authors

Wayne L. Westcott, PhD, CSCS, is fitness research director at the South Shore YMCA in Quincy, Massachusetts. With more than 38 years in strength training as an athlete, coach, teacher, professor, researcher, writer, and speaker, Westcott is recognized as a leading authority on fitness.

Westcott has served as a strength training consultant for numerous national organizations and programs, including Nautilus, the President's Council on Physical Fitness and Sports, the National School Fitness Foundation, the International Association of Fitness Professionals, the American Council on Exercise, the YMCA of the USA, and the National Youth Sports Safety Foundation. Through his work with these organizations, he has also received numerous awards, including the Hall of Fame Award from the International Fitness Professionals Association, Fitness Industry Leader Award from the National Strength Professionals Association, five National Fitness Profession Leadership Awards, the Massachusetts Governor's Council Lifetime Achievement Award, the IDEA Lifetime Achievement Award, the President's Council Healthy American Fitness Leader Award, and the Alumni Recognition Award from Pennsylvania State University.

Westcott has authored or coauthored 20 books on strength training, including *Building Strength & Stamina, Strength Training for Seniors,* and *Complete Conditioning for Golf.* In addition, he has served on the editorial boards of *Prevention, Shape, Men's Health, Fitness, Club Industry, American Fitness Quarterly, Nautilus,* and *Fitness Management.* He is currently a columnist for *South Shore Senior News* and *The Patriot Ledger.* Westcott also serves on advisory boards for the Senior Fitness Association and the American Association for Health and Fitness.

Westcott lives in Abington, Massachusetts, with his wife, Claudia.

Thomas R. Baechle, EdD, CSCS, *D; NSCA-CPT, *D, competed in Olympic-style weightlifting and powerlifting and was an instructor of weight training and a strength and conditioning coach for 20 years. Currently he is a professor and chair of the exercise science and athletic training department at Creighton University, where he directed phase III cardiac rehabilitation for 16 years. He is a cofounder and past president of the National Strength and Conditioning Association (NSCA) and for 20 years was the executive director of the NSCA Certification Commission.

Baechle has been recognized as the force behind the creation of the Certified Strength and Conditioning Specialist and NSCA-Certified Personal Trainer examination programs. He has received the NSCA's most coveted awards, Strength and Conditioning Professional of the Year and Lifetime Achievement. Baechle also served as president of the National Organization of Competency Assurance, currently serves as a commissioner on the National Commission for Certifying Agencies, and has served on various other regional, national, and international boards. This book is one of 12 texts authored, coauthored, or edited by Baechle, some of which have been translated into 10 languages.